Human Performance and Productivity:

Human Capability Assessment

Volume 1 of a 3 Volume Series

Human Performance and Productivity:

Human Capability Assessment

Edited by

MARVIN D. DUNNETTE
Personnel Decisions Research Institute and
the University of Minnesota
Minneapolis, Minnesota

EDWIN A. FLEISHMAN
Advanced Research Resources Organization
Washington, D.C.

Volume 1 of a 3 Volume Series

Series Editor

EDWIN A. FLEISHMAN

Psychology Press
Taylor & Francis Group

New York London

First Published by
Lawrence Erlbaum Associates, Inc., Publishers
365 Broadway
Hillsdale, New Jersey 07642

Transferred to Digital Printing 2009 by Psychology Press
270 Madison Avenue, New York NY 10016
27 Church Road, Hove, East Sussex BN3 2FA

Library of Congress Cataloging in Publication Data
Main entry under title:

Human capability assessment.

  (Human performance and productivity : v. 1)
  Bibliography: p.
  Includes indexes.
  1. Employees, Rating of.   2. Personnel management.
3. Labor productivity.   I. Dunnette, Marvin D.   II. Fleish-
man, Edwin A.   III. Series.
HF5549.5.R3H85   658.3′125   81-9911
ISBN 0-89859-085-X (v. 1)   AACR2

Publisher's Note
The publisher has gone to great lengths to ensure the quality
of this reprint but points out that some imperfections in the
original may be apparent.

Contents

Contents of Volume II

Information Processing and Decision Making

Contents of Volume III

Stress and Performance Effectiveness

Preface

This series of volumes reviews the state of the art in several areas of human performance research. These areas are human capability assessment, information processing and decision making, and job stress. It was recognized that these have been active research areas, but work in these areas has not previously been linked directly to national concerns about productivity. The focus is on implications for improving productivity and for recommending research in these areas that should have impact on productivity.

The series is a product of a National Science Foundation grant (DAR-7707886) to the Advanced Research Resources Organization (ARRO), under the title "A critical path for formulating research and policy on human performance and productivity relevant to national needs" (E. A. Fleishman, Principal Investigator).

The structure of the project included the establishment of a research panel that served as a steering committee for the project. Besides the Principal Investigator, this panel included two members of the ARRO staff, and the chairperson selected for each of the three major areas. The chairpersons selected were Dr. Marvin D. Dunnette, University of Minnesota (human capability assessment); Dr. William C. Howell, Rice University (information processing and decision making); and Dr. Earl A. Alluisi, Old Dominion University (stress and performance effectiveness). Each is an acknowledged leader in the field he represented, and I am grateful for these contributions. I am pleased to acknowledge the assistance of Dr. Albert S. Glickman and Dr. Joyce C. Hogan of the ARRO staff, who also served on this panel.

The panel met early in the project to identify needs and priorities, to select subareas for intensive review, and to nominate exceptional researchers in each of the subareas. The individuals selected are listed as the authors of the various chapters in these volumes. Each is expert in the area identified, and has published extensively in his respective topic.

During the period of the project, each author prepared a chapter reviewing the designated subarea. The area subgroups held meetings with the chairperson of that area to discuss drafts and to deal with overlap and omission of relevant content and suggested revisions and implications. Each area chairperson served as a Section Editor, integrating the chapters for this series of volumes.

A major activity of this project was a conference organized by the Principal Investigator. The Conference, entitled "Human Performance and Productivity: A Critical Path for Research and Policy," was held at the Washington Hilton on June 2, 1978. A brochure announcing the Conference was sent to a selected list of researchers and practitioners in both the public and private sectors, who are concerned with problems of productivity. Approximately 100 participants, representing industry, universities, governmental and other public agencies, and research institutes attended.

The Conference had two primary purposes. One was to disseminate the thinking and recommendations of the overall effort to a larger audience of researchers in related areas and to individuals who need to apply the findings. The second purpose was to obtain feedback from these groups for possible utility in revising sections of the report. The format consisted of three major presentations, representations by the Principal Investigator, and by the three area chair persons. This was followed by five concurrent workshops of specialized interest. These workshops and their leaders included:

- Individual Capability, Team Performance, and Productivity
  Bernard M. Bass, Ph.D., State University of New York, Binghamton
- Applying the Information Processing Approach to Human/Operator Computer Interactions
  Robert C. Williges, Ph.D., Virginia Polytechnic Institute
- Utility Considerations in Productivity Assessment
  Frank L. Schmidt, Ph.D., Personnel R & D Center, U.S. Civil Service Commission
- Training and Human Performance
  Irwin L. Goldstein, Ph.D., and Virginia Buxton, Ph.D., University of Maryland
- Temporal Factors in Human Performance and Productivity
  Ben B. Morgan, Jr., Ph.D., Old Dominion University

Following these workshops, a plenary session was held in which a workshop member summarized the discussions of their workshop for the entire audience. The luncheon speaker was Dr. Vaughn L. Blankenship, Division Director for Intergovernmental Science and Public Technology, National Science Foundation. Dr. Blankenship described NSF's interests in this area in the context of the total applied science program. I wish to express my appreciation to him and to Dr. Frank Scioli, Section Head, Social and Behavioral Sciences, National Science Foundation, for their continued support of this effort.

I am indebted to Ms. Ellen Eisner and Dr. Joyce C. Hogan of the ARRO staff for their assistance in the arrangements and administration of this conference.

It is felt that these volumes represent authoritative statements by leading scholars in their respective fields, regarding the state of the art in these areas of human performance. The individual chapters present the implications of research for productivity enhancement and the directions of needed human performance research likely to impact on productivity. I am indebted to these authors and editors for their contributions. In addition to individuals already mentioned, I wish to acknowledge the contributions of Dr. Jerrold Levine of the ARRO staff and Dr. Arthur Siegel and Dr. Martin Lautman, Applied Psychological Services, who influenced our earlier thinking on needs in this area.

I am especially indebted to Dr. Neil S. Dumas, then Program Director for Advanced Productivity Research and Technology, National Science Foundation, who was project officer at NSF and was particularly supportive of this effort.

Edwin A. Fleishman

Introduction

Edwin A. Fleishman
Advanced Research Resources Organization
Washington, D.C.

The universal goal of continuous improvement in *quality of life* is keyed to the enhancement of productivity. In simplest human terms, increased productivity translates as improvement in output generated by each unit of effort, with concommitant reduction in unit cost. The assumption is that, as the people who constitute a social and economic entity generate more output than other comparable entities, their relative standard of living will improve. For the unit of effort they expend, more goods and services become available, the amount of free time they have available to make use of these goods and services is increased, and the choice of alternative uses of the products and services is expanded—(i.e., life's quality is improved).

In industrial societies, increases in productivity are accounted for largely by capital investment strategies. Machinery multiplies man's output many fold. Theoretically, therefore, more people can be released from the "bondage of labor" for more time to "enjoy life."

However, though we hail the advent of the postindustrial society, in which substantially all our essential human needs will be produced without a great amount of human effort, the fact remains that the millennium is not here yet. Human beings are not yet obsolescent as important contributors to the productive process. The quality of performance by men and women, whether in manufacturing or servicing, still accounts for a very large part of the variation in productivity, however one chooses to define the criteria of productivity—and this condition will continue to prevail far into the future. As a matter of fact, as our social and economic system becomes proportionately less oriented to the production of goods and more to the provision of services, the "human element" takes on added importance and new meaning—including perhaps some revision of the conventional definitions of "productivity." Furthermore, as reserves of natural resources decline and the rate of population growth declines as well, productivity will indeed take on new meaning and added importance.

The need for attention to performance and productivity seems clear. During the past decade, output per man hour within the U.S. has dropped to a level of only 1.4% growth per year—the lowest rate in recent history. In addition to the rapidly changing expectations of American employees, the economy is confronted with slowed growth, high energy costs, foreign competition, and persistent unemployment. The productivity level of increasingly costly labor has become one of the key factors in the equation.

Over the past 50 or more years, "scientific" study of productivity has been a prominent feature of the work of many professions, including economists, psychologists, engineers, and accountants. Its applications have been the concern of those responsible for industrial relations, management, and public policy. The literature on the subject is extensive. Nonetheless, particularly as regards the relation of human performance to productivity, it is still difficult to generalize principles, procedures, and policies because of the ad hoc nature of so much of the work that has been done. For the most part, each effort has been designed to fit special circumstances and available data, employing unique terminology and giving special emphasis to different aspects of human performance and different criteria of productivity. Furthermore, most criteria of human performance and productivity, as well as the inferences as to the relationships between the two, have been cast in a short time frame. Time dependencies inherent in the relationships have been largely neglected. Consequently, productivity-seeking changes have been pushed into a symptom-treating, patchwork pattern by the focus upon immediate "results," to the virtual exclusion of plans of attack that are rooted in scientific methodology instead of technical improvisation. To provide the impetus for advances in understanding that go beyond conventional wisdom, and in applying new knowledge and theory of human performance related to productivity, in consonance with national needs, a more unified conceptual framework and research agenda is called for.

There is a need to lay out more clearly and more consistently the relations between productivity and human performance as a prerequisite to more systematic and comprehensive policy planning and research to enhance productivity— and the quality of life. The objective of this book and the others in this series is to focus attention on some issues of productivity from some new perspectives provided by recent research on human performance.

Concern for productivity enhancement is not new, although major national priority for research in this area is relatively recent. Certainly, behavioral and social scientists have been intimately involved with these issues. However, we decided to emphasize some areas from experimental, engineering, and personnel psychology that we feel had not received sufficient attention in this context. Previous work in the social and behavioral services dealing with productivity have often stressed motivational, social, attitudinal, and organizational factors. Recent publications by the *Work in America Institute,* for example, have stressed topics such as worker alienation, social-psychological aspects relevant to older populations, product quality and worker attitudes, *all critically* important issues. Yet, there are active areas of research in several fields of human performance that need to be examined for their implications for productivity enhancement and research. These areas, as we identified them, include *human capability assessment, information processing and decision making,* and *stress effects on performance.* Until now, it was the feeling of many of us that not enough attempt has been made to link the research in these areas to issues of work productivity.

This book, and the other two volumes in this series, bring together, in a joint enterprise, the views of scholars nationally recognized for their work in selected areas of human performance. They were asked to review the state of the art in their areas of expertise, with a view to implications for improving productivity and for recommending research in these areas that should have impact on problems of productivity. During the year, these scholars and the editors have been meeting and exchanging views. A conference was held to disseminate and share some of these findings and to obtain reactions from knowledgeable individuals concerned with research and application in these areas. The book and the accompanying volumes reflect their inputs and offer some conclusions and recommendations about future directions.

In the typical organizational context, the conventional management perspective sees the principal questions involved as centering upon the matching of requirements and resources, mostly in personnel terms. This starts with task analysis to set requirements in terms of the specific skill, knowledge, ability, and activity requirements imposed upon the people who are to be engaged in the work to be done. Analytic processes are employed in order to establish selection and training requirements. Recent developments have taken place in taxonomizing categories of tasks and skills, and new methodologies have emerged to create a "common language" for dimensionalizing resources and requirements in consistent, operationally translatable terms (Fine, 1955, 1957, 1962; Fine & Wiley, 1971; Fleishman, 1967, 1975a, 1975b; McCormick, 1975; Theologus & Fleishman, 1971). New emphases have also been given to ways of measuring worker perceptions of job components related to both proficiency and motivation to perform (Hackman & Lawler, 1971).

The task requirements having been set, personnel requirements are then established, and selection and assignment processes are employed to identify from the pool of available personnel those most suitably qualified, or those who can be equipped through training, with the abilities and knowledge necessary to perform the required tasks. The next step is to distribute these personnel resources to the jobs available so as to optimize the allocation of human resources as nearly optimally as circumstances permit. The recent advances in dimensionalizing task requirements and resource characteristics have facilitated new developments in creating efficient allocation models (Dunnette, 1976).

The outcomes of these processes are reflected in the level and quality of human performance in the job–task situation. Emphasis is on work measurement and on interfaces with the equipment, facilities, environment, and organization, which determine the overall system or subsystem performance (Howell & Goldstein, 1971; Landy & Trumbo, 1976). To the extent that the abilities of the individual worker can be enhanced on the one hand by improvements in training, and on the other hand by design of the equipment, facilities, environment, and organization, the output of the system can be improved. Much of the work to be discussed in this series of volumes comes to focus at this point of interface. Recent emphases include the identification of different categories of skill affected by these factors and new developments in standardization of work measurement methods (Alluisi, 1967; Dunnette, 1976; Fleishman, 1975b).

The three foundation areas selected for discussion in the series of volumes are rooted in bodies of active research and developing methodology in the human performance domain but have not yet been brought together under the same conceptual structure in a systematic way to deal with the special issues of enhanced productivity. Recent handbooks (Dunnette, 1976, *Handbook of Industrial and Organizational Psychology;* Dubin, 1976, *Handbook of Work, Organization, and Society*) have few entries on "productivity." The information available needs to be refocused. The organization of this series of books is built upon examination of the following three areas:

1. *Human capability assessment.* This area evaluates the improved techniques to identify, measure, train, and evaluate human capabilities needed. This includes the development of concepts relating to individual and team performance.

2. *Information processing and decision making.* This area attempts to define the parameters and limits of the human as a processor and integrator of information and as a decision maker in operating systems.

3. *Stress and performance effectiveness.* This area examines aspects of human performance under environmental, social, situational, and organismic stressors. The goal of this effort would be to reduce or prevent the degradation of performance effectiveness in the presence of conditions that are stressful.

Each volume in this series[1] deals with one of these areas. The authors of the individual chapters within each volume are active researchers at the leading edge

[1]The other two volumes in this series are (Vol. 2) Howell, W. C. & Fleishman, E. A. (Eds.), *Human performance and productivity: Information processing and decision making.* Hillsdale, N.J.: Lawrence Erlbaum Associates, 1982; and (Vol. 3) Alluisi, E. A. & Fleishman, E. A. (Eds.), *Human performance and productivity: Stress and performance effectiveness.* Hillsdale, N.J.: Lawrence Erlbaum Associates, 1982.

of their research fields. They are in a unique position to assess the status of each area and to recommend what needs to be done next to advance the state of the art in human performance research and the consequent impact on productivity.

ACKNOWLEDGMENT

The contribution of Albert S. Glickman to these initial formulations is gratefully acknowledged.

REFERENCES

Alluisi, E. A. Methodology in the use of synthetic tasks to assess complex performances. *Human Factors*, 1967, *4*, 375-384.

Dubin, R. Theory building in applied areas. In M. D. Dunnette (Ed.), *Handbook of industrial and organizational psychology*. Chicago: Rand McNally, 1976.

Dunnette, M. D. (Ed.) *Handbook of industrial and organizational psychology*. Chicago: Rand McNally, 1976.

Fine, S. A. Functional job analysis. *Personnel Administration and Industrial Relations*, Spring 1955.

Fine, S. A. U.S.E.S. Occupational classification and Minnesota occupational rating scales. *Journal of Counseling Psychology*, 1957, *4*, 3.

Fine, S. A. *Functional job analysis as a method of indirect validation: A study in synthetic validity*. Unpublished doctoral dissertation, The George Washington University, June 1962.

Fine, S. A., & Wiley, W. W. *An introduction to functional job analysis*. Kalamazoo, Mich.: W. E. Upjohn Institute, 1971.

Fleishman, E. A. Performance assessment based on an empirically derived task taxonomy. *Human Factors*, 1967, *9*, 349-366.

Fleishman, E. A. Toward a taxonomy of human performance. *American Psychologist*, 1975, *30*, 1127-1149.(a)

Fleishman, E. A. Taxonomic issues in human performance research. In W. T. Singleton & P. Spurgeon (Eds.), *Measurement of Human Resources*. New York: Halsted Press, 1975.(b)

Hackman, J. R., & Lawler, E. E. Employee reactions to job characteristics. *Journal of Applied Psychology Monograph*, 1971, *55*, 259-286.

Howell, W. C., & Goldstein, I. L. *Engineering psychology: Current perspectives in research*. New York: Appleton-Century-Crofts, 1971.

Landy, F. J., & Trumbo, D. A. *Psychology of work behavior*. Homewood, Ill.: Dorsey Press, 1976.

McCormick, E. J. Job and task analysis. In M. D. Dunnette (Ed.), *Handbook of Industrial and Organizational Psychology*. Chicago: Rand McNally, 1976.

Theologus, G. C., & Fleishman, E. A. *Development of a taxonomy of human performance: Validation study of ability scales for classifying human tasks*. Washington: American Institutes for Research, April 1971.

Human Performance and Productivity:

Human Capability Assessment

Volume 1 of a 3 Volume Series

1 Critical Concepts in the Assessment of Human Capabilities

Marvin D. Dunnette
Personnel Decisions Research Institute
and
The University of Minnesota
Minneapolis, Minnesota

MATCHING PERSONS AND JOBS IN WORK SETTINGS

Productivity in organizational work settings can be increased by many methods. Accommodation—improving the match between worker characteristics and job requirements—is the process common to all such methods. On the organizational side, equipment may be designed differently, jobs may be changed, patterns of work flow may be restructured, or control and reward systems changed. On the individual worker's side, improved matching may be accomplished by training, selection and job placement, vocational counseling, or team development. Whether one or many of these accommodating methods is used, the starting point must be an evaluation of human capability, assessed in the context set by circumstances of particular work settings. The following six chapters consider a variety of critical concepts relevant to human capability assessment in work settings.

A Job/Person Characteristics Matrix

Fig. 1.1 is a section of the matrix formed from the two taxonomies that invariably are involved in the various methods of accommodation mentioned previously. The matrix is presented here in order to highlight critical issues in the assessment of human capability as they impact on the success or failure of efforts to increase productivity in work settings. Cell entries in the matrix provide quantitative estimates of the usefulness of particular personal characteristics for fulfilling the task requirements of particular classes of job characteristics.

Requirements for Constructing and Using the Matrix.   A central assumption underlying this matrix is that we either know or can learn information required to

1

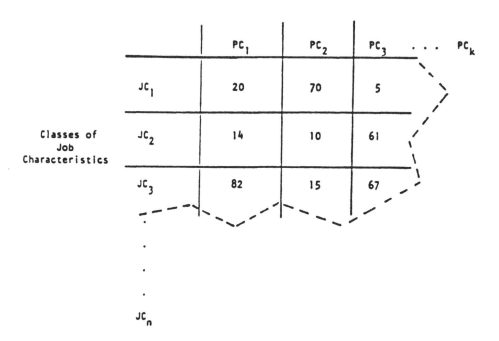

Classes of

Person Characteristics

FIG. 1.1.   A Job/Person Characteristics Matrix.

Note: Numbers in the cells of the matrix are shown without designating what they are. They might be validities, estimates of overlap, variance percentages, probabilities, or any other quantitative estimate of the relative usefulness of various classes of personal characteristics for carrying out various classes of job characteristics.

define and measure the taxonomic categories and to fill in the cells of the matrix. Even after the matrix has been constructed, we need to learn how its information may be most efficiently used for accomplishing improved accommodations between persons and jobs, and how estimates of the level of benefits likely to be realized from such improvements may be made.

The many issues and questions implied by these last comments have been considered by authors of the following six chapters. Each of the critical issues involved in developing and successfully using the job/person matrix becomes apparent to the reader, as we now summarize briefly what each of the following chapters is about.

MEASURING TASK PERFORMANCE

To be useful as a basis for human resources decisions, entries in the cells of the matrix must show in some way how personal characteristics are related to levels of effectiveness in performing classes of tasks and to varying levels of individual and group productivity. Muckler gives extended attention in Chapter 2 to methods and issues in productivity assessment and human performance measurement. He addresses critical concepts in measuring both individual job performance and organizational or system productivity. He argues persuasively that the commonly held distinction between so-called "objective" and "subjective" criterion measures is, in actuality, a false dichotomy and shows how human judgment is involved at some point in *all* programs focusing on performance measurement and productivity assessment. Finally, Muckler identifies and discusses a number of standards for evaluating performance measures and suggests that these standards should be applied, henceforth, in planning, designing, or evaluating programs directed toward productivity assessment. Muckler's chapter builds on, but does not repeat unnecessarily, what is already known about performance and criterion analysis. He deals much more directly than most with productivity per se and avoids many of the more mundane issues, such as differences between rating scale formats, problems of perceptual bias, and rater training techniques. His chapter is especially useful in presenting many examples of actual productivity assessment programs carried out in specific work settings ranging from retail sales, teaching, and research to logging, foundry work, and data management. Finally, Chapter 2 presents a general process model or flow diagram to guide practitioners and researchers in developing productivity assessment and measurement systems in the particular production settings that they may be studying.

TAXONOMIES

Earlier, Fleishman and his associates reviewed the issues in developing taxonomies of task performance and provided some alternative directions (Farina, 1973; Fleishman, 1967, 1975; Fleishman & Stephenson, 1972; Theologus & Fleishman, 1973; Wheaton, 1973). In Chapter 3, Peterson and Bownas provide a comprehensive overview of what is known concerning taxonomies of tasks in work settings and taxonomies of measurable characteristics making up individual knowledges, skills, abilities, and orientations (KSAOs).

Classes of Person Characteristics. Their review of relevant literature suggests that a useful starting point for describing individuals might well utilize 12 cognitive abilities, 18 psychomotor/physical abilities, 15 modes of interpersonal orientation (personality), and 6 modes of vocational orientation (interests). To these 51 classes of person characteristics should be added the 14 personal background (biographical) dimensions mentioned by Schoenfeldt in Chapter 4. In essence, then, 65 discrete categories or classes of personal characteristics provide a good characterization of the person side of the job/person matrix shown in Fig. 1.1.

Classes of Job Characteristics.   In Chapter 3 Peterson and Bownas report less consensus and fewer truly comprehensive studies of task taxonomies making up jobs. Examples of the most general and broadly useful taxonomy are based on extensive studies undertaken by E. A. Fleishman and E. J. McCormick and their associates. Fleishman provides a comprehensive abilities taxonomy and methods for describing any job in terms of 37 different abilities (Fleishman, 1975; Fleishman & Hogan, 1978; Theologus & Fleishman, 1973). McCormick and others have developed the Position Analysis Questionnaire (McCormick, 1976; McCormick, Jeanneret, & Mecham, 1972). Depending on the level of generality or specificity desired, it appears that any given job may be described with the Position Analysis Questionnaire according to 12 quite general categories (e.g., clerical tasks, supervision tasks, physical tasks, etc.) or according to 32 much more specific categories (e.g., decision-making tasks, vigilance tasks, physical coordination tasks, etc.).

We may conclude from Peterson's and Bownas's review that much is now known about the taxonomies necessary to begin constructing the full job/person matrix. So far, however, little is known about how cells making up the full matrix might be merged. If *all* person categories and *all* job categories were utilized, the full matrix would contain a total of 2860 cells—too many to be manageable. A most pressing area for further taxonomic investigation involves learning which cells may be merged without serious loss or distortion of information bearing on cellular estimates of the usefulness of particular KSAO categories for carrying out certain classes of tasks.

PSYCHOMETRIC EVALUATION OF MEASURES

Constructs

In addition to Muckler's conceptual guidelines for developing and evaluating productivity measures, there exist certain strictly psychometric considerations requiring attention when measures of either task or personal characteristics are being considered. Such considerations are given extended treatment by Peterson and Bownas in Chapter 3 and by Schoenfeldt in Chapter 4. Peterson and Bownas summarize the process of construct validation as it applies to developing both task and person measures and decisions about the number and nature of categories sufficient to describe both taxonomic domains. They also present marker tests or measures for each of 51 cognitive, motor, physical, personality, and interest measures and brief summaries of the psychometric evidence available for each.

Intralndividual Variation.   Schoenfeldt, in Chapter 4, considers issues involving patterns of variation *within* persons and the implications of such variability for evaluating the dimensions and cell entries of the job/person matrix. One obvious form of within-person variation is simply due to errors of measurement; that is, KSAO measures, job performance measures, or both invariably are measured with less than perfect reliability. Schoenfeldt's concern is *not* with this form of intraindividual variation.[1] Instead, Schoenfeldt's concern is with stable aspects of differences within single measures and between different measures within persons. He notes that persons may differ in a reliable way in the variance of scores obtained on a single measure taken at several different times[2] and suggests that such differences in *intraindividual variability* could have implications for any number of personnel decisions such as job design, training procedures, and selection. In fact, Muckler also cites work by Rothe in which an index of Productivity Consistency (based on the ratio of Intraindividual Consistency to Interindividual Consistency) proved potentially useful in studying the effects of programs designed to decrease performance variability in foundry work. Schoenfeldt also notes that persons may differ in a reliable way according to the patterning or configuration of KSAO's or performance measures characterizing them[3] and suggests that such differences in *intraindividual trait variation* need to be much more thoroughly explored in order to develop richer characterizations of the levels of individuality shown by different persons. Obviously, both types of indices of intraindividual variation deserve emphasis in research studies designed to evaluate aspects of the job/person matrix.

ENHANCING TASK PERFORMANCE

As stated earlier, one widely acknowledged and frequently attempted strategy oriented toward individual workers for improving the match between worker

---

[1]The reader should note, however, that Hunter and Schmidt, in Chapter 7, do discuss effects of measurement nonreliability on the magnitudes of cell entries in the matrix and the implications of such effects on the generalizability of inferences related to a science of human resource allocation.

[2]For example, two hypothetical persons, Dick and Jane, might differ in the consistency (or variance) of hourly measures of output on a job requiring hand assembly of electronics components.

[3]For example, Dick and Jane may also differ from each other in the variance of scores each obtains on a number of different measures of personal characteristics or different dimensions of job performance. Schoenfeldt argues that the mean variance of scores within persons may well exceed the mean variance of scores on the same trait across persons.

characteristics and job requirements is training. In Chapter 5, Goldstein and Buxton provide an extended discussion of both the potential of training approaches and the problems encountered in efforts to implement such approaches as a means of enhancing productivity in industrial work settings. The authors present a model known as Instructional Systems Development (ISD) that proves useful, both for guiding their discussion and as a framework for use by practitioners and researchers as they set out to design and evaluate training approaches in organizations. Unfortunately, the authors, after considering the current state of training technology according to their ISD model, are forced toward pessimistic conclusions concerning the state of the art in training technology. They conclude that documentation of productivity enhancing outcomes of training programs is almost nonexistent; moreover, training as currently practiced in most organizational settings suffers frequently from unspecified goals, muddled analyses of organizational and individual learning requirements, organizational conflicts, and deplorable evaluation methodology. Readers are advised to give special attention to research suggestions made by Goldstein and Buxton as a means of guarding against making some of the same conceptual and methodological errors that have been prevalent for so long in the design and implementation of training approaches in work settings.

TEAM PERFORMANCE AND TEAM PRODUCTIVITY

In Chapter 6, Bass examines in detail what is known and what needs to be learned about relationships between factors affecting individual work performance and productivity and performance/productivity outcomes of team effort. Bass considers team performance according to differences in the distribution of individual capabilities of team members, the distribution of work assignments, importance of roles, conditions imposed on the team, and the nature of interaction processes between team members. After describing an effective work team as consisting of capable and highly motivated individuals who are highly interdependent, cooperative, and whose coordination is facilitated by a free flow of information, Bass presents a model that serves as an heuristic both for summarizing previous research findings and for guiding new research concerning team productivity. Bass's considerations can best be entered into the framework of the job/person matrix by introducing new categories for the taxonomies already discussed. Thus, team characteristics and individual characteristics relevant to team performance need to be added to the taxonomy of person characteristics. And, classes of job characteristics need to be developed that take account of work requirements in relation to organizing and structuring processes required for properly accomplishing the organization's performance and productivity goals.

DEVELOPING AND INTERPRETING COMBINING RULES: VALIDITY AND UTILITY

Methods for Estimating Cell Entries

As already mentioned, operational usefulness of the job/person matrix depends on filling in the cells of the matrix with quantitative estimates of linkage between classes of personal characteristics and classes of job characteristics. Several methods for developing such estimates and psychometric considerations related to them are given in the last third of Chapter 3 and throughout Hunter's and Schmidt's Chapter 7. In Chapter 3 Peterson and Bownas classify several methods and present examples of how they have been utilized. Thus, cells of the matrix have been filled in for many jobs and many personal characteristics by judgments from experts (psychologists and personnel officers) in relation to task dimensions derived from the Position Analysis Questionnaire; or, cells of the matrix have been completed for task dimensions comprising only one job (e.g., firefighter or corrections officer) by expert judgments (from job incumbents and psychologists) that have then been subjected to empirical scrutiny in the form of criterion-oriented validity studies.

Generality of Results

The examples given by Peterson and Bownas do confirm the practical usefulness of the job/person matrix concept; however, the generality of entries within the cells would still need to be demonstrated. In other words, will it be necessary to develop many such job/person matrices, differing according to classifications of situations or special organizational circumstances? Approaching the issue at a different level of abstraction, Hunter and Schmidt present psychometric evidence in Chapter 7 in support of arguments against situational specificity. Their contention is that situational parameters have not been shown to affect in any systematic or ordered way the magnitudes of validity estimates relating classes of person characteristics to classes of task characteristics. Their evidence argues strongly that observed variability in such quantitative estimates as validity coefficients is almost exactly what would be predicted on the basis of wide differences between studies in random sampling error, errors of measurement, range restriction in measures, computational errors, and various constant errors in criterion development and measurement.

The net effect of their view, if correct, would be that the quantitative estimates linking personal characteristics to job performance characteristics could, in fact, be regarded as *constants* within fairly broad groupings of task classes and person trait classes. What is necessary, therefore, is to conduct a series of parametric investigations based on large numbers of persons and carefully conceived and highly reliable measures of person characteristics and task performance. The outcome could well be a kind of periodic table comprised of cells containing fundamental constants portraying levels of congruence between traits and aspects of work performance and productivity.

Utility.   The chapter by Hunter and Schmidt is a rich store of information tracing the development of thinking about the concept of utility in personnel classification. They show the great gain to be expected from measures of even modest validity, when they can be used with appropriate prediction equations to aid in developing programs of human resources allocation or job *classification* as opposed to strictly selection decisions. An exciting aspect of their chapter is their hypothetical, but conservative, illustration of the substantial gain in the nation's productivity that might be realized by using a few simple tests (general ability, spatial aptitude, perceptual speed) of moderate validities to establish guidelines for assigning persons tentatively to one of four broad occupational groupings (professional/managerial, skilled, clerical, and unskilled or semiskilled). Even under the most conservative of assumptions, the gain in productivity could amount to over $700 per worker or a total of nearly $75 billion per year throughout the total labor force.

AREAS OF NEEDED RESEARCH

Methodologies, results, and speculations reported by authors of these six chapters lead to an optimistic view of how human resources can be allocated and utilized to improve both individual work performance and our economy's total productivity. Significant advances have been made in the technologies of job analysis, human capability assessment, productivity measurement and assessment, job–person matching, and new formulations of validity generalization. We seem to be at the threshold for adopting systematic procedures of human resource allocation that give equal and proper attention to both the specialized individualities of all persons in society and to the society's institutional/organizational requirements for increased productivity.

Authors of each of the following chapters specify areas of continuing investigation necessary to continue the advances already made. The reader is urged to give particular attention to each of the authors' recommendations for continued studies. Taken together, they constitute a kind of research agenda defining areas of human capability assessment most likely to result in a fully operational and practical theory of human resource allocation. These areas of needed research are summarized briefly below:

1. We need to learn what the minimum number of necessary cells may be for the job/person matrix. Studies need to consider the degree of generalizability of

cell entries across different task classes and across different trait classes. Such studies, as mentioned, should be performed with large numbers of subjects and make use of highly reliable measures that can be shown to be conceptually free from constant error variance arising from such factors as response set biases, criterion contamination, and incomplete domain sampling.

2. We need to learn more about the nature of relationships between traditional measures of work performance and measures of actual productivity expressed as dollars. A good beginning has been made for a few occupations by using experts to estimate productivity differences (in dollars) between high-performing and low-performing job incumbents. Such estimating procedures need further attention, and results need to be confirmed by independent methods of analysis.

3. Productivity indices currently used are diverse, somewhat primitive, and often unclear. Many have only limited diagnostic value, and their use for administrative or policy decision making is frequently questionable. Even so, increasing numbers of studies have shown that careful development of operational assessment systems in field settings can yield rich dividends, and they can serve as most fruitful sources for improving productivity assessment in the years ahead. Further studies of such operational assessment systems need to be carried out, and their results thoroughly documented.

4. Taxonomies comprising entry categories for the job/person matrix need to be broadened to include dimensions on the task side related to team performance and interdependencies between particular tasks and to include dimensions on the person side related to propensities toward team effort as contrasted with strictly individual effort.

5. Patterns of individuality defined according to differences in *intraindividual trait variation* and *intraindividual variability* should be studied more extensively according to their magnitude, stability, and behavioral correlates. Studies should be performed on both traits and tasks and on configurations of interactions between traits and tasks. The potential yield from such studies is likely to be greater in relation to intra-individual trait variation than in relation to intraindividual variability.

6. Much research must be done on methods of determining training needs in work settings. Information of this type is sorely needed in order to assure better and more accurate specification of both training goals and training procedures. In addition, a critical need exists for developing training evaluation methodology that takes better account of the many practical constraints within organizations that hamper the collection of relevant training-program evaluation information.

7. Relations between individual capability, team performance, and team productivity need continued investigation. First, results of field research studies should be systematically compiled and subjected to further analysis. Second, dynamic computer simulation models should be developed and used to study effects on team productivity of simultaneously varying such group parameters as

individual abilities and motivation, constraints on team assignments, nature of interaction processes, and many others.

8. Performance acquisition and performance change should be studied in the context of the job/person matrix. In particular, studies of processes of skill acquisition should be carried out to discover how configurations of traits governing performance increments may change during different stages of knowledge, skill, and task proficiency acquisition. In such studies, performance measurement on the task side of the matrix may be somewhat different than in the case of performance measurement for fully trained job incumbents. It should still be possible, however, to merge such differing measures in the form of productivity estimates stated in the form of dollars.

9. As additional research information in all these areas continues to accumulate, it will be desirable to establish a source data base for all published productivity studies. At present, such studies appear in a tremendous variety of settings and publication outlets. An integration of all such information will prove most helpful in providing knowledge of where productivity studies have been carried out, when measures have proved to be useful and why, and what strategies have been successfully employed in productivity enhancement programs.

The nine broad areas of needed research summarized above are outlined in much greater detail by various of the authors of the following chapters. We urge readers to give special attention to their recommendations and to regard them as a research agenda for guiding future investigations in human capability assessment and productivity measurement.

REFERENCES

Farina, A. J., Jr. Development of a taxonomy of human performance: A review of descriptive schemes for human task behavior. JSAS *Catalog of Selected Documents in Psychology*, 1973, *3*, 23 (Ms. No. 318).

Fleishman, E. A. Performance assessment based on an empirically derived task taxonomy. *Human Factors*, 1967, *9*, 349–366.

Fleishman, E. A. Toward a taxonomy of human performance. *American Psychologist*, 1975, *30*, 1127–1149.

Fleishman, E. A., & Hogan, J. C. *A taxonomic method for assessing the physical requirements of jobs: The physical abilities analysis approach* (ARRO Technical Report 3012/R78-6). Washington, D.C.: Advanced Research Resources Organization, June 1978.

Fleishman, E. A., & Stephenson, R. W. Development of a taxonomy of human performance: A review of the third year's progress. JSAS *Catalog of Selected Documents in Psychology*, 1972, *2*, 40–41 (Ms. No. 113).

McCormick, E. J. Job and task analysis. In M. D. Dunnette (Ed.), *Handbook of Industrial and Organizational Psychology*. Chicago: Rand McNally, 1976.

McCormick, E. J., Jeanneret, P. R., & Mecham, R. C. A study of job characteristics and job dimensions as based on the position analysis questionnaire (PAQ). *Journal of Applied Psychology*, 1972, *56*, 347–368.

Theologus, G. C., & Fleishman, E. A. Development of a taxonomy of human performance: Validation study of ability scales for classifying human tasks. JSAS *Catalog of Selected Documents in Psychology*, 1973, *3*, 29 (Ms. No. 326).

Wheaton, G. R. Development of a taxonomy of human performance: A review of classificatory systems relating to tasks and performance. JSAS *Catalog of Selected Documents in Psychology*, 1973, *3*, 22–23 (Ms. No. 317).

2 Evaluating Productivity

Frederick A. Muckler
Canyon Research Group, Inc.

"It is quality rather than quantity that matters."
—Seneca

DEFINITIONS OF PRODUCTIVITY

A Definition of Productivity

The term *productivity* is used in many way; it is used here as follows: Productivity is the amount of goods and/or services produced per hours of human labor. The purpose of this chapter is to explore problems associated with both the *measurement* of productivity and the *evaluation* of productivity measures. Productivity assessment is concerned with the latter; it is the evaluation and the meaning of productivity that is of prime importance. Productivity assessment goes beyond human output per se and must be viewed in terms of the impact of productivity on the system of which the human is a part. Productivity assessment will be limited by the nature and conditions of productivity measurement, but it cannot be determined by human output alone.

Productivity: Good or Bad?

It is a widely held assumption, particularly in business and economic circles, that more productivity is always better. For several years, there has been much concern that the productivity of the U.S. worker is diminishing. McConnell

13

(1979), for example, cites statistics that show a decline in output growth as follows:

1948-1966:   3.3% productivity increase per year average
1966-1973:   2.1% productivity increase per year average
1973-1977:   1.2% productivity increase per year average

a decrease that compares unfavorably with such nations as Canada, Japan, France, West Germany, and Italy, and favorably only with the United Kingdom. The situation is automatically interpreted as "bad."

Conversely, there is the almost universal belief that only continual increases in productivity are "good" for a firm and a nation and it's economy. In simplistic terms: More is better. Further, it is frequently assumed fervently that the ills of an economic system will disappear if only increased productivity is achieved.

The position taken here is that increased (or decreased) productivity is neither good nor bad in itself. What is important in productivity changes are the uses to which increased productivity is directed. For example, increased productivity in a cigar factory (i.e., an increase in cigars produced per hour by each production worker) is "good" only in so far as the firm is able to sell that increase in the market. That which cannot be sold must go to the warehouse, where it serves neither the worker nor the firm. The first major qualification in productivity assessment, therefore, must be that productivity is *usable*. Increased productivity may be either "good" or "bad" depending on the *use* to which the product or services are put.

To assume that increased productivity is an automatic good in itself is to ignore much of recent history. Following the U.S. Civil War, the period of approximately 1870 to 1900 saw a constant oscillation of underproduction and overproduction (Rodgers, 1978). The supply of goods frequently exceeded consumption of those goods resulting in, among other things, a glut of goods on the market, business depressions, lowered prices below cost, high unemployment, and very severe labor strife. The full impact of the Industrial Revolution in technology combined with new uses of labor resulted in increased productivity that could not be absorbed by the then-existing societal system. The inability of the system to cope with these changes often resulted in societal catastrophes, the echoes of which are still heard today.

Further, from the point of view of the societal system, there is the fundamental question of the effective *distribution* of productivity between positive and nonpositive uses. Melman (1970, 1971, 1974), for example, has argued that, since World War II, the military sector of the U.S. economic system has absorbed too much of the total available resources for what he considers essentially nonuseful ends. However one feels about the validity of this argument, we are dealing here with the fundamental resource allocation problem for individuals, groups, businesses, or nations: How should available resources be usefully distributed? Increased productivity may, or may not, relieve this problem, depending on how new resources are used.

Finally, mention should be made of the growing feelings of many that the earth societal system may be approaching finite resource limits. If this is true, then it follows that increased productivity will only accelerate the rate at which resources are used—with catastrophic results (Meadows & Meadows, 1972). In this set of beliefs, increased productivity may well be "bad."

The point to be made here is that increased or decreased productivity defined in terms of worker output is neither good nor bad. Productivity is a system input; the positive or negative impact of that input is determined elsewhere in the system.

What is "Productivity"?

From a measurement and evaluation standpoint, it may be worthwhile to take a somewhat closer look at the various meaning of "productivity." In short, what is it that we are trying to measure and evaluate? As Judson (1976) points out: "There are too many loose definitions of productivity [p. 62]." He continues to make an important distinction among technical, economic, and social productivity. These three kinds of productivity depend on where the observer looks and, influence the consequences of increased or decreased productivity.

1. Technical productivity is that associated with the workplace and concerns the direct goods or services produced by individuals or work groups coupled with the tools of the workplace. Most discussions are concerned with this level of productivity and, of course, enhancing it.

2. Economic productivity will not automatically result from increased technical productivity—as is so commonly assumed. Greater investment in the workplace for increased technical productivity may result in increased and noncompetitive costs for the products or services. It would appear, for example, that this trend may be the central problem in the sharp increase in health service and system costs. Health technology has shown remarkable advances in technical productivity; there is some question, however, whether the economic system can afford these improvements.

3. Social productivity refers to the desirability and/or usefulness of the products or services produced, a point already made here. Increased "social" productivity may be a societal evil, if the demand considerably and consistently exceeds the supply of scarce resources.

In the broadest sense, productivity assessment must take into account all levels of productivity: technical, economic, and social. Obviously, this is very difficult to do. The emphasis of this chapter is oriented toward technical (and principally the labor component) productivity and it's measurement and evaluation. But that this emphasis is incomplete should never be overlooked. Enhancing technical productivity can lead to economic and social disaster for an individual, an organization, or a society. Further, increasing labor productivity alone will not automatically insure positive economic and/or social benefits. Labor productivity is a part of the measurement and evaluation problem; never is it all of the problem.

SOME GENERAL MEASUREMENT PROBLEMS

Like most areas of measurement in the behavioral and social sciences, productivity assessment involves some extremely difficult measurement and data interpretation issues. Although specific issues are discussed in the following section in the context of different classes of work, it may be of value to note and discuss some general measurement problems that may occur in any application of productivity assessment.

Collection and Dissemination of Productivity Measures

Public Law 94-136 (National Productivity and Quality of Working Life Act of 1975) charged the Federal Government with the responsibility of collecting and disseminating national productivity measures. The National Center for Productivity and Quality of Working Life, created by this act, is an attempt to satisfy this and other objectives in the goal of improving national productivity. This goal, as might be expected, has turned out to be a very substantial and difficult task (General Accounting Office, 1978a).

The General Accounting Office (1978b) has pointed out that: "Currently no unified system exists for the collection, processing, analysis, and dissemination of information, documents, and material in the field of productivity (p. 5)." The development of a National Productivity Clearinghouse is proposed "to provide national and international data and knowledge on various aspects of productivity—effective methods, their costs, how long they take to provide results, etc. (p. 5)" In the meantime, there exists no substantial body of detailed productivity data except the aggregate numbers provided by the U.S. Bureau of Labor Statistics.

In the ideal, it is possible to imagine a national data center to which all segments of American society could input productivity data. One of the first problems of such a (presumably computerized) national productivity data bank would be standardization of what should be measured, how the processes should be measured, and how the data should be interpreted. None of these steps have been accomplished, and the only detailed sources of productivity data are isolated case histories, field demonstrations, and research papers. Standardization of measurement simply does not exist.

Resistance to Productivity Measures

Most measurement systems can be developed without getting the acceptance of the "processes" being measured. Productivity assessment appears to be an exception. Several authors have insisted upon the participation of the worker (the "process" being measured) in measurement development (Delamotte, 1975, pp. 412–4). Judson (1976) is typical: "Any measurement of improved productivity must use a method agreed upon between management and employees (p. 67)."

The reason is obvious: Productivity measurement by it's very nature is an evaluation of worker performance, and, as Usilaner (1978) comments: "No one wants to be held accountable (p. 61)." Resistance to productivity measurement can be expected in any application. It is vital that the measurement data be valid (A. Campbell, 1978, p. 41) and that the measurement be *perceived* as valid and fair. If it is not seen as such by the worker, the impact of productivity assessment may be negative and harmful to productivity.

Some of the possible negative consequences have been known for over a century in industrial manufacturing through the phenomena of worker "limitation of output" or "systematic soldiering" (Lupton, 1976). If the worker believes productivity measurement will be used for work "speedup," informal group limitation of work output will very probably occur. It is possible, therefore, that the very act of measuring productivity may result in decreased productivity.

General or Specific Measurement?

There have been many criticisms that commonly used productivity measures are too general and abstract (A. Campbell, 1978, p. 41). John Campbell (1978) has stated the need for specific measurement strongly:

> It is very dangerous to develop measures of any organizational characteristics without keeping firmly in mind the *specific* decisions for which the data are to be used. Thus, before indices of productivity or motivation are monitored, the organization must have a very clear idea of why it wants the information and how the information is to be used . . . At every stage in the process, three questions must be asked: What questions do we want to answer? Will the data base toward which we are moving answer the questions we want it to answer? Are we inadvertently moving toward asking the same data to serve conflicting aims?

He continues:

> competence, or performance, can only be assessed by referring to a long list of highly specific task objectives. Specification of these objectives serves as a rigorous definition of what it is we want the individual performer to be able to do [pp. 68–69].

Many lines of evidence, some of which are mentioned later, support these statements.

This requirement for measurement specificity places many demands on a productivity measurement and assessment system. First, it assumes a detailed analysis of worker performance dimensions that can probably only be achieved by extensive task analysis (McCormick, 1976). Second, it will probably impose an in-depth and very costly measurement system. Third, management must set specific standards for which kinds of and how much outputs are expected: This may be the most difficult problem of all.

How Will the Numbers be Used?

We do not normally measure for the sake of measuring. Measurement is a process and not an end goal. We measure for information that is usable. Indeed, assessment, as distinguished from measurement, is the application of standards and meaning to measurement. Assessment comes from outside the measurement system and is, in part, determined by the uses to which the numbers will be used. In this literature, the problem is not finding uses to which to put the measures; rather the problem is making sense out of the many possible uses. Some of the pertinent areas are as follows.

Productivity Data as a Motivator.   It would seem obvious that productivity data, first and foremost, are used to measure worker output. But even this has been questioned; Judson (1976), for example, feels that productivity measurement "must involve measurement at motivating workers and only secondarily to appraise progress [p. 76]." It is very clear that the main stated purpose of productivity measurement and assessment is improving worker productivity and not measurement of productivity per se (Glaser, 1980; Sutermeister, 1976; and many others).

The use of productivity measures to motivate workers raises many fascinating measurement problems. At a minimum, the numbers must not be threatening to the workers in that increasing productivity should not penalize them—a condition difficult to meet in many cases (Fein, 1974).

Feedback of Productivity Data.   Further, the numbers may be used in the workplace as feedback to the employee. How feedback should be accomplished is a complex matter. Pritchard, Montagno, and Moore (1978) uncovered from the literature 14 possible feedback conditions that might influence productivity. Experimentally, they studied five: (1) high versus low specificity; (2) personal (evaluative) versus impersonal (nonevaluative); (3) delayed versus immediate feedback; (4) group versus individual; and (5) public versus private feedback. Of interest here is the possible significance of the results for requirements to be placed on future productivity assessment systems. For example, feedback was superior to nonfeedback in performance effects; this means that mechanisms for productivity assessment systems should assume feedback modes. Further, high specificity feedback was superior to low feedback. Pritchard, Montagno, and Moore (1978) have stated: "Gross feedback on quality and quantity of performance indeed appears to have motivating properties, but more information is needed by the workers in order to know how to change their behavior to be more productive [p. 32]." As noted earlier, this means very precise measurement. Finally, how quickly results should be fedback is important, because it will determine how fast the data have to be processed. This study found delayed feedback superior to immediate feedback, a finding not consistent with the general literature and current reinforcement theory. One essential factor in the design of a productivity assessment system would be how fast processed data must be available; the current literature provides no consistent guidelines for making that decision.

Two other points from this study are illustrative for measurement:

1. Both quality and error scores were recorded in an attempt to measure both *quantity* and *quality* of worker performance. As might be expected, there appeared to be a low correlation, if any, between quantity and error scores (a finding not inconsistent with other reports, such as Seashore, Indik, & Georgopoulus, 1960). For example, with public versus private feedback, there were no differences. On the other hand, high specificity feedback resulted in a slight increase in quantity but a marked reduction in errors. Much more work is needed on the relationships between quantity and quality measures.

2. In addition to quantity and quality of performance, Pritchard, Montagno, and Moore (1978) measured job satisfaction. It would appear that the trend of the literature and actual practice is that a second major measurement domain pertaining to worker's attitudes toward the job must be assumed; performance data are not enough (Muckler, 1977b).

Measures of the Quality of Working Life.   These measure sets in turn may go beyond job satisfaction directly associated with specific work factors into all conditions surrounding work (Locke, 1976, Table 3, p. 1315) and into the more general problem of the measurement of the total quality of working life. Dyer and Hoffenberg (1975), Goodale, Hall, Burke, and Jayner (1975) Lawler (1975), Seashore (1975), Sheppard (1975), and Walton (1975) have produced a stimulating set of articles on the issue of the definition and measurement of the quality of working life.

The main theme of these articles is the measurement to determine the worker's perception of working life in it's totality and even as a part of the worker's total life space. This assumes that we cannot understand and assess job performance without this information. In short, if we are to understand job performance, we must understand the individual who performs the job. This requirement would place a tremendous burden on the measurement system underlying productivity assessment. It is difficult even to estimate the total number of dimensions that might be included except to guess that it would be very large.

Measurement for Whom?   Seashore (1975, Table 1) makes an important distinction among three kinds of measures of "work role effectiveness [p. 110]," as seen from the perspective of the worker, the employer, and the community or society. Each segment might require different kinds of data. For example, at the higher policy levels, one goal for information from research is to Srivastra, (1975): "the *identification of action levers*, variables which can be manipulated to create desirable changes in satisfaction and productivity [p. 6].": but these are aggregate variables for national policy decisions. At any rate, for these three categories, Seashore defines 21 measurement dimensions, all of them complex. The development and implementation of a productivity assessment system based on all these measures would be a formidable undertaking; no such system exists today, or even an approximation of it, to the knowledge of this writer.

A few additional words could be said about measures of interest to the employer. To be sure, quality and quantity of output are primary measures. But indirect measures of counterproductive behavior, turnover, absences, and transfer rates add more relevant information. These are of interest not only to the employer, but they may also be related to employee satisfaction or dissatisfaction, although the connection is not clear (Kilbridge, 1974a).

Human Resources Accounting.   One step further allows us to combine all these measurement issues into one general topic area: Human Resources Accounting (HRA), a notion stemming from the work of Likert (1967). As Dierkes and Coppock (1975) have described this concept, it allows for the measurement, monitoring, and evaluation of all aspects of manpower and personnel utilization in the working environment. HRA would provide a measurement base for all pertinent decisions in the three areas defined by Seashore (1975): the employee, the employer, and the community or society. It is essential for evaluating technical, economic, and social productivity. At present, HRA is a dream in the literature, and one that has it's critics (Cannon, 1974; Swann, 1978). But, theoretically, HRA could provide a rational framework for productivity. At the least, it would give some meaning to productivity assessment and, in turn, would help in defining a measure set that would be usable.

The major difficulty with the state of the art of productivity assessment today is that it is composed of specific measures and part solutions that may be useful in very specific cases. But, as a general approach for cost-effective measurement (of which more later), it is ineffective if not harmful. What is needed is a framework like HRA to establish decision and information needs and then the best-measurement system to meet those needs.

Personnel Actions: The Problem of Pay.   In the meantime, thousands of personnel actions per day must be made. One of the most critical is compensation. The question to be noted here briefly is: What numbers are used (needed) to determine pay? Traditional wisdom assumes that the worker is paid in direct proportion to performance and the value of that performance to the organization. Further, many wage and salary plans stress both past performance and predictions of future performance enhancement. In short, pay plans (wages, incentives, bonuses, raises, profit sharing, etc.) are often perceived (by management) as motivators for increased future productivity (Katzell & Yankelovich, 1975).

There is a reasonable amount of evidence suggesting that if pay is closely tied to performance, pay can be an effective motivator (Lawler, 1971, 1973). But, there are at least two general cautions:

1. The performance data must be perceived by the employees as reasonably specific, complete, valid, and representing attainable goals. And, pay increases for increased productivity should not lead to future negative personnel actions, such as layoffs created by increased productivity. Finally, it may well be that effective wage, salary, bonus, and/or profit-sharing plans will be effective only in so far as the plans are jointly developed by employees and employers (O'Toole, 1973). This, hopefully, would create some shared perceptions between labor and management.

2. Pay or bonus increments must be perceived as meaningful and satisfying to the employee. What may seem to be a significant raise by the employer may not seem so to the employee.

From the standpoint of productivity measurement and assessment, these conditions create two demands. First, the performance measurement system must be acceptably valid, reliable, complete, and fair. Second, the perceptions of the workers concerning compensation must be measured in addition to performance. For example, depending on the pay system used, it is possible to get both higher worker motivation and decreased satisfaction with the job (Schwab, 1974). Further, the numbers alone are necessary but not sufficient. Fair standards of performance must be established by management or labor-management participative teams; these standards will not automatically be generated by the productivity assessment system itself.

Fair pay methods can be dramatically successful. Salvendy (1976), for example, has reported in a production situation significant increases in productivity coupled with remarkable decreases in absenteeism, grievances, and labor turnover. Much of this success hinged on workers' perceptions of fair pay and certainly not on the productivity measurement system.

A Comment.   In productivity assessment, the numbers are only a beginning. They are part of a total information and decision system. At present, there is no detailed system measurement theory matching uses, information needs, and measure sets. Even if such theory did exist, the success of any productivity measurement system would largely depend, in practice, on the perceptions of the individuals involved and the conditions under which they system is applied. It is doubtful that the productivity measurement and assessment system would even account for a large portion of the variance associated with worker behavior.

Measuring Change: System and Measurement Stability

The validity and reliability of measurement of any system will be determined, in part, by the stability of the system being measured. The more stable the system, the easier measurement becomes. A basic question, therefore, in this area is: How stable can we expect the system to be for productivity assessment? In the work environment, we can reasonably expect both continual change and great complexity. Any method of productivity assessment, therefore, must be sensitive to possible instability of working conditions. Measurement must be designed accordingly, with increased measurement demands as change and complexity increase.

From the standpoint of total workplace output (i.e., technical productivity), the phenomena of changing output levels is well-known in production "learning" or "experience" curves (Bodde, 1976). With experience, production normally becomes more efficient. It is doubtful, however, that any production system becomes completely stable, and some productivity variance can be expected at any time (Kola & Hitchings, 1973). Further, in any work situation, certain required operations may be viewed as "nonproductive," such as unexpected tool handling and operator movements in and around the workplace that are not easy to predict (Kilbridge, 1974b). Greater variability may be expected at the beginning of production runs (Beged Dov & Gregory, 1972). All these factors, and many others, combine to make for a highly variable and relatively unstable technical productivity output. Much variance can be expected even in those production lines that have been in place for some time.

One significant source of variance will always be variability in worker output. For over 50 years, industrial psychologists have reported data on operator variability in production that may be due either to the worker or the system of which the operator is a part (Salvendy & Seymour, 1973, pp. 197–202). A recent study, for example, by Rothe (1978) showed that week to week output variability can be markedly influenced by the presence or absence of an incentive system, but, that under any case: "a rather long period of time is needed to produce a reliable criterion of output: A very short period such as a few days or weeks will not supply a reliable output criterion [p. 45]." The data cited by Bodde (1976, p. 59) confirms this comment with the indication that productivity changes due to incentive systems may continue over several months of operations.

Certain kinds of organizational demands may be expected to shift worker output levels significantly. For example, input load demands exceeding the worker's capabilities may be perceived as stressors (McGrath, 1976) with uncertain consequences but with reasonably certain variability. Rotations of shiftwork may result in the worker not being present at all (Nicholson, Jackson, & Howes, 1978). It might be noted that these findings are not limited to blue-collar production-line work. Research and development, for example, is notoriously unpredictable, unstable, and poorly productive in part, perhaps, because the process is so little understood (Carlsson, Keane, & Martin, 1976).

For productivity assessment, the most important measurement implications of these facts are in the duration, frequency, and specificity of productivity measurement. Due to cost, among other factors, continuous measurement is not desirable; work sampling methods are normally used (Grillo & Berg, 1959; Hansen, 1960). As Salvendy and Seymour (1973) have noted, in production situations, this is normally the responsibility of the industrial engineer: "who observes the work of a typical operator, selected to represent the characteristics of the average operator [p. 204]." Work sampling in this manner is a technique the validity and reliability of which has not been spectacularly successful. With the possible exception of the work of Moskowitz (1965), there has been little extensive methodological work to establish standardized methods of work sampling that would specify duration, frequency, and depth of measurement.

Further, with the current emphasis of techniques introduced to improve productivity, the basic experimental design and measurement model is a before and after method. A baseline of productivity must be established (before) to measurement the productivity impact (after) of the techniques used. There is certainly no current standardization of the duration of "before" and "after" measurement periods, if, indeed, such standardization is possible. In light of high work instability and such well-known phenomena as the "Hawthorne Effect," very precise measurement and care over how the measurement is performed will be essential to understanding the meaning of productivity changes when they occur (Parsons, 1974).

Data Sources: "Subjective" or "Objective"?

Fundamental to productivity assessment is the productivity measurement data base. The question is: What kinds of numbers are collected and how are they collected? Many alternatives are available in practice to develop a specific productivity measurement system.

Data Collection.   There are at least three basic ways of collecting productivity measures: (1) from the system output directly; (2) from worker self-reports; and (3) from observation.

1. Most practitioners would probably prefer measurement derived directly from some part of the system process. In many cases, this is indeed possible where a clear-cut outcome occurs. In production lines with discrete, sequential, and countable events, the measurement problem appears to be relatively simple.

The classic case of bricklayers and number of bricks laid per hour (or any unit of time) has often been cited. In addition, if automated instrumentation is available to count the events, the measurement system should derive large quantities of "objective" data.

In practice, there are at least three problems with this measurement approach. First, many jobs do not lend themselves to clear and discrete units. For example, supervision and management tasks are very difficult to categorize satisfactorily. Second, for many jobs, the effective output is not immediate and available for easy counting. Quantity scores may have to be combined with subsequent scores of quality. Where the process is a long-term one (e.g., research or teaching), years may be involved before a good assessment is possible. This frequently leads to the enormously unsatisfying step of measuring immediate or inter-mediate "process" rather than the final outcome. This problem has been widely recognized, and lamented, in all areas of training and training devices. Third, for many systems applications, there is often a reluctance to include such measure-ment in the process. This resistance is often vague but, perhaps, is a reflection of an apparently general feeling that performance measurement is to be avoided if possible.

2. It would seem simple to reject productivity measures from the self-report of the workers themselves on the grounds that such measures would be highly subjective and, perhaps, highly distorted in favor of the workers. Yet, there is some evidence (Murrell, 1969, 1974; Hartley, Brecht, Pagery, Weeks, Chapanis, & Hoecker, 1977) that subjective self-reports are a feasible alternative in at least some cases. It would appear that the accuracy of such estimates depends on the kinds of activities the workers perform and the kinds of judg-ments that have to be made (McCormick, 1976; Klemmer & Snyder, 1972). The more quantitative the judgments, the less accurate they will be. A self-report method widely used in some areas is the "work diary," in which the individual keeps an on-going log of activities as they occur. How accurate work diaries are is not known, but if they are shown to be reasonably reliable, they might well be an inexpensive source of raw productivity numbers.

3. Productivity measurement by observation of worker performance is in some disrepute. It is widely known that the observation of the work of an individual or team by another individual or team will probably affect the indi-vidual or team performance. By analogy to the Heisenberg Principle, the mea-surement of work in this way affects the process being measured. This may be particularly true where the observational methods are being used to establish "work standards" against which the worker will be evaluated. Parenthetically, many observational methods have been tested for this purpose (Salvendy & Seymour, 1973, Chapter V), all of which are subject to serious difficulty. Yet, research and practical interest continues in the area of standardized observation, at least with respect to job content if not for performance measurement (Jenkins, Nadler, Lawler, & Cammann, 1975).

"Subjectivity" Versus "Objectivity".   It is apparently axiomatic that "objective" measures are to be preferred to "subjective" measures. The latter are any measures contaminated by human action during the act of measurement. Objective measures come from measurement independent of the human observer and are, presumably, "true" measures. Thus, self-report or human observation must generate subjective measures. At least one observer (Muckler, 1977a) has suggested that this distinction is false and that, in fact, it is not possible to measure anything without the intervention of the human at some point in the measurement process. In brief, there are four fundamental steps in all measurement, no matter what is being measured: selecting measures, collecting data, analyzing data, and interpreting data. Human intervention is rampant in all four of these steps. In short, there is no such thing as objective measurement in the strict sense of the term. Rather, the emphasis should be on the characteristics of the measures derived in terms of at least six criterion measures of the measure: validity, reliability, precision, nonreactivity, generalizability, and cost.

Productivity Indices

Much of the confusion about productivity assessment has come from the wide variety of usages that the term *productivity* enjoys. To Vough and Asbell (1979, p. 4) productivity is the following ratio:

$$\text{Productivity} = \frac{\text{Output (in goods or services)}}{\text{Input (in dollars, both direct and indirect)}} \tag{1}$$

This is surely a global measure for a total production system and contains all the resources that are needed for both inputs and outputs to the total system. Labor productivity is a submerged subset within both. It is much more common to restrict the term *productivity* to the human resource of the organization or system. In a global (i.e., national) sense, Malkiel (1979) defines productivity as:

$$\text{Productivity} = \frac{\text{Total Output of Economy (Real Gross National Product)}}{\text{Total Civilian Employment}} \tag{2}$$

Or, simply, a relationship of output per labor hour worked. It is this kind of number that is so often used to demonstrate the declining (or increasing) productivity of nations and industries.

Sibson (1976) is one of the few who has distinguished among productivity indices in terms of four such ratios:

$$\text{Productivity} = \frac{\text{Physical Output}}{\text{Total Man-Hours of Work}} \tag{3}$$

Sibson (1976, p. 48) states that this is the "traditional" index of productivity that is too simple for modern complex organizations. A second index, Key Productivity, gives a finer look at the outputs:

$$\text{Key Productivity} = \frac{\text{Output Product A} + \text{Output Product B} + \ldots}{\text{Total Man-hours of Work}} \tag{4}$$

that purports to look more closely at the key products of the system or organization. A third index translates input and output into money terms in "dollarized productivity":

$$\text{Dollarized Productivity} = \frac{\text{Total Sales (\$)}}{\text{Total Payroll (\$)}} \tag{5}$$

But, Sibson (1976, p. 49) states that a more informative measure is "productiveness" rather than productivity:

$$\text{Productiveness} = \frac{\left(\begin{array}{c}\text{Correctness}\\\text{of Action}\end{array} + \begin{array}{c}\text{Measure}\\\text{of Output}\end{array}\right) - \begin{array}{c}\text{Disruptive}\\\text{Effect}\end{array}}{\text{Hours of Work}} \tag{6}$$

that takes into account the value of the work done, the efficiency with which the work is done, and the degree to which work performed might have a disruptive effect on other elements in the system.

A variation of Sibson's "productiveness" index has been subjected to extensive empirical test by Hanes and Kriebel (1978). In their terms, productivity is measured by:

$$\text{Productivity} = \frac{\sum_{j=1}^{J} (V_j - \Sigma \Delta E_j)}{L + C + R + M} \tag{7}$$

where V_j =   total value to user of each j products or services
   ΔE_j =   cost penalty for each factor causing inefficiences
      C =   capital cost
      L =   labor cost
      R =   materials cost
      M =   cost of miscellaneous supplies and services

Assuming that V_j and E_j can be given satisfactory dollar values, this is an extremely sophisticated dollarized productivity index. The index was tested at three computer centers. It is interesting that a key instrument for measuring V_j and E_j was a subjective rating questionnaire. It may be that, as Sibson (1976) comments: "Ultimately the measure of productivity in today's contemporary business is qualitative [p. 49]."

A number of comments can be made about these indices that reflect the difficulty they generate in application:

1. It would be desirable if some standardization was developed so that the term *productivity* could have some common meaning. The word is used so freely that it is difficult to know what the word means at all.

2. The input denominators may refer to all the inputs in the system or to labor inputs only. As equation (7) makes clear, the output is a function of many kinds of inputs of which labor is only one. Only equation (3) is limited to labor input and output performance.

3. The resulting ratio numbers may be so gross as to obscure critical differences in productivity within industries or groups. Data were cited at the beginning of this chapter on declines in U.S. productivity over the period of 1973–1977. But, other data, shown in Table 2.1, show a much different picture, when productivity figures are given for selected U.S. industries. These data show that some industrial groups are demonstrating substantial growth and not decline.

4. When, as in equation (4), the outputs are combined, the sum may obscure significant differences between product output and the groups that produce them.

5. There appears to be no escape from some "value" judgment about the value of the product. Both equation (6) and (7) contain value terms.

6. The equations make the confusion stated at the beginning of this chapter among technical, economic, and social productivity (Judson, 1976). In practice,

TABLE 2.1
Output Growth Per Employee
Hour: 1972–1977

Industry Group	Average Annual Percent Change
Hosiery	+10.2%
Malt Beverages	+7.0
Mattresses and Bedsprings	+5.0
Motor vehicles and equipment	+4.0
Canning and preserving	+2.9
Tobacco products	+2.0
Nonmetallic minerals	0
Retail food stores	−1.0
Candy	−2.7
Iron and coal mining	−3.5

Source: Department of Labor, Bureau of Labor Statistics, Bulletin 2002, 1978.

there have been two primary uses for productivity measures. First, some continuous measure is needed to express labor effectiveness. Second, some measure is required to show the economic value (dollarized productivity) of labor. None of these indices provide an uncontaminated and clear measure of either.

7. It may well be that a technical productivity index that concentrates on labor inputs and work outputs is not feasible. This is reflected in equation (7) that recognizes that output is a function of more than labor input. This is a recognition that, in modern technology, output is rarely, in either goods or services, a simple and direct result of what people do.

Causation and Uses

Productivity measures are not collected just for the sake of collecting numbers. Like all measures, they must serve some purpose. Two issues are of importance here: (1) productivity measures as an indication of the causes of productivity decline or increase; and (2) productivity measures as tools for increasing employee productivity.

1. Where productivity shows an increase or a decline one immediate question is: Why? Why is it, as shown in Table 2.1, that some industrial groups are showing marked increases in productivity, whereas others are in marked decline? One purpose of productivity assessment might well be *diagnostic;* that is, the measurement should provide some indication of the reasons for productivity change. Unfortunately, all the available evidence points to a remarkable complexity in the specific determinants of labor productivity. In the most detailed analysis to date, Sutermeister (1976) has suggested some 33 possible determinants that may affect job productivity. These are roughly divided into such general categories as individual needs, physical conditions, social conditions, organizational variables, leadership, and so forth. And, it is very probable that for every real-life situation, many of these determinants are acting together in some unknown amounts.

Trends in the literature appear to concentrate on single variables or small clusters of variables. For some years, there has been substantial interest in such items as: (1) job satisfaction and productivity (Dunn & Stephens, 1972); (2) quality of working life (Herrick, 1975); (3) consumer behavior and productivity (Lovelock & Young, 1979); (4) job redesign (Pritchard, Montagno, & Moore, 1978); (5) team pressures (Pepinsky, Pepinsky, & Pavlik, 1960); (6) environmental variables and productivity (Young & Berry, 1979), and so forth. What all these studies seem to indicate is that individual and team productivity is a very complicated matter.

From the standpoint of productivity assessment and with a diagnostic measurement goal, it becomes very difficult to specify what particular measures should be in the total measure set. The primary technique at the present time is that the author includes those measures he or she thinks are relevant, which turn out to be those measures of the variables that are perceived to be important. Even worse, there is a substantial economic point of view that reduced productivity is due to factors other than labor, such as reduced investment for R & D, and government regulations (Malkiel, 1979, p. 82). How one measures all of this is unknown. But, surely, numbers such as that shown in Table 2.1 give no diagnostic information whatsoever.

2. As has been described previously, productivity measures have long been used as a tool for changing productivity. If they are to be used properly, they must be tied in some way to causal dimensions in the work situation. And these dimensions may be complex. For example, if the focus is on quality of working life, very extensive measurement can be required (Herrick, 1975), and measures covering the whole organization must probably be taken (Glaser, 1980).

Thus, when productivity measures are directly used in the work situation, there are a number of measurement requirements that must be observed. First, the measures should be specific to major job dimensions. Second, they will probably have to be in depth to insure that the measures reflect the actual process. Third, they must be credible to the individual and the organization. Fourth, they must be reasonably complete in the sense of covering all essential elements. Lawler (1978) has noted:

> When you start fiddling around with just one thing, say job design, in a complex interrelated system, if you are not prepared to go and look at other aspects, you are going to do more harm than good, because the system usually is in some kind of balance even though it may not be the best balance [p. 91].

This demands very thorough measurement both in depth and scope.

Performance Objectives

A critical part of any measurement set is a statement of performance objectives. Performance objectives come in two parts: (1) What behaviors are important?; and (2) What levels of behaviors are desired? It is surprising that many workers do not know what critical aspects of the job the management or organization desires. Many of the modern performance appraisal systems attempt to be very specific on this point. On the other hand, some supervisors are reluctant to state performance objectives in the possibility that employees will work to those objectives and not others. Technically, the problem from a measurement standpoint is criterion deficiency, when the key performance dimensions are not (or cannot be) identified. For measurement to be reasonable, system states must be established. Careful measurement of nose length will not give adequate estimates of body height.

Traditionally, the desired amounts of production have been derived from either: (1) estimation of physiological or psychological limits in the workplace; or (2) estimates based on observed performance in the workplace (Salvendy & Seymour, 1973, Chapter 5). For some purposes, this has been satisfactory, and, indeed, a great deal of time and effort is spent in the development of "work standards." But, as may be seen from equation (6) and (7) earlier, there appears to be an increasing requirement to assess the "value" of production. It is not just what is done but the value of doing it. How value is to be measured is a very difficult problem, but it is probably an inevitable part of future measurement (Messick, 1975).

Organizational Criteria

Productivity assessment must take place in some organizational setting (Campbell, Bownas, Peterson, and Dunnette, 1974). In addition to the normal psychometric criteria about measures, some organizational criteria can also be stated (Moore, 1970; Muckler, 1979). They are eight in number, and they apply to productivity assessment in any organization:

1. *Suitability.* Are the measures relevant, and do they support the purpose and mission of the organization?
2. *Feasibility.* Are the measures theoretically attainable within the organization?
3. *Acceptability.* Will the management accept the measures and provide the resources to collect the measures?
4. *Value.* Are these measures the best buy for the money?
5. *Achievability.* Can, in fact, the measures be collected?
6. *Measurability.* Can the measures be quantified in terms of quality, quantity, time, and cost?
7. *Adaptability and Flexibility.* Can we change the measures to reflect changing organizational environments and management needs?
8. *Commitment.* Does everybody in the organization want to do it?

It is probable that any applied productivity system will be evaluated against most if not all of these criteria either formally or informally.

SOME PRODUCTIVITY ASSESSMENT EXAMPLES

It may be useful to illustrate some of these general measurement problems with specific examples. Further, productivity assessment difficulties within the examples can be noted.

Retail Sales

A very common metric for retail sales productivity is that given earlier as equation (5) for dollarized productivity. As a measure of organizational productivity, this is:

$$\text{Organizational Productivity} = \frac{\text{Total Sales (\$)}}{\text{Total Payroll (\$)}}$$

This is certainly an indicator of the proportion of payroll costs that are involved and may be useful in assessing that percentage. In most organizations, payroll costs are the most significant cost element. This number could well be useful across departments, companies, and industries.

This measure is also commonly used for measuring individual performance. In this case, the ratio becomes:

$$\text{Individual Productivity} = \frac{\text{Total Individual Sales (\$)}}{\text{Individual Payroll Cost (\$)}}$$

Such a measure is often used to indicate the sales effectiveness of individuals.

The dollarized productivity index, however, has three possibly major deficiencies in evaluating retail sales:

1. As shown in equation (7) earlier, payroll costs are not the only key cost in total sales. Material costs, for example, will vary widely depending on the particular product. One must know what other costs are involved in total sales dollar figures.

2. Payroll costs in themselves are complex. Often, only direct wages are considered. But, in current labor markets, fringe benefits may assume a significant portion of the total payroll cost of an individual to an organization.

3. As a measure of individual productivity, the measure fails to take into account sales demands. In retail sales, it is obvious that total sales will depend in large part on how many customers are available. Setting of, and achieving, daily sales quotas in dollars is dependent not only on how many sales are made to customers but on how many customers are available. In retail sales, therefore, the system is open-loop; the input load is highly variable and, in many cases, apparently only very partially predictable. Even where the worker has a high level of motivation, there may be little opportunity to increase productivity for factors over which the worker has no control (Herman, 1973). To use this kind of number to measure individual sales effectiveness may be seriously unfair. Some measure such as the ratio of sales contacts to actual sales may be required.

Production Examples

There has been a continuing increase in practice to measure individual productivity; indeed, one may suspect that millions of numbers are collected per day
for this purpose. A very small amount of these data, of course, are available in
published form. What does appear in the public record has a number of interesting features. First, there are a vast variety of productivity measures and indices.
Second, they tend to be system-specific. Third, they tend to show high variability, suggesting that long sample periods are necessary to understand the data.
Fourth, better data are now appearing as a result of planned interventions to
improve worker productivity. Four examples may be noted:

1. Latham and his associates have published a number of studies on planned
interventions in logging operations. The main purpose of these studies was a test
of the impact of goal setting on performance. In the first study, the productivity
measure was the "percent legal net weight of 36 logging trucks" that transported
the logs cut by the crews (Latham & Baldes, 1975). This measure is particularly
useful, because, when a large increase in productivity was shown over a 9-month
period, the results could be translated directly into dollar savings. And, of particular interest is the fact that the intervention took 4 months to have a substantial
impact. In a second study (Latham & Yukl, 1975), the productivity measure
shifted to "cunits"—or 100 cubic feet of wood—per week. The primary interest
of the study concerned the education of the loggers and three methods of goal
setting. Performance objectives were set before the study, and it is interesting
that under even the best conditions, only 55% of the performance objectives were
achieved. In a third study, yet a third measure of productivity was used: "Output
rate was measured by dividing the number of cords (each cord, or pile of wood,
is 4 feet × 4 feet × 8 feet) delivered by each crew by the total man-hours
worked." (Latham & Locke, 1975, p. 525) In this case, the principal variable
was a restriction of the times the wood could be sold. With such restriction,
productivity increased.

2. Rothe (1978) has described the impact of individual and team pay incentives on the output of foundry employees. Here, the measure of productivity was
percent performance of standard by week. The important finding did not seem to
be the amount of productivity improvement but, rather, the consistency of production. Based on unpublished work by Benningson, Rothe proposes a productivity consistency ratio:

$$\text{Productivity Consistency} = \frac{\text{Intraindividual Consistency}}{\text{Interindividual Consistency}}$$

where intraindividual consistency is the ratio of the individual's highest output
divided by lowest output over the entire sampling period, and interindividual

consistency is the ratio of highest to lowest employee output per week. For future studies on the effect of intervention techniques, it may be useful to consider preintervention and postintervention performance consistency as well as the absolute amounts of performance enhancement. At the very least, in the setting of work standards and pay incentive systems, degree of allowable performance variability should be considered.

3. Daily variation in worker output is a phenomena long established in the literature. Monk and Conrad (1979) found, in general, afternoon performance to be superior to morning performance for clerical workers. But, this appears to be dependent on the type of task. In some cases (e.g., speed and accuracy of typing), there was no significant differences between morning and afternoon. This study is interesting because: (1) it attempted to sample by eight different tests what clerical workers do; and (2) the results suggest that daily task scheduling might improve productivity.

4. Gross (1978) reports on the effect on productivity of an organizational development program for maintenance personnel in communications and electronics. Productivity here is a group measure:

$$\text{Group Productivity} = \frac{\text{Actual Productive Work Hours}}{\text{Total Work Hours Available}}$$

To derive this ratio, it was necessary: (1) to specify carefully the detailed maintenance tasks performed; and (2) to establish a "fair work standard" that is necessary to determine "productive" work hours. It may be seen that a ratio of 1.0 would indicate that all the available work hours were productive. Sometimes, however, it was possible to obtain a ratio score of more than 1.0 that suggests some measurement difficulties in any productivity measure derived from average "fair" work standards.

Comment. The studies cited previously are of excellent quality for applied settings. But, they illustrate that, from a measurement standpoint, there is no standardization in the selection of productivity measures. It may be that standardization is impossible; measurement may have to be system-specific and situation-specific. Or, it may not be. Authors feel free to manipulate the productivity data in many kinds of ratios: there is some real question what these ratios mean. On one thing, all authors seem to be in agreement: The measurement of productivity requires substantial periods of time.

Data Management Centers

Reference has already been made to the work of Hanes and Kriebel (1978) in the development of equation (7) for computer data management centers. Because data processing is becoming a significant service industry, measurement in this specific case is of considerable interest. Peeples (1978) reports a case history of productivity measurement across 14 data centers. For this measurement system, seven basic objectives were assumed: (1) Establish performance objectives; (2) Record and report total performance; (3) Provide a basis of comparison; (4) Maintain historical records; (5) Measure and compare performance; (6) Foster competitive spirit; (7) Provide management and customer visibility. The measures themselves were divided into two classes: (1) data center measures; and (2) system development measures. The first included measures of efficiency and effectiveness; the former those concerned with internal center performance, the latter with outside service provided by the centers. System development measures included development in scheduling and maintenance. In all, 26 measures were taken. In the data reported by Peeples (1978, p. 224), time periods under measurement varied from 18 months to 6 years. In 25 of the 26 measures, substantial productivity improvement was shown. In addition to identifying critical dimensions, variable weighting was provided to each of the 26 measures reflecting the importance of each to management. For example, *effectiveness* was weighted essentially twice that of *efficiency*, denoting that the data management centers are service centers for others and do not exist simply to process numbers. This reflects the important distinction between process and product.

Programming Productivity. In every data processing center, or for that matter any computer-based system, a significant amount of time and resources will be spent programming or reprogramming. Current experience suggests: (1) that it is very difficult to measure programming productivity; and (2) that it is almost impossible to predict how much time and effort programming will require.

Research and Development

The scientific community, either in basic research or in applied research and development, has been subjected to increased emphasis on relevance, productivity, and accountability. This seems to be due primarily to the amounts of money that are being invested in research and development. Thurow (1978, p. 68) shows that in 1974 the United States investment in R & D exceeded 30 billion dollars. Lipetz (1965) demonstrated that in 1930 research and development investment was less than .2 percent of the U.S. gross national product, rising to 2.8 percent by 1962. Gibson (1979) has summed up the measurement problem: "Performance measurement in research, even by experts, is difficult and controversial ... Undoubtedly, there is resistance in the research community to the concept of direct evaluation of the quality of research."

Classes of Measures. One can distinguish three general classes of productivity measures for research and development; (1) planning and process performance; (2) indirect performance measures such as impact; and (3) direct performance evaluation. Some comments on each might be appropriate:

1. Increasing emphasis is being given to how well R & D is planned, and how well the research is conducted based on the plan. This is obviously a process kind of number (efficiency), and how these kinds of numbers would relate to product efficiency is not known. One such number is time allowed for research completion; some data (Andrews & Farris, 1972) suggest that time pressures are directly related to research productivity.

2. There has been increasing emphasis on indirect measures, such as impact of research. A measure that purports to measure impact is number of citations. How these numbers can be used is discussed in depth by Endler, Rushton, and Roediger (1978), based on an analysis of psychology departments using the 1975 Social Science Citation Index. Productivity is measured by the number of publications; impact by frequency of citation. In this case, both individuals and institutions were ranked by number of citations. Among several findings, it is interesting that a relatively small number of psychologists generate a very large portion of the citations. The third highest ranked individual (of 102) is the author of a widely used statistics handbook; one might question the nature of that "impact."

3. In a sense, number of citations is a measure of direct performance evaluation in that it suggests how widely used the work of an individual may be—at least for the period of time covered by the citation count. That there may be a variety of other measures is shown from an extensive study of scientific productivity across research units in six countries. Andrews (1979), in that study, lists some 30 measures that were taken for research units. These are shown in Table 2.2. As may be seen there, the measures are divided into product and quality estimates. These numbers were weighted and used, in turn, in a composite measure of R & D effectiveness, stressing: (1) general contribution of the unit to science and technology; (2) recognition given the unit; (3) social effectiveness of the unit; (4) training effectiveness of the unit; (5) administrative effectiveness of the unit; (6) R & D effectiveness of the unit; (7) applications effectiveness of the unit.

This measure set, as shown in Table 2.2, reflects all three classes of measures: process, indirect, and direct performance evaluation. Many of the measures can only be derived from subjective ratings. And, it reflects an apparent need to measure many different aspects of the scientific process beyond numbers of publications; other metrics (James & Ellison, 1973) have also stressed the need for multidimensional measurement.

Some Problems.   From a measurement standpoint, there are many problems connected with scientific productivity assessment. Only four will be noted here:

TABLE 2.2
Measures of Unit Scientific Productivity

PRODUCT
   1. Number of books
   2. Original articles published within unit's country
   3. Original articles published outside unit's country
   4. Patents within unit's country
   5. Patents outside unit's country
   6. Algorithms, blueprints, flowcharts, drawings, etc.
   7. Published reviews, bibliographies
   8. Internal reports on original R&D work
   9. Routine internal reports
 10. Other written reports
 11. Experimental prototypes of devices, instruments, etc.
 12. Experimental materials
 13. Prototype computer program
 14. Audiovisual materials
 15. Other undocumented products
QUALITY
 16. Productiveness
 17. Innovativeness
 18. R&D effectiveness
 19. Training effectiveness
 20. Effectiveness for non R&D objectives
 21. International reputation
 22. Demands for publications
 23. Social value of work
 24. Usefulness
 25. Success in meeting quality requirements
 26. Success in meeting schedules
 27. Success in staying within budget
 28. General contribution to science and technology
 29. Application of research results
 30. Use made of development activities

Note: Andrews (1979, p. 35)

1. Multidimensional sets such as those shown in Table 2.2 are probably not dimensionally clean. To return to an earlier point, the system states are not clear; intercorrelations between measures do not present a consistent pattern.

2. Impact measures such as citation references do not take into account (as presently used) the possibility of further delayed impact. The work of Mendel and Doppler may be cited as two cases where the impact of the original work was not felt for long periods of time. Further, what is popular today may not stand the test of time—which seems to be important in scientific knowledge.

3. It is in the nature of research that a certain percentage of risk (failure) can be expected. In one accounting study, it was shown that "only" 62% of the

research products were used; this may in fact be a spectacular record of application (or an indication that the research was not risky enough). The question is: What performance expectations should be placed on research considering the risk of failure?

4. There is a strong desire to translate R & D productivity results into dollarized indices that represent the return on investment or cost-benefit of research. Yet, Thurow (1978), an economist, suggests that this may not be wise; Thurow (1978) states: "It is impossible to know the exact cost and the precise benefits of any given R & D project. Setting a single dollar estimate is fundamentally misleading because it masks this uncertainty; at best only ranges of possible costs and benefits can be determined [p. 67]."

What does appear clear is that the societal units that pay for research and development are increasingly demanding measurement of R & D productivity. Measures are being imposed that may not properly reflect scientific outputs; an alternative is for the scientific community to provide better measures.

Faculty Performance

Far more pressure appears to be brought currently on evaluating the productivity of educational institutions (Anderson, Ball, & Murphy, 1975; Wittrock & Wiley, 1970). Here, attention is given to evaluation of faculty performance with emphasis on higher educational levels. As is seen, much more than teaching performance per se is involved. Of the many problems in assessing performance of educational institutions, it might be noted in passing that once again the question of delayed impact beyond instruction may be the primary measurement focus. What happens in college would seem to be less important than what happens to the student after he or she leaves college (Kulik, Kulik, & Cohen, 1979, p. 313; Pace, 1979, pp. 48–113).

Productivity Measures.   To many, the principal function of a faculty member is to teach. It is unfortunate, then, as Dressel (1976,) puts it: "There is no agreement among faculty members as to what constitutes good teaching [p. 341]." Be that as it may, there has evolved a large technology on evaluating teaching productivity. Three kinds of measures may be stressed. First, there are evaluations of the course content (Miller, 1979). Second, there are administrative measures such as course load and student/staff ratios. Third, there are direct rating estimates of teaching effectiveness provided by student ratings, self-assessment, and evaluation by colleagues (Centra, 1979). Posteducational measures of outcome are often mentioned but seldom measured.

But, there are many that would raise two objectives. First, there is doubt that any process measures are fair. For example, there is some question as to whether students have the knowledge to rate anything about a class except whether it pleased and/or entertained them. Second, it appears to many faculty members that pay and promotion—and particularly critical tenure decisions—depend far less on teaching skill than on other faculty activities. There is doubt that the measurement is either fair or complete.

A Model System.   One (anonymous) institution of higher learning has attempted to resolve many of these problems with the following model system. First, the institution makes it clear that it values four basic activities for a faculty member:

1. Performance as a teacher.
2. Creative contributions.
3. Service to the university.
4. Service to the community.

This is a management statement of performance objectives. Further, the four are weighted equally, and it is a management commitment that all of them are of value in assessing faculty performance.

Choices of measurement for each of these dimensions is left to the individual faculty member. For example, service to the community may be the local, state, federal, or civil communities. And, for the evaluation of teaching effectiveness, the faculty member may select classroom visits by peers, student evaluations, self-appraisal, important instructional materials, or, for that matter, any procedure that is acceptable to the Personnel Committee.

The individual faculty member is required to keep a continuous performance log with entries relevant to the four dimensions. These logs are examined annually by the Personnel Committee with a written evaluation from the Committee. That evaluation is subject to appeal to university management. Pay and promotion decisions must take into account the Personnel Committee evaluations.

Comment.   It appears to this writer that too much attention has been given to the instruments of evaluation and not enough to the process and goals of faculty evaluation. First and foremost, it is essential that the institution state explicitly its performance objectives and the relative value that it places on them. Second, it seems very desirable that the individual faculty member be given a wide range of options for demonstrating performance in each of the areas of objectives. Third, mechanisms for formal evaluation must be explicit with participation and appeal rights for the individual. Fourth, there must be some perceivable relation between evaluation and personnel decisions. If the process is not clear and fair, no psychometric elegance of a particular rating form will make it acceptable.

In passing, it might be noted that many institutions—organizational and otherwise—stress loyalty to the organization as a prime performance objective. It might be interesting further to note that Jauch, Gluech, and Osborn (1978) found that research productivity of 84 college professors was unrelated to organizational loyalty. On the other hand, professional commitment was highly related to research productivity.

GUIDELINES FOR A PRODUCTIVITY ASSESSMENT SYSTEM

Development of a Productivity Assessment System

It is not possible at this time to specify exact productivity assessment measurement systems except to copy those that have been used. One of the purposes of this chapter has been to identify the available literature and the systems that have been used for a variety of applications. It is possible, however, to suggest a method by which such measurement systems may be developed. Figure 2.1 shows a suggested development process for generating a productivity-assessment measurement system. The comments that follow pertain to the numbered boxes in Fig. 2.1:

1. It has been mentioned several times in this chapter that the uses to which the data will be put is a central and guiding part of any measurement system. "Information Need Analysis" refers to the answers to the questions: What do you want to know?; and what are you going to do with the information once you have it?

2. Much has also been made here of the question of performance objectives. As in the case of faculty assessment, the organization must decide what behaviors are valued, the relative importance of the behaviors, and the requirements for each behavior. This is by no means a simple process, but, in its absence, measurement has little focus and meaning.

3. In many cases, manipulations of the basic data will occur, frequently, as has been seen earlier, in the form of productivity indices. It is important at the start to get some idea of what kinds of indices will be used.

4. Sufficient information now exists to state a specification for the measurement dimensions that will be used in this system. This is a statement of "what" will be measured but not "how."

5. For any measurement dimensions there are always several alternative measures that can be used to express that dimension. This step defines the alternative measures—the "how" of measurement. Some of the criteria that may be applied to selecting from alternative measures are shown in Fig. 2.1. Some are classic psychometric tests of measures (e.g., validity and reliability); others pertain to how the measure will be used (e.g., generalizability and acceptability).

6. It is often difficult to convince organizations that preliminary tests of a measurement system are essential. But, it is particularly true in this application.

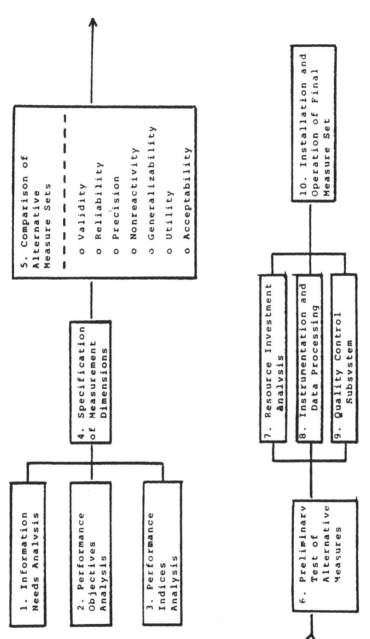

FIG. 2.1. Suggested process for developing a productivity assessment measurement system.

One critical problem will be the selection of adequate sampling periods; the available literature gives no indication of adequate sampling times.

7. Given a measurement set, it is now time to evaluate what resources must be generated to produce the measurement system. One serious problem is that the time spent operating the final productivity-assessment system must be a small part of available time and resources. Examination of some current teacher-reporting systems for local, state, and federal-government information needs has suggested that up to 35% of the teacher's time can be spent in preparing reports. This is time not spent teaching.

8. For many of the systems that have been mentioned here, automated instrumentation and data processing packages were used. In some cases (e.g., the data management centers), the equipment is already available; in many cases, it will not be present. It does not necessarily follow that any such tools will be needed; it depends on the data and processing loads required.

9. It is useful in these kinds of systems to consider a requirement for a data quality-control subsystem. This allows for periodic checks internally in the data base to ensure that good data are being put into the system. In some current measurement systems with multisource input reporting, the initial data-entry error rate can exceed 10%.

10. Before installation and operation of the final measure set, it may be necessary to iterate within the steps shown in Fig. 2.1. For example, it may be that the resource investment analysis shows that some measures are too costly in time and/or resources to obtain.

A Data and Cost Minimization Objective

Many present-day measurement systems are far too elaborate for the information and decision-making needs they serve. There are at least three reasons for this: (1) techniques for data acquisition have improved remarkably over the past 2 decades; (2) computers are readily available for processing of data; and (3) there is continually increasing emphasis on accountability through performance data. But, more is not necessarily better; collection and processing of data should be evaluated on a minimization goal. In some cases, very general data may be adequate for the kinds of decisions that must be made. On the other hand, it is probable that some kinds of data must be very precise; incentive pay programs are an example.

Privacy Constraints

Any measurement system for human behavior must take into account possible constraints due to the right of the individual to privacy. For most of the systems described here, this should be no particular problem, because it pertains to on-the-job performance. In some cases (e.g., faculty-member activities outside the educational institution), the privacy problem may arise. At any rate, by following the process shown in Fig. 2.1, the final measurement set selected and developed can be shown to be specifically job relevant through the analysis of step 1, 2, and 3. It is probable, for example, that the Performance Objectives Analysis will have to be developed from job and task analysis.

PROBLEMS FOR FUTURE RESEARCH AND PRACTICE

This discussion has assumed that productivity assessment is a specific example of the general case of system and human performance measurement. Some of the current problems in productivity assessment are measurement problems; some are specific to the area itself:

1. As many have commented, the term *productivity* is used in many different ways. It pertains either to evaluation of the performance of labor in a system or the performance of the entire system or parts of both. It would be very useful to get some sort of general concensus on how the term should be used. Measurement will be inherently ambiguous, until this terminological problem is resolved.

2. Productivity indices are primitive and unclear. The aggregate numbers cited for the total economy are gross and confounded. They have little diagnostic value; indeed, they may be misleading. There is no sound and detailed information as to why productivity has declined over the past decade. Further, there is no basis in these data for concluding that increases in productivity will solve any fundamental economic problems.

3. The use of presently available productivity data for administrative, managerial, or policy decision making is often questionable. Only in a few cases are the data rationally and sensibly tied to decision-making processes. The procedure outlined in Fig. 2.1 demands a closer look at the relationship between productivity measures and the decisions they serve.

4. There has been considerable interest in the development of a national productivity data base. It has been shown here that productivity numbers may to a great extent be system and situation specific. How all of these different kinds of numbers would be combined into a total data base across jobs and industries and products may be a very formidable challenge. Surely some commonality can be found, but what that might be has yet to be demonstrated.

5. Everyone agrees that productivity data are highly variable. Most agree that fairly substantial periods of time are needed to get a data base that is comprehensible. Rules for selecting adequate sampling periods do not exist.

6. For productivity assessment, certain key elements must be defined outside the measurement system. Much has been made here, for example, of the system specification of performance objectives. No measurement system in itself can

provide these objectives, although the measures will certainly assist in refinement of objectives.

7. In all cases, value judgments will be needed to evaluate productivity-assessment data. This will necessarily insert a "subjective" element into assessment. The real issue is not whether value judgments will be made, but, how they will be made.

8. Some of the most interesting data noted here has been derived from field demonstrations and actual operational assessment systems. It may be that in the future these will serve as the most fruitful sources for improving productivity assessment. If so, it is particularly important that they be reported in the public literature and in considerable detail. The growing literature on organizational development studies is valuable in this regard; these studies are usually longitudinal, providing preintervention and postintervention data; they are system oriented, and the measurement is usually in considerable depth.

9. At present, it would very desirable to establish a source data base for all published productivity studies. As may be seen in the reference list, these studies appear in a tremendous variety of settings and published sources. At the very least, there should be a continuing accumulation of what has been done. We should know not only where productivity has been measured but *how* it has been measured as well.

REFERENCES

Anderson, S. B., Ball, S., & Murphy, R. T. *Encyclopedia of educational evaluation.* San Francisco: Jossey-Bass, 1975.

Andrews, F. M. The international study: its data sources and measurement procedures. In F. M. Andrews (Ed.), *Scientific productivity: The effectiveness of research groups in six countries.* Cambridge: Cambridge University Press, 1979.

Andrews, F. M., & Farris, G. F. Time pressure and performance of scientists and engineers. *Organizational Behavior & Human Performance,* 1972, *8*(2), 185-200.

Beged Dov, A. G., & Gregory, W. R. The effect of operator learning rate on shrinkage allowances: An operations research analysis. *International Journal of Production Research,* 1972, *10*(2), 101-112.

Bodde, D. L. Riding the experience curve. *Technology Review,* March/April 1976, *78*(5), 53-59.

Campbell, A. The impact of Civil Service reform on productivity and motivation. In L. A. Broedling & R. Penn (Eds.), *Military productivity and work motivation: Conference proceedings.* U.S. Navy: NPRDC SR 78-15, August 1978, pp. 37-42.

Campbell, J. P. Organizational effectiveness: How can military organizations monitor improvements in motivation and productivity? In L. A. Broedling & R. Penn (Eds.), *Military productivity and work motivation.* U.S. Navy: NPRDC SR 78-15, August 1978, pp. 65-71.

Campbell, J. P., Bownas, D. A., Peterson, N. G., & Dunnette, M. D. *The measurement of organizational effectiveness.* U.S. Navy: NPRDC TR 75-1, July 1974.

Cannon, J. Human resource accounting—a critical comment. *Personnel Review,* 1974, *3*(3), 14-20.

Carlsson, B., Keane, P., & Martin, J. B. R & D organizations as learning systems. *Sloan Management Review,* 1976, *17*(3), 1-15.

Centra, J. A. *Determining faculty effectiveness.* San Francisco: Jossey-Bass, 1979.

Delamotte, Y. P. Union attitudes toward quality of working life. In L. E. Davis & A. B. Cherns (Eds.), *The quality of working life* (Vol. 1): Problems, prospects, and the state of the art. New York: The Free Press, 1975.

Dierkes, M. & Coppock. R. Human resources accounting: A tool for measuring and defining manpower utilization in a business environment. In W. T. Singleton & P. Spurgeon (Eds.), *Measurement of human resources.* New York: Halstead Press, 1975.

Dressel, P. L. *Handbook of academic evaluation.* San Francisco: Jossey-Bass, 1976.

Dunn, J. D., & Stephens, E. C. *Management of personnel.* New York: McGraw-Hill, 1972.

Dyer, J. S., & Hoffenberg, M. Evaluating the quality of working life—Some reflections on production and cost and a method of problem definition. In L. E. Davis & A. B. Cherns (Eds.), *The quality of working life* (Vol. 1). New York: The Free Press, 1975.

Endler, N. S., Rushton, J. P., & Roediger, H. L., III. Productivity and scholarly impact (citations) of British, Canadian, and U.S. departments of psychology (1975). *American Psychologist,* 1978, *33*(12), 1064-1082.

Fein, M. Job enrichment: A reevaluation. *Sloan Management Review,* 1974, *15*(2), 69-88.

General Accounting Office. The federal role in improving productivity—Is the National Center for Productivity and Quality of Working Life the proper mechanism? Washington: U.S. Government General Accounting Office (Report FGMSD-78-26), 23 May 1978. (a)

General Accounting Office. Development of a National Productivity Clearinghouse. Washington: U.S. Government General Accounting Office (Report FGMSD-79-4), 12 December 1978. (b)

Gibson, J. E. Performance evaluation of academic research. *Science,* 26 October 1979, *206*(4417), Editorial.

Glaser, E. M. Productivity gains through worklife improvement. *Personnel,* January/February 1980, 71-77.

Goodale, J. G., Hall, O. J., Burke, R. J., & Jayner, R. C. Some significant contexts and components of individual quality of life. In L. E. Davis & A. B. Cherns (Eds.), *The quality of working life* (Vol. 1). New York: The Free Press, 1975.

Grillo, E. V., and Berg, C. J. *Work measurement in the office.* New York: McGraw-Hill, 1959.

Gross, A. C. *Human factors in productivity improvement project.* San Diego: City of San Diego and U.S. Department of Housing and Urban Development Innovative Projects Program Grant H-2579-RG, 1 December 1978.

Hanes, L. J., & Kriebel, C. H. (Eds.), *Research on productivity measurement system for administrative services: Computing and information services.* National Science Foundation Grant No. APR75-20546, July 1978 (Vol. 2): Final Technical Report.

Hansen, B. L. *Work sampling for modern management.* Englewood Cliffs, N.J.: Prentice-Hall, 1960.

Hartley, C., Brecht, M., Pagery, P., Weeks, G., Chapanis, A., & Hoecker, D. Subjective time estimates of work tasks by office workers. *Journal of Occupational Psychology,* 1977, *80,* 23-36.

Herman, J. B. Are situational contingencies limiting job attitude-job performance relationships? *Organizational Behavior & Human Performance,* 1973, *10,* 208-224.

Herrick, N. Q. The quality of work and its outcomes: Estimating potential increases in labor productivity. Columbus, Ohio: The Academy of Contemporary Problems, 1975.

James, L. R., & Ellison, R. L. Criterion composites for scientific creativity. *Personnel Psychology,* 1973, *26,* 147-161.

Jauch, L. R., Gluech, W. F., & Osborn, R. M. Organizational loyalty, professional commitment, and academic research productivity. *Academy of Management Journal,* 1978, *21*(1), 84-92.

Jenkins, C. D., Jr., Nadler, D. A., Lawler, E. E., III, & Cammann, C. Standardized observations: An approach to measuring the nature of jobs. *Journal of Applied Psychology,* 1975, *60*(2), 171-181.

Judson, A. S. New strategies to improve productivity. *Technology Review*, July/August 1976, 61-67.

Katzell, R. A., Yankelovich, D., et al. *Work, productivity, and job satisfaction.* New York: The Psychological Corporation, 1975.

Kilbridge, M. D. Indirect measures of worker job satisfaction. In T. O. Prenting & N. J. Thomopoulos (Eds.), *Humanism and technology in assembly line systems.* Rochelle Park, N.J.: Hayden, 1974. (a)

Kilbridge, M. D. Nonproductive work as a factor in the economic division of labor. In T. O. Prenting & N. J. Thomopoulos (Eds.), *Humanism and technology in assembly line system.* Rochelle Park, N.J.: Hayden, 1974. (b)

Klemmer, E. J., & Synder, F. W. Measurement of the time spent communicating. *Journal of Communication,* 1972, *22,* 142-158.

Kola, R., & Hitchings, G. G. The effects of performance time variance on a balanced, four-station manual assembly line. *International Journal of Production Research,* 1973, *11*(4), 341-353.

Kulik, J. A., Kulik, C. C., & Cohen, P. A. A meta-analysis of outcome studies of Keller's personalized system of instruction. *American Psychologist,* 1979, *34*(4), 307-318.

Latham, G. P., & Baldes, J. J. The "practical significance" of Locke's theory of goal setting. *Journal of Applied Psychology,* 1975, *60*(1), 122-124.

Latham, G. P. & Yukl, G. A. Assigned versus participative goal setting with educated and uneducated woods workers. *Journal of Applied Psychology,* 1975, *60*(3), 299-302.

Latham, G. P., & Locke, E. A. Increasing productivity with decreasing time limits: A field replication of Parkinson's Law. *Journal of Applied Psychology,* 1975, *60*(4), 524-526.

Lawler, E. E., III. *Pay and organizational effectiveness: A psychological viewpoint.* New York: McGraw-Hill, 1971.

Lawler, E. E., III. *Motivation in work organizations.* Monterey, Calif.: Brooks/Cole, 1973.

Lawler, E. E., III. Measuring the psychological quality of working life: The why and how of it. In L. E. Davis & A. C. Cherns (Eds.), *The quality of working life* (Vol. 1). New York: The Free Press, 1975.

Lawler, E. E., III. Summary address. In L. A. Broedling & R. Penn (Eds.), *Military productivity and work motivation.* U.S. Navy (NPRDC SR 78-15), August 1978. pp. 91-93.

Likert, R. *The human organization, its management and value.* New York: McGraw-Hill, 1967.

Lipetz, B. A. *The measurement of efficiency of scientific research.* Carlisle, Mass.: Intermedia, 1965.

Locke, E. A. Nature and causes of job satisfaction. In M. D. Dunnette (Ed.) *Handbook of industrial and organizational psychology.* Chicago: Rand McNally, 1976.

Lovelock, C. H., & Young, R. F. Look to consumers to increase productivity. *Harvard Business Review,* May/June 1979, 168-178.

Lupton, T. Shop floor behavior. In R. Dubin (Ed.), *Handbook of work, organization, and society.* Chicago: Rand McNally, 1976.

Malkiel, B. G. Productivity—the problem behind the headlines. *Harvard Business Review,* May/June 1979, 81-91.

McConnell, C. R. Why is U.S. productivity slowing down? *Harvard Business Review,* March/April 1979, 36-38.

McCormick, E. J. Job and task analysis. In M. D. Dunnette (Ed.), *Handbook of industrial and organizational psychology.* Chicago: Rand McNally, 1976.

McGrath, J. E. Stress and behavior in organizations. In M. D. Dunnette (Ed.), *Handbook of industrial and organizational psychology.* Chicago: Rand McNally, 1976. Chapter 31, 1351-1395.

Meadows, D. H., & Meadows, D. H. *The limits to growth.* New York: New American Library, 1972.

Melman, S. *Pentagon capitalism.* New York: McGraw-Hill, 1970.

Melman, S. *The war economy of the United States.* New York: St. Martin's Press, 1971.

Melman, S. *The permanent war economy*. New York: Simon & Schuster, 1974.

Messick, S. The standard problem: Meaning and values in measurement and evaluation. *American Psychologist*, 1975, *30*(10), 955-966.

Miller, R. W. *The assessment of college performance*. San Francisco: Jossey-Bass, 1979.

Monk, T. H., & Conrad, M. C. Time of day effects in a range of clerical tasks. *Human Factors*, 1979, *21*(2), 191-194.

Moore, R. F. (Ed.), *AMA management handbook*. New York: American Management Association, 1970.

Moskowitz, A. D. A monograph for work sampling. *Work Study and Management Services*, 1965, *9*, 349-350.

Muckler, F. A. Selecting performance measures: "Objective" versus "subjective" measurement. Symposium Proceedings: Productivity Enhancement. U.S. Navy (NPRDC, 12-14), pp. 169-178 October 1977. (a)

Muckler, F. A. Human factors and the nature of work. Proceedings of 21st Annual Meeting of Human Factors Society, San Francisco, 17-20 October 1977. (b)

Muckler, F. A. Navy efforts in criterion development for job performance evaluation. In C. J. Mullins & W. R. Winn (Eds.), *Criterion development for job performance evaluation*. USAF (AFHRL-TR-78-85), February 1979, pp. 39-48.

Murrell, H. Performance rating as a subjective judgment. *Applied Ergonomics*, 1974, *5*(4), 201-208.

Murrell, K. F. H. On the validity of work measurement techniques. *Work Study*, 1969, *18*(4), 25-31.

Nicholson, N., Jackson, P., & Howes, G. Shiftwork and absence: An analysis of temporal trends. *Journal of Occupational Psychology*, 1978, *51*, 127-137.

O'Toole, J., & others. *Work in America*. Cambridge: The MIT Press, 1973.

Pace, C. R. *Measuring outcomes in college*. San Francisco: Jossey-Bass, 1979.

Parsons, H. M. What happened at Hawthrone? *Science*, 1974, *183*, 922-932.

Peeples, D. E. Measure for productivity. *Datamation*, May 1978, *24*(5), 222-230.

Pepinsky, P. N., Pepinsky, H. B., & Pavlik, W. B. The effects of task complexity and time pressure upon team productivity. *Journal of Applied Psychology*, 1960, *44*(1), 34-38.

Pritchard, R. D., Montagno, R. V., & Moore, J. R. *Enhancing productivity through feedback and job design*. USAF (AFHRL-TR-78-44), August 1978.

Rodgers, D. T. *The work ethic in industrial America: 1850-1920*. Chicago: The University of Chicago Press, 1978.

Rothe, H. F. Output rates among industrial employees. *Journal of Applied Psychology*, 1978, *63*(1), 40-46.

Salvendy, G. Effects of equitable and inequitable financial compensation on operator's productivity, satisfaction, and motivation. *International Journal of Production Research*, 1976, *14*(2), 305-310.

Salvendy, G. & Seymour, W. D. *Prediction and development of industrial work performance*. New York: John Wiley, 1973.

Schwab, D. P. Conflicting impacts of pay on employee motivation and satisfaction. *Personnel Journal*, 1974, *53*(3), 196-200.

Seashore, S. E. Defining and measuring the quality of working life. In L. E. Davis & A. B. Cherns (Eds.), *The quality of working life* (Vol. 1). New York: The Free Press, 1975.

Seashore, S. E., Indik, B. P., & Georgopoulus, B. S. Relationships among criteria of job performance. *Journal of Applied Psychology*, 1960, *44*(3), 195-202.

Sheppard, H. L. Some indicators of quality of working life: A simplified approach to measurement. In L. E. Davis & A. B. Cherns (Eds.), *The quality of working life* (Vol. 1). New York: The Free Press, 1975.

Sibson, R. E. *Increasing employee productivity*. New York: AMACON, 1976.

Srivastra, S., et al. *Job satisfaction and productivity: An evaluation of policy related research on productivity, industrial organization, and job satisfaction: Policy development and implementation.* Cleveland, Ohio: Case Western Reserve University, Department of Organizational Behavior, 1975.

Sutermeister, R. A. *People and productivity* (3rd ed.). New York: McGraw-Hill, 1976.

Swann, H. V. Human resource accounting: Some aspects that require psychologists' attention. *Journal of Occupational Psychology,* 1978, *51,* 301–304.

Thurow, L. C. Eight imperatives for R & D. *Technology Review,* January 1978, *80*(3), 64–71.

Usilaner, B. Comments. In L. A. Broedling & R. Penn (Eds.), *Military productivity and work motivation: Conference proceedings.* U.S. Navy (NPRDC SR 78-15), August 1978, pp. 60–61.

Vough, C. F., & B. Asbell. *Productivity: A practical program for improving efficiency.* New York: AMACON, 1979.

Walton, R. E. Criteria for quality of working life. In L. E. Davis & A. B. Cherns (Eds.), *The quality of working life* (Vol. 1). New York: The Free Press, 1975.

Wittrock, M. C., & Wiley, D. E. (Eds.), *The evaluation of instruction: Issues and problems.* New York: Holt, Rinehart, & Winston, 1970.

Young, H. H., & Berry, G. L. The impact of environment on the productivity attitudes of intellectually challenged office workers. *Human Factors,* 1979, *21*(4), 399–407.

3

Skill, Task Structure, and Performance Acquistion

Norman G. Peterson
David A. Bownas
Personnel Decisions Research Institute
Minneapolis, Minnesota

THE JOB-REQUIREMENTS MATRIX

A complete, universally applicable information system for human resources allocation requires three components: information about work tasks, information about task environments, and information about desirable or required human characteristics (knowledges, skills, abilities, and orientations). An idealized model for such a system must, therefore, include fundamental taxonomies for classifying tasks, human characteristics, and task situations. This chapter focuses on what we know about two of these three taxonomies—task and human characteristics—their content, methodologies for developing them, and their role in determining and evaluating job requirements, performance, and productivity.

Specifications and Problems

A job-requirements system can be represented in two dimensions. Thus, the job-requirements matrix contains rows defined by types or classes of tasks and columns defined by classes of human abilities.[1] Each cell of the matrix indicates the level of contribution to performance in a class of tasks made by a particular class of abilities, or, alternatively, the degree to which the ability class is required for performing the task class. Such a matrix, constructed for a wide assortment of task and ability classes, has several important implications for

---

[1]Throughout this chapter, we use the terms *abilities, attributes,* and *characteristics* as shorthand designations for all human characteristics, including knowledges, aptitudes, experiences, proficiencies, interests, personality orientations, background factors, etc.

personnel management in general and productivity enhancement in particular. Specifically, such a matrix could greatly simplify selection procedures. If techniques could be developed for reliably determining from which task classes a given job was sampled, the matrix would provide an immediate source of synthetically validated selection procedures, including the combining weights to be applied to each ability measure. If the matrix could be proven to apply to jobs in a variety of environmental or contextual settings, or if the impact of known contextual factors on the matrix could be specified, organizations could legitimately adopt appropriate ability-class measures with little or no special requirements or expenses for local and specific validation.

Moreover, if ability classes are defined with sufficient specificity, the job-requirements matrix can provide information relevant to the design of training programs for particular task classes. By identifying the principal ability classes required for performing tasks in the target job, training programs could be designed quickly and efficiently to develop those skills that are essential for task performance. Ability requirements could be summed or otherwise combined across task classes, perhaps weighted for task criticality, to establish training priorities. If levels of task proficiency could be reliably linked to ability levels, criterion-referenced training requirements could also be established, and trainees failing to attain these levels of achievement could be provided with additional training.

Three important and somewhat interrelated problems or obstacles stand in the way of creating an operational job-requirements matrix. The first involves the difficulty of identifying generally applicable taxonomies of tasks and abilities that are sufficiently precise to facilitate training design or to allow diagnostic evaluation. Task and ability classes defined with sufficient generality to apply across several jobs may be so vague that few reliable linkages can be made between tasks and abilities. Furthermore, several distinct measures might appear conceptually to be relevant to a single broad ability class, even though their intercorrelations might be small. In addition, excessive generality could make it extremely difficult to have much confidence that training or development applied to a given ability class would actually suit the proficiency requirements of the corresponding task class.

More specific taxonomic classes would provide more information but could rapidly become unmanageably profuse and diverse. How serious a problem this may be will remain uncertain until considerably more research has been performed, especially in constructing task taxonomies. Research and theorizing in the domain of human cognitive abilities at one time suggested an enormous number of cognitive factors (Guilford, 1959). Subsequently, researchers have become convinced that fewer independent dimensions actually account for the bulk of test score variation (Ekstrom, 1973).

A second problem threatening to limit the potential of a job-requirements matrix involves the procedures required for developing the taxonomies. The basic problem lies in selecting methods for generating taxonomic classes when no strong a priori basis exists for classifying tasks or abilities. The extensive program of Fleishman and his associates has reviewed these issues and provided a number of provisional alternatives (Fleishman, 1975; Fleishman, Kinkade, & Chambers, 1972; Fleishman & Stephenson, 1972; Fleishman, Teichner, & Stephenson, 1972; Wheaton, 1973). A major difficulty is conceptually grasping a sufficiently large sample of jobs or human attributes, so that both similarities and differences between tasks or between abilities can become apparent. The nature of both empirically and conceptually derived taxonomies is determined to a great degree by the domain of elements being considered, in much the same way that factor analytic results depend on the domain of variables being factored. For example, if only clerical jobs are investigated, several task dimensions including sorting/filing, typing, and computing might emerge. However, if clerical tasks are pooled with elements from a wider range of jobs, a general clerical dimension would probably emerge along with such probable factors as mechanical, administrative/organizational, and interpersonal dimensions. Although this issue is not likely to be resolved solely through speculative discussions, it has obvious implications for designers of taxonomic research. In an empirical sense, the question becomes one of when to stop extracting factors, and when and how to determine that a solution at some given level of specificity is optimal. The best answer for the time being is that researchers must make every effort to define the relevant domains of both tasks and abilities thoroughly and to sample from them carefully and systematically.

The third problem in developing the job-requirements matrix has been discussed at some length by Dunnette (1976): Task and ability taxonomies to date have been developed from two quite different bodies of data. Task classes have been derived mostly from responses to job-oriented task check lists, whereas ability taxonomies have largely originated from paper and pencil measures of various cognitive abilities, or inventoried attributes conceived with only limited reference to the world of work. As a result, although understandable and internally consistent task and ability dimensions have been devised, linkages between the two are not obvious and are difficult to determine.

Programs of research specifically aimed at identifying and explicating the communalities between the two taxonomic worlds of tasks and abilities need to be undertaken (Fleishman, 1975).

Validation of the Job-Requirements Matrix

Construct Validation: Constructing Taxonomies.   To be useful in human resource planning and programming, the validity of a job-requirements matrix needs to be demonstrated. Validation entails a three-step construct-oriented investigation.

Construct validation (Cronbach & Meehl, 1955) is an ongoing process of investigating the relationships between operational measures of the constructs. Construct validity can never be "proved"; rather, validation is a continuing process of reducing uncertainty about the pattern of influences affecting a group of constructs. Ultimately, a program of construct validation should lead to a specification of "rules" describing patterns of relationships between constructs being studied. Cronbach & Meehl refer to this pattern of descriptive rules as the "nomological net"—the matrix of laws governing (or describing) construct interrelationships.

The first step in validating a job-requirements matrix must be a series of decisions that combine specific abilities and tasks into relatively independent classes or constructs that are presumed to "summarize" performance or proficiency covariances across the individual tasks and abilities. Multivariate statistical procedures may be used to perform this sorting empirically, or persons knowledgeable about the contents of the tasks and abilities can be instructed in making a priori categorizations. Fleishman and associates have described the taxonomy construction process in some detail (Theologus & Fleishman, 1973; Theologus, Romashko, & Fleishman, 1973; Wheaton, 1973).

Once a preliminary taxonomy has been constructed, the quality of the taxonomic structure can be evaluated in two stages. The principal criterion will be high correlations between measures of abilities or of task proficiency for task or ability elements classed in the same category. This essentially requires high internal consistency between elements within each taxonomic class. The second, somewhat weaker, requirement is that measures from different classes should be relatively independent. Whereas statistically independent taxonomic classes are extremely unlikely, if ability or task proficiency measures consistently correlate higher with members of another class than with those of their own, one should question the appropriateness of their placement.

If expert judgments are the principal criterion for task or ability categorization, interjudge agreement is also an appropriate measure of taxonomy quality. Our bias, however, is to give primary weight to correlations between actual test or task performance measures, and to consider correlations between experts as ancillary evidence.

Construct Validation: Developing Measures.   The second step in evaluating the construct validity of a job-requirements matrix is to obtain valid operational measures of proficiency in each task or ability class. This initially entails a representative sampling of the tasks or abilities constituting each class. The measures are subject to revision, however, based on results of operational use. Cronbach and Meehl pointed out that it is from the relationships among these measures that we may develop inferences about the nature of the nomological net enmeshing the underlying constructs. As our knowledge about the nature of the constructs changes, however, the measures will be modified to conform to changes in the construct system.

A second and less-direct process for developing measures of taxonomic classes is to infer the general constructs that seem to underlie all tasks or abilities that have been grouped together, and to develop measures of these constructs. For example, rather than measuring proficiency in a class of tasks directly by administering a sample of standardized task simulations to individuals, one might infer that all tasks in a class share some feature (e.g., operating business machines, or making mathematical computations). Tests of the common features could then be developed (or existing tests selected) to measure the underlying construct. Such construct-based measures would, of course, require further validation to confirm that inferences leading to their development or selection were correct. This validation process would include investigating the agreement between alternate forms of measures and predicting and evaluating relationships between the focal measures and measures from other taxonomic classes. When this process is followed, it is difficult to distinguish construct validation of class measures from the construct validation of the classes themselves. Perhaps the critical factor is not the researcher's activities but his or her intentions, and, principally, the relative amount of confidence placed in the class as a valid construct versus the measure as a valid operation. If the hypothesized patterns of relationships fail to appear, either the researcher can revise the measures in the hope of bringing the empirical results more in line with predictions or he or she can alter the hypotheses about the nature of relationships among the classes.

Construct Validation: Comparing and Linking Taxonomies. As already suggested, the third step of validation of the job-requirements matrix is the most extensive and, so far, the least investigated. The taxonomy of abilities must be linked empirically with the taxonomy of tasks. Here, the researcher seeks to determine the "rules" governing ability contributions to task proficiency. Initially, this is done by predicting patterns of ability–task class relationships and carrying out empirical tests of these hypotheses. Fleishman and associates have already shown how experiments can be carried out to establish how variations in task characteristics are related to classes of ability requirements (Fleishman, 1957; Wheaton, Eisner, Mirabella, & Fleishman, 1976). As more data become available, investigations can be made to explore previously unpredicted relationships among taxonomy classes. Additional studies replicating such preliminary findings would need to be conducted.

Finally, to provide a fully generalized job-requirements matrix, a taxonomy of contexts or situations probably should be developed to investigate the impact of situational classes on ability–task relationships. One situational aspect—the nature of the subjects on which results are based—is typically evaluated in studies today. Some have expressed concern that results obtained for groups of whites may not generalize to groups of minorities; researchers have become sensitized to this possibility and have studied such factors as subgroup membership with increased frequency. Other contextual factors, such as the nature and extent of training provided, the closeness of supervision, or the quality of physical surroundings, could similarly affect how particular patterns of abilities may or may not be utilized in performing tasks, but these factors have not been extensively investigated even within the simple prediction models used in selection research today. The idea of such "situational specificity" (i.e., the belief that relationships between ability and task measures may change according to situational parameters) has been more or less accepted for some time, even though research so far has produced no generally usable situational taxonomy against which to evaluate the belief. However, recently Schmidt and Hunter (1977) have questioned this widely held "doctrine" of situational specificity. They argue convincingly that the wide variation in sizes of validity coefficients reported for particular ability–job combinations is almost exactly what would be expected by chance, given that studies have varied greatly in such validity attenuating factors as random sampling error, criterion unrealiability, range restriction in both ability and job proficiency measures, and levels of criterion contamination and deficiency.

Because of the paucity of systematic research on situational taxonomies and their impact on ability contributions to task proficiency, we consider only two dimensions of the job-requirements matrix, tasks and abilities, and give no further systematic attention to the possible impact of situational parameters.

In sum, then, development and validation of a job-requirements matrix can be viewed as a sequence of three steps: Taxonomic classes must be identified that are internally consistent and that reflect covarying subclusters of abilities and tasks; reliable measures of these classes must be developed; and the interrelationships among classes making up each of the taxonomies must be explored.

The result of such investigations will be an extremely powerful tool for selecting, training, and diagnostically evaluating employees. Increases in overall productivity can be dramatic, as evidence of this type becomes available to guide human resources planning and allocation.

TASK AND ABILITY TAXONOMIES

We turn now to consider what we know about task and ability taxonomies, and how this knowledge can be used in developing the job-requirements matrix.

Task Taxonomies

Three types of task taxonomies can be assumed to impinge directly on patterns of job performance and skill acquisition. The first is relevant to selection on jobs where no postemployment training is provided. Here, all tasks classed in a single cell should possess similar technical content. For selection, work samples could be used to evaluate a person's potential for doing tasks in each category. Scores on the samples would provide information about applicants' qualifications for a major part of the job. Such an approach is obviously based on a content-validity selection model. The taxonomic structure of tasks is useful in generalizing predicted performance across tasks within cells. The taxonomy defines independent components of the performance domain to be sampled in achievement or job-proficiency testing.

When posthire training is provided, it is inappropriate to screen applicants on any knowledges or skills that will be learned on the job. It is, however, appropriate to select applicants on the basis of abilities that can be shown to contribute to job performance or job learning. Here, a task taxonomy could group together all tasks that require the same or highly similar abilities. Once these abilities have been identified and linked with relevant task categories, administrators can use the results to predict job-component performance with some accuracy.—

The third type of task taxonomy also applies to jobs where training is provided after hire. In this case, however, the problem is to identify groups of tasks that incumbents can be expected to learn by similar training methods. Thus, one group of tasks may require classroom lectures, others may be more readily mastered by using massed practice trials in a simulator, and others may best be learned through an on-the-job apprenticeship program. These considerations would require a two-stage research program: one stage to identify the knowledges and skills to be learned and a second stage to explore the optimal training strategies for each required proficiency.

In the following sections, we review the major existing task taxonomic systems, and how each addresses the issues mentioned earlier. Farina (1973) has reviewed a number of earlier attempts.

Functional Job Analysis.   Fine's (1963) Functional Job Analysis (FJA) procedure classifies jobs according to levels of complexity required by the job incumbent in dealing with *data, people,* and *things.* The version incorporated in the U.S. Department of Labor's (1972) *Handbook for Analyzing Jobs* includes seven levels of data handling (ranging from "Comparing" to "Synthesizing"), nine levels of dealing with people (ranging from "Taking instructions/helping" to "Mentoring"), and eight levels of dealing with inanimate objects (ranging from "Handling" to "Setting up"). This model could, therefore, be regarded as containing 504 taxonomic classes of jobs, although many cells probably have few or no entries, and the majority of highly populated occupations in this country probably fit into no more than a few dozen cells.

The FJA model classes jobs as a whole, rather than investigating task structures within jobs. Although some within-job differentiation is considered (i.e., level of involvement with people, with data, and with objects), it seems unlikely that these rather broad constructs will offer much value in determining specific job or task requirements. More specifically, FJA, by itself, provides no empirical information about the abilities required for task performance other than estimates by job analysis. Thus, it contributes in only a limited way to either work sample development or training design and course development. The FJA approach could, nonetheless, be used to infer which human abilities might be most important in screening applicants for jobs, but to be maximally useful, much more research needs to be done showing linkages between abilities and performance in each of the most heavily populated cells of the FJA taxonomy.

McCormick's Position Analysis Questionnaire. The second research program aimed at developing a task taxonomy and identifying the abilities related to its elements is the work performed by McCormick and his colleagues (McCormick, 1976; Mecham & McCormick, 1969a, 1969b) with the Position Analysis Questionnaire (PAQ).

The PAQ evolved from an initial attempt to determine rationally all activities engaged in by workers. The resulting instrument focuses most heavily on work behavior in blue-collar skilled and semi-skilled manual jobs. McCormick, Jeanneret, and Mecham (1969a) describe the development of the current version of the PAQ (Form B). The PAQ comprises 183 items or elements with standard scale responses, and an additional 11 open-ended or nonstandard elements. Each standard element describes "a general work activity, work condition, or job characteristic." Raters use standard scales (usually 5-point scales) to indicate the extent of use, amount of time spent, importance, possibility of occurrence, or applicability of each element. Twenty-one items have unique special scales (e.g., degree of responsibility; amount of supervision given).

The PAQ is divided into six conceptual sections; the section titles, subsection titles, and illustrative items are shown in Table 3.1. Several empirical studies of the PAQ's dimensionality have been conducted, producing generally similar results. In all these studies, the researchers have factor analyzed the element intercorrelation matrix for various numbers of jobs. The elements within each of the six divisions are factored separately, with a seventh analysis performed on all 183 standard items taken together. The original study (McCormick, Jeanneret, & Mecham, 1969b), using PAQ data from 536 jobs, identified a total of 27 "divisional" factors and five general (i.e., across all item) factors. A second study by Marquardt and McCormick (1974) found 31 within-division and 14 general factors for data based on 3700 PAQ protocols. In discussing a more recent study, McCormick, Mecham, and Jeanneret (1977) report finding 32 divisional factors and 13 general factors from a sample of 2200 jobs that they feel are more representative of occupations in the U.S. than were the 3700 jobs in the 1974 analysis. Table 3.2 shows the factor titles from the three studies for each division, and for the general factors. Although comparing factor titles is not a very satisfactory method for evaluating factor solution comparability, item factor loadings are not presently available for either the 1969 or the 1977 studies, so a more rigorous and precise comparison is not possible. Given the large numbers of jobs on which these results are based, however, and especially considering the representativeness of the 1977 sample of 2200 jobs, the factors involved probably constitute stable descriptions of job activity dimensions, within the broad range of jobs in which the PAQ has been used.

The principal focus of the PAQ elements is on physical and perceptual work activities highly characteristic of skilled and semiskilled blue-collar jobs. Fewer elements are included that focus on dealing with other people, handling paper work, making decisions in the field, and other areas. Although such functions are covered in the PAQ, they do not receive the intensive sampling that manual activities do. Thus, whereas the majority of elements could apply to many different levels of jobs (e.g., extent of and use of written materials, importance of color vision, level of education required), there are at least 55 items that appear to deal exclusively or primarily with manual trades (e.g., importance of nonprecision tools, importance of machines/equipment, importance of setting up/adjusting machines, time spent in dirty environment), and only about 20 elements that seem to deal primarily with relatively high-level, white-collar positions (e.g., importance of combining or synthesizing information, importance of advising or counseling others, importance of writing [composing] information, number of persons supervised or responsible for). Whereas some coverage is thus provided for higher-level and white-collar activities, most of the PAQ's discriminatory power is centered on blue-collar positions.

The most significant step taken in work with the PAQ is reported in a pair of studies (Marquardt & McCormick, 1972; Mecham & McCormick, 1969a, 1969b) linking a total of 76 human attributes (knowledges, abilities, interests, personality factors) to expected proficiency in each job element. To do this, a large number of industrial psychologists were given lists of elements and defi- nitions of attributes and asked to estimate the relevance of each attribute for performing well in each job element. A mean of nine raters responded to each element-attribute pair; the mean rating vector across elements was extremely stable, with intraclass correlation reliabilities ranging from .67 to .96 across the 76 attributes, with one exception. Attribute 58, "ability to adjust to working alone," showed an intraclass coefficient across 180 job elements of only .04. In general, then, the resulting median ratings provide a reliable indication of how each attribute contributes to performing each element. By weighting these attribute-element contributions by elements factor loadings, it is possible to identify which attributes are most relevant for predicting or altering performance in each of the job-element factors described in Table 3.2.

One of McCormick's primary hopes in designing the PAQ was to develop a standardized job analysis procedure that would identify the critical attributes required for performing any job being analyzed. The next step would be to develop procedures for developing tests or inventories to measure each of the attributes or to identify existing tests that can be shown to be adequate measures of the attributes. So far, no such systematic steps have been carried out. Until accepted measures for each of the 76 attributes are agreed upon, the power of

TABLE 3.1
Division and Subdivision Titles and Sample Items
from the PAQ

1. Information Input
   1.6 Sources of job information
      1.1.1 Visual sources of job information
         1. Use of written materials
      1.1.2 Nonvisual sources of job information
         15. Use of verbal (spoken) sources
   1.2 Sensory and perceptual processes
      20. Degree of detail required in near visual differentiation
   1.3 Estimation activities
      28. Importance of estimating speed of moving parts
2. Mental Processes
   2.1 Decision making, reasoning, and planning/scheduling
      36. Level of decision making involved in the job
   2.2 Information processing activities
      40. Importance of analyzing information or data
   2.3 Use of learned information
      45. Importance of short-term (e.g., less than ½ hour) memory
3. Work Output
   3.1 Use of devices and equipment
      3.1.1 Hand-held tools or instruments
         50. Importance of using precision tools/instruments
      3.1.2 Other hand-held devices
         56. Importance of using drawing and related devices
      3.1.3 Stationary devices
         61. Importance of operating stationary machines
      3.1.4 Control devices
         62. Importance of hand- or foot-operated activation controls
      3.1.5 Transportation and Mobile Equipment
         70. Importance of nonpowered vehicles
   3.2 Manual activities
      78. Importance of setting up/adjusting machines or equipment
   3.3 Activities of the entire body
      85. Importance of balancing
   3.4 Level of physical exertion
      87. Level of physical exertion required on the job.
   3.5 Body positions/postures
      88. Amount of time spent sitting
   3.6 Manipulation/coordination activities
      93. Importance of finger manipulation
4. Relationships with Other Persons
   4.1 Communications
      4.1.1 Communicating by speaking
         99. Importance of advising others
      4.1.2 Communicating by written/printed material
         107. Importance of writing letters, reports, articles, etc.
      4.1.3 Other communications
         109. Importance of code communications (e.g., telegraph)

(Continued)

TABLE 3.1 *(Continued)*

4.2 Miscellaneous interpersonal relationships
      110. Importance of entertaining others
4.3 Amount of personal contact
      112. Frequency of required contact with others
4.4 Types of job-required personal contact
      113. Importance of dealing with corporate executives/officials
4.5 Supervision and coordination
    4.5.1 Supervision/direction given
      128. Number of nonsupervisory personnel supervised by respondent
    4.5.2 Other organizational activities
      131. Importance of supervising nonemployees (students, patients)
    4.5.3 Supervision received
      134. Level of supervision received by respondent
5. Job Context
  5.1 Physical working conditions
    5.1.1 Out-of-door environment
      135. Amount of time spent out of doors
    5.1.2 Indoor temperatures
      136. Amount of time spent in high indoor temperatures (85-90°)
    5.1.3 Other physical working conditions
      138. Amount of time spent in air contamination
  5.2 Physical hazards
      144. Possibility of minor injuries
  5.3 Personal and social aspects
      148. Importance of dealing with frustrating situations
6. Other Job Characteristics
  6.1 Apparel worn
      154. Expected to wear business suit or dress
  6.2 Licensing
      160. Licensing/certification required
  6.3 Work schedule
    6.3.1 Continuity of work
      162. Irregular work (depending on weather, season, etc.)
    6.3.2 Regularity of working hours
      164. Variable shift work (work shift varies from time to time)
    6.3.3 Day-night schedule
      166. Work typical day hours
  6.4 Job demands
      169. Importance of maintaining specified work pace
  6.5 Responsibility
      183. Amount of responsibility for safety of others
  6.6 Job structure
      186. Degree to which job activities are structured for the worker
  6.7 Criticality of position
      187. Criticality of position (impact of worker on the organization, the public, or other people)
  6.8 Pay/Income
      188. Amount of weekly, biweekly, monthly, or annual salary

TABLE 3.2
Job Dimensions Based on Principal Components Analyses of PAQ Data

Division	Dimensions based on data from 536 jobs (McCormick et al., 1969b)		Dimensions based on data from 3700 jobs (Marquardt & McCormick, 1974)		Dimensions based on data from 2200 jobs (McCormick et al., 1977)	
	Dim. No.	Dimension Title	Dim. No.	Dimension Title	Dim. No.	Dimension Title
1. Information Input	1.	Visual input from devices/materials	3.	Visual input from devices/materials	3.	Visual input from devices/materials
	2.	Perceptual interpretation	1.	Perceptual interpretation	1.	Perceptual interpretation
	3.	Information from people				
	4.	Visual input from distal sources				
	5.	Evaluation of information from physical sources	2.	Evaluation of sensory input	4.	Evaluating/judging sensory input
	6.	Environmental awareness	5.	Environmental awareness	5.	Environmental awareness
			4.	Input from representational sources	2.	Input from representational sources
					6.	Use of various senses
	7.	Awareness of body movement/posture				
2. Mental Processes	8.	Decision making	6.	Decision making	7.	Decision making
	9.	Information processing	7.	Information processing	8.	Information processing
3. Work Output	10.	Machine/process control				
	11.	Manual control/coordination activities	8.	Manual/control activities	13.	Controlled manual/related activities
	12.	Control/equipment operation	12.	Adjusting/operating machines/equipment		

13. General body activity
14. Handling/manipulating activities
15. Use of finger-controlled devices versus physical work
16. Skilled technical activities

4. Relationships with Other Persons
17. Communication of decisions/judgments
18. Job-related information exchange
19. Staff/related activities
20. Supervisor-subordinate relationships
21. Public/related contact

10. General body activity
11. Handling/manipulating activities
13. Skilled technical activities
9. Physical coordination in control/related activities
14. Use of miscellaneous equipment/devices
15. Interchange of ideas/judgments/related information
20. Job-related communications
16. Supervisory/staff activities
17. Public/related personal contact
18. Communicating instructions/directions/related job information
19. General personal contact

10. General body activity
15. Handling/manipulating/related activities
12. Skilled technical activities
16. Physical coordination
11. Control and related physical coordination
14. Use of miscellaneous equipment/devices
9. Using machines/tools/equipment
17. Interchange of judgmental/related information
20. Job-related communications
19. Supervisory/coordination activities
21. Public/related personal contact
18. General personal contact

(Continued)

TABLE 3.2 (Continued)

Division	Dim. No.	Dimensions based on data from 536 jobs (McCormick et al., 1969b) Dimension Title	Dim. No.	Dimensions based on data from 3700 jobs (Marquardt & McCormick, 1974) Dimension Title	Dim. No.	Dimensions based on data from 2200 jobs (McCormick et al., 1977) Dimension Title
5. Job Context	22.	Unpleasant/hazardous environment	21.	Stressful/unpleasant environment	22.	Stressful/unpleasant environment
			22.	Hazardous job situations	24.	Hazardous job situations
	23.	Personally demanding situations	23.	Personally demanding situations	23.	Personally demanding situations
	24.	Businesslike work situation	28.	Work/protective vs. business clothing	26.	Businesslike work setting
	25.	Attentive/discriminating work demands	24.	Attentive job demands		
6. Other Job Characteristics			25.	Vigilant/discriminating work activities	32.	Vigilant/discriminating work activities
	26.	Unstructured vs. structured work	26.	Structured vs. unstructured work activities	31.	Structured vs. unstructured job activities
	27.	Variable vs. regular work schedule	27.	Regular vs. irregular work schedule	29.	Regular vs. irregular work schedule
			29.	Specific vs. nonspecific clothing	27.	Optional vs. specified apparel
			30.	Continuity of work load	25.	Nontypical vs. typical day work schedule
			31.	(undefined)	28.	Variable vs. salaried compensation
					30.	Job demanding responsibility

Overall
(all PAQ items
factored
together)

1. Decision/communication/ social responsibilities
2. Skilled activities
3. Physical activities/ related environmental conditions
4. Equipment/vehicle operation
5. Information processing activities

1. Decision/communication/ social responsibilities
2. Environmental demands/ general body coordination
3. Equipment/machine operation
4. Environmental awareness
5. Manual control activities
6. Office/related activities
7. Evaluation of sensory input
8. General/public/related personal contact
9. Use of technical/related materials
10. General physical vs. sedentary activities
11. Hazardous/personally demanding situations
12. Attentive/vigilant work activities
13. Routine/controlled work activities
14. Supervision/coordination

1. Decision/communication/ general responsibilities
2. Machine/equipment operation
8. Environmental awareness
3. Clerical/related activities
11. Public/customer/related contact activities
4. Technical/related activities
9. General physical activities
12. Unpleasant/hazardous/demanding environment
7. Routine/repetitive work activities
10. Supervising/coordinating other personnel
5. Service/related activities
6. Regular day vs. other work schedules
13. (Undefined)

McCormick's work for synthetically validating selection batteries will not be fully realized.

Other Task Taxonomy Approaches.   Several approaches have been followed for identifying and classifying tasks within jobs. The job-inventory technique, systematized by the U.S. Air Force (Christal, 1974), is used almost exclusively in the armed services. In this method, tasks are identified through a combination of reviewing existing job documentation, observing workers, interviewing workers and supervisors, and having preliminary lists reviewed, edited, and modified by job experts. The final task list is submitted to a large number of job incumbents, and each task is rated on any of several factors, including whether the task is performed at all, the level of involvement in performing the task (e.g., helper versus doer), the task's criticality, the impact on mission accomplishment of failing to perform the task, the difficulty of performing the task, the amount of training time required to perform the task proficiently, the proportion of time spent performing the task, the frequency with which the task is performed, etc. The particular rating factors used depend on the purposes of the job analysis. Thus, various task difficulty measures (number of tasks performed, task difficulty, amount of training required to learn the task) are useful for job evaluation, whereas task criticality and frequency measures seem most relevant for job description, and criticality and difficulty together provide information for training design.

Task taxonomies can be developed by performing multivariate analyses on any of these task ratings, although task criticality or frequency ratings seem the most sensible of those mentioned. The resulting task clusters or dimensions represent groups of tasks that tend to co-occur on jobs and hence can be potentially useful in identifying job components for synthetic validation studies.

The present authors have found a different task rating approach to be useful in generating task-performance dimensions in several occupations. In selection research, the focus of job analysis is to identify all critical aspects of performance and to determine which knowledges, skills, abilities, and orientations (KSAO's) contribute to proficiency in each. To assist in this determination and to increase performance rating reliability, we wished to identify task dimensions that were homogeneous with respect to contributory KSAO's, and hence with respect to levels of performance. To accomplish this, we have tried two procedures; for both, the goal is to estimate the task-performance covariance matrix.

In the first procedure, the list of nontrivial tasks (those above average in task criticality, task frequency, or both) is randomly divided into manageable subsets of 10 to 15 tasks, and the subsets are assigned to each of several job experts (incumbents or immediate supervisors) for rating. Each task in the subset assigned to a rater is represented by a hypothetical worker, whose performance on that task is either above average or below average. Thus, a rater might be asked to consider an incumbent who is below average on task A, a second incumbent who is above average on task B, a third who is above average on task C, and so on, through 10 to 15 hypothetical performers of the subset of tasks. The rating instructions stress that different hypothetical workers are described for the different tasks, and hence that task performance is to be considered for only one task at a time. The raters confronted with each hypothetical incumbent are asked to estimate the incumbent's expected proficiency on each of the *remaining* tasks. A typical rating scale has five points:

2. The incumbent described would definitely be above average on this task.
1. The incumbent described would probably be above average on this task.
0. The incumbent described could be either above average or below average; no way of knowing one way or the other.
−1. The incubent described would probably be below average on this task.
−2. The incumbent described would definitely be below average on this task.

This scale approximates the correlation between performance on pairs of tasks. Given an above-average hypothetical performer on a stimulus task, a "2" rating for some other task suggests that performance on the stimulus task and the rated task is highly correlated. A "1" rating suggests a moderate correlation, and a "0" rating suggests a correlation of zero between the tasks, because knowledge of performance on one task provides no information about expected proficiency on the other. Similarly, for a *below*-average stimulus, a "−2" rating indicates a high between-task correlation, a "−1" rating suggests a moderate relationship, and a "0" rating suggests no between-task correlation. As would be expected, we have found no cases where high performance on one task implied low performance on another.

The assignment of task-stimulus subgroups and of above- and below-average stimuli to raters is such that: (1) all tasks serve as stimuli an equal number of times; (2) each task is presented to an equal number of raters as an above-average and a below-average stimulus; and (3) each rater considers an equal number of above- and below-average stimuli.

The result, when data from all raters have been pooled, is a matrix of similarity measures, of determinable reliability, reflecting expected performance similarity between all possible task pairs. The matrix values can readily be submitted to factor or cluster analyses to identify salient dimensions or clusters of task performance, based on the perceptions of job experts.

The second procedure for determining task performance similarity is less demanding but provides less control over the task comparison process. In this method, job experts are first imbued with the notion of task-performance similarity and then asked to sort cards containing nontrivial task statements into stacks, based on the tasks' expected performance similarity. Between-task similarity is indexed by the proportion of raters who cocluster each task pair. The resulting task-similarity matrix may again be submitted to multidimensional analyses to identify performance dimensions based on covariance in expected task proficiency.

On the occasions when we have performed such analysis, the resulting task dimensions appeared far more homogeneous in terms of task contiguity and in terms of contributory KSAO's than did dimensions derived from task criticality or frequency ratings.

Both procedures yield task-based performance dimensions with determinable mean task criticality and frequency values, and which are readily amenable to behaviorally anchored scaling for performance rating measures. Further, the resulting dimensions have proved to be homogeneous with respect to ratee performance, which contributes substantially to raters' cognitive comfort and to rating reliability.

Although such task taxonomies have to date been restricted in scope, applying to only a single job, applications in cooperative industry-wide research into high-volume jobs (Taylor, 1978) can produce task taxonomies with broad relevance. At the same time, focusing on a limited range of job classifications permits the resulting taxonomies to be far more precise and explicit in detailing job activities than, for example, the more broadly aimed PAQ and, thus, permits a clearer link between job tasks and required KSAO's.

Human-Characteristics Taxonomies

In the immediately preceding section, we noted that task analysis might generate three types of task groupings including: (1) tasks where little or no postemployment learning is required, and applicants are evaluated according to work samples, achievement, or proficiency measures; (2) tasks that involve postemployment training, and applicants are evaluated according to characteristics inferred to be required for effective task learning and/or task performance; and (3) tasks grouped according to the learning context (type of training) used in helping an incumbent attain task proficiency.

Levels of Generality. Now, as we consider taxonomies of human characteristics, we may ask whether or not we require separate taxonomies in abilities corresponding to each of the types of task taxonomies mentioned earlier. We do not believe such correspondence is necessary. We do believe, however, that ability taxonomies may be required at *two* levels—the levels differing according to their relative specificity or generality. Abilities classed at the more specific level would be those proficiencies usually thought of as *acquired* through previous learning or experience. For example, steel workers who must work several hundred feet above the ground will have learned certain specific cognitive and physical skills associated with the tools and materials of their trade, and they will have developed a rather specific temperamental accommodation to working high above the ground. The characteristics comprising his or her qualifications for the job will be quite specific and nearly indistinguishable from the work-sample task statements relevant to the first kind of task taxonomy mentioned previously.

Ability taxonomies at the more general level will contain those characteristics usually thought to be more "basic", those that are not specific to only a single job or task grouping but that include those cognitive, physical, and temperamental dimensions that are commonly viewed as being relatively "untrainable." We believe that the taxonomic cells of human characteristics belonging to this more general level are relevant to both the second and third types of task taxonomy mentioned earlier.

It appears to us that the more general level of classification holds most promise for an early return on an investment of research in developing the job-requirements matrix. It is more immediately applicable to studies aimed at linking the ability columns of the matrix to the more general of the task rows of the matrix. In addition, it may be useful to regard the "work samples" that define the clusters of the first kind of task taxonomy as job-performance criteria, in which case the more general (or "basic") ability taxonomy, which we favor, can be linked to the elements of that task taxonomy via the usual strategies of predictive or concurrent validation.

This section is, therefore, devoted to presenting and discussing a general taxonomy of all human characteristics that appear to be relevant for human performance and productivity. We have reviewed results from programs of research aimed at identifying and classifying human characteristics according to internal consistency within cells, and cell to cell independence. The taxonomy presented in these pages includes only those characteristics for which operational measures exist; thus, the reader may note that some prior suggested taxonomies have been excluded. Such exclusion is not inadvertent; our intention is to present only those domains for which measures have been developed, so that research suggested by the job-requirements matrix that emerges may go forward with all due haste. Finally, because our central concern in this chapter is with productivity, we also have restricted our gaze to measures relevant to relatively healthy, "normal" people. No attempt has been made to include measures aimed primarily at abnormality or disease, either psychological or physical.

Human Cognitive Abilities.   Dunnette (1976) and others (Ekstrom, 1973; Theologus, Romashko, & Fleishman, 1973) have provided reviews of cognitive taxonomies. Such taxonomies have moved from a singular idea of cognitive ability or general intelligence, such as Spearman's (1904) general factor or g, to the idea of a few abilities (Thurstone's 1938 seven aptitudes) to many abilities (Guilford's 1967 Structure of Intellect model), and back to few (Ekstrom's review suggests that about a dozen cognitive abilities seem to cover the domain quite well).

Dunnette listed and briefly defined 10 cognitive abilities that he felt sum-marized Ekstrom's review (Dunnette, 1976, p. 483). Following is an abstraction of that review:

1. *Flexibility and speed of closure:* the ability to "hold in mind" a particular visual percept and find it embedded in distracting material; and the ability to "take in" a perceptual field as a whole, to fill in unseen portions with likely material and thus to coalesce somewhat disparate parts into a visual percept.

2. *Fluency:* a combination of four different fluencies; associative, producing words from a restricted area of meaning; expressional, supply proper verbal expressions for ideas already stated or finding a suitable expression that would fit a given semantic frame of reference; ideational fluency, quickly producing ideas and exemplars of an idea about a stated condition or object; word fluency, producing isolated words that contain one or more structural, essentially phonetic, restrictions without reference to the meaning of the words.

3. *Inductive reasoning:* ability in forming and testing hypotheses directed at finding a relationship among elements and applying the principle to identifying an element fitting the relationship.

4. *Associative (rote) memory:* ability to remember bits of unrelated material.

5. *Span memory:* ability to recall perfectly for immediate reproduction a series of items after only one presentation of the series.

6. *Number facility:* ability to manipulate numbers in arithmetical operations rapidly; facility in performing elementary arithmetical operations (typically under speeded conditions).

7. *Perceptual speed:* speed in finding figures, making comparisons, and carry-ing out other very simple tasks involving visual perception.

8. *Syllogistic (deductive) reasoning:* ability to reason from stated premises to their necessary conclusion; ability in formal reasoning from stated premises to rule out nonpermissible combinations and thus to arrive at necessary conclusions.

9. *Spatial orientation and visualization:* ability to perceive spatial patterns or to maintain orientation with respect to objects in space and the ability to manipu-late or transform the image of spatial patterns into other visual arrangements.

10. *Verbal comprehension:* knowledge of words and their meaning as well as the application of this knowledge in understanding connected discourse.

Ekstrom and other researchers at the Educational Testing Service have con-tinued to investigate the realm of cognitive ability. They have published a report of an attempt to confirm five recently identified cognitive factors (Ekstrom, French, & Harman, 1975). In this study, they reported the development of "factor-referenced" or "marker" tests for the five newly identified factors and their possible relationships to factors already established. They concluded that two of these new factors, verbal closure and figural fluency, were successfully identified, and that visual memory had been adequately replicated. The new factor of integrative processes appeared to be closely related to a number of previously established reasoning factors, and the fifth factor, concept attainment, failed completely to be replicated. From this study, it appears that three more cognitive abilities could be added to the prior list of 10. The three new cognitive factors are:

Verbal closure: the ability to solve problems requiring the identification of words, when some of the letters are missing, disarranged, or mixed with other letters.

Figural fluency: the ability to produce a response quickly by drawing a number of examples, elaborations, or restructurings based on a given visual or descriptive stimulus.

Visual memory: the ability to remember the configuration, location, and orientation of figural material.

We group Figural fluency with the four other Fluency factors earlier identified and add Verbal closure and Visual memory, giving us 12 cognitive factors. All these cognitive factors have so-called "marker" tests developed by the ETS researchers (these are listed in Fig. 3.3). Most, if not all, of these tests display adequate psychometric properties. Thus, it is possible to administer these marker tests to individuals and obtain scores for each of the cognitive abilities.

Psychomotor Abilities and Physical Proficiencies. Fleishman and his colleagues also have conducted a comprehensive program of research aimed at identifying and defining human abilities (Fleishman, 1964, 1972b). Like the ETS researchers, they extensively reviewed past research to identify ability domains. They originally identified a list of 19 cognitive or perceptual abilities (Theologus, Romashko, & Fleishman, 1973) and an even larger number of psychomotor, physical proficiency, and sensory abilities. From an original list of 50 cognitive, perceptual, psychomotor, physical proficiency, and sensory abilities, they settled on 37 abilities after reviewing results from two pilot studies.

Nineteen of these 37 abilities dealt primarily with the cognitive domain and overlap a great deal with the cognitive abilities we have listed previously. A major goal of Fleishman and his colleagues was to develop a set of rating scales for each of the abilities, so that job experts could reliably rate tasks according to how important the abilities are in performing those tasks.

Excluding the 19 abilities involving the cognitive domain (we prefer the ETS taxonomy because each of the ETS cognitive abilities is backed up with one or more psychometrically sound "marker" measures), we are able to use the definitions of 18 abilities within the domain of psychomotor skill and physical proficiency provided by Fleishman and his colleagues. These names and definitions are listed in Fig. 3.1. In this series of studies, Fleishman used a combina-

1. Static strength

   This ability involves the *degree* of muscular force exerted against a fairly immovable or heavy *external object* in order to lift, push, or pull that object. Force is exerted *continuously* up to the amount needed to move the object. This ability is general to different muscle groups (e.g., hand, arm, back, shoulder, leg). This ability does not extend to prolonged exertion of physical force over time and is not concerned with the number of times the act is repeated.

2. Explosive strength

   This is the ability to expend energy in one or a series of explosive muscular acts. The ability requires a mobilization of energy for a *burst* of muscular effort, rather than continuous strain, stress, or repeated exertion of muscles. The ability may be involved in propelling the body as in jumping or sprinting or in throwing objects for distance.

3. Dynamic strength

   This ability involves the power of arm and trunk muscles to repeatedly or continuously support or move the *body's own weight*. Emphasis is on resistance of the muscles to performance decrement when put under repeated or continuous stress.

4. Stamina

   This ability involves the capacity to maintain physical activity over *prolonged* periods of time. It is concerned with resistance of the *cardiovascular system* (heart and blood vessels) to breakdown.

5. Extent flexibility

   This is the ability to extend, flex, or stretch muscle groups. It concerns the *degree of flexibility* of muscle groups but does *not* include repeated or speeded flexing.

6. Dynamic flexibility

   This is the ability to make repeated trunk and/or limb flexing movements, where both *speed* and *flexibility* of movement are required. It includes the ability of these muscles to recover from the strain and distortion of repeated flexing.

7. Gross body equilibrium

   This is the ability to maintain the body in an upright position or to regain body balance especially in situations where equilibrium is threatened or temporarily lost. This ability involves only *body balance*; it does *not* extend to the balancing of objects.

8. Choice reaction time

   This is the ability to select and initiate the appropriate response relative to a given stimulus in the situation where *two or more stimuli* are possible, and where the appropriate response is selected from *two or more* alternatives. The ability is concerned with the *speed* with which the appropriate response can be *initiated* and does not extend to the speed with which the response is carried out. This ability is independent of mode of stimulus presentation (auditory or visual), and also of type of response required.

9. Reaction time

   This ability involves the *speed* with which a *single motor response*

FIG. 3.1. Eighteen psychomotor and physical proficiency abilities identified by Theologus, Romashko, and Fleishman (1973).

can be initiated after the onset of a *single stimulus*. It does *not* include the speed with which the response or movement is carried out. This ability is independent of the mode of stimulus presentation (auditory or visual), and also of the type of motor response required.

10. Speed of limb movement

    This ability involves the *speed* with which discrete movements of the arms or legs can be made. The ability deals with the speed with which the movement can be carried out after it has been initiated; it is not concerned with the speed of initiation of the movement. In addition, the precision, accuracy, and coordination of the movement is not considered under this ability.

11. Wrist–finger speed

    This ability is concerned with the speed with which discrete movements of the fingers, hands, and wrists can be made. The ability is not concerned with the speed of the initiation of the movement. It is only concerned with the speed with which the movement is carried out. This ability does not consider the question of the accuracy of the movement; nor does it depend on precise eye-hand coordination.

12. Gross body coordination

    This is the ability to *coordinate* movements of the *trunk and limbs*. This ability is most commonly found in situations where the entire body is in motion or being propelled.

13. Multilimb coordination

    This is the ability to coordinate the movements of two or more limbs (e.g., two legs, two hands, one leg, and one hand). The ability does *not* apply to tasks in which trunk movements must be integrated with limb movements. It is most common to tasks where the body is at rest (e.g., seated or standing) while two or more limbs are in motion.

14. Finger dexterity

    This is the ability to make skillful, coordinated movements of the fingers where manipulations of objects may or may not be involved. This ability does *not* extend to manipulation of machine or equipment control mechanisms. Speed of movement is *not* involved in this ability.

15. Manual dexterity

    This is the ability to make skillful, coordinated movements of a hand, or a hand together with its arm. This ability is concerned with coordination of movement within the limb. It may involve manipulation of objects (e.g., blocks, pencils) but does not extend to machine or equipment controls (e.g., levers, dials).

16. Arm-hand steadiness

    This is the ability to make precise, steady arm-hand positioning movements, where both strength and speed are minimized. It includes steadiness during movement as well as minimization of tremor and drift while maintaining a static arm position. This ability does *not* extend to the adjustment of equipment controls (e.g., levers, dials).

17. Rate control

    This is the ability to make timed, anticipatory motor adjustments relative to *changes* in the speed and/or direction of a continuously

FIG. 3.1. (*Continued*)

moving object. The purpose of the motor adjustments is to intercept or follow a continuously moving stimulus whose speed and/or direction vary in an *unpredictable* fashion. This ability does not extend to situations in which both the speed and direction of the object are perfectly predictable.

18. Control precision
   This is the ability to make controlled muscular movements necessary to adjust or position a machine or equipment control mechanism. The adjustments can be anticipatory motor movements in response to changes in the speed and/or direction of a moving object whose speed *and* direction are perfectly predictable.

FIG. 3.1.   (*Continued*)

tion of experimental and factor analytic studies to isolate and define the underlying dimensionality of the abilities shown there. For each of these underlying dimensions of abilities, Fleishman has identified marker tests. These marker tests and their reliabilities are shown in Fig. 3.3.

Personality.   Several excellent reviews of measures of personality have been done (French, 1953, 1973; Goldberg, 1971), and Gough (1976) recently reviewed personality measurement from a more applied viewpoint.

French (1973) listed 28 personality factors that had been identified in at least three studies carried out in at least two different laboratories. These are listed and defined in Fig. 3.2 that is derived from French's report. French limited his review to "first-order" factors, or those factors that first appear when a wide variety of items or sets of items are factored.

An examination of French's review and of Fig. 3.2 suggests that a few personality dimensions are missing that have been identified in certain widely used personality inventories. For example, French cites none of the work with the *California Psychological Inventory* (Gough, 1956) or the *Personality Research Form* (Jackson, 1967). French's review also relies on factor analytic studies completed before 1973. Browne and Howarth (1977) contend that all those studies are inconclusive because they relied on small sample sizes.

In addition, Browne and Howarth believe that many factors attributed to published questionnaires are difficult to replicate and are probably illusory. For example, Sells, Demaree, and Will (1970) found that a pool of marker items drawn from Cattell's and Guilford's inventories do not load on factors they have been assumed to represent. They concluded that 400 of the 600 source items should be classified on different factors from those they had been purported to represent. Eysenck and Eysenck (1969) factored 108 Eysenck Personality Inventory (EPI) items and found 13 factors instead of only the two that have been claimed to represent the response variance in the EPI. This finding was confirmed by Howarth and Browne (1972), when they derived a 13-factor solution

1. Factor *Ac*: General Activity
   A. Moves rapidly, quick in physical performance vs. slow
   B. Busy, active in projects or (nonsocial) affairs vs. uninvolved, gets overburdened
   C. Accomplishes things rapidly vs. indolent, unmotivated
2. Factor *Ag*: Agreeableness
   A. Interested in people's welfare vs. prefer lone intellectual contributions
   B. Cooperative, supportive, forgiving vs. irritated by people, vengeful
   C. Adaptable, tends to agree, submissive vs. negativistic, domineering, aggressive
   D. Trustful, confides in people vs. suspicious, keeps distance
   E. Friendly, likeable, outgoing vs. aloof, unpleasant, withdrawn
3. Factor *Al*: Alertness
   A. Alertness to immediate surroundings, attentive vs. unaware, engrossed, deep in thought, absent minded
4. Factor *Au*: Autistic Tendency
   A. Daydreams vs. has practical thoughts
   B. Anxiety and worry that leads to autistic thinking vs. relaxed, adjusted, realistic thoughts
   C. Bothered by daydreams or autistic distractions vs. enjoys these things
5. Factor *Ca*: Calmness vs. Anxiety
   A. Relaxed, stable, at ease vs. anxious, worried (about self), edgy, uneasy, nervous, tense, restless (without cause)
   B. Takes time to think, deliberate vs. overreacts, impulsive, jittery
   C. Confident about the world vs. having fears or worries about outside influences
6. Factor *Co*: Concentration
   A. Concentration on study or reading, restraint leading to maintenance of attention vs. mind wanders, bored, forgets names
7. Factor *De*: Dependability
   A. Likes rules, follows plans vs. likes freedom of choice, likes change
   B. Dependable, punctual, keeps promises vs. careless about promises and details
   C. Self-sentiment control, control of own feelings vs. actions and thoughts are swayed by emotions
8. Factor *Do*: Dominance
   A. Takes charge socially, wants power vs. submissive, willing to serve
   B. Egoistic, pushes own ideas vs. respects others' ideas, self-effacing
   C. Rights conscious, complaining vs. tolerant
9. Factor *E*: Emotional Stability
   A. Emotionally stable, tolerant, stolid vs. emotionally sensitive, irritable
   B. Optimistic, faces problems vs. worrying, dwells on problems, escapist
   C. Healthy, feels vigorous vs. tired, intermittent loss of energy, hypochondriacal
   D. Life is good, life is worthwhile vs. feels frustrated, dissatisfied
10. Factor *Em*: Emotional Maturity
   A. Patient, adjusts to frustration vs. verbally aggressive, demanding
   B. Modest, shuns attention, outwardly directed vs. self-centered, seeks attention, egotistical

FIG. 3.2. Twenty-eight personality factors identified by French (1973).

C. Satisfied, cooperates with authority vs. asserts independence from authority, stubborn
11. Factor *Gs*: Gregariousness
    A. Likes to be with people physically vs. likes to be alone
    B. Interest in occupations with people vs. interest in occupations isolated from people
    C. Likes work or socializing with people vs. likes work alone or isolated activities
12. Factor *Me*: Meticulousness
    A. Meticulous, orderly, neat, careful, particular about personal effects vs. messy, careless, impulsive
13. Factor *Mo*: Morality
    A. Law-abiding, obedient, well-mannered, patriotic vs. free progressive, liberal
    B. Moral, knows right from wrong, resists temptation vs. pleasure seeking
    C. Generous, helpful, fair, gives to causes vs. selfish, uncharitable
14. Factor *Na*: Need for Achievement
    A. Likes to do his best, works hard, persists until successful vs. play before work
    B. Likes success in competition, likes getting ahead vs. dislikes competition
    C. Strives for accomplishment, wants to produce something great vs. no motivation to do good or to help people
15. Factor *O*: Objectivity vs. Paranoid Tendency
    A. Objectivity and fairness attributed to others vs. paranoid delusions about others
    B. Credit is given by others vs. blame by others is unfair
    C. Depends on others for help, advice, and sympathy vs. not interested in others, independent
16. Factor *Om*: Open-Minded vs. Authoritarian
    A. Believes many different philosophies (religious or political views) can be reasonable vs. rigid belief in one philosophy, no tolerance of compromise
    B. Respect for and interest in the religious and political philosophies of other people vs. strong belief in the rightness or wrongness of principles
    C. Innovative, readiness for new ideas, flexible, foresighted vs. highly conservative, conventional, and unchangeable in ideas
17. Factor *Pe*: Persistence
    A. Persistent, persevering, determined vs. quitting, fickle, needs change, gets discouraged
    B. Likes stable tasks, interests are stable vs. likes changing tasks, interests change
    C. Conscientious, careful, exacting, tidy, orderly vs. relaxed, carefree, nonchalant
18. Factor *Po*: Poise vs. Self-Consciousness
    A. Enjoys group attention, exhibitionistic, poised vs. dislikes being in front of people

FIG. 3.2. *(Continued)*

    B. Enjoys performing in public, feels pride in speaking to a group vs. dislikes performing in public

    C. Seeks comment and attention from important people vs. self-conscious with superiors, avoids criticism

19. Factor *Re*: Relaxed vs. Nervous

    A. Physically relaxed vs. fidgets, has nervous habits, twitches, has restless movements

    B. Tolerant of physical, nonhuman or situational annoyances vs. irritated by mishaps and frustrating circumstances

20. Factor *Rt*: Restraint vs. Rhathymia

    A. Planning vs. acting without thought, impulsive

    B. Serious, responsible vs. lively, carefree, irresponsible, no thought of the future

    C. Enjoys stable pursuits vs. wants excitement, change, wildness

21. Factor *Sc*: Self-Confidence

    A. Feels confident physically, personally, and career-wise vs. needs encouragement, feels inferior, afraid of failure

    B. Claims to have abilities, skills, and good experiences vs. claims handicaps, ineptitude, and unfavorable experiences

    C. Perceives others as having been positive toward him vs. negative

22. Factor *Se*: Sensitive Attitude

    A. Warm, soft, cooperative, kind, considerate vs. hard, stern, bossy

    B. Emotionally sensitive, empathic, delicate, quiet vs. robust, noisy, active, tough, fearless

    C. Interest in people's welfare, religion vs. interest in people for companionship or fun

    D. Interest in imaginative ideas, music, esthetics, literature vs. interest in practical, technical, political, and economic ideas

23. Factor *So*: Sociability

    A. Competent socially, social organizer, enjoys attention vs. withdrawn, fears public speaking and social responsibilities

    B. Glib talker, has superficial social know-how vs. aloof, doesn't know or care what should be said

    C. Hardened socially, confident in social contacts vs. shy, socially insecure

24. Factor *Ss*: Self-Sufficiency

    A. Self-sufficient, likes to be alone in stress, in planning, in facing problems, makes own plans, dislikes being served, self-reliant, decisive vs. dependent, needs help from others, group dependent

    B. Desires to be different, individualistic, free vs. needs approval of others, conforms, accepts social order, agrees with group, likes affiliation, complies

    C. Unusual ideas, unconventional, idealistic, reflective vs. has majority opinions, tends to have same feelings as others

    D. Emotional independence vs. needs love, friends, succorance, and protection

25. Factor *Su*: Surgency vs. Repression

    A. Exuberant, enthusiastic, cheerful vs. repressed, reserved, inhibited

FIG. 3.2. (*Continued*)

       B. Likes to stimulate and cheer up people vs. quiet stay at home

       C. Talks without inhibition, expressive, frank vs. cautious in talking, precise, secretive

26. Factor *T*: Thoughtfulness
       A. Likes to think, reflect, meditate vs. prevented from doing it by social or business activity
       B. Likes to think about people or with people vs. enjoys the company of people without analyzing them
       C. Thinks about self vs. carefree about self
       D. Intellectual interests vs. active interests

27. Factor *To*: Tolerance of Human Nature and Things vs. Criticalness
       A. Naive, impunitive, believes people are honest and fair vs. believes people lie and are unfair to gain an advantage
       B. Believes people are capable of good work vs. critical, fault finding
       C. Tolerant of human nature vs. cynical about human nature
       D. Tolerates or respects people vs. feels hostility (covert, not overt) against people or groups of people
       E. Tolerates the imperfections in things vs. feels hostility toward things that fail to work

28. Factor *Wb*: Well-being vs. Depression
       A. Has feeling of well-being, happy vs. depressed, blue, lonely
       B. Hopeful, interested in life vs. fear and worry about doom or vague dangers
       C. Confident, can stand criticism vs. guilt prone, feels worthless and spurned, worries about himself

FIG. 3.2. *(Continued)*

from the matrix of correlations based on responses from 1319 persons to the EPI. Howarth and Browne (1971) also factored items from the 16PF (Cattell, Eber, & Tatsuoka, 1970) and found 13 factors rather than the 16 claimed by the authors of the 16PF. Jernigan and Demaree (1971) performed a similar analysis of the Guilford–Zimmerman Temperament Survey (GZTS) (Guilford & Zimmerman, 1949) and, again, concluded the GZTS was not measuring traits according to the structure claimed previously. Browne and Howarth (1977) concluded from their review that there was a need to conduct a study using a comprehensive item pool and a variety of factor rotation methods in an attempt to identify the basic or primary personality constructs. (They point out that such a study was only recently made possible by advances in computer technology, making possible the handling of large data matrices.) Their review also casts some doubt on the adequacy of the 28-factor structure developed by French, because his work also was dependent on many of the previous investigations reviewed by Browne and Howarth.

Howarth and Browne set out, therefore, to conduct the study they felt was needed to overcome the serious shortcomings in previous efforts to identify a comprehensive taxonomy of personality dimensions. As just mentioned, they determined to evaluate underlying taxonomies with several types of factor analytic approaches and to examine the dimensionality of a much more extended and complete item pool than had been used in any previous investigation. Accordingly, they included 1726 items (after redundant items were eliminated from an original pool of 3029 items) collected from 16 questionnaires[2] that had been used extensively for either clinical or research purposes over the past 5 decades. These 1726 items were assigned to 20 Putative Factor Hypotheses (PFH's) that were seen as representative of the factor structure indicated from a review of the literature. Twenty items were selected as most representative of each of the 20 PFH's, the selection being based on a consideration of available item-factor studies. The items were rewritten where necessary to conform to a common format, and the direction of item scoring was balanced (10 and 10) for each PFH by reversing the wording of statements where necessary to achieve such balancing. The 400 items were placed in two 200-item questionnaires, and both questionnaires were administered to 1600 college students in 13 Canadian colleges. Questionnaires with more than 2% items blank were deleted, leaving 1003 completed questionnaires, 488 from female students and 515 from male students.

The resulting 401 × 401 correlation (sex was the 401st variable) matrix was factor analyzed. Twenty factors were extracted and examined via two orthogonal and two oblique rotations. Examination of these results led Howarth and Browne to conclude that 15 of the 20 PFH's were recovered and were robust across the differing rotation methods. The authors listed the five highest loading items for each factor and also briefly discussed the nature of each factor. We have made a crude comparison of these descriptions of the 15 robust Browne and Howarth factors with the description of French's 28 factors. This comparison shows an apparently similar factor in French's list for each of the 15 Browne and Howarth factors. Five factors appear to have a single French factor that was similar; six appear to be similar to two French factors, and four appear similar to three French factors. Thus, apparently the Browne and Howarth factors are circumscribed within French's conceptual review. There is, however, no straightforward, one-for-one mapping of the Browne and Howarth solution onto French's list. (Obviously, the Browne and Howarth solution does not circumscribe the list of factors by French. Indeed, there appear to be eight factors listed by French that have no similar factor in the Browne and Howarth solution.)

---

[2]The questionnaires were: Heidbreder's List (1926); Neymann-Kohlstedt Test (1929); Stagner and Pessin Inventory (1934); Minnesota Multiphasic Personality Inventory (Hathaway & McKinley, 1943); Guilford–Zimmerman Temperament Survey (1949); California Psychological Inventory (Gough, 1956); Heron Scale (1956); Maudsley Personality Inventory (Eysenck, 1956); Pittsburgh Scales of Social Extraversion-Introversion and Emotionality (Bendig, 1962); Eysenck Personality Inventory, Forms A and B (Eysenck & Eysenck, 1963); Sensation Seeking Scale (Zuckerman, Kolin, Price, & Zoob, 1964); Omnibus Personality Inventory, Form F (Heist & Yonge, 1968); PEN Scale (Eysenck & Eysenck, 1968); Sixteen Personality Factor Questionnaire (Cattell, Eber, & Tatsuoka, 1970); Comrey Personality Scales (1970); Howarth Personality Questionnaire 2 (Howarth, 1971).

The 15 factors identified in their study appear to be the most useful and justifiable taxonomy of personality available. The factors are nearly orthogonal, replicate across several rotational methods, and are based on the most comprehensive pool of items that has been used in factor analytic work. Moreover, the data were collected from a large population of adults.

Comparison of the Browne and Howarth structure with the French structure does, of course, suggest that some personality dimensions may be missed. Nonetheless, the French list suffers from being merely a conceptual review of many previous studies often based on rather small samples. Thus, we are convinced that the Browne and Howarth taxonomy is the best starting point. Obviously, it can be expanded or modified as further research information accumulates, concerning its overall usefulness.

Names of their factors, brief descriptions of them, and the mean eigenvalues obtained for each across the four rotation methods are shown in Fig. 3.3.

Vocational Preferences.   Holland (1976) reviews a great deal of evidence concerning vocational preferences. He concludes that four-to-eight categories or dimensions of interest encompass most interest inventory scales, and that the relationships between these dimensions tend to have a characteristic order. He also cites evidence showing consistent, moderate correlations between interest dimensions and several other domains: aptitude, personality, perception, etc. He concludes that the same four-to-eight personal dispositions may account for current knowledge of vocational preference, vocational interests, vocational choices, and occupational membership. He feels that traditional personnel functions could benefit by capitalizing on vocational preference classification schemes. If we accept Holland's conclusions, it would seem prudent to include a set of vocational preference dimensions in our taxonomy of human characteristics.

There are several inventories available to measure vocational preferences, but the two most widely used are the Strong-Campbell Interest Inventory (SCII), (Campbell, 1971), and the Kuder Preference Record (Kuder 1970). Both of these can be scored for the six basic scales that correspond to Holland's six-category typology: Realistic, Investigative, Social, Conventional, Enterprising, and Artistic. (These are described in Fig. 3.3.) For purposes of our human characteristics taxonomy, then, either of these inventories could be used to produce scores for these six major vocational preference dimensions. Holland's review shows, however, that these dimensions are not orthogonal, either with each other or with other constructs we already have discussed. Because our aim has been to identify a minimum number of independent (orthogonal) constructs describing the domain of human characteristics, the lack of orthogonality within the vocational preference domain may be a problem.

Nonetheless, vocational preferences constitute conceptually a very distinct domain that seems to us to warrant separate attention. Constructs included in our

Ability	Measure(s)

1. Flexibility and Speed of Closure	Flexibility
	  Hidden Figures (.82M, .80F)[a]
	  Hidden Patterns (.91M, .89F)
	Speed
	  Gestalt Completion (.85)
	  Concealed Words (.83)

2. Fluency	Associative Fluency
	  Controlled Associations Test (.83)
	  Opposites Test (.82)
	Expressional Fluency
	  Making Sentences (.80)
	  Arranging Words (.68)
	Ideational Fluency
	  Topics Test (.81)
	  Theme Test (.80)
	Word Fluency
	  Word Endings Test (.70)
	  Word Beginnings Test (.86)
	Figural Fluency
	  Ornamentation Test (.85)
	  Elaboration Test (.86)

3. Inductive Reasoning	Letter Sets Test (.84) Locations Test (.75) Figure Classification (.88)
4. Associative (Rote) Memory	Picture Number Test (.83) Object Number Test (.76)
5. Span Memory	Auditory Number Span Test (.63) Auditory Letter Span Test (.65)
6. Number Facility	Addition Test (.93) Division Test (.94) Subtraction and Multiplication Test (.92) Addition and Subtraction Correction (.86)
7. Perceptual Speed	Finding A's Test (.73) Number Comparison Test (.82) Identical Pictures Test (.87M, .81F)
8. Logical Reasoning (formerly Syllogistic Reasoning)	Nonsense Syllogisms Test (.64) Diagramming Relationships (.79) Inferences Test (.76M, .78F)

FIG. 3.3. A tentative taxonomy of cognitive abilities, psychomotor and physical proficiency abilities, personality factors, and vocational preference dimensions pertinent to skill and task performance acquisition

Cognitive Abilities

Ability	Measure(s)
9. Spatial Orientation and Visualization	Orientation Card Rotation Test (.86M, .89F) Cube Comparison Test (.77) Visualization Form Board Test (.81) Paper Folding Test (.84) Surface Development (.92)
10. Verbal Comprehension	Vocabulary I and II (.94, .84) Advanced Vocabulary I and II (.79, .83)
11. Verbal Closure	Scrambled Words (.83) Hidden Words (.84) Incomplete Words (.85)
12. Visual Memory	Shape Memory Test (.68) Building Memory Test (.80) Map Memory (.77)

Psychomotor and Physical Fitness Abilities*

Ability	Measure(s)
1. Static Strength	Weight Lift (.80, r_{tt})[b] Dynamometer (.83, r_{tt})
2. Explosive Strength	Ten yard sprint (.62, r_{tt}) Jumps (.90, r_{tt})
3. Dynamic Strength	Pull-ups (.93, r_{tt})
4. Stamina	600 yard run–walk (.80, r_{tt})
5. Extent Flexibility	Twist and Touch Test (.90, r_{tt})
6. Dynamic Flexibility	Floor Touch Test (.92, r_{tt})
7. Gross Body Equilibrium	Rail Walk Test (not available)
8. Choice Reaction Time	Choice Reaction (.68, r_{sh})[c]
9. Reaction Time	Simple Reaction (.86, r_{tt})
10. Speed of Limb Movement	Speed of Arm Movement or Plate Tapping (.99) Two-foot Tapping (unavailable)
11. Wrist–Finger Speed	Tapping (.94, r_{sh})
12. Gross Body Coordination	Cable Jump (.70, r_{tt})
13. Multilimb Coordination	Complex Coordination Test (.68, r_{sh})
14. Finger Dexterity	Purdue Peg Board (.76, r_{tt})
15. Manual Dexterity	Minnesota Rate of Manipulation Test (.87 placing, .79 turning, r_{sh})

*Drawn largely from Fleishman, 1964, 1972b.

FIG. 3.3. (*Continued*)

16. Arm-Hand Steadiness	Track Tracing Test (.88, r_{th})
17. Rate Control	Single Dimension Pursuit Test (.84, r_{th})
18. Control Precision	Rotary Pursuit (.92, r_{th})

Personality Dimensions: Names, Brief Descriptions, and Variances[d]

Social Shyness. Hesitancy to engage in social interactions with a lack of initiative in making new friends. Variance = 12.42

Sociability. Enjoyment of and engagement in social activities; liking to be around and with people. Variance = 7.53

Mood-swings Readjustment. Strong emotional moods without apparent cause, feeling listless and tired for no good reason, swings of happiness to depression, and often feeling just miserable. Variance = 6.5

Adjustment–Emotionality. Nervous, easily rattled or upset, and worrying over possible problems. Variance = 6.18

Impulsiveness. Impulsive actions, acting on the first thought that comes into one's head, being an "impulsive person," etc. Variance = 5.63

Persistence. Persisting on a job until it is completed even when others have given up, not giving up easily, capability of working at a problem for more than an hour or two at a stretch. Variance = 5.45

Hypochondriac–Medical. Complaints about state of physical health. Variance = 5.18

Dominance I. Being easily downed in an argument, considered submissive, seldom fighting for one's rights, etc. Variance = 5.75

Dominance II. Taking command, exerting leadership, swaying a group. Variance = 5.03

General Activity. Interest in action and energy expenditure; preferring and enjoying many types of sports and sports that have "lots of action." Variance = 4.83

Trust versus Suspicion. Combines a carefree attitude about life with a tendency toward paranoid sensitivity. Variance = 4.35

Superego. A "social conscience" in terms of feeling that most people do an honest day's work for a day's pay, too many people take too much and give too little back to society, etc. Variance = 3.90

Social Conversation. Talking with others a great deal, being considered a talkative person. Variance = 8.03

Inferiority. Feelings of inferiority, not being successful, and failure to make favorable impressions on people. Variance = 7.05

Cooperativeness–Considerateness. Inconveniencing one's self to oblige others, being a "Good Samaritan", becoming easily involved in straightening out other people's problems, etc. Variance = 4.10

Vocational Preference Dimensions

Dimension	Description[e]	Reliability[f]
1. Realistic	rugged, robust, practical; good motor coordination and skills but lacking interpersonal and	.87, .91

FIG. 3.3. (Continued)

81

Vocational Preference Dimensions

Dimension	Description[e]	Reliability[f]
	verbal skills; practical, natural, stable, and persistent	
2. Investigative	scientifically oriented, introspective, social; enjoy ambiguous tasks and prefer to work independently; possess unconventional attitudes and values; confident of scholarly and intellectual abilities but not leadership or persuasive abilities	.84, .90
3. Artistic	impulsive, creative, expressive, original, intuitive, introspective, nonconformist, and independent; value aesthetic qualities; dislike highly structured problems or use of gross physical skills; perform well on standard measures of creativity	.91, .93
4. Social	sociable, responsible, humanistic, and religious; like working in groups; prefer to solve problems through feelings and interpersonal manipulations; see themselves as understanding, responsible, idealistic, and helpful	.86, .89
5. Enterprising	possess verbal skills suited to selling, dominating, and leading; have strong drive to reach organizational goals or economic gains; concern for power, status, and leadership; see themselves as aggressive, self-confident, cheerful, and sociable	.85, .85
6. Conventional	prefer well-ordered environments and systematic verbal and numerical activities; usually conform and prefer subordinate roles; see themselves as conscientious, efficient, calm, orderly, and practical	.84, .91

[a] These measures are all tests developed by ETS. The figures are alpha coefficients, an M following the figure indicates it was computed for males only, F indicates computation for females only.

[b] These tests were developed or identified by Fleishman and his colleagues. r_{tt} indicates a test–retest coefficent.

[c] r_{sh} indicates a split-half coefficient.

[d] This portion of the figure is abstracted from Browne and Howarth's (1977) description of the 15 factors which replicated across four rotations. The "Variance" value given for each dimension refers to the mean eigenvalue obtained for that factor across the four separate solutions.

[e] These descriptions are abstracted from the Strong–Campbell Interest Inventory Manual (Campbell, 1971).

[f] These are test–retest reliabilities; the first figure is for a 30-day interval, $N = 102$; the second is for a two-week interval, $N = 180$ (Campbell, 1971).

FIG. 3.3. (Continued)

taxonomy from the other domains (cognitive, personality, etc.) came close to orthogonality *within* each domain, but it is likely that constructs show small to moderate correlations across different domains. In effect, then, inclusion of vocational preference dimensions does not seem to do undue damage to our stated aims.

In addition, vocational preferences, as implied, provide much that may be of considerable empirical and conceptual usefulness to our overall taxonomy. Specifically, we believe that they may assume two different roles in thinking about and empirically linking classes of human characteristics to classes of task and performance dimensions. First, it is possible that they may serve in the role of stable suppressor variables. Evidence collected by many investigators (summarized by Campbell, 1971) indicates that vocational preferences are highly stable (after age 21) for individuals over long periods of time (up to 25-30 years). They also are reasonably effective predictors of future occupational classification for persons—especially within broad occupational families as opposed to highly specific occupations. On the other hand, vocational preference constructs have only rarely shown much predictive validity against criteria of performance effectiveness within occupations. Finally, recall the earlier finding that vocational preferences do show a number of consistent, moderate correlations with other human characteristics (like those in our taxonomy), which *do* predict job performance. This set of findings follows exactly the statistical configuration defining suppressor variables (i.e., low or zero correlation with a criterion, and moderate to high correlation with other valid predictors of the criterion). In this role as suppressor variables, vocational preference constructs would be entered directly into the empirical prediction equation with the other human characteristic constructs.

A second possible role for vocational preferences is that of a moderator variable. A moderator variable has been defined by Guion (1976) as one that improves prediction of a criterion on the basis of subgrouping persons according to scores on the moderator. Such an approach is especially feasible for vocational preference constructs, because ''scores'' may be derived on such constructs for both persons and jobs.

For example, large numbers of occupations already have been classified into vocational preference categories, according to scores achieved by members of the occupation on the six vocational preference dimensions measured by the Strong-Campbell Interest Inventory (SCII, Campbell, 1971). Persons can also be classified according to the same six dimensions on the basis of their responses to either the SCII or the Kuder Preference Record (Kuder, 1970). Thus, either jobs, persons, or both can be classified into categories based on vocational preferences, and separate prediction equations can be developed within the separate groups. Note that subgrouping can be accomplished on the criterion side of the equation as well as on the predictor side. We can either classify jobs (criterion side) into homogeneous groups according to vocational classification and seek prediction functions for persons either in or entering those jobs; or, we could classify persons into homogeneous groups and seek various prediction functions for them. In this moderator variable role, vocational preference constructs would not be entered *directly* into the empirical prediction equations as they would in their role as suppressor variables. In fact, of course, vocational preference constructs may find use in either or both of these ways. Therefore, they represent potentially powerful instruments in bringing about the eventual linkages between human characteristics, on the one hand, and task dimensions on the other.

This line of thinking suggests the intriguing possibility that the world of work might be classified into a relatively few, quite coarse groupings—roughly equivalent, for example, to the six areas defined by Holland's work in the vocational preference domain. In fact, recent work by Schmidt (1978) suggests that minor task differences from job to job may be of less consequence in "moderating" validity coefficients between cognitive measures and job performance criteria than has been assumed. In effect, then, such an approach might be seen as a step toward evaluating whether or not some useful portion of variance due to so-called "situational specificity" might be captured by grouping occupations according to categories approximating those suggested by vocational preference considerations. Task classes would, of course, still be developed within each of the coarse groupings, and research would be devoted to examining the relative gain in predicted performance variance that might be accomplished by fine tuning the regression equations (i.e., equations more and more specific to particular task clusters) developed for the broadly classified and coarse groupings of jobs chosen initially.

A Tentative Taxonomy of Human Characteristics. We have presented taxonomies based on cognitive abilities, physical and psychomotor abilities, personality dimensions, and vocational preferences. These dimensions are listed and briefly defined in Fig. 3.3. In addition, the figure lists certain measures available for each along with estimates of their reliabilities.

There are about 12 well-established cognitive factors, and each has a number of reliable operational measures. As mentioned, these abilities have been defined through a long history of developmental work and especially with the relatively recent studies by the ETS researchers (Ekstrom, 1973; Ekstrom, French, & Harman, 1975). Although there may be additional cognitive abilities beyond these 12, this set provides an adequate beginning point for measuring human cognitive abilities. Figure 3.3 lists the twelve cognitive abilities and their marker tests. Note that their reliabilities (alpha coefficients) range from .63 to .94 with 36 of the 51 coefficients being .80 or greater.

Psychomotor and physical abilities appear well defined and measured by the work done by Fleishman (Fleishman, 1954, 1958, 1963, 1964). There are about 18 abilities in this domain, and operational measures are available for each of them. As can be seen, reliability coefficients for these measures are comparable to those in the cognitive domain.

The area of human personality is relatively less well defined and measured. It appears that a promising set of existing measures may be the personality factors isolated by Browne and Howarth. The intercorrelations of these factors are quite low, even with solutions using oblique rotation (mean correlation = .164). Their instrument does not, of course, possess the long empirical tradition and the hundreds of studies that supply greatly enhanced interpretive power to its measures in the same way as with such instruments as the *Minnesota Multiphasic Personality Inventory*, the *California Psychological Inventory*, and others. However, the Browne and Howarth scales were derived from the items from both the MMPI and the CPI, and most other major personality inventories that have been used over the last 50 years. The factors verified on the Browne and Howarth instrument were hypothesized a priori based on past personality measurement research. For the personality part of our tentative taxonomy, therefore, we use the Browne and Howarth factors. Fig. 3.3 contains the names and brief descriptions of each of them. One possible measure for each of these factors is, of course, the corresponding scale from the Browne and Howarth instrument. These authors, however, did not report any reliability information concerning these scales.

We already have suggested the special role that might be played by vocational preference dimensions in the development and validation of the job-requirements matrix and have mentioned that several current inventories can be used to derive operational scores for six primary vocational-preference dimensions. Fig. 3.3 presents one of these inventories, the Strong–Campbell Interest Inventory, as the operational measure. This instrument has a long history of development and careful research behind it. The test–retest reliabilities for the measures of the six major vocational-preference dimensions are excellent, ranging from .84 to .93.

These 51 constructs and their corresponding measures represent a broad taxonomy of general human characteristics. We feel confident that by applying the operational measures of these constructs we can obtain an adequate descriptive profile of any given person. Such a profile provides information about each person's strengths and weaknesses, according to a number of human characteristics relevant to differences in various aspects of task performance and work productivity.

As stated earlier, the trick in developing an operational, efficient, human-characteristic taxonomy with measures likely to be predictive of performance is to determine an appropriate level of abstraction. The taxonomy we put forth here possesses a fairly high level of abstraction. Even so, it possesses sufficient specificity to allow potentially powerful differential predictions concerning productivity on different task groupings (e.g., productivity in engineering versus manual labor, etc.). It also possesses sufficient specificity between various characteristics to allow good differential predictions between relatively similar groupings (e.g., engineering versus skilled trades), but it probably would not provide specific differential predictions for different types of engineers, different types of clerical activities, different types of lawyers, etc.). As levels of task specificity increase, it may be necessary to develop additional layers of ability taxonomies geared to finer and finer levels. At some point, of course, we will find that we can no longer distinguish predictor performance from that which is being predicted. At that point, our prediction system must begin to rely on work samples as means of evaluating candidates.

Finally, we are aware that our tentative taxonomy was not structured around any a priori rational scheme, such as the one developed by Dawis (1977). We have simply selected constructs and measures that appear empirically to meet the requirements of high internal consistency within ability classes and relative independence between classes. Thus, we believe this tentative taxonomy does contain concepts and measures that can be used to characterize the uniqueness of persons. The taxonomy is *not* dependent on subjective judgments; thus, we can expect individual characterizations to show reasonably high stability over time. To be sure, it may not yet include *all* possible human characteristics relevant to productivity, but this is probably because most research going into the development of such measures has been for the purpose of measuring humans, not for the purpose of measuring humans *at work*. As this taxonomy comes to be used within the conceptual framework of the job-requirements matrix, its strengths as well as its shortcomings will rather quickly become highlighted.

COMPLETING THE JOB-REQUIREMENTS MATRIX

We have presented and discussed methods used in developing task and human-characteristics (abilities) taxonomies and have presented tentative taxonomies for both tasks and abilities. Now, it is necessary to consider how two such taxonomies may be linked. Linkage is necessary in order to produce an operationally useful job-requirements matrix. Our goal is to define the matrix, so that each cell will indicate the level of contribution made to performance in a class of tasks by a particular class of abilities; or, alternatively, the degree to which the ability class is required for performing the task class. Obviously, this step constitutes the payoff for using the job-requirements matrix to enhance human performance and productivity in work settings.

Methodology and Results

To date, most methods of linking human characteristics to task performance have used some form of expert judgment. Because it is usually easier to teach job experts definitions of human characteristics than to teach equal numbers of psychologists about specific jobs, most studies have relied on people knowledgeable about the jobs or tasks being studied (e.g., supervisors or job incumbents) to provide the necessary judgments. Note, however, that some important exceptions exist, including McCormick's work on the PAQ (Marquardt & McCormick, 1972), where personnel and industrial psychologists rated the importance of characteristics for performing various job elements.

Classification of Methods. One way of classifying different methods for determining task-ability linkages is shown in Fig. 3.4. This model consists of a four-cell classification, depending on whether sets of abilities and of tasks used in the method are fixed, standard items intended to apply to all appropriate jobs, or are generated specifically for each job or job type studied and thus represent systematic samples from some universe or domain of possible job activities.

Methods using fixed sets of abilities or tasks are typically based upon some underlying theory or model of human ability and performance, thereby offering greater potential for contributing to an understanding of human work behavior at a theoretical or construct level. Such models, although applicable to many jobs, need be developed only once, and hence more resources can be devoted to building theoretically elegant and methodologically sound models of job performance and human characteristics than is usually possible in studies of the specific skills required for performance in a single job. In addition, methods based on fixed ability or task taxonomies can be used to evaluate very different kinds of jobs, enabling researchers to collect normative data on similarities and differences among abilities, tasks, and ability–task links relevant for performance in different settings.

One potential disadvantage of such "fixed element" procedures for describing jobs and identifying ability requirements is that task activities must be stated broadly in order to ensure their applicability to a wide variety of jobs, thereby losing potentially important specificity in developing job descriptions. Schmidt (1978), however, contends that this is not a problem but an advantage. He believes that detailed and fine-tuned task analyses are not necessary for identifying abilities required for effective job performance, though his arguments, so far, have been restricted to cognitive abilities.

Tasks	Abilities			
	Fixed		Sampled	
Fixed	Position Analysis Questionnaire	I	Individual Job Choice	III
Sampled	Ability Analysis Scales	II	Job Element Procedure PDRI	IV

FIG. 3.4. Taxonomy of job/ability analysis procedures classification of methods for linking abilities and tasks.

Position Analysis Questionnaires (Cell I).   The best-known procedure for establishing task–ability linkages using fixed task and ability domains has been the work done on the PAQ (Marquardt & McCormick, 1972; McCormick et al., 1969a). It will be remembered that Mecham and McCormick (1969a) and Marquardt and McCormick (1972) obtained reliable ratings of the importance of each of 76 characteristics for performing effectively in each of 180 task elements. The resulting matrix of characteristic-task element mean importance ratings (presented in Marquardt & McCormick, 1972) provides a ready linkage between task information based on PAQ responses and a comprehensive list of human characteristics. Now, therefore, a standard product available when the PAQ is used to analyze a job is a listing of human characteristics judged to be important for performing the task elements making up the job that has been analyzed.

Ability Analysis Scales (Cell II).   It will also be remembered that Fleishman and his colleagues identified 37 independent cognitive and psychomotor abilities. An important part of their research included the development of a series of scales, the Ability Analysis Scales, for defining each of the 37 abilities and distinguishing different levels of proficiency on each (Fleishman, 1975; Fleishman & Hogan, 1978; Theologus & Fleishman, 1973). One of their scales is shown in Fig. 3.5. In evaluating job-ability requirements, job experts read the ability definitions and defining anchors and decide what level of proficiency on each ability is required for successful performance in the job being considered. The positions of the task examples have been determined empirically. In practice, raters usually consider overall job performance, but there is no reason why more specific performance components or tasks could not be evaluated separately within each job.

Because the expert ratings on the Ability Analysis Scales indicate specific *levels* of required ability, and because the ability dimensions themselves are based on factor analyses of specific tests and psychomotor tasks, it should be possible to use such ratings to estimate levels of test performance (cutting scores) required to ensure that selectees will possess ability levels required for minimally acceptable performance on any job that has been rated. The only limits to the accuracy and fairness of these cutting scores are the adequacy and clarity of the behavioral anchors used in distinguishing levels of proficiency, the reliabilities of experts' ratings, and the reliabilities of the tasks.

Individual Job Choice. (Cell III).   No widely used procedures for institutional decision making about human resources have been developed, according to the Fixed-Sampled cell (Cell III) of Fig. 3.4. Taxonomies of human characteristics are not typically "sampled," because research on them has been so thorough and so widely communicated that they have, by now, come to be seen as reasonably fixed or constrained within the 50 or so dimensions we presented and discussed earlier in this chapter.

STATIC STRENGTH

This is the ability to use muscle force to lift, push, pull, or carry objects. This ability can involve the hand, arm, back, shoulder, or leg.

HOW STATIC STRENGTH IS DIFFERENT FROM OTHER ABILITIES:

Use muscle to exert force against *objects*.	vs.	Dynamic Strength (4) and Trunk Strength (5): Use muscle power repeatedly to hold up or move the body's own weight.
Use *continuous* muscle force, without stopping, up to the amount needed to lift, push, pull or carry an object.	vs.	Explosive Strength (3): Gather energy to move one's own body to propel some object with *short bursts* of muscle force.
Does *not* involve the use of muscle force over a long time.	vs.	Stamina (6): *Does* involve physical exertion over a long time.

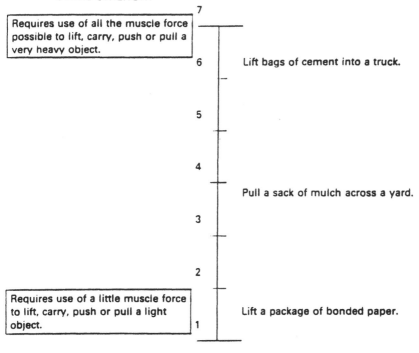

STATIC STRENGTH

Requires use of all the muscle force possible to lift, carry, push or pull a very heavy object.

7

6 Lift bags of cement into a truck.

5

4

Pull a sack of mulch across a yard.

3

2

Requires use of a little muscle force to lift, carry, push or pull a light object.

Lift a package of bonded paper.

1

FIG. 3.5.   Sample ability rating scale (from Fleishman & Hogan, 1978)

However, another way of looking at Cell III is in terms of an individual applicant's perspective. In one sense, each individual is comprised of a unique sampling of human characteristics drawn from the total population taxonomy of such characteristics. Thus, studies relevant to Cell III would, in effect, carry out a thorough analysis of *one* individual's unique configuration or profile of knowledges, skills, abilities, and orientations for the purpose of determining the optimal linkage between his or her ability profile and the many task classes defined by the world of work. Such study is essentially what happens in processes usually called "counseling," "vocational guidance," or the like. The purpose basically is to aid that individual as he or she seeks to come to a wise and appropriate choice concerning his or her job, occupation, or career.

Though obviously of great importance, this area of investigation is not directly relevant to the types of linkages between tasks and abilities that we have been pursuing in our efforts to fill out the cells of the job-requirements matrix. The reader may recognize, however, that methods are available whereby individuals may be grouped according to their level of similarity across a number of attributes to form "typologies" of relatively homogeneous persons. Studies of the job choices or levels of task performance of persons belonging to the same so-called person type would certainly constitute a research strategy appropriate to Cell III. In fact, such research has been done by a number of investigators. One large-scale research program of this kind (using biographical information as the classifying measure) is discussed in Schoenfeldt's chapter on intraindividual variation.

Individual Job Requirements (Cell IV).   The final type of job/ability linkage technique is used when one wishes to tailor the linkage to components of one specific job. Persons thoroughly familiar with the job are asked to identify characteristics contributing to successful performance on the job and to estimate the contribution of each such attribute, either to overall effectiveness, to performance in specific job components, or both.

Job-Element Method.   The Job-Element method (Primoff, 1975) is a standardized procedure for identifying required or desirable characteristics and for determining whether each such characteristic: (1) distinguishes among inadequate, adequate, and superior performers; and (2) is a practical job requirement in terms of the proportions of applicants likely to possess various levels of proficiency in the characteristic. Primoff desctibes ways of combining experts' ratings of characteristics' discrimination power and practicality to estimate the weight each characteristic should receive in selecting applicants. In addition, Primoff shows how the overall validities of predictor batteries chosen in this way may be estimated.

A second method associated with the lower right cell of Fig. 3.4 is typified by the "traditional" criterion-related validity study. Researchers consider a single job, perform a sufficiently detailed job analysis to identify homogeneous components or dimensions of performance, form and hopefully document hypotheses about abilities and other characteristics contributing to each job performance component, and test these hypotheses empirically.

Job Components and Human Attributes (Cell IV).   Bownas and Heckman (1976), Bownas, Rosse, and Dunnette (1977), and Peterson, Holtzman, Bosshardt, and Dunnette (1977) have developed procedures for linking human characteristics with job-performance dimensions and with specific tests and scales to establish conceptual linkages between test scores and job performance.

Job-performance components and classes of required human attributes are identified according to methods outlined previously in this chapter. Such procedures can, of course, be applied to an overall job proficiency construct, but Dunnette (1963) has argued that a more accurate model of job performance is provided by considering several homogeneous performance dimensions within each job, rather than relying solely on just one overall performance criterion for a job.

Examples of two performance dimensions identified for the job of firefighter are shown in Fig. 3.6, and examples of characteristics required for carrying out various components of the firefighter job are shown in Fig. 3.7.

Job experts, either immediate supervisors of the position, training personnel, or higher-level administrative personnel who are very familiar with the job's task and ability demands, are given definitions of the performance dimensions and of the potentially relevant attributes. They then rate, typically on a five-point rela-

Dimension I.   PERFORMING RESCUE OPERATIONS

Locating and rescuing victims trapped in burning, smoke-filled buildings. Carrying or assisting conscious, unconscious, or deceased victims up and down ladders and stairs, using drags, slings, cots, scoops, chairs, stretchers, or improvised equipment. Locating and digging to free victims trapped or unconscious in tunnels, pipes, excavations, cave-ins, etc. Moving heavy objects or materials to free or to gain access to trapped victims or bodies. Hoisting or lowering victims using rope, knots, or blocks and tackles. Removing victims using life-guns, lines, and lifebelts. Rescuing drowning persons, or recovering bodies using poles, ropes, buoys, hooks, and boats. Calming distraught victims, relatives, or spectators at emergency scenes.

Dimension II.   DEALING WITH THE PUBLIC

Meeting civilians in the station, and conducting station tours or giving directions to people who are lost. Giving fire prevention and other demonstrations to educate the public and to "sell" the department. Making nonemergency courtesy calls (freeing children locked in rooms, cleaning water from burst pipes).

FIG. 3.6. Definitions of two dimensions of firefighter performance (from Bownas & Heckman, 1976.)

1. *Physical strength:* ability to make and sustain strenuous exertions; ability to lift, carry, or control heavy weights; ability to maintain physical exertion over a long period of time.
2. *General body coordination:* ability to maintain balance while moving; ability to coordinate the movement of one's limbs with visual inputs; ability to move one's arms and legs quickly.
6. *Verbal skills:* ability to read, write, understand spoken messages, and speak fluently.
8. *Problem-solving ability:* ability to perceive small details and size up situations quickly and accurately; sensitivity to cues that indicate problems; ability to focus on a task and ignore distractions; preparing for potential problems before they arise; creativity in solving problems.
10. *Courage:* willingness to work in dangerous situations; ability to work in high or closely confining quarters; willingness to continue working despite physical discomfort.
11. *Resistance to stress:* ability to perform coolly and efficiently during crisis and emergency situations and under extremely tight time pressure.
12. *Teamwork:* ability to work with others as part of a team; anticipating what others will do, and cooperating with them.
14. *Responsibility:* being conscientious, responsible, and dependable; willingness to seek and accept responsibility.
16. *Getting along with people:* liking to be with other people; having a sense of humor; ability to accept hazing, ribbing, practical jokes, etc.; being outgoing and friendly; ability to understand the motives and behavior of others; ability to deal openly and comfortably with strangers.
17. *Honesty:* being honest and trustworthy.

FIG. 3.7. Sample attributes required of entry-level firefighters (from Bownas & Heckman, 1976.)

tive scale, how important each attribute is for adequate performance in each job dimension. The resulting matrix suggests how each attribute should be weighted to predict dimension performance. If the relative contribution of each job-performance dimension to overall job proficiency is known, the weights of attributes for dimensions can be combined with this knowledge to form estimates of each attribute's contribution to overall job proficiency. It would be preferable to obtain a less-relative index of attribute importance than that used so far; ideally, we would like to estimate the proportion of variance overlap between the attribute construct and the performance construct, but such an estimate seems implausible for most applied situations.

Judgments of which tests or inventories may be the best measures of the various human attribute constructs are made by psychologists who are familiar with the kinds of attributes being considered and with a wide range of possible measures of these attributes. These people are given definitions of the attributes to be measured, and the titles and some descriptive information (e.g., reliabilities, correlations with other measures, developer's conclusions regarding construct validity) about potential tests or measures of these attributes. After reviewing this information for all attributes and measures, they make three sets of judgments for each attribute-measure pair. First, they estimate the test's accuracy or thoroughness as a measure of the attribute, using the 8-point scale shown in Fig. 3.8. This scale estimates the proportion of trait or attribute variance that is measured by the test.

The second judgment for each attribute-test pair estimates the efficiency with which the test measures the attribute. The scale used is shown in Fig. 3.9. This scale essentially estimates the proportion of test variance measuring things *not* related to the attribute being rated; scores on a personality scale requiring reading proficiency at a twelfth-grade level, for example, would be ''contaminated'' to a fair extent by reading ability, and such a test would receive a relatively high rating on the second scale (e.g., a 3.5 or a 4.0).

In the third judgment, test experts estimate the form and direction of the relationship between test or scale scores and standing on the target attribute. In most cases, these relationships are linear, and either positive (e.g., between the attribute ''responsibility'' and the *Re* (Responsibility) scale of the CPI) or negative (e.g., between ''responsibility'' and the Lability scale of the Gough Adjective Checklist). In a few cases, nonlinear relationships may be indicated (e.g., up to some score, the Danger Seeking scale from Tellegen's (1976) Differential Personality Questionnaire probably measures ''courage'', but extremely high scores probably are more indicative of foolhardiness).

Results from two studies using these methods suggest that job and test experts can and do provide reliable estimates of job attribute requirements and attribute measurement accuracy and efficiency. In the firefighter study (Bownas & Heckman, 1976), Hoyt coefficients of agreement among job experts on the importance of 20 attributes for performing 16 performance dimensions ranged from .91 to .99, with a median of .97. In a selection study for correctional officers (Peterson et al., 1977), reliabilities of importance ratings for 18 attri-

Extent of Measurement of the KSA Construct

The KSA construct is *not measurable at all* by the test.			The KSA construct is measured *partly* (about half) by the test.			The KSA construct is *entirely measured* by the test.		
0	1	2	3	4	5	6	7	8
Levels 0, 1, and 2 suggest that the test, scale, or item is *almost useless* for measuring the KSA construct.			Levels 3, 4, and 5 suggest that the test, scale, or item is *of some use* for measuring the KSA construct.			Levels 6, 7, and 8 suggest that the test, scale, or item is *highly useful* for measuring the KSA construct.		

FIG. 3.8. Scale used to estimate accuracy or thoroughness of tests as measures of attributes or constructs (from Bownas, Rosse, & Dunette, 1977.)

Amount "Left Over" in Measurement Potential for the Test, Scale, or Item

0	1	2	3	4	5	6
Nothing at All (0%)	A Little (1–19%)	Less than Half (20–39%)	About Half (40–50%)	More than Half (60–79%)	A Lot (80–99%)	Every-thing (100%)

FIG. 3.9. Scale used to estimate efficiency of tests as measures of attributes (from Bownas, Rosse, & Dunette, 1977.)

butes and 79 tasks ranged from .86 to .96, with a median of .93. These high values indicate that the importance means for both sets of data are extremely stable and can be used to estimate attribute contributions to task or dimension performance with a good deal of confidence.

Test ratings in these studies were also quite reliable. In the firefighter study, with test experts rating 53 tests for 15 attributes, Bownas et al. (1977) obtained interrater reliabilities ranging from .50 to .98, with a median of .84 for the first (accuracy) test rating, and from .50 to .97, with a median of .78 for the second (efficiency) rating. Similarly, Peterson et al. obtained interrater reliabilities ranging from .61 to .96, with a median of .90 for ratings of the accuracy with which 51 tests measured 20 attributes.

Table 3.3 shows the results of fire service experts' ratings of the importance of 20 attributes for performance in 16 firefighter job dimensions. Within each dimension, attributes' values are proportional to their mean importance rating. Dimension marginals (the Total row), however, have been adjusted to reflect the dimensions' relative importance, derived from ratings by a different group of experts. The Overall column (attribute or ability marginals) reflects each attribute's contribution to overall performance, where overall performance is defined as the sum of dimension performances, weighted by dimensions' relative importance. Finally, the values in Table 3.3 were rescaled to sum to 100, so that the attribute marginals could be interpreted as percentages in developing a test weighting plan for screening firefighters applicants. In Table 3.3, we can easily see that many attributes contribute to performing in some dimensions (e.g., Dimensions 4, 9, and 10), whereas only a few attributes contribute to others (e.g., Dimensions 2, 5, 6, and 14). Where only one or two attributes almost completely determine performance in a critical dimension, such as Dimension 6 in Table 3.3, these attributes receive considerable weight, both in the sixth column and in the Overall column. This is appropriate because the attribute largely determines performance on a major component of the job. Where more attributes contribute to performing even a very critical dimension, such as Dimension 8 in Table 3.3, a relatively low level in any one attribute can be compensated for by higher levels in other attributes; hence, no single attribute contributes preponderantly to the Overall column.

TABLE 3.3
Weighting Plan for 20 Attributes and 16 Performance Dimensions, Based on Ratings of Attribute Importance for Adequate Performance

Attribute	1 Rescue	2 Salvage	3 Ladders	4 Entry	5 Ventilation	6 Safety	7 Technical knowledge	8 Fire suppression	9 Apparatus	10 Medical	11 Public	12 Fire safety inspection	13 Training	14 Cleaning equipment	15 Station routine	16 Dealing with peers	Overall
1	.66	1.94	.91	.51	2.05			1.23									7.3
2	.63		.96	.50				1.19	.53	.45							4.3
3	.58		.83	.48				1.12	.51	.47							4.0
4			.84	.50				1.17	.51	.49							3.5
5							.99		.54								2.1
6										.46	1.14	.61	.82			.91	4.0
7																	.5
8	.60			.49			1.01		.53	.48		.66	.80				4.5
9				.52					.55								1.1
10	.69		.89	.47					.51								1.6
11	.65	2.05	.85	.51			.95		.51	.49		.59					3.9
12	.67		.99		2.14	3.56		1.29	.49	.50			.83			1.03	14.1
13	.59			.48				1.17					.81				3.1
14	.61			.48			1.02		.54	.52	1.00	.61	.80	5.66		.91	12.2
15	.60			.47		3.54	.96		.52	.50		.63	.94			.91	9.1
16										.45	1.09	.60	.85		1.90	1.12	6.0
17	.58	2.39									1.10	.66	.80		1.95	1.12	8.6
18										.52	1.17	.63			2.16	1.05	5.5
19										.57							.6
20				.50	2.07		.97					.64					4.2
Total	6.86	6.38	6.27	5.91	6.26	7.10	5.90	7.17	5.74	5.90	5.50	5.63	6.65	5.66	6.01	7.05	100.0

Note: Attributes are as follows: (1) Physical strength; (2) General body coordination; (3) Quickness; (4) Dexterity; (5) Visual acuity; (6) Verbal skills; (7) Math skills; (8) Problem solving ability; (9) Mechanical ability; (10) Courage; (11) Resistance to stress; (12) Teamwork; (13) General activity level; (14) Responsibility; (15) Desire to learn; (16) Interpersonal skills; (17) Honesty; (18) Cleanliness; (19) Medical interest; (20) Construction trade interest.

Fig. 3.10 and 3.11 compare the results of job and test experts' ratings for two rather dissimilar firefighter performance dimensions. Note the different kinds of characteristics rated as important for performance in the physical/technical "Rescue" dimension (Fig. 3.10), and in the interpersonal "Deal with the public" dimension (Fig. 3.11). Psychologists' ratings suggest that the scales used to measure required attributes are of about equal quality for the two dimensions. In administering tests to individuals, where several tests or scales were judged to be useful for measuring a single characteristic, scores on the several scales were converted to standard scores, the standard scores summed across tests and the sums restandardized to obtain an attribute score for each individual. The attribute standard scores were multiplied by the weights shown in Table 3.3 to estimate performance in each dimension, and overall job proficiency. These estimated scores were then correlated with supervisors' ratings of performance on each dimension and on overall proficiency for over 600 firefighters from 19 different departments.

The resulting correlations, after correcting for criterion unreliability and predictor restriction of range, ranged between .10 and .32 for the 16 dimensions. These values, though not as high as one might hope, are of sufficient size to

Required Personal Characteristic (Construct)	Firefighters' Estimate Of Importance Characteristic For Rescue (5 point scale)	Psychologists' Estimate of Quality of Measure for Measuring Construct (0 to 1.0)	Psychological Measure
BODY COORDINATION	3.8		—Not Assessed—
PHYSICAL STRENGTH	4.0		—Not Assessed—
COURAGE	4.2	.81	.DPQ Danger Seeking
		.61	.DPQ Stress Reaction
TEAMWORK	4.0	.67	.ORI Interaction
		.65	.ACL Nurturance
		.63	.ACL Affiliation
		.61	.DPQ Social Closeness
		.57	.Gough Personnel Reaction Blank
RESISTANCE TO STRESS	3.9	.78	.DPQ Stress Reaction
		.72	.Comrey Emotional Stability
PROBLEM SOLVING ABILITY	3.6	.57	.CPI Self-Acceptance
		.63	.CPI Intell. Eff.
		.54	.FIT Judgment and Comprehension

FIG. 3.10. Portion of the chain of inference between *performing rescue operations*, required personal characteristics and measures of those characteristics.

Required Personal Characteristic (Construct)	Firefighters' Estimate Of Importance For Dealing With The Public (5 point scale)	Psychologists' Estimate of Quality of Measure for Measuring Construct (0 to 1.0)	Psychological Measure
VERBAL SKILLS	4.1	.90	EAS Verbal Comprehension
		.71	FIT Judgment and Comprehension
RESPONSIBILITY	3.6	.84	CPI Responsibility
		.61	ACL Nurturance
		.65	Gough Personnel Reaction Blank
		.60	ACL Self Control
		.58	DPQ Hard Work
		.52	ORI Task Orientation
GETTING ALONG WITH PEOPLE	3.9	.71	DPQ Social Closeness
		.68	CPI Sociablity
		.60	ORI Interaction
		.59	ACL Affiliation
HONESTY	3.9	.48	Gough Personnel Reaction Blank

FIG. 3.11. Chain of inference between *dealing with the public,* required personal characteristics and measures of those characteristics.

suggest good utility for using these tests and inventories in screening firefighter applicants, where the selection ratio is typically very low (.05 or less) and the costs of inadequate performance potentially extremely high.

Peterson et al. (1977) are currently conducting a predictive follow-up study to assess the validity and utility of the screening test battery identified in their application of this task-attribute linkage procedure.

This method has several characteristics that should be noted. Tests and scales are not linked directly with task-performance measures. Instead, job experts connect job or task constructs with attributes, and testing experts *independently* judge which scales provide the best measures of the attributes. Thus, the attributes or hypothetical ability constructs serve as the common ground between job experts and test experts. Three elements are essential to the success of this procedure: Job experts must be thoroughly familiar not only with the tasks performed by incumbents but with the job's ability requirements as well; similarly, test experts must be very familiar with both the tests and scales they are evaluating, and with the attributes for which they are considering them; and the attributes, the linking pin between test and job experts, must be defined sufficiently clearly that both psychologists and nonpsychologist job experts can readily understand exactly what is, and what is not, included in each attribute. The high levels of reliability we obtained in two studies for both job and test experts ratings suggest that these three requirements can be met without excessive difficulty.

The test weighting plan obtained by combining job and test experts' ratings should not constitute the sole source of validity evidence for a test battery. Such a plan does, however, offer strong evidence that the selected set of worker characteristic measures is a "best bet" for predicting task performance and should enhance the odds of obtaining useful validity results in subsequent empirical research.

RESEARCH DIRECTIONS

Here, we outline important considerations related to future research centered around the job-requirements matrix. The discussion focuses on research in two areas: employee selection and placement and performance acquisition.

Employee Selection and Placement

A Grand Design.   An optimal design for empirically linking a human characteristic taxonomy with a task/job taxonomy would be a large-scale predictive validity study. Measures of each of the 51 human characteristics comprising our human ability taxonomy would be administered to a large population of individuals. These individuals would then be randomly assigned to jobs. At several points in each individual's career, measures would be obtained of his or her work performance and productivity. These measures would consist of work samples, scores on objective work knowledge tests, achievement in training, or some other fairly objective criterion that reflect productivity and success at the task, job, or occupational group level.

Several years after collecting the initial human-characteristics scores, we would have available scores reflecting productivity and success for each individual with regard to tasks, jobs, and occupational groups. We could then compute equations relating scores on variables in the taxonomy of human characteristics to scores of productivity at the task, job, and occupational group level in the task/job taxonomy. Many statistical techniques could be used to capture such relationships. The particular technique would depend on the nature of the resulting job-requirements matrix, the linkages of greatest interest, the differentiations to be made, and the potential cost/benefit patterns of particular selection and job-placement decisions, both for institutions and individuals, implied by cells of the matrix.

Such a body of data, it is clear, could lead directly to an allocation of individuals across occupational groups, across jobs within occupational groups, or even across tasks within jobs, that would optimize overall productivity. From the individual's point of view, it could provide valuable information about his likelihood of becoming a highly productive (or successful) member of several occupational groups or jobs. This design would lead to the same sort of information for cognitive abilities, psychomotor abilities, and personality factors that is now generally available with regard to vocational preferences.

This design is really nothing new, of course. It is basically similar to work begun by Dvorak (1935) and Paterson and Darley (1936), which led to the Occupational Ability Patterns or the General Aptitude Test Battery. That work, however, relies on testing persons currently employed in jobs and identifying patterns of ability existing within those groups of persons. The design presented here uses a predictive model, obtaining ability scores at Time 1 and criterion scores at later times. Ghiselli's (1966, 1973) reviews of validity studies of various types of tests for various occupations represent a summary of information that has been collected piecemeal but ultimately might result in a specification of tests useful for prediction for various occupations—a sort of job-requirements matrix. Indeed, the OAP's and Ghiselli's reviews constitute useful starting points for developing hypotheses that could be directly tested with the design we are presenting.

Practical Constraints.   These are considerable. Note that we assume a large population of individuals all measured with a very extensive battery at the same point in their career, all randomly assigned to jobs and all tracked and measured at the same points in their careers on similar criteria of productivity and success. The only population that appears to have (or could have) most of these characteristics is the Armed Forces. Even if this population were available, we could not reasonably expect random assignment of individuals to occupational groups, though perhaps we could for jobs within occupational groups.

If we assume at least a modicum of validity for present occupational group assignments, then the absence of random assignment is perhaps less worrisome. It simply means that part of our work is already completed—that is, distinctions between individuals in terms of human characteristics that account for productivity and success in different occupational groups are already known. To the extent that these initial allocations are less valid, we come closer to the random allocation model. The essential feature is the requirement that all individuals be measured with regard to all cells in the human-characteristics taxonomy.

A More Modest Design.   An alternative to the admittedly grand design presented previously would be a series of smaller studies at the job or task level. Here we would administer only those measures of human characteristics that previous evidence suggest are the most likely predictors of productivity. These designs could use the concurrent model utilized in developing occupational ability patterns but should certainly maintain the use of objective and detailed criteria of success and/or productivity. In addition, some common tests should be utilized in these studies to enhance the usefulness of comparisons of results across studies. Using this tactic, the job-requirements matrix could be built from the bottom up, rather than from the top down. Such an approach is more practical and easily implemented, but the results are less compelling and more difficult to integrate.

In perhaps the ultimate dilution of the grand design, we could simply postulate hypothetical taxonomies of human characteristics and tasks/jobs and hypothetical relationships between the two based on available knowledge. (In a sense, this chapter is one step toward that postulation.) This hypothetical job-requirements matrix could then become a communication device to record and report past, present, and future studies conducted by many investigators that (by design or happenstance) offer tests of the hypotheses inherent in the matrix.

Skill and Performance Acquisition

One final concern regarding taxonomies of abilities and tasks is their impact on skill acquisition. Books have been written discussing optimum training strategies to capitalize on different kinds of trainee ability patterns, and to facilitate learning different kinds of tasks (see e.g. Gagné, 1965; Cronbach & Snow, 1977). An excellent review of the training field, with additional references for more intensive reading, is Hinrichs's (1976) discussion of personnel training theory and practice. Instead of attempting to repeat such a general presentation, we suggest only a few points that seem to be most directly relevant to the topics we have mentioned so far.

Taxonomies of human abilities affect skill acquisition and training design in several ways. Perhaps the most obvious connection is that training programs must be geared to the ability levels of the target trainee population. Hinrichs (1976) emphasizes how important it is for trainees to experience success early in the training cycle. Positive subjective outcomes for the trainee, especially perceptions of mastery, seem critical for maintaining trainee interest in, and enthusiasm for, learning in both formal training and on-the-job settings.

A more intriguing consideration is Fleishman's (1957, 1972a) findings that different abilities can be involved in performing tasks that vary only very slightly, and that different abilities may contribute to success in training at different stages of the training process. For example, high performers during *early* practice trials for some tasks tend to be people with high verbal skills, who readily understand the task to be performed, and with high perceptual abilities, who can quickly and accurately detect and interpret (at a cognitive level) incoming signals. During later trials, after the task itself has been practiced to the point that signal detection and interpretation are automatic processes, motor skills and skills highly specific to the task become the principal determinants of performance.

These results have several important implications for training design and evaluation. The most obvious, and perhaps the most critical, is that learning should not be assessed nor training terminated, until the trainee has had enough practice so that *terminal* skills or abilities are controlling performance, for these are the particular attributes that eventually are most important in determining task proficiency on the job.

A second implication is related to screening people for training programs. Employers could require applicants to be high on *both* skills that affect early performance and those that contribute to performance after practice. This strategy would allow a faster pace of training, but at the cost of rejecting some trainees who could eventually learn to perform at high levels after getting over the hump imposed by earlier learning requirements. The alternative would be to screen primarily on the skills determining *terminal* performance, and then to tailor the rate of training during early stages to the ability levels of the individual trainees. The greatest error would be to select only on those skills that determine the *rate* of performance acquisition, and to ignore the terminal skills that govern the eventual *level* of task proficiency.

Task and ability structures can jointly affect training and evaluation programs. The job-requirements matrix is extremely valuable for discovering which fundamental abilities are prerequisite to successful task acquisition, for determining which patterns of training will best facilitate learning transfer between related tasks, and for guiding research into the dynamic interactions among abilities contributing to learning across training practice trials and across tasks of different types. Such a matrix, with sufficient supporting research, can be used in a combined selection–placement–training program in which: (1) candidates' levels in essentially nontrainable abilities can be assessed to determine for which task types they are ineligible; (2) candidates' attribute profiles can be compared with the profiles of attribute requirements for the types of tasks present in the organization, to determine which task types the candidates will best fit; and (3) information on candidates' attribute profiles and task skill requirements can be combined to develop an individual training program to build the candidate's task performance to stable levels as efficiently as possible.

Although such a job information center will remain an ideal, distant goal for some time, it will be possible to explore some limited portions of a job-requirements matrix over the next decade, and such research should be strongly encouraged and supported.

REFERENCES

Bendig, A. W. The Pittsburgh scales of social extraversion–introversion and emotionality. *Journal of Psychology*, 1962, *53*, 199–209.

Bownas, D. A., & Heckman, R. W. *Job analysis of the entry-level firefighter position*. Minneapolis: Personnel Decisions, Inc., 1976.

Bownas, D. A., Rosse, R. L., & Dunnette, M. D. *Construct validation of a selection battery for the entry-level firefighter position.* Minneapolis: Personnel Decisions Research Institute, 1977.

Browne, J. A., & Howarth, E. A comprehensive factor analysis of personality questionnaire items: a test of 20 positive factor hypotheses. *Multivariate Behavioral Research,* 1977, *12,* 399–427.

Campbell, D. P. *Handbook for the Strong Vocational Interest Blank.* Stanford, Calif.: Stanford University Press, 1971.

Cattell, R. B., Eber, H. W., & Tatsuoka, M. M. *Handbook for the Sixteen Personality Factor Questionnaire.* Champaign, Ill.: Institute for Personality and Ability Testing, 1970.

Christal, R. E. *The United States Air Force Occupational Research Project* (Technical report AFHRL-TR-73-75). Brooks Air Force Base, Tex.: Air Force Human Resources Laboratory, 1974.

Comrey, A. L. *Comrey Personality Scales.* San Diego, Calif.: Educational and Industrial Testing Service, 1970.

Cronbach, L. J., & Meehl, P. E. Construct validity in psychological tests. *Psychological Bulletin,* 1955, *52,* 281–302.

Cronbach, L. G., & Snow, R. E. *Aptitudes and instructional methods: a handbook for research on interactions.* New York: Halstead Press, 1977.

Dawis, R. V. *A model, method, and taxonomy for the selection of tests as predictors.* Draft manuscript. Minneapolis: Minneapolis Civil Service Commission, 1977.

Dunnette, M. D. A note on *the* criterion. *Journal of Applied Psychology,* 1963, *47,* 251–254.

Dunnetee, M. D. Basic attributes of individuals in relation to behavior in organizations. In M. D. Dunnette (Ed.), *Handbook of Industrial and Organizational Psychology.* Chicago: Rand Mc-Nally, 1976.

Dvorak, B. J. *Differential occupational ability patterns.* Bulletin 8. Employment Stabilization Research Institute. Minneapolis: University of Minnesota, 1935.

Ekstrom, R. B. *Cognitive factors: Some recent literature* (Technical Report No. 2, ONR Contract N00014-71-C-0117, NR 150-329). Princeton, N.J.: Educational Testing Service, 1973.

Ekstrom, R. B., French, J. W., & Harman, H. H. *An attempt to confirm five recently identified cognitive factors* (Technical Report No. 8, ONR Contract N00014-71-C-0117, NR 150-329). Princeton, N.J.: Educational Testing Service, 1975.

Eysenck, H. J. The questionnaire measurement of neuroticism and extraversion. *Rivista di Psicologica,* 1956, *50,* 113–140.

Eysenck, H. J. & Eysenck, S. B. G. *Eysenck Personality Inventory.* London: University of London Press, 1963.

Eysenck, H. J., & Eysenck, S. B. G. *Personality structure and measurement.* London: Routledge & Kegan Paul, 1969.

Eysenck, S. B. G., & Eysenck, H. J. The measurement of psychoticism: A study of factorial stability and reliability. *British Journal of Social and Clinical Psychology,* 1968, *7,* 286–294.

Farina, A. J., Jr. Development of a taxonomy of human performance: A review of descriptive schemes for human task behavior. JSAS *Catalog of Selected Documents in Psychology,* 1973, *3,* 23. (Ms. No. 318).

Fine, S. A. *A functional approach to a broad scale map of work behaviors.* HSR-RM-63/2. McLean, Va.: Human Sciences Research, September, 1963.

Fleishman, E. A. Dimensional analysis of psychomotor abilities. *Journal of Experimental Psychology,* 1954, *48,* 437–454.

Fleishman, E. A. Factor structure in relation to task difficulty in psychomotor performance. *Educational and Psychological Measurement,* 1957, *17,* 522–532.

Fleishman, E. A. Dimensional analysis of movement reactions. *Journal of Experimental Psychology,* 1958, *55,* 438–453.

Fleishman, E. A. Factor analysis of physical fitness tests. *Educational and Psychological Measurement,* 1963, *23,* 647–661.

Fleishman, E. A. *The structure and measurement of physical fitness.* Englewood Cliffs, N.J.: Prentice Hall, 1964.

Fleishman, E. A. On the relation between abilities, learning, and human performance. *American Psychologist,* 1972, *27,* 1017-1032. (a)

Fleishman, E. A. Structure and measurement of psychomotor abilities, Chapter 4. In R. N. Singer (Ed.), *Psychomotor domain: Movement behavior.* Philadelphia: Lea & Febiger, 1972. (b)

Fleishman, E. A. Toward a taxonomy of human performance. *American Psychologist,* 1975, *30,* 1127-1149.

Fleishman, E. A., & Hogan, J. C. *A taxonomic method for assessing the physical requirements of jobs: The physical abilities analysis approach* (ARRO Technical Report 3012/R78-6). Washington, D.C.: Advanced Research Resources Organization, June 1978.

Fleishman, E. A., Kinkade, R. G., & Chambers, A. N. Development of a taxonomy of human performance: A review of the first year's progress. JSAS *Catalog of Selected Documents in Psychology,* 1972, *2,* 39. (Ms. No. 111).

Fleishman, E. A., & Stephenson, R. W. Development of a taxonomy of human performance: A review of the third year's progress. *JSAS Catalog of Selected Documents in Psychology,* 1972, *2,* 40-41. (Ms. No. 113).

Fleishman, E. A., Teichner, W. H., & Stephenson, R. W. Development of a taxonomy of human performance: A review of the second year's progress. JSAS *Catalog of Selected Documents in Psychology,* 1972, *2,* 39-40.

French, J. W. *The description of personality measurements in terms of rotated factors.* Princeton, N.J.: Educational Testing Service, 1953.

French, J. W. *Toward the establishment of noncognitive factors through literature search and interpretation.* Princeton, N.J.: Educational Testing Service, 1973.

Gagné, R. M. *The Conditions of learning.* New York: Holt, Rinehart and Winston, 1965.

Ghiselli, E. E. *The validity of occupational tests.* New York: Wiley, 1966.

Ghiselli, E. E. The validity of aptitude tests in personnel selection. *Personnel Psychology,* 1973, *26,* 461-477.

Goldberg, L. R. An historical survey of personality scales and inventories. In P. McReynolds (Ed.), *Advances in Psychological Assessment.* New York: Science and Behavior Books, 1971.

Gough, H. G. *Manual for the California Psychological Inventory.* Palo Alto: Consulting Psychologists Press, 1956.

Gough, H. G. Personality and personality assessment. In M. D. Dunnette (Ed.), *Handbook of Industrial and Organizational Psychology.* Chicago: Rand McNally, 1976.

Guilford, J. P. Three faces of intellect. *American Psychologist,* 1959, *14,* 469-479.

Guilford, J. P. *The nature of human intelligence.* New York: McGraw-Hill, 1967.

Guilford, J. P., & Zimmerman, W. S. *Manual for the Guilford-Zimmerman Temperament Survey.* Beverly Hills, Calif.: Sheridan Supply Company, 1949.

Guion, R. M. Recruiting, selection, and job placement. In M. D. Dunnette (Ed.), *Handbook of Industrial and Organizationl Psychology.* Chicago: Rand McNally, 1976.

Hathaway, S. R., & McKinley, J. C. *Manual for the Minnesota Multiphasic Personality Inventory.* New York: Psychological Corporation, 1943.

Heidbreder, E. Measuring introversion and extraversion. *Journal of Abnormal and Social Psychology,* 1926, *21,* 120-134.

Heist, P., & Yonge, G. *Manual for the Omnibus Psychological Inventory, Form F.* New York: Psychological Corporation, 1968.

Heron, A. A two part measure for use as a research criterion. *British Journal of Psychology,* 1956, *47,* 243-251.

Hinrichs, J. R. Personnel training. In M. D. Dunnette (Ed.), *Handbook of Industrial and Organizational Psychology.* Chicago: Rand McNally, 1976.

Holland, J. L. Vocational preferences. In M. D. Dunnette (Ed.), *Handbook of Industrial and Organizational Psychology.* Chicago: Rand McNally, 1976.

Howarth, E. *Howarth Personality Questionnaire 2*. Edmonton: University of Alberta, 1971.

Howarth, E., & Browne, J. A. An item-factor analysis of the 16PF. *Personality*, 1971, *2*, 117-139.

Howarth, E., & Browne, J. A. An item-factor-analysis of the Eysenck Personality Inventory. *British Journal of Social and Clinical Psychology*, 1972, *11*, 162-174.

Jackson, D. N. *Personality Research Form Manual*. Goshen, N.Y.: Research Psychologists Press, 1967.

Jernigan, L. R., & Demaree, R. G. Item-factor-analysis of the Guilford-Zimmerman Temperament Survey. *Proceedings of the 79th Annual Convention of the American Psychological Association*, 1971, 111-112.

Kuder, G. F. *Manual for Occupational Interest Survey, Form DD*. Chicago: Science Research Associates, 1970.

Marquardt, L. D., & McCormick, E. J. *Attribute ratings and profiles of job elements of the Position Analysis Questionnaire (PAQ)*. Lafayette, Ind.: Occupational Research Center, Department of Psychological Sciences, Purdue University, Report No. 1, 1972.

Marquardt, L. D., & McCormick, E. J. *The job dimensions underlying the job elements of the Position Analysis Questionnaire (PAQ)*. Lafayette, Ind.: Occupational Research Center, Department of Psychological Sciences, Purdue University, Report No. 4, June, 1974.

McCormick, E. J. Job and task analysis. In M. D. Dunnette (Ed.), *Handbook of Industrial and Organizational Psychology*. Chicago: Rand McNally, 1976.

McCormick, E. J., Jeanneret, P. R., & Mecham, R. C. *The development and background of the Position Analysis Questionnaire*. Lafayette, Ind.: Occupational Research Center, Purdue University, Report No. 5, 1969. (a)

McCormick, E. J., Jeanneret, P. R., & Meacham, R. C. *A study of job characteristics and job dimensions as based on the Position Analysis Questionnaire*. Lafayette, Ind.: Occupational Research Center, Purdue University, Report No. 6, 1969. (b)

McCormick, E. J., Mecham, R. C., & Jeanneret, P. R. *Technical Manual for the Position Analysis Questionnaire (PAQ)* (System II). Logan, Utah: PAQ Services, 1977.

Mecham, R. C., & McCormick, E. J. *The rated attribute requirements of job elements in the Position Analysis Questionnaire*. Lafayette, Ind.: Occupational Research Center, Purdue University, Report No. 1, 1969. (a)

Mecham, R. C., & McCormick, E. J. *The use of data based on the Position Analysis Questionnaire in developing synthetically derived attribute requirements of jobs*. Lafayette, Ind.: Occupational Research Center, Purdue University, Report No. 4, June, 1969. (b)

Neymann, C. A., & Kohlstedt, K. D. A new diagnostic test for introversion-extroversion. *Journal of Abnormal Social Psychology*, 1929, *23*, 482-487.

Paterson, D. G., & Darley, J. G. *Men, women, and jobs*. Minneapolis: University of Minnesota Press, 1936.

Peterson, N. G., Holtzman, J. S., Bosshardt, M. J., & Dunnette, M. D. *A study of the correctional officer job at Marion Correctional Institution, Ohio: Development of selection procedures, training recommendations, and an exit information program*. Minneapolis: Personnel Decisions Research Institute, 1977.

Primoff, E. S. *How to prepare and conduct job element examinations* (Technical Study No. TS-75-1), Personnel Research and Development Center, U.S. Civil Service Commission, Washington, D.C., 1975.

Schmidt, F. L. *Validity generalization: Recent data and their implications for personnel selection practices*. Paper presented to the Minnesota Pro-Seminar, Minneapolis, November 15, 1978.

Schmidt, F. L., & Hunter, J. E. Development of a general solution to the problem of validity generalization. *Journal of Applied Psychology*, 1977, *62*, 529-540.

Sells, S. B., Demaree, R. G., & Will, D. P., Jr. Dimensions of personality: I. Conjoint factor structure of Guilford and Cattell trait markers. *Multivariate Behavioral Research*, 1970, *5*, 391-422.

Spearman, C. "General intelligence" objectively determined and measured. *American Journal of Psychology*, 1904, *15*, 201-293.

Stagner, R., & Pessin, J. The diagnostic value of introversion-extraversion items. *American Journal of Psychology*, 1934, *6*, 321-324.

Taylor, L. R. (chairman). *Industrywide approaches to the study of validity generalization*. Symposium presented at the Annual Convention of the American Psychological Association, Toronto, Ontario, Canada, 1978.

Tellegen, A. The Differential Personality Questionnaire. Unpublished manuscript, Department of Psychology, University of Minnesota, Minneapolis, 1976.

Theologus, G. C., & Fleishman, E. A. Development of a taxonomy of human performance: Validation study of ability scales for classifying human tasks. JSAS *Catalog of Selected Documents in Psychology*, 1973, *3*, 29. (Ms. No. 326).

Theologus, G. C., Romashko, T., & Fleishman, E. A. Development of a taxonomy of human performance: A feasibility study of ability dimensions for classifying human tasks. JSAS *Catalog of Selected Documents in Psychology*, 1973, *3*, 25-26.

Thurstone, L. L. Primary mental abilities. *Psychometric Monographs*, 1938 (No. 4).

Uniform Guidelines on Employee Selection Procedures. *Federal Register*, 1978, *43*, 38290.

U.S. Department of Labor. *Handbook for analyzing jobs*. Washington, D.C.: U.S. Government Printing Office, 1972.

Wheaton, G. R. Development of a taxonomy of human performance: A review of classificatory systems relating to tasks and performances. JSAS *Catalog of Selected Documents in Psychology*, 1973, *3*, 22-23. (Ms. No. 317).

Wheaton, G. R., Eisner, E. J., Mirabella, A., & Fleishman, E. A. Ability requirements as a function of changes in the characteristics of an auditory signal identification task. *Journal of Applied Psychology*, 1976, *61*, 663-676.

Zuckerman, M., Kolin, E., Price, L., & Zoob, I. Development of a sensation-seeking scale. *Journal of Consulting Psychology*, 1964, *28*, 477-482.

4 Intra-Individual Variation and Human Performance

Lyle F. Schoenfeldt
Rensselaer Polytechnic Institute

INTRODUCTION

Individuals differ in the kinds of capabilities they bring to the work situation. These capabilities are related to how well or how rapidly they will learn new tasks, how much they will benefit from different kinds of training, and to the level of performance they will eventually achieve (see Fleishman, 1966, 1972). The previous chapter dealt with issues of identifying classes and measures of human capabilities and establishing their linkages with measures of performance in job tasks. The emphasis was on the description and measurement of differences *between* individuals in human abilities and skills (*inter-individual variation*) and on the relation of these differences to job performance. The present chapter focuses on some additional issues concerning the relation of human capabilities to task performance. These issues concern variations in capabilities which occur *within* the individual, which we will call *intra-individual variation*.

Specifically, two kinds of *intra-individual* variations are identified. The first is concerned with the *organization* of different attributes or performance capacities within individuals. Interest here is on the person's *pattern* of attributes, rather than on his or her relative standing in the population with respect to a particular attribute (e.g. verbal ability). It represents a profile of attributes for that individual and is measured by the variance of several types of performance obtained from one individual at a single time. We will designate this kind of intra-individual variation as *intra-individual trait variation*.

The second kind of intra-individual variation is concerned with behavioral *consistencies*, *changes*, or *fluctuations* in human attributes or performance capabilities over time. Here we are dealing with variations in performance of an

107

individual obtained on different occasions. We have designated this kind of variation *intra-individual variability* and it is measured by the variance of an individual's performance on the particular attributes on capacities obtained at two or more different times.

Throughout this chapter, the two terms intra-individual trait variations and intra-individual variability are used according to these definitions. The term *intra-individual variation* is used, in a general sense, to refer to either or both types of such within-person variation. Individuals can differ in both the organization of the attributes they possess and in the changes in these attributes which occur over time. Obviously, these types of variations are highly relevant to issues involving human performance and productivity.

THE ORGANIZATION OF HUMAN ATTRIBUTES

Quantification of human behavior had its beginning late in the 19th century and proliferated greatly during the first quarter of the present century. It was natural that much effort should come to be devoted to developing alternate explanations of the organization of human attributes according to patterns of correlations between behavior measures and test scores. Some conceptualizations were based on different substantive orientations, such as educational, clinical, occupational, or experimental psychology. Other conceptualizations were based on theoretical notions concerning the structure of behavior. Still other systems were based on the types of responses typically demanded by different measuring instruments, such as questionnaire formats, experimental apparatuses, types of test items, and the like. Increased statistical sophistication over the years played an important role in developing various classifications of human attributes.

After considerable effort devoted to developing an organizational framework of human attributes over a more than 50-year period, a consensus has been reached. The resulting outline is shown in Table 4.1 and includes three main divisions of behaviors, each discussed briefly in the following sections. More detailed classifications of human attributes have been presented in Chapter 3.

Abilities

The abilities, also termed maximum performance behaviors, are characterized by measurement procedures for which high scores always indicate more of the ability in question. Each person tested is presumed to try as hard as he or she can, and the resulting score represents the maximum performance of which he or she is capable. In the case of school achievement, tests or grades are the measures of the amount learned, and, again, high scores always indicate the acquisition of more knowledge.

TABLE 4.1
Organization of Human Attributes

Examples of Abilities or Maximum Performance Behaviors
  Intelligence
  School achievement
  Special aptitudes
    Verbal abilities
    Numerical abilities
    Spatial abilities
    Perceptual abilities
    Sensory capacities
    Memory
    Motor abilities
    Physical abilities
    Mechanical, clerical, and other special aptitudes
Examples of Measures or Typical Behaviors
  Personality
  Interests
  Values
  Choice behaviors
  Attitudes
  Opinions
Examples of Stylistic Measures
  Field dependence-independence
  Conceptual tempo
  Reflectivity-impulsivity
  Leveling-sharpening

Although the abilities listed in Table 4.1 give the range of behaviors included, the actual number that could be listed is much larger (Ekstrom, French & Harmon, 1976; Theologus, Romashko & Fleishman, 1973). For example, a battery of tests exists for the measurement of 11 separate motor abilities and 9 physical abilities (Fleishman, 1962, 1964). Other catagories have been refined in a similar manner. Subcomponents of perceptual and cognitive abilities exist. Categories of memory have been hypothesized and translated to measurement procedures. Each area has been the subject of extensive research and has been carefully refined.

Typical Behaviors

The strength and direction of a person's interests, attitudes, and values are related to that person's performance. Measures of these behaviors are typically comprised of questions or statements concerning how the respondent reacts to his or her day-to-day circumstances. Thus, scores on such personality measures or interest inventories are intended to represent an individual's *typical behavior* predispositions or tendencies, instead of his or her maximum performance potentialities. The measurements in these areas are concerned with the quantification of these generalized tendencies or motivational directions. For reviews of measures in these areas see Anastasi, 1976; Cronbach, 1970; Dermen, French, and Harman, 1978; Holland, 1973; Super and Crites, 1962, as well as the previous chapter.

Stylistic Measures

Bridging the gap between the aforementioned major groupings of attributes are measures that draw something from both groupings. Stylistic differences and measures of them have been researched to a lesser degree than behaviors and measures in the other two areas. What has begun to attract research attention is the analysis of cognitive and perceptual styles (e.g., Holzman & Gardner, 1960; Kagan, 1966; Kogan, 1971; Witkin, et al, 1962; Witkin & Goodenough, 1977). When several individuals face a problem for which they must develop a solution, they do not attack it in the same way. One proceeds deliberately, examining all aspects of the problem before trying out possible solutions. Another leaps in, gives an answer, and then, if it turns out to be wrong, keeps trying others until one works. Some people characteristically take greater risks than others or approach problems actively rather than passively, and so forth. Some persons have to differentiate objects from their background (field independent) in contrast to those who are unable to separate field and yield to the power of background effects (field dependent) (see Witkin & Goodenough, 1977). Thus, stylistic attributes draw on one's abilities but are also a product of interests, personality characteristics, and other typical behavior attributes. They may represent fundamental and pervasive ways of responding to stimuli and may be related to a wide range of human performances.

Implications

Structural Considerations.   As can be seen, the number of possibilities for organizing human attributes in different ways is great, if not limitless. Various researchers have suggested structural models for specific aspects of the human attribute spectrum. One example is Vernon's (Vernon, 1950) hierarchical conception of cognitive abilities shown in Fig. 4.1. As can be seen, four levels are indicated. The most general level is *g* or *general mental energy*, a term first used by Spearman (Spearman, 1927). The major group factors include *V:ED*, or verbal–educational abilities and *K:M*, or knack-mechanical abilities. In addition, each test measures minor group factors, such as numerical ability, spatial ability,

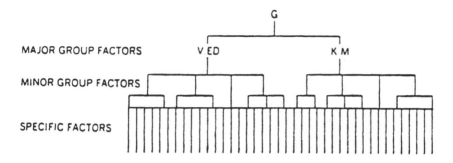

FIG. 4.1.   Diagram illustrating the hierarchical structure of mental abilities. (Vernon, 1950, p. 22)

and so forth, as well as information specific to that test alone, such as specific talents. Vernon's hierarchical conceptualization is illustrative of the potential complexity embedded in test scores. In his view and that of most other structural theorists, test scores can be viewed as additive combinations of various subelements. Other structural conceptualizations include the Primary Mental Abilities model of Thurstone (1938) and the Structure of Intellect model of Guilford (1967) that posits 120 distinct maximum performance abilities in cognitive and perceptual domains and the taxonomies of Fleishman (1964, 1972) in the physical and psychomotor domains. Ekstrom, French, and Harman (1976) have provided a list of reference measures for well established categories of cognitive abilities. Many models or structural conceptualizations have also been suggested and demonstrated for the typical behavior and stylistic domains (see e.g. Anastasi, 1976; Dermen, French, Harman, 1978; Goldberg, 1975). However, for our purposes, the categorization of human attributes into abilities (maximum performance), typical behavior, and stylistic attributes provides a suitable guide for discussing research bearing on the relevance of intra-individual trait variation and intra-individual variability for human performance and human productivity.

Intra-Individual Trait Variation.   Obviously, people differ greatly from one another on each of the measurable constructs making up abilities, typical performance, and stylistic attributes. Such differences have obvious implications for what some persons can or cannot do or will or will not do in different work settings. However, if these constructs were highly correlated *within* persons (i.e., if some persons possessed attributes equipping them for almost all jobs, whereas others possessed attributes equipping them for almost no jobs), then questions of human performance capability in work settings would be reduced to a simple matter of identifying, in a general sense, society's most capable and least capable persons.

Anastasi (1958) points out, however, that studies (De Voss, 1925; Hull, 1927; Tilton, 1947) have shown that intra-individual trait variation is almost as great as the range of individual differences in single traits across different persons. The typical study has involved the administration of a large number of tests and inventories to a large representative sample of normal persons. All test and inventory scores are then expressed in comparable units, such as standard scores. It is then possible to compute each individual's variability around his or her own mean and to compare that variability (intra-individual trait variation) with measures of variability for each of the scores across all the persons tested. Whenever this has been done, the mean level of intra-individual trait variation has been shown to be 75 to 80% as large as the mean level of trait variability across all persons tested. Such results have been obtained on groups of school children, high school and vocational-school students, and adults. It is also of great interest that the amount of intra-individual trait variation itself varies widely from person to person. Of even greater interest is the fact that the studies reviewed by Anastasi were all done with ability measures only. The likelihood is great that studies utilizing a full complement of human attribute measures (abilities, typical behavior, and stylistic measures as well as ability tests) would show that intra-individual trait variation, on the average, actually exceeds the average level of individual differences (inter-individual variation) by a considerable degree.

The importance of these results and speculations concerning the magnitude of intra-individual trait variation cannot be overemphasized. In essence, individual uniqueness may be expressed in an infinity of configurations. An understanding of an individual's work performance and its organizational analogue, productivity, requires knowledge of: (1) *how much* of each of a myriad of attributes that person possesses; (2) the *configuration* or organization of those attributes within that person; and, (3) *which* attributes or combinations of attributes have been or are in the process of being developed into job-relevant competencies or proclivities.

As implied previously, the nature of an individual's uniqueness varies over time. Measurement of within-person change and the impact of such change on human performance and productivity is considered on the pages that follow.

INTRA-INDIVIDUAL VARIABILITY AND BEHAVIORAL CONSISTENCY

General Concerns

Intra-individual variability has been defined as the mean of variances over time for each of several of an individual's attributes.[1] One difficulty in documenting

---

[1] As indicated earlier, within-person or intra-individual variation is measured by the variance of a person's several scores either at a single time (intra-individual trait variation) or over different times (intra-individual variability). If several types of performance are obtained for an individual on two or

and understanding intra-individual variability derives from the necessity that observations be tied to constructs underlying tests used in measuring the attributes.

Other constraints mentioned by Fiske (1957) include aspects of the testing situation. Fiske reviews a number of studies suggesting that the variability of a person's scores on a test over several occasions is inversely related to the amount of structure of the test situation for that person. The amount of structure of a test situation for a person may be related to one or more of several factors. First, some individuals have a tendency to avoid certain types of responses. For example, on continuous scales, some subjects confine their responses to the middle of the scale, whereas others prefer the extremes of the scale. A second factor is a tendency to prefer certain types of responses. For example, it is "socially desirable" to select self-enhancing responses in describing one's typical behavior. A third aspect of the test situation that may influence consistency is the individual's position on the variable being assessed. On ability and achievement tests, responses are most inconsistent at or near the threshold of ability on the item. Thus, for a question with two alternatives (such as true or false), the closer a person's probability of passing is to .50, the more inconsistent or variable he or she will be on that question. The fourth and final factor mentioned by Fiske (1957) as contributing to the degree of structure in a test situation for a person is the person's perception of the test. For example, a negative, unfavorable, or uncooperative attitude has been found to be frequently associated with low variability.

Other factors have been mentioned as influencing intra-individual variability. Johnson and Kotaskova (1969) defined a rate of growth factor and examined individuals deviating from the line of best fit. With this reference point, it was possible to examine tempo of growth. Although the application of this approach was with infants, it could also be used with mature individuals as a way of relating age to differences in intra-individual variability.

A final general concern involves the relationship between reliability and intra-individual variability. High reliability implies consistency of measurements and, one would think, precludes intra-individual variability. This is not necessarily the case, however. *Intra-individual variability is not intended to be the same as error of measurement.* In the context of the present discussion, the concern is for estimating *true score differences* over time (i.e., real differences on the traits over time).

A recent reanalysis by Whitely (1978) of data initially reported by Berdie (1969a, 1969b) bears on the relationship between intra-individual variability to both reliability and behavioral predictability. In the Berdie (1969a, 1969b) studies, each of 79 subjects was tested during 20 successive days on parallel

---

more occasions, the mean of the variances computed separately for each of the types of performance can be taken as an overall index for that person of intra-individual variability. In addition, of course, separate estimates of intra-individual trait variation can be computed for each occasion and their mean taken as a single estimate of that individual's overall intra-individual trait variation.

forms of six tests. Berdie (1969a) found moderate correlations among the variability measures obtained from the six traits, thus providing some support for the generalizability of intra-individual variability. Berdie (1969b) hypothesized that intra-individual variability should be negatively related to actual and predicted college grades, and although some significant correlations were found, the relationship depended on both the specific index of variability and behavioral predictability. To eliminate the confounding of level and individual inconsistency with change, Whitely (1978) developed three parameters for each subject by regressing trait scores on occasions: (1) the intercept; (2) the slope; and (3) the standard error of estimate. The three regression scores for each trait, a total of 18 scores, constituted the independent variables for the reanalysis of the Berdie data. The results showed some support for generalizability of intra-individual variability, although the trait-specific contribution to variability was, on average, four times as large as the generalizable component. Separating short-term variability from change did not lead to stronger results in the predictability of grades. Whitely (1978) concluded a more limited definition of the intra-individual variability component—most short-term fluctuation was measurement error rather than systematic individual differences in response variability.

In summary, the concern of the present review revolves around the observation that some individuals change over time, whereas others do not. Intra-individual variability is assumed to be a meaningful characteristic of test responses. It can be clouded by characteristics of the test, the test situation, the trait being measured, or other factors; hence, one must assume potential difficulty in decoding intra-individual variability information.

Some time ago, Fiske (1957) pointed out that consistency (or intra-individual variability) is a function of the intensities of the stimuli used to elicit scores. When stimuli are of low intensity, an organism shows marked variability of behavior. On the other hand, moderate levels of stimuli result in more consistent responses. Although couched in terms of experimental observation, this finding has applicability in terms of more general performance, including job performance. If schooling and society provide a low level of stimulation with respect to some ability or skill, people may be expected to be inconsistent in their performance. For example, society as a whole does less in providing opportunity to develop skills required in the combat infantry; hence, intra-individual variability would be expected to be large in these skills during basic training. In contrast, schools emphasize development of reading and computational skills, and this moderate to high level of stimulation would be expected to enhance individual consistency. (Note that such an argument has no implications for the final level of performance achieved, only for consistency over time.)

Behavioral Consistency

Most intra-individual variability research has examined changes in the relation of test scores to criterion performance over time. One of the best studies examined performance consistency in terms of changes over time in ability factors underlying performance. Fleishman (1957) and Fleishman and Hempel (1954) measured performance by means of a Complex Coordination device, requiring the subject to manipulate feet and hand controls in response to successive changes in patterns of lights. The study involved 64 2-minute trials. As might be expected, performance continued to improve from trial to trial, since considerable practice on such devices is required before one can show his or her full skill attainment and individuals differ in their rate of learning the skill. In this study, subjects were administered a battery of ability tests and scores on the Complex Coordination task and scores on the several ability measures were factor analyzed at each of several different stages over the entire period of practical trials. Results of the factor analysis are shown in Fig. 4.2.

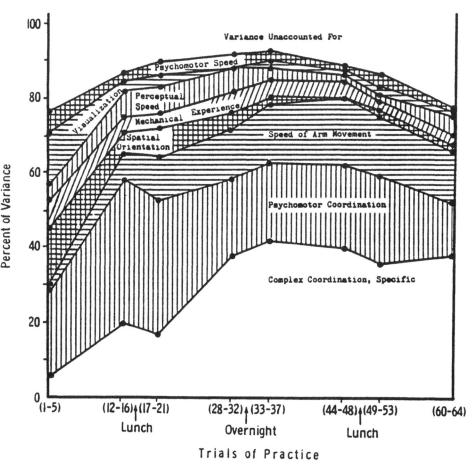

FIG. 4.2. Composition of complex coordination task as a function of time (Adapted from Fleishman & Hempel, 1954).

The areas between the curves in Fig. 4.2 show the proportion of performance variance accounted for by each factor after removing error variance and unidentified minor factors. It is apparent that the abilities that play a role in performance vary from trial to trial in a consistent and meaningful way. In the early stages, cognitive factors (e.g., visualization, mechanical experience, and spatial orientation) account for almost 50% of performance differences. Speed of arm movement accounts for less than 5% of the variance, while multilimb coordination accounts for up to 35%. A factor specific to the task accounts for a small amount of the variance. After 128 minutes of practice, spread over two days, coordination factors account for 50% of the variance, with the specific factor being the single most prominent source (35%). Speed of arm movement also has an increased role, to 20%. Cognitive sources, although the largest contributor originally, end up accounting for less than 10% of the performance differences. The early trials seem to measure adaptation to the new task, and intellectual factors play a large part in the performance differences. At the end, speed and coordination have become the most prominent source of performance differences.

This study is significant in that it shows how changes over time in contributions of individual attributes may be related to changes in levels of performance on more complex measures encompassing several different underlying abilities. Subsequent work by Fleishman and associates (Fleishman, 1962, 1972) has confirmed these findings with a variety of different attributes and tasks.

We turn now to research related to findings concerning intra-individual variability in the domains of abilities, typical behaviors, and stylistic measures.

Abilities.   Review of the literature over the course of the past 12 years uncovered relatively few articles that could be considered as contributing to knowledge about intra-individual variability in the ability realm. Most of these articles concern psychomotor skills, with the others dealing with vigilance.

Wilson, Tunstall, and Eysenck (1971) used a finger-tapping task in a partial replication of the Fleishman and Hempel (1954) study. Subjects were given the Otis Quick-Scoring Mental Ability Test, the Raven Standard Progressive Matrices Test, the Need Achievement Test of the Thematic Apperception Test, and the Eysenck Personality Inventory. Various test variables changed in the degree and direction of their association with tapping performance as a function of time through the session, presumably reflecting motivation or persistence to continue.

Carron and Bailey (1969) repeatedly administered a reaction time task to a group of subjects. Intra-individual variabilities differed substantially across different subjects. This led the authors to suggest that such differences might reflect differences in biological variability from subject to subject.

Stelmach (1969) studied the effect of practice on intra-individual variability. On a large muscle motor task, individual differences increased, whereas intra-individual variation remained unaffected by massed practice.

In a study of children working on the pursuit rotor, Eckert (1974) found that variability increased with age and ease of task, contradicting previous findings toward less variability. Relative intra-individual variability seemed the most appropriate index of developmental variability. Intra-individual variability decreased with age and increased with task complexity within age, confirming the hypotheses of other experimenters.

Along these same lines, Carron (1971) examined intra-individual variability in motor performance as a function of age. The amount of intra-individual variability was high, and there was no evidence for generality in motor response intra-individual variability at any age.

Drinkwater, Flint, and Cleland (1968) focused on performance of 20 general aviation pilots in a series of simulated instrument flights under stress and nonstress conditions. Intra-individual variability of masseter muscle activity and eye blink rate were uniform and low across all conditions.

Intra-individual variability in a vigilance performance task was examined by Parasuraman (1976). Specifically, consistency of performance on different tasks was strongly dependent on task factors, as defined within the abilities classification system. Thus, by classifying the different monitoring tasks on the basis of two primary abilities, perceptual speed and flexibility of closure, and two secondary abilities, it was possible to predict levels of individual consistency in monitoring performance. This confirmed an earlier study be Levine, Romashko, and Fleishman (1973) which showed that predictions about monitoring performance was enhanced when classified according to the primary ability measured.

Typical Behavior Measures.   Research in intra-individual variability in the realm of personality, interest, values, attitudes, etc. has been dominated by concern for the extent to which inconsistency is a function of failure to take situational specificity into account. Much of the impetus for the emphasis on situational factors and environmental contingencies was stimulated by Mischel's article titled "Continuity and Change in Personality" (Mischel, 1969). Within this framework, Shweder (1975) questioned the applicability of the conceptualization that personality consists of stable internal factors that make one person's behavior consistent across situations and different from the behaviors of other persons in comparable situations.

Alker (1972) examined and rejected Mischel's (1969) claims concerning the situational specificity of personality. According to Alker, the facts of situational specificity used to support Mischel's argument supported only the claim that the same person makes different responses in different situations. Alker suggests a new paradigm that incorporates facts of situational specificity into a more general contrast between organized and disorganized personalities.

Another study related to the situational specificity is more central to the topic of the present review. Ace (1972) assessed two aspects of response inconsistency measures as intra-individual variability and the relationships among response inconsistency and five demographic variables. A total of 56 undergraduates responded to a questionnaire on two occasions 4 weeks apart. Results showed no support for convergent validity and only meager and inconsequential correlations between demographic variables and intra-individual variability. Ace concluded that intra-individual variability is the result of situation specific and unstable factors.

All this research prompted the following statements from Phares and Lamiell (1977) in their review of personality:

> The interaction between personality and the situation along with the consistency and generality of behavior are hot topics of debate today. . . . All too often the literature seems to imply that it is necessary to prove or disprove the existence of personality and its stability, consistency, and generality. Actually the issue seems more one of utility . . . More observational studies of behavior are needed in order to better deal with questions of consistency in behavior . . . We also need to devote more attention to the manner in which we define consistency . . . We need a theoretical schema that will enable us to define consistency in advance of prediction and not afterward [p. 115].

A study by Hatfield (1972) involved showing 36 experienced and 36 inexperienced gymnastic judges a film containing 20 gymnastic performances, each of low, moderate, and high caliber. Judges received complete, partial, and no feedback of information concerning the ratings of other judges. Inexperienced judges were individually more variable in their ratings than experienced judges, and more intra-individual variability was displayed within ratings of low-level performances.

A study by Berdie is of interest. He found (Berdie, 1968) that correlations between intra-individual variability indices based on repeated testing with the MMPI ranged from -0.53 to -0.88. The distribution of correlation coefficients suggested that they reflect covariation of personality characteristics to a greater extent than variations related to mode of response.

Finally, a study by Parker (1971) evaluated the usefulness of conceptualizing intra-individual stability as a personality construct. The feasibility of developing a psychometric scale that might be used to predict individual stability in self-description was investigated, using the Adjective Check List (ACL). The ACL was administered to a group of subjects, and the variance in each scale score was computed for each person. The average variability furnished an overall index of self-description stability. The effort was only partially successful in that the high-versus low-stability groups tended to represent social desirability differences as much as anything else.

In summary, intra-individual variability research efforts in this domain have been confined almost exclusively to personality. Most of the studies on personality have concentrated on attempts to explain intra-individual variability in terms of situational or environmental differences. Thus, instead of attempting to converge on the construct of intra-individual variability in the personality realm, most research has been devoted to an effort to provide convincing evidence that situational specificity is the primary contributor to intra-individual variability in patterns of typical behavior tendencies.

Stylistic Measures.   Stylistic behaviors draw on one's abilities and at the same time are a product of interests, personality, and other typical behaviors. The behaviors falling in this domain have been researched less than in either the cognitive or noncognitive areas. Even so, emphasis seems to be increasing, as suggested by the discovery of five fairly recent studies bearing on intra-individual variability in style.

A study involving the free recall of four preschool children was reported by Baumeister and Luszcz (1976). Each child was tested repeatedly over many sessions with various experimental manipulations interspersed with baseline sessions. Among the findings were the results that subjects adopted consistent strategies in their approaches to problems. The strategies differed for different subjects but were consistent over time for a given subject. Considerable variation in performance was observed for individual subjects.

In another study, North and Gopher (1976) examined attention capabilities and the validity of these capabilities in predicting success in flight training. The testing system included digit processing, reaction time, and a one-dimensional compensatory tracking task. Among the findings were consistent scores across time in these tasks.

In a somewhat different study, Levin, Divine-Hawkins, Krest, and Guttmann (1974) developed an instrument to determine whether an individual learns relatively better from pictures or from words. The paired-associate learning task (group administered) consisted of lists of both pictorial and verbal items from which different types of learners were identified. Based on data from fourth and sixth graders, repeated classifications of the subjects were found to be quite consistent. In other words, those who performed better on the visual paired associates were consistent over trials, and vice versa.

Florek (1973) examined heart rate during creative activity. Changes in the heart rates of 15 artistic undergraduates were measured during rest and during four stages of creative activity. Subjects were given a stimulus painting, asked to examine and interpret it, to paint a representation of their ideas about it, and then to evaluate their own work. It was found that heart rate was a more sensitive index for judging differences in the stages of creative process than intra-individual variability.

The final study in the stylistic domain was by Higgins, Peterson, and Dolby (1968). Inconsistency in preference behavior was predicted on the basis of variability in cognitive control. Twenty-eight students performed an aesthetic preference task and were subsequently assessed for intra-individual variability on the cognitive-control dimension of breadth of categorization. The results supported the hypothesis that variability in preference behavior was related to variability on the control task.

Summary Comments

The studies reviewed here offer only limited, if any, hope for relating intra-individual variability in any consistent or meaningful way to actual measures of job performance or productivity. Studies have failed to separate with any precision that part of variability that may be due to errors of measurement and other artifactual components from that which might legitimately be regarded as due to true score changes over time. Researchers have debated issues revolving around the so-called reality status of personality traits, and the relative importance of situational specificity in determining behavioral outcomes. However, even those who argue most strongly for the situational viewpoint offer almost nothing that can be seen as useful for understanding the impact of such specificity on performance or productivity measurement in work settings. The upshot of all this is that even though most scholars agree that individuals *do* change over time, and from time to time in reliable and important ways, we do not know enough about the impact of such changes within individuals on performance variability, levels of performance effectiveness, or productivity in work settings.

Such lack of knowledge is indeed distressing; nonetheless, certain complex models of work performance have been suggested that may offer some speculative utility to thinking about the impact, if any, of intra-individual variation on performance. These models and their possible usefulness in the context of inter-individual variation are discussed later.

MODELS OF HUMAN PERFORMANCE AND PRODUCTIVITY

Industrial psychologists have always been interested in predicting human performance in work settings, although the shape and form of the interest has changed over the years. Early interest was predominantly empirical; but, over the last 15 years, a second class of prediction models has surfaced. These might be termed *Person-Process-Product models*, in that they attempt to examine productivity as a complex outcome of interactions between individual attributes and organizational requirements within work processes.

Toward Complex Models

Figure 4.3 is a schematic portrayal of a prediction model adapted from one suggested earlier by Guetzkow and Forehand (1961). It was designed in an effort to take into account complex interactions that may occur between various predic-

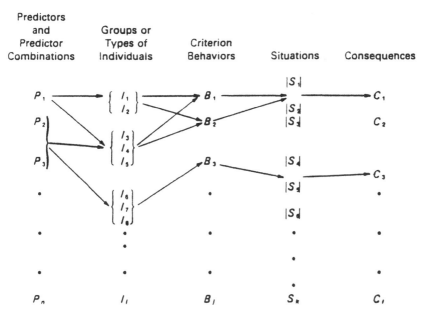

FIG. 4.3. A model for estimating performance outcomes (consequences) from individual characteristics. (Adapted from Dunnette, 1963, p. 319)

tor combinations, different groups or types of individuals, different behaviors, and the consequences of these behaviors relative to productivity. As Dunnette (1963) has stated:

> The model permits the possibility of predictors being differentially useful for predicting the behaviors of different subsets of individuals. Further, it shows that similar . . . behaviors may be predictable by quite different patterns of interaction between grouping of predictors and individuals, or even that the same level of performance on predictors can lead to substantially different patterns of . . . behavior for different individuals. Finally, the model recognized the annoying reality that the same or similar . . . behaviors can, after passing through the situational filter, lead to quite different . . . consequences [p. 315].

An updated version of the previous model is shown in Fig. 4.4. As the model in Fig. 4.4 indicates, job performance is viewed as a product of the person impacting with various organizational forces. The individual is represented as a configuration of abilities, special skills, interests, personality traits, attitudes, expectancies, and reward preferences.

Looking at the model from the individual point of view, a job involves task demands, which are objective lists of expectancies or priorities imposed upon the

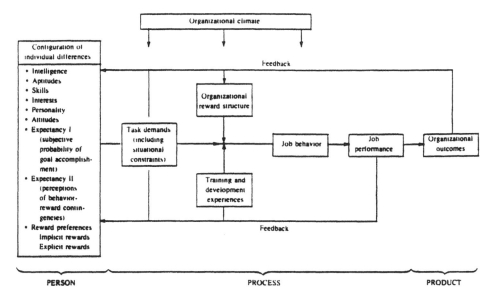

FIG. 4.4.   Model for prediction of job effectiveness. (From Campbell, Dunnette, Lawler, & Weick, 1970, p. 475).

individual in an attempt to alter behavior in specified ways. The result is job behavior, which includes all emitted responses, and job performance, which includes those aspects of job behavior related to organizational climate. The result or product of the individual's effort is a contribution to the organizational outcome, the generalized result of job performance.

Implications.   The models shown in Fig. 4.3 and 4.4 are two of several that summarize the relationship between individual characteristics and job performance. The implications are significant. Job behavior is seen as the complex product of cognitive, noncognitive (including motivational tendencies), and stylistic abilities. Expenditures of energy are the product of motivational forces. The level of motivation determines whether goal oriented behavior occurs or not. Once an individual is motivated, the effectiveness of performance is determined by the cognitive capabilities, stylistic tendencies, and configurations (intra-individual trait variation) of such attributes within the individual. Over time, consistency or reliability of performance will depend, at least in part, on the nature and range of attribute changes (intra-individual variabilities) within the individual from time to time and over time.

Capturing Individuality Through Statistical Analysis (Moderator Variables).   A study by Berdie (1961) suggested that persons differing in intra-individual trait variation (on measures of mathematics proficiency) might be differentially predicted to be successful or unsuccessful in engineering studies. Thus, intra-individual trait variation was thought to "moderate" performance predictions. Other examples of efforts to discover moderators in predictions are given by studies by Fiske (1957) and Fiske and Rice (1955), both of which were similar to the Berdie (1961) study. In addition, studies by Cleary (1966), Frederiksen and Melville (1954), Ghiselli (1956, 1960a, 1960b), Lee (1961), and Rock (1969) are relevant. In each case, the dominant theme has been an effort to identify persons who are consistently more and less predictable with particular sets of predictors or subgroups of persons requiring different prediction procedures.

The procedures cited previously are statistical in that they involve variations of frequently employed statistical techniques. Although some of the procedures are more difficult to implement than others, unlike the models shown in Fig. 4.3 and 4.4, all have been attempted in one or several studies.

Recently, it has become unfortunately apparent that moderate prediction approaches do not do much better than traditional linear methods of prediction. Zedeck (1971), for example, showed that initially favorable results usually fail to maintain their superiority upon cross-validation. In discussing such statistical strategies, Dunnette and Borman (1979) conclude that:

> Selection research must devote increased effort toward reducing sources of both variable error (measurement and sampling error) and constant error (such as perceptual biases) in the development of instruments and in the design of studies. Nonlinear models may someday once again warrant attention but not until such errors have been reduced sufficiently to overcome the inherently superior robustness of the simple linear model [p. 495].

Capturing Individuality by Studying Aptitude × Treatment Interactions.   Interest in bringing together individual differences and performance outcomes has led to the aptitude–treatment–interaction (ATI) model as a vehicle for prediction. General discussions of the importance of combining the "two disciplines of scientific psychology," as Cronbach (1957) has been recommending, have been published by Owens (1968, 1971), Vale and Vale (1969), and others. But by far the most comprehensive and penetrating review of the whole field is to be found in a book by Cronbach and Snow (1976) and in an article by Cronbach (1975). The authors presented background into the nature and history of the problem as well as the statistical and methodological difficulties involved. The results of the ATI approach to date have not been impressive. Evidence for significant interactions is scarce and fragmentary. Second- or third-level interactions tend to cloud any simple person-performance relationships, or at least render relationships inconsistent from sample to sample. In Cronbach's (1975) words:

> The line of investigation I advocated in 1957 no longer seems sufficient. Interactions are not confined to the first order; the dimensions of the situation and the

person enter into complex interactions. . . . Taking stock today, I think most of us judge theoretical progress to have been disappointing [p. 116].

Later in the same article, Cronbach (1975) states:

> When ATIs are present, a general statement about a treatment effect is misleading because the effect will come or go *depending on the kind of person treated*. When ATIs are present, a generalization about aptitude is an uncertain basis for prediction because the regression slope will depend on the treatment chosen. . . . An ATI result can be taken as a general conclusion only if it is not in turn moderated by further variables. If Aptitude × Treatment × Sex interact, for example, then the Aptitude × Treatment effect does not tell the story. Once we attend to interactions, we enter a hall of mirrors that extends to infinity. However far we carry our analysis—to third order or fifth order or any other—untested interactions of a still higher order can be envisioned (emphasis add) [p. 119].

Thus, in Cronbach's own words, the ATI path he has walked in an effort to predict performance has not been fruitful. Gains were made, as reported in the 1975 publication, but these were of less magnitude than had been hoped might materialize. These reservations had led Cronbach (1975) to propose abandonment of the ATI approach as a potential explanatory model for predicting performance behavior.

The Assessment-Classification Model

Although the list of approaches to predicting performance outcomes could extend ad infinitum, one further procedure, namely the Assessment-Classification model described by Schoenfeldt (1974), is worthy of mention. The Dunnette (1963) model, and virtually all the approaches discussed in this section, sought to improve prediction by the identifying subsets of persons for whom predictors were differentially useful, for whom situational factors varied, and so forth. On the basis of these concerns, as well as in the interest of an alternative to the ATI model, Owens (1968, 1971) reported on his development-integrative model. The Assessment-Classification model, shown in Fig. 4.5, is the logical extension of the Owens' developmental-integrative approach, the version most suitable for matching people with jobs in such a manner as to enhance productivity and performance. Thus, it incorporates the evaluation of person, process, and product (as suggested by the models in Fig. 4.3 and 4.4) with the subgroup conception formulated by Owens (1968).

Inventorying the psychological capabilities the individual brings to the job market has two aspects. The first involves utilizing standard predictors found to be valid for the jobs in question, the individual differences variables of the Campbell, Dunnette, Lawler, and Weick (1970) model. The second aspect involves implementation of the approach described by Owens (1968), involving

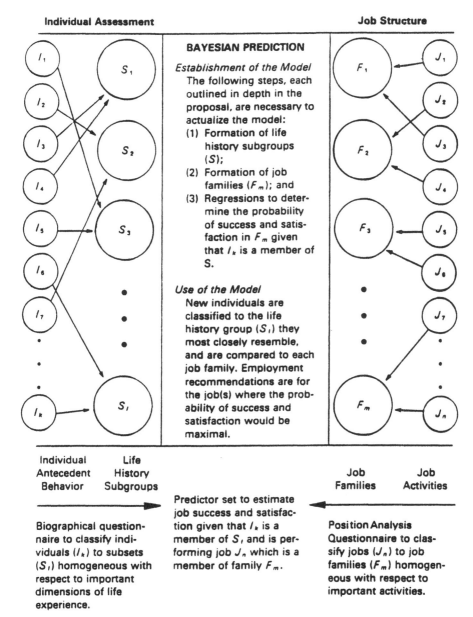

Individual Assessment

Job Structure

I_1 I_2 I_3 I_4 I_5 I_6 I_7 I_k

S_1 S_2 S_3 S_l

BAYESIAN PREDICTION

Establishment of the Model
The following steps, each outlined in depth in the proposal, are necessary to actualize the model:
(1) Formation of life history subgroups (S);
(2) Formation of job families (F_m); and
(3) Regressions to determine the probability of success and satisfaction in F_m given that I_k is a member of S.

Use of the Model
New individuals are classified to the life history group (S_l) they most closely resemble, and are compared to each job family. Employment recommendations are for the job(s) where the probability of success and satisfaction would be maximal.

F_1 F_2 F_3 F_m

J_1 J_2 J_3 J_4 J_5 J_6 J_7 J_n

Individual Antecedent Behavior	Life History Subgroups		Job Families	Job Activities

Predictor set to estimate job success and satisfaction given that I_k is a member of S_l and is performing job J_n which is a member of family F_m.

Biographical questionnaire to classify individuals (I_k) to subsets (S_l) homogeneous with respect to important dimensions of life experience.

Position Analysis Questionnaire to classify jobs (J_n) to job families (F_m) homogeneous with respect to important activities.

FIG. 4.5. The assessment-classification model for enhancing job performance. (Adapted from Schoenfeldt, 1974, p. 584)

125

the formation of subgroups with respect to the major dimensions of antecedent behavior and relating the subgroups to relevant criteria. This would involve administering a biographical questionnaire to assess the antecedent behaviors. On the basis of their responses, the individuals would then be classified accord- ing to life history subgroups or subsets homogeneous with respect to important dimensions of life behavior.

Undoubtedly, the subgroups formed (Fig. 4.5) would have intra-individual variation implications, although none of the studies done to date has addressed this matter as directly as was done by Berdie (1961). However, the subgroups are constructed on the basis of bringing together individuals who have reported similar background patterns. To the extent that intra-individual variation is re- lated to previous experiences, the subgroups would be expected to embody these individual characteristics. Thus, the resulting subgroups would be expected to differ from one another according to both intra-individual trait variation and intra-individual variability.

The other aspect of the model (Fig. 4.5) concerns the careful measurement of job requirements and the development of a job structure. Several instruments have been developed and found to be of use for measuring jobs in terms of the psychological demands required for successful performance (Cunningham, 1969; McCormick, Jeanneret, & Mecham, 1969). Thus, in the same way that individu- als are placed in subgroups homogeneous with respect to past behavior, jobs can be classified into families homogeneous with respect to their performance re- quirements and desirable configurations of attributes among job incumbents.

Unlike the conceptual models in Fig. 4.3 and 4.4 that do not lend themselves to statistical evaluation, or the statistical models that have been tried and found lacking, the results with the Assessment-Classification model have been positive. Schoenfeldt (1974) examined the validity of the model with a large sample of students ($N = 1934$) working toward college degrees. Subgroups, formed on the basis of previous behavioral data collected during the freshman year, differed with respect to criterion (major, grade point average, and so forth) measurements taken 4 years later. More important, the subgroups differed with respect to the curricular paths walked during college. The results indicated that it was possible to differentiate people in meaningful ways, to identify "job families," and to match people with jobs.

Two industrial tryouts have been reported using the Assessment-Classification model. In the first, Morrison (1977) tested the model's efficacy in making placement decisions in an industrial setting with nonexempt employees. Eight developmental-interest dimensions describing life choices, values, and interests of 438 blue-collar workers were formulated. Job analysis identified two clusters of positions that were homogeneous within and differentiated between each other on relevant job attributes. One cluster consisted of process operator positions and had 102 incumbents with more than 6-months service. The other cluster was composed of heavy equipment operator positions that had 148 incumbents. A discriminant function was calculated on a validation group of incumbents in an effort to develop a linear combination of the life history factors that maximally differentiated the two-job families. Cross validation demonstrated that three psychologically meaningful dimensions discriminated among the groups at both statistical and practical levels of significance. The process operators were more likely to be raised in an urban environment, to have a more favorable self-image, and to prefer standardized work schedules.

The second study was by Brush and Owens (1979) and utilized a total of 1987 nonexempt employees of a U.S. oil company. Each employee completed an extensive biographical inventory. Hierarchical clustering of the resulting biographical profiles produced 18 subgroups of employees, such that within any one subgroup, background experiences and interests were similar, and among subgroups, they were different. A similar methodology was applied to job anaylsis data in creating a structure of 19 job families for 939 office and clerical jobs. Significant relationships were found between biodata subgroups and critera, such as sex, educational level, termination rate, job classification, and, most important, performance rating.

Summary

This review has shown that our knowledge of job performance has advanced more rapidly than our knowledge of the effects of intra-individual variation. Good conceptual and practical models exist of how human attributes may interact with job requirements to result in performance. These models have made it possible to relate attributes (cognitive, noncognitive, and stylistic behaviors) of people to job outcomes. Some models have shown more potential than others, but taken together, they offer a measure of knowledge about how individual characteristics translate to job performance.

Intra-individual variation research has, however, proceeded slowly and has offered only limited information relevant for an understanding of performance and productivity measurement. Although some of the research has had implications for performance in what might be considered jobs or job-like tasks, most research has focused exclusively on test scores. The two domains of research have not yet been brought together, although models of job performance could and should incorporate intra-individual variation conceptions and measures.

It is also unfortunate that the early results by Fleishman and Hempel (1954), showing how performance changes during learning are accompanied by changes in the organization of abilities, have not been pursued more fully. Despite the encouraging results shown by Fleishman and his associates in a variety of complex job simulations and actual job settings (Fleishman, 1966, 1972; Fleishman & Fruchter, 1960; Parker & Fleishman, 1960, 1961), extension of this work is needed.

NEEDED NEXT STEPS

This chapter has been an updating of what we know about intra-individual variation in traits and behaviors—skills, abilities, personality dimensions, and domains of job performance. The presentation has summarized the organization of traits in the various domains and defined two different concepts involving intra-individual variation. Finally, the chapter has examined the relevance of intra-individual variation in traits and behaviors to issues involving productivity and human performance.

Our discussion now focuses on answers to four general questions concerning the nature and effects of intra-individual variation:

1. What do we know?
2. What is wrong with what is known?
3. What needs to be learned?
4. How will we learn what we need to know?

What do We Know?

By far the most intriguing result of research studies in this area is that the extent of intra-individual trait variation is extremely large, probably as great as and very likely exceeding the average level of variability shown across persons on single traits. Implications of these findings for the vast array of patterns of individuality relevant to performance and productivity enhancement in work settings cannot be overstated. Nonetheless, research beyond the single fact of learning about the relative magnitude of intra-individual trait variation has been sparse and of relatively limited usefulness.

Research has, of course, also shown the widespread existence of intra-individual variability across virtually all human attributes. In these studies, the basic measure of intra-individual variability has been the variance of an individual's responses on two or more occasions. There is some evidence, though not extensive, that intra-individual variability exists over and above variability due to errors of measurement. The fact that intra-individual variability scores have sometimes shown consistent relationships with trait scores and with external criterion measures, or that they can be used meaningfully in other analyses, is usually taken as indicative that such scores contain variance above and beyond errors of measurement. It appears to be the case that variability on a test is not entirely specific to that test. Variability scores from two or more tests may be positively related, the degree of association usually depending on levels of similarity among the tests.

With respect to the traits examined, most research has concentrated on motor skills and personality, especially the relationship between variation in personality scores and specific situational features. Fiske (1957), on the basis of research completed to that point, concluded that although variability scores do intercorrelate, variability is *not* an important general trait of the cognitive, noncognitive, or stylistic domains. None of the research reported in the past 20 years has been sufficient to challenge the accuracy of Fiske's conclusion.

Performance and productivity models have proliferated during the past 15 years. Taken together, these models represent a substantial contribution to the theoretical and practical understanding of how individual traits become translated into performance outcomes. Unfortunately, most of this research has been without regard to examination of intra-individual variation research.

What is Wrong with What Is Known?

With respect to all aspects of intra-individual variation research, much could be done to pull things together. Those doing work in intra-individual variation have not been as oriented to the applied (productivity-performance) areas as they might be. In turn, those doing work in applied areas have not been as oriented toward or concerned with intra-individual variation as they might be. There is no basic aversion on the part of the more theoretical or more applied to cross over to the other area, as is demonstrated by several notable researchers who have "crossed over," especially in the attempts to take into consideration situational aspects in personality. However, the modest results in generalizing one or several variability traits, or in using variability as a means of prediction, has not encouraged extensive further research in the area. Thus, intra-individual variation research continues at a rather modest level, and seldom in the type of organized programmatic way that is required to reach the next plateau of knowledge.

In summary, what is known tends to be fragmented in scope and modest in significance. As a result, the sum of what is known about intra-individual variation tends to be largely specific to the special circumstances of each study and of limited generalizability.

What Needs To Be Learned?

The use of intra-individual variability scores as predictors, or in a quasi-actuarial design, is *not likely* to be a profitable avenue of research. A number of good studies have been done on the prediction of predictability, including studies where the predictability groups were formed on intra-individual variability scores, and the results have been modest at best.

On the other hand, many of the domains of the person portion of the Campbell et al. (1970) model are known to vary over time. Perhaps intelligence, aptitudes, and skills would be expected to show the least intra-individual variability over time, especially in the absence of intervening factors, such as training programs and the like. On the other hand, interests and personality are typically expected to show more intra-individual variability. Attitudes, expectancies, and reward preferences could vary within individuals on a day-to-day or even within-day basis, although this is usually taken on faith rather than as a result of systematic research. These areas of variability have not been given much attention in seeking to pinpoint components of the person-process-product equation. Much research needs to be done to evaluate those aspects of intra-individual variability in typical and stylistic attributes that can definitely be regarded as systematic, non-error variation. It is within this arena of research that we may learn much more than we now know about such matters as adaptation patterns in relation to organizational requirements and job performance demands, developmental sequences in individual patterns of work performance, and individualized strategies of productivity enhancement.

How Will We Learn What We Need to Know?

Three approaches should receive top priority in further research concerning the impact of intra-individual variation on performance and productivity.

First, much more needs to be learned, both parametrically and in a behavioral sense, concerning the vast array of individual configurations stemming from increased attention and greater precision of measurement of intra-individual trait variation, along with the job placement and work performance implications of such emphases.

Second, the approach pioneered by Fleishman and his associates (see Fleishman, 1966) should be pursued more completely. Their work had the appearance of a ''breakthrough,'' suggesting that complex performance changes might be understood according to changes in the underlying mix of constructs related to that performance. These studies in this program have shown that individual differences in certain abilities predict performance early in learning complex skills, but that other combinations of abilities may be predictive of more advanced skill levels at later stages of training and performance (Fleishman, 1962, 1966, & 1972). These investigators, (see, e.g. Fleishman, 1972) have also suggested leads for the identification and measurement of new abilities especially predictive of high levels of proficiency. These include ability to integrate previously learned proficiencies and individual differences in kinesthetic sensitivity. Fleishman and Rich (1963) have already demonstrated that a test of kinesthetic sensitivity increased in prediction of performance on a two-hand coordination task, as practice on this task continued, while predictions from a spatial measure decreased. As a follow up, Fleishman (1978) was able to develop a battery of kinesthetic sensitivity measures to explore a new ability area with potential for predicting individual differences at higher levels of proficiency in perceptual-motor tasks. Parker and Fleishman (1961) also have provided encouraging results showing that performance can be enhanced by training those abilities known to be critical at high performance levels.

Finally, increased and more widespread attention should be given to the performance models that have been discussed in this chapter. More specifically, the models shown in Fig. 4.3, 4.4, and 4.5 should be modified to incorporate intra-individual variation into their paradigms. Such steps are not done without some difficulty, however. Several problems exist. First, the Dunnette (1963) (Fig. 4.3) and Campbell et al. (1970) (Fig. 4.4) models have never been implemented; that is, they have not been statistically actualized with real data. Thus, statistical incorporation of measures of intra-individual variation into their conceptions may not be regarded as highly likely.

The Assessment-Classification model (see Fig. 4.5) is somewhat different. The focus is on matching people to jobs, and only indirectly on production. In other words, the attempt is to match people to positions in such a way that we might expect them to be both productive and satisfied. The Assessment-Classification model *has* been shown to be statistically usable, as is evident from studies already completed. Further, measures of intra-individual variation may already be incorporated indirectly into the subgroup structure of the Assessment-Classification model. This should be investigated, because even if the group structures, as currently developed, do not incorporate intra-individual variation on the specific traits used so far, it should be easy to include such measures in further studies guided by the model.

In summary, then, these three areas of research involve more focused attention on developing and investigating more sophisticated measures of both intra-individual trait variation and intra-individual variability. The context of study should be within the framework of a model, such as the Assessment-Classification model and should emphasize studies of multiple traits as opposed to the simplistic variable-by-variable approach used so frequently in past studies. Finally, *changes* in performance (as might be expected during programs of productivity enhancement), viewed in a learning or developmental sense and taking account of the concomitant changes in underlying patterns of trait constructs, should receive heavy emphasis.

REFERENCES

Ace, M. E. Some validity assessments of response inconsistency. *Proceedings of the Annual Convention of the American Psychological Association*, 1972, 7 (Part 1), 1-2.

Alker, H. A. Is personality situationally specific or intraphysically consistent? *Journal of Personality*, 1972, 40, 1-16.

Anastasi, A. *Differential Psychology* (3rd ed.). New York: MacMillan, 1958.

Anastasi, A. *Psychological Testing* (4th ed.). New York: MacMillan, 1976.

Baumeister, A. A., & Luszcz, M. A within-subjects analysis of free recall with preschool children. *Child Development*, 1976, 47, 729-736.

Berdie, R. F. Intra-individual variability and predictability. *Educational and Psychological Measurement*, 1961, 21, 663-676.

Berdie, R. F. Perhaps mode of response does not explain intra-individual variability. *Psychological Reports*, 1968, 23, 40-42.

Berdie, R. F. Consistency and generalizability of intra-individual variability. *Journal of Applied Psychology*, 1969, 53, 35-41. (a)

Berdie, R. A. Intra-individual temporal variability and predictability. *Educational and Psychological Measurement*, 1969, *29*, 235-257. (b)

Brush, D. H. & Owens, W. A. Implementation and evaluation of an assessment-classification model for manpower utilization. *Personnel Psychology*, 1979, *32*, 369-384.

Campbell, J. P., Dunnette, M. D., Lawler, E. E., III, & Weick, K. E., Jr. *Managerial behavior, performance, and effectiveness.* New York: McGraw-Hill, 1970.

Carron, A. V. Motor performance and response consistency as a function of age. *Journal of Motor Behavior*, 1971, *3*, 105-109.

Carron, A. V., & Bailey, D. A. Evidence for reliable individual differences in intra-individual variability. *Perceptual and Motor Skills*, 1969, *28*, 843-846.

Cleary, T. A. An individual differences model for multiple regression. *Psychometrika*, 1966, *31*, 215-224.

Cronbach, L. J. The two disciplines of scientific psychology. *American Psychologist*, 1957, *12*, 671-684.

Cronbach, L. J. *Essentials of Psychological Testing. (3rd edition).* New York: Harper & Row, 1970.

Cronbach, L. J. Beyond the two disciplines of scientific psychology. *American Psychologist*, 1975, *30*, 116-127.

Cronbach, L. J., & Snow, R. E. *Aptitudes and instructional methods.* New York: Irvington, 1976.

Cunningham, J. W. A conceptual framework for the study of job similarities. In J. W. Cunningham (Ed.), The job-cluster concept and its curricular implications. *Center for Occupational Education Monograph*, 1969 (No. 4).

Dermen, D., French, J. W., & Harman, H. *Guide to factor-reference tempermental scales.* Princeton, N.J.: Educational Testing Service, 1978.

De Voss, J. C. Specialization of the abilities of gifted children. In L. M. Terman (Ed.), *Genetic studies of genius.* Stanford University: Stanford University Press, 1925.

Drinkwater, B. L., Flint, M. M., & Cleland, T. S. Somatic responses and performance levels during anticipatory physical-threat stress. *Perceptual and Motor Skills*, 1968, *27*, 539-552.

Dunnette, M. D. A modified model for test validation and selection research. *Journal of Applied Psychology*, 1963, *17*, 317-323.

Dunnette, M. D., & Borman, W. C. Personnel selection and classification systems. In L. Porter (Ed.), *Annual Review of Psychology*, Palo Alto, Calif.: Annual Reviews, Inc., 1979.

Eckert, H. M. Variability in skill acquisition. *Child Development*, 1974, *45*, 487-489.

Ekstrom, R. B., French, J. W., & Harman, H. H. *Kit of factor referenced cognitive tests.* Princeton, N.J.: Educational Testing Service, 1976.

Fiske, D. W. The constraints of intra-individual variability in test response. *Educational and Psychological Measurement*, 1957, *17*, 317-337.

Fiske, D. W., & Rice, L. Intra-individual response variability. *Psychological Bulletin*, 1955, *52*, 217-250.

Fleishman, E. A. A comparative study of aptitude patterns in unskilled and skilled motor performances. *Journal of Applied Psychology*, 1957, *41*, 263-272.

Fleishman, E. A. The description and prediction of perceptual-motor skill learning. In R. Glaser (Ed.), *Training research and education.* Pittsburgh, Pa.: University of Pittsburgh Press, 1962.

Fleishman, E. A. *The structure and measurement of physical fitness.* Englewood Cliffs, N.J., Prentice-Hall, 1964.

Fleishman, E. A. Human abilities and the acquisition of skill. Chapter in E. A. Bilodean (Ed.), *The acquisition of skill.* New York: Academic Press, 1966.

Fleishman, E. A. On the relation between abilities, learning, and human performance. *American Psychologist*, 1972, *27*, 1017-1032.

Fleishman, E. A. *Kinesthesis: A neglected area of human performance research.* Presidential address, Society of Engineering Psychologists, American Psychological Association, 1978.

Fleishman, E. A., & Fruchter, B. Factor structure and predictability of successive stages of learning Morse Code. *Journal of Applied Psychology*, 1960, *44*, 97-101.

Fleishman, E. A., & Hempel, W. E., Jr. Changes in factor structure of a complex psychomotor test as a function of practice. *Psychometrika*, 1954, *19*, 239-252.

Fleishman, E. A., & Rich, S. Role of kinesthetic and spatial-visual abilities in perceptual-motor learning. *Journal of Experimental Psychology*, 1963, *66*, 6-11.

Florek, H. Heart rate during creative activity. *Studia Psychologica*, 1973, *15*, 158-161.

Fredericksen, N., & Melville, S. D. Differential predictability in the use of test scores. *Educational and Psychological Measurement*, 1954, *14*, 647-656.

Ghiselli, E. E. Differentiation of individuals in terms of their predictability. *Journal of Applied Psychology*, 1956, *40*, 374-377.

Ghiselli, E. E. The Prediction of Predictability. *Educational and Psychological Measurement*, 1960, *20*, 3-8. (a)

Ghiselli, E. E. Differentiation of tests in terms of the accuracy with which they predict for a given individual. *Educational and Psychological Measurement*, 1960, *20*, 675-684. (b)

Goldberg, L. R. *Toward a taxonomy of personality descriptive terms*. Eugene, Ore.: Oregon Research Institute Tech. Report, 1975.

Guetzkow, H., & Forehand, G. A. A research strategy for partial knowledge useful in the selection of executives. In R. Taguiri (Ed.), *Research needs in executive selection*. Boston: Harvard Graduate School of Business Administration, 1961.

Guilford, J. P. *The nature of human intelligence*. New York: McGraw-Hill, 1967.

Hatfield, F. C. Effect of prior experience, access to information and level of performance on individual and group performance ratings. *Perceptual and Motor Skills*, 1972, *35*, 19-26.

Higgins, J., Peterson, J. C., & Dolby, L. L. Variability in cognitive control. *British Journal of Psychology*, 1968, *59*, 127-129.

Holland, J. L. *Making vocational choices: A theory of careers*. Englewood Cliffs, N.J.: Prentice-Hall, 1973.

Holzman, P. S., & Gardner, R. W. Leveling-sharpening and memory organization. *Journal of Abnormal Social Psychology*, 1960, *61*, 176-186.

Hull, C. L. Variability in amount of different traits possessed by the individual. *Journal of Educational Psychology*, 1927, *18*, 97-104.

Johnson, J., & Kotaskova, J. Development of intelligence. *Human Development*, 1969, *12*, 169-177.

Kagan, J. Developmental studies in reflection and analysis. In A. Kidd and J. Rivoire (Eds.), *Perceptual and conceptual development in children*. New York: International Universities Press, 1966, 487-522.

Kogan, N. Educational implications of cognitive styles. In G. S. Lesser (Ed.), *Psychology and educational practice*. Glenview, Ill.: Scott, Foresman, 1971.

Lee, M. C. Interactions, configurations, and nonadditive models. *Educational and Psychological Measurement*, 1961, *21*, 797-805.

Levin, J. R., Devine-Hawkins, P., Krest, S. M., & Guttman, J. Individual differences in learning from pictures and words: The development and application of an instrument. *Journal of Educational Psychology*, 1974, *66*, 296-303.

Levine, J. M., Romashko, T., & Fleishman, E. A. Evaluation of an abilities classification system for integrating and generalizing findings about human performance: The vigilance area. *Journal of Applied Psychology*, 1973, *58*, 149-157.

McCormick, E. J., Jeanneret, P. R., & Mecham, R. C. *The development and background of the Position Analysis Questionnaire (PAQ)*. Occupational Research Center, Purdue University, June, 1969.

Mischel, W. Continuity and change in personality. *American Psychologist*, 1969, *24*, 1012-1018.

Morrison, R. F. A multivariate model for the occupational placement decision. *Journal of Applied Psychology*, 1977, *62*, 271-277.

North, R. A., & Gopher, D. Measures of attention as predictors of flight performance. *Human Factors*, 1976, *18*, 1-14.

Owens, W. A. Toward one discipline of scientific psychology. *American Psychologist*, 1968, *23*, 782-785.

Owens, W. A. A quasi-actuarial prospect for individual assessment. *American Psychologist*, 1971, *26*, 992-999.

Parasuraman, R. Consistency of individual differences in human vigilance performance: An abilities classification analysis. *Journal of Applied Psychology*, 1976, *61*, 486-492.

Parker, G. V. C. Prediction of individual stability. *Educational and Psychological Measurement*, 1971, *31*, 875-886.

Parker, J. F., Jr., & Fleishman, E. A. Ability factors and component performance measures as predictors of complex tracking behavior. *Psychological Monographs*, 1960, *74*, (16, Whole No. 503).

Parker, J. F., Jr., & Fleishman, E. A. Use of analytical information concerning task requirments to increase the effectiveness of skill training. *Journal of Applied Psychology*, 1961, *45*, 295-302.

Phares, E. J., & Lamiell, J. T. Personality. *Annual Review of Psychology*, 1977, *29*, 113-140.

Rock, D. A. The identification and utilization of moderator effects in prediction systems. Research Bulletin 69-32. Princeton, N.J.: Educational Testing Service, 1969.

Schoenfeldt, L. F. Utilization of manpower: Development and evaluation of an assessment-classification model for matching individuals with jobs. *Journal of Applied Psychology*, 1974, *59*, 583-595.

Shweder, R. A. How relevant is an individual difference theory of personality. *Journal of Personality*, 1975, *43*, 455-484.

Spearman, C. E. *The abilities of man*. New York: Macmillan, 1927.

Stelmach, G. E. Individual differences and intra-individual variability in motor performance under continuous-practice conditions. *Human Factors*, 1969, *11*, 201-206.

Super, D. E., & Crites, J. O. *Appraising vocational fitness by means of psychological tests*. (Rev. ed.) New York: Harper, 1962.

Theologus, G. C., Romashko, T., & Fleishman, E. A. Development of a taxonomy of human performance: A feasibility study of ability scales for classifying human tasks. American Psychological Association, Washington, D.C. JSAS Catalogue of selected documents in psychology. 1973, 3, 29 (ms. 326).

Thurstone, L. L. *Primary mental abilities*. Psychometric Monograph No. 1. Chicago: University of Chicago Press, 1938.

Tilton, J. W. The relation between IQ and trait differences as measured by group intelligence tests. *Journal of Educational Psychology*, 1947, *38*, 343-352.

Vale, J. R., & Vale, C. A. Individual differences and general laws in psychology. *American Psychologist*, 1969, *24*, 1093-1108.

Vernon, P. E. *The structure of human abilities*. London: Methuen, 1950.

Whitely, S. E. Individual inconsistency: Implications for test reliability and behavioral predictability. *Applied Psychological Measurement*, 1978, *2*, 571-579.

Wilson, G. D., Tunstall, O. A., & Eysenck, H. J. Individual differences in tapping performance as a function of time on the task. *Perceptual and Motor Skills*, 1971, *33*, 375-378.

Witkin, H. A., Dyk, R. B., Paterson, H. F., Goodenough, D. R., & Karp, S. A. *Psychological differentiation*, New York: Wiley, 1962.

Witkin, H. A., & Goodenough, D. Field dependence and interpersonal behavior. *Psychological Bulletin*, 1977, *84*, 661-689.

Zedeck, S. Problems with the use of "moderator" variables. *Psychological Bulletin*, 1971, *71*, 295-310.

5 Training and Human Performance

Irwin L. Goldstein and Virginia M. Buxton
University of Maryland

INTRODUCTION

Throughout each person's life, learning experiences provide a potent source of stimulation. Thus, infants learn to eat with a spoon; school children learn the three R's; and adults learn the requirements of a job. This chapter is concerned with the systematic modes of instruction that are designed to produce environments that mold or shape behavior to satisfy stated objectives. In this sense, training can be defined as the systematic acquisition of skills, rules, concepts, or attitudes that results in improved performance in another environment. Thus, the school environment is designed to enable the primary school child to read books in the home, and the dental student to repair caries in the office. Similarly, training programs are planned to produce a more considerate supervisor or a more competent electronics technician in the working environment.

If an opinion on the relationship of training programs to performance and productivity is entirely based upon the criteria of hours of effort or funds expended, then it would be necessary to agree that training must be an extremely efficient approach. For example, consider the following illustrations gleaned from a variety of time periods and instructional approaches:

1. Most surveys indicate that over 90% of private corporations have some type of systematic training program. One large corporation reported that they were spending over $75 million annually on the salaries of nonmanagement employees while they were undergoing training. This figure did not include the costs of the training program or the facilities involved (Holt, 1963).

135

2. A catalogue released by the U.S. Civil Service Commission (1971) presenting training programs for use by educationally disadvantaged employees lists over 50 basic reading programs. There are similar lists for language arts, mathematics, world of work, and consumer education.

3. Estimates for the fiscal year 1967 show that the U.S. Office of Education spent over $800 million just on instructional materials and media (Grayson, 1972).

4. An analysis of the program of the Department of Defense for fiscal year 1977 indicates that over $6 billion are allocated for military training efforts (Orlansky, 1977).

These efforts are expended on training efforts, because there is an inherent faith that such instructional efforts provide results in terms of better job performance and increased productivity. Indeed, most of these financial awards are for the development of expensive new techniques (e.g., flight simulators), and very little attention is given to need assessment techniques or evaluation efforts to determine the utility of the approaches. However, before turning to these issues, it is first necessary to detail the potential uses of training and instructional technology that lead to such outpourings of both confidence and money.

POTENTIAL OF TRAINING APPROACHES

Training as a Learning–Performance Strategy

When most individuals or organizations consider the potential benefits of training, they are usually referring to the placement of trainees in an instructional program where the learning that takes place will transfer to the job. Most available training analyses and data are relevant to this learning–performance strategy, and this chapter focuses on this topic. A few illustrations are presented here to clarify this approach.

First, it should be noted that well-conceived training programs can have a beneficial effect on productivity. One early illustration of this approach is provided by Lindahl, who in 1944 analyzed a disc-cutting operation and determined the correct foot patterns to use in a complex hand-foot coordination task. One analysis used to evaluate this program concerned the number of wheels broken by the operator while operating the disk-cutting machine. Since the wheels were costly and the production time lost during the changing period could be as much as 30 minutes, Lindahl considered this to be an important measure of the success of his program. As can be seen from Fig. 5.1, the trainees damaged 24% of their wheels during the first week. By the third week, they were breaking fewer than those operators with 9 months experience. Lindahl reported similar data using

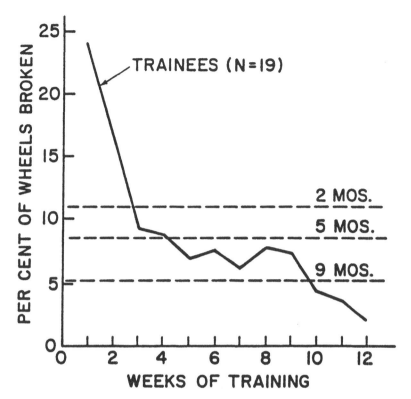

FIG. 5.1. Percentage of wheels broken by disc-cutter trainees. Dotted lines represent average percentage of wheels broken for first 2 weeks by groups with an average of 2, 5, and 9 months experience at start of training. From Lindahl, L. G. Movement analysis as an industrial training method. *Journal of Applied Psychology*, 1945, *29*, 430.

other performance measures and comparisons with operators who were already on the job.

Similar results are found in: (1) more recent studies; (2) studies that employ a variety of techniques from simulation to computer-assisted instruction to sensitivity training; and (3) studies that focus on a variety of behaviors from motor skills to managerial responses and worker safety behavior. However, as this chapter indicates, the promise of training as a learning–performance technique is mainly a search for the isolated, well-conceived training program mired in a mass of training programs that are poorly constructed and thoughtlessly evaluated. The reasons for this state of affairs are complex and range from a lack of research on applicable job-analysis techniques to an organizational belief that training can solve all problems. As indicated earlier, most of the remainder of this chapter focuses on these issues and the use of training as a learning–performance strategy. However, before the presentation of that material, two other potential uses of training approaches must be acknowledged—uses that are not usually considered, but which have the promise of substantial benefits.

Training as a Predictor of Future Performance

Data obtained during training can be utilized to predict the later on-the-job performance of trainees. Measures collected during training can be employed in a prediction equation just as initial selection tests are used to predict performance. There are various ramifications to this type of strategy, including the matter of cost. The collection of training data usually occurs later in the occupational process than initial selection tests. Thus, in some cases, individuals would have to go through training before being selected which, in some cases, could be prohibitively costly. As serious as that problem may be, there is still the question of cost-benefit analysis. For example, does a strategy that utilizes training as a predictive device improve prediction to the extent that the extra cost is worthwhile? Also, it fails to consider methods that might be used to reduce the cost associated with hiring everyone into the training program, as well as less costly ways of developing training prediction strategies.

The major current issue to be addressed in considering training as a predictor is whether or not there is any support for such an approach. Conceptually, Wernimont and Campbell (1968) have argued that it might be fruitful to focus on meaningful samples of relevant behaviors as the best potential predictors of future behavior. It is possible to generalize from this finding and suggest that those training performances that are similar in nature to the actual performances required on the job will be good predictors of those criteria. Some empirical evidence that training behavior will predict future job performance does exist. Thus, in field settings, assessment-center research with simulation exercises has demonstrated the usefulness of this approach (Bray & Campbell, 1968; Bray & Grant, 1966; Hinrichs, 1969). Also, Bartlett and Goldstein (1974) found that a road test conducted as part of a driver-training program predicted accidents ($r = .52$) and customer complaints ($r = .51$). Interestingly, a study by Kraut (1975) indicated that several peer ratings obtained from managers attending a month-long training course predicted several criteria, including future promotion and performance appraisal ratings. Thus, it is also possible that trainees are able to predict the success of their cohorts based upon their performances in the training program. The usefulness of this approach is dependent on whether the validity coefficients obtained are an improvement over the disappointing validity typically found in most predictor-performance research.

There is also the question of the cost of putting all individuals into a training program. Where cost is not a factor, then the issue is based on where the best prediction is likely to occur. Where cost is a factor, an alternative model is to predict training performance first and then use training performance to predict on-the-job performance. These issues are addressed by Bartlett and Goldstein (1974) as follows:

> If the training costs are not prohibitive one of the best strategies in selecting successful bus drivers would be to allow applicants into the training program and select future bus drivers on the basis of performance in the training program. Another alternative would be to use tests to predict successful training performance. By utilizing this strategy, tests which predict performance in training could be used to select individuals for the training program. Then, performance on the training measures could be used to select bus drivers [p. 14].

This model has an additional assumption; namely, it must be demonstrated that it is possible to predict training performance as well as using training performance to predict on-the-job behavior. There is some evidence to indicate that trainability criteria are not only predictable but also may be more easily predicted than job performance. In a review that compared the use of aptitude tests for trainability and job-performance criteria, Ghiselli (1966) found that the average validity for training criteria was .30 and for proficiency criteria .19. Further support for this view may be found in laboratory research on individual differences and motor learning. Fleishman (1972) suggests that measures that predict performance during the learning period tend to change as the learner becomes more experienced. Thus, general-ability measures predict early performance, whereas assessments of the actual habits and skills required to perform the task are more useful later in training. In this situation, it might be possible to predict initial performance in the training program with one measure, and later on-the-job performance with an actual training measure.

Another approach is based upon the belief that persons who learn and perform some sample of the tasks involved in the job are the same individuals who will also be able to perform the actual job. This approach has followed two paths: The first is the actual design of miniature job-training tasks as potential predictors, and the second path is the examination of early performance on the less-complex tasks in a training program as predictors of later on the job performance.

Miniature Job Training.   An illustration of the miniature job-training approach (MJT) is provided by Siegel's research (1978). One study (Siegel & Bergman, 1975) was conducted with Navy men assigned to the Machinist Mate "A" School. A basic requirement for participation in the MJT was that subjects must have failed the entry tests for the Machinist Mate School, but the subjects were unaware of this and of their special selection for the research program.

Based on a job analysis, a list of critical behaviors for the journeyman-level machinist-mated job were identified. These behaviors then served as the foundation for developing training situations and associated tests. The situations were: tool identification and use, gasket cutting, meter reading, trouble shooting, equipment operation, and assembly. The predictive validity of the MJT and its evaluative situations was assessed in two follow-up periods. One was conducted after subjects had been in the fleet 9 months, and the second follow-up was completed after 18 months. The criteria at both points were identical tests of job-sample performance.

Results revealed that for the first follow-up, five of the six performance criteria were predicted better by the MJT and evaluative situations than by the Navy selection tests, but for the second follow-up, exactly opposite results were obtained. The authors suggest that this result may be due to the fact that this study was not conducted as a test development program and if it had been, different steps would have been taken. Instead, it was intended to explore the merits of the MJT technique. Siegel (1978) reports a review of several similar studies on miniature job training with equal or more promising results.

Early Training Performances. An illustration of the second approach in which early training performance serves as predictors can be found in a study designed to predict trainability (Gordon & Cohen, 1973). The study did not attempt to predict future job performance. It is important, however, because it presents results that point to the possibility of obtaining high validities for predicting trainability.

The training program studied involved a welding program that was part of a larger manpower development project aimed at training unemployed and under-

TABLE 5.1
Correlations between the Time to Completion for Various Segments
of the Course and Total Time Required to Complete the
Plate-Welding Course

	Correlation of Task			
	1 with finish	*1 –2 with finish*	*1 –3 with finish*	*1 –4 with finish*
I (N = 21)	0.55	0.76	0.81	0.84
II (N = 19)	0.70	0.83	0.94	0.96
III (N = 18)[a]	0.09	0.18	0.77	0.78
Total (N = 58)	0.69	0.79	0.87	0.87

Note: Group I, II, and III differed in their starting dates.

[a]A word of explanation is due regarding the poor predictability of tasks 1 and 2 in Group III. Discussion with the training supervisor of the welding program indicated that illness had caused two of his three instructors to be absent for most of the period during which Group III was learning tasks 1 and 2. Consequently, the amount of supervision and guidance provided was necessarily below normal. It is probable that this temporary understaffed situation changed the usual conditions of learning and caused the correlations observed in Group III to be unlike those recorded for Groups I and II. Reprinted from Gordon, M. E. and Cohen, S. L. Training behavior as a predictor of trainability. *Personnel Psychology,* 1973, *26*, 261–272.

employed individuals from the East Tennessee area. The program consisted of 14 different tasks that fell into four categories and ranged in difficulty from simple to complex. Advancement from one task to the next was dependent on successful completion of all previous tasks. Thus, trainees progressed at a rate commensurate with their ability to master the material to be learned. For each trainee, data were collected on the amount of time spent on each of the tasks. The correlations between the completion times for the four categories of tasks and total time to complete the plate-welding course are given in Table 5.1.

Gordon and Cohen (1973) indicate that the results show: "that early performance in the lab generally is an excellent predictor of final performance. Furthermore, the greater the number of tasks included in our predictor, the better our prediction will become. It is possible, therefore, to identify those trainees who will take longer than average to complete the plate welding course by simply examining their performance on the first few tasks [p. 268]."

These various approaches warrant further research consideration. Obviously, if it is possible to predict future performance while efficiently providing the learning experiences necessary to perform job-related tasks, then the usefulness of training programs will be substantially enhanced, as will the final levels of work performance and productivity attained.

Training as a Provider of Realistic Expectations

A third major potential use of training is in providing trainees with "realistic" expectations about the job. As indicated previously, the most common purpose of training programs is to teach the knowledge and skills necessary to perform the tasks required on the job. Unfortunately, little attention is paid to those attitudes and perceptions that affect performance, both in training and on the job. These attitudes may have been brought by the trainee into the training program, they may be learned during the course of the training, or they may change as a result of having completed training. Such attitudes and perceptions can be considered from one viewpoint as unintended outcomes of the training program.

One attitude variable that has recently received a large amount of attention is expectations. The focus of the expectation literature has concentrated mainly on two issues: (1) the effects of expectations on organizational choice; and (2) the effects of recruitment on an individual's expectations. However, it is also possible to consider the relationship of training to expectations.

An individual enters a training program with certain expectations of what the organization will be like, what the job will involve, what tasks must be performed, what kinds of workers there are, etc. These entering expectations will affect the individual's perceptions of what occurs in the training program and what occurs will in turn affect the attitudes and perceptions. It is possible, and probably likely, that during the course of the program some, if not all, of these entering expectations will change, and they may well change again when the person is placed in a new situation, that is, on the job. The congruency of the training and organizational environments may largely determine the extent of change in individual expectations once the individual is on the job.

Expectations from Navy Training.   Research conducted by Hoiberg and Berry (1978) has examined the effects of expectations and perceptions along 10 dimensions on performance within Navy environments of recruit training, six training schools, and subsequent fleet duty assignment. Within the first 48 hours of attendance, subjects enrolled in recruit training and the six Navy schools were administered questionnaires regarding their expectations of the recruit or school training. At the midpoint of the various training programs, a questionnaire on perceptions was given. Upon graduation, students were also given expectation questionnaires about fleet duty, and at the end of one year, all subjects still on active duty were given a perceptions questionnaire and asked to describe what their present duty stations were like.

Performance effectiveness was measured different ways. For recruit training, effectiveness was defined as graduation from training. For the other six training schools and for the 2-year survival period, effectiveness was defined as persons who graduated from school and remained on active duty for at least 2 years.

The results indicated that, in recruit training, expectations were significantly related to graduation. Recruits with expectations for innovative training methods and minimal emphasis on efficiency and control were met with a situation incongruent to these expectations. Ultimately, these unrealistic expectations were related to failure to graduate. The findings relative to the technical schools indicated that those schools that emphasized less pressure to complete work tasks and more opportunities for personal growth, support from instructors, and innovative teaching methods had larger percentages of effective students.

These findings reemphasize the concept that the greater the congruency between actual and expected conditions, the greater the performance effectiveness. Based on such results, a case can be made for attending to the context of training and organizational settings. As the authors (Hoiberg & Berry, 1978) point out in their discussion: "another recommendation would be to more accurately prepare and train individuals for the work that they will actually perform in the school and work setting. A coordinated effort to align recruiting and training materials with actual work environments and job requirements would be expected to reduce discrepancies between expectations and preceptions [p. 15]."

Expectations and Recruitment.   Another area of research on expectations has dealt with the effects of certain recruitment practices on expectations; specifically, the realistic job preview and, certainly, providing realistic job previews is one of the potentials of training. Wanous (1977) reviewed the literature on realistic job previews and concluded that: "the use of realistic job previews in the recruitment of new members has shown consistent results in reducing the turn-over of newcomers for a wide variety of organizations. Conclusions about the effect of realism on other facets of the entry process must remain tentative, however [p. 615]."

Assuming that enrollment in training is a point of entry into an organization, then the organization has the opportunity at that point in time to provide the incoming trainee with a realistic view of what to expect from the organization. If the training program provides all the necessary and accurate information required for the trainee to perform effectively in the new position, then some of the later "reality shock" of entering the new organization may be eliminated.

If the training program is designed to provide not only the necessary skills and knowledge but also realistic expectations, then the probability of future job success may be enhanced. In addition, the use of training as a method for providing realistic expectations may help to alleviate some of the negative consequences of unrealistic expectations of new job holders. As Wanous (1977) pointed out, one of the most common consequences of job holders with unrealistic expectations is turnover. An employee who has exaggerated beliefs about what the new job holds is likely to be disappointed and thus seek employment elsewhere. Unrealistic expectations may also result in poor transfer of training to the job, poor attitudes, and poor performance on the job.

It is interesting to note that the previous section on the use of training as a predictor and this section on realistic expectations suggest some interesting research interactions between the two approaches. For example, it is possible to consider miniature job training not only as providing prediction data to the organization but also as providing realistic information to the potential job holder. Thus, it provides the individual with the opportunity to see what abilities are required, and what the new job situation will be like. In this way, it may enable the person to make a more valid organizational choice. Although these sections on prediction and realistic expectations are based upon a limited number of research findings, it is clear that future support for such efforts may expand our conception of the usefulness of training programs.

An Instructional Model

A useful framework that can be used to consider the interactive components of training programs is known as *instructional systems development* (ISD) or *instructional technology*. The terms as used here do not refer to the development of hardware but rather to the systematic development of training programs. This systems approach to training emphasizes careful need assessment, specification of instructional objectives, precisely controlled learning experiences designed to achieve the instructional objectives, use of performance criteria, and obtaining evaluative information. As specified by Goldstein (1974), other instructional system characteristics are:

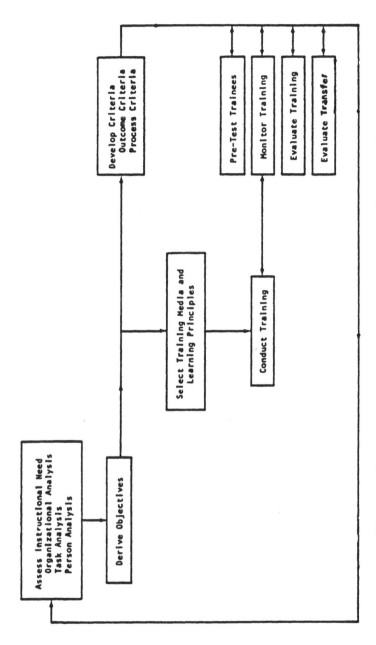

FIG. 5.2.   An instruction system adapted from Goldstein, I. L. *Training: Program development and evaluation.* Monterey, California: Brooks/Cole, 1974.

144

1. In order to reduce static instructional programs, the systems approach emphasizes the continuous use of feedback to modify the instructional process. From this perspective, training programs are never considered finished products but rather continually adaptive to information that indicates the extent to which the program is meeting its stated objectives.

2. The approach recognizes the complex nature of the interactions among the components of the system. It accepts the likelihood that one particular media, like television, might be effective in achieving one set of objectives, whereas another media might be preferable for a second set of objectives. Similar interactions could involve media characteristics, learning variables, and specific individual characteristics of the learner. The systems view stresses a concern with the total system rather than the objectives of any single component.

3. Systematic analysis provides a frame of reference for planning and for reamining on target. It implies that a research approach is necessary to determine which programs are meeting their objectives.

4. The ISD view recognizes that the instructional system is just one of a whole set of interacting systems. Instructional programs in industry are part of a larger system involving corporate policies (e.g., selection, management, philosophy) that in turn affect and interact with the training program. Similarly, educational programs like the Sesame Street T.V. program are affected by the social values of the society that the program is designed to meet.

Although these characteristics represent goals that are highly valued by most of the training-research community, it is important to note that most of the characteristics of ISD (e.g., needs assessment, criterion development, and evaluation methodology) are not brand new. That view is basically correct, and those individuals who have considered the ISD approach a new magic wand that will solve all previous problems have been bitterly disappointed. The systems approach offers a model that emphasizes the important training system components and their interactions and provides a sense of direction and organization. As such, it provides a useful tool to organize the material in this section and provides a framework that can be used to evaluate the present state of the art. The ISD model is shown schematically in Fig. 5.2. The next section on need assessment deals with the left-hand side of the model; other parts of the model are discussed in later sections.

ASSESSMENT OF INSTRUCTIONAL NEED

A first step in deciding upon a training program is the assessment of instructional need. This step provides the input necessary to design the entire training program. Thus, instructional objectives are based upon need assessment, and the program should be designed to meet these objectives. Also, the criteria used to evaluate the program stem from the same source.

The assessment stage should consist of three complimentary analyses. They are: organizational analysis, job or task analysis, and person analysis. The organizational analysis requires a consideration of the organization's goals, both short- and long-term, as well as an assessment of the organizational setting within which the job performance will take place. The job analysis requires the consideration of the specific tasks that must ultimately be performed by trainees. Finally, the person analysis requires a consideration of the human attributes necessary for effective performance. In addition, the person analysis must take into account the target population of trainees and their existing capabilities and abilities. It is clear then that the assessment phase must look at the entire organization, its people, and its jobs. Descriptions of each of the various analyses and some of the techniques used in conducting them follows.

However, before that presentation, it is important to note that there are two types of state of the art questions related to this material. The first question concerns commentary on the present state of knowledge concerning the various instructional components (e.g., how do we perform organizational analysis?). The second set of questions concerns the use of the knowledge presently available in the design and implementation of training programs. Obviously, there is an interaction between these two questions. However, the present section describes the components of instructional programs and comments on the present state of knowledge. A later section discusses the utilization of the present state of knowledge.

Organizational Analysis

One of the first steps in the assessment phase of the training model is an examination of the organization. The training program does not exist in isolation but instead is merely a subsystem of the entire organization. If this larger environment is ignored, then many of the objectives that should be included may be ignored, and the training program may ultimately fail to meet certain requirements.

The analysis should include an examination of the goals of the organization, its resources, and the organizational environment. This process is intended to help ensure that the training program will be designed to meet organizational needs and also to help match the training program to organizational reality (i.e., to provide congruence between the training and the organizational settings).

The first step in the organization-wide analysis is the specification of organizational goals. Campbell, Dunnette, Lawler, and Weick (1970) suggest that considering training needs is not enough. The goals of the whole organization must first be examined to see the extent to which the identified training needs are relevant to these goals. An individual may be very deficient in a certain set of skills, but if such skills are irrelevant to the organization's goals, they may be an inappropriate goal for training. Also, it may be far more important to institute training for an aspect of job performance that is judged less deficient than some other aspect, if the former is many times more important for the organization than the latter. The importance of the training needs must be assessed relative to the organization's goals.

Another step in the organizational analysis is an examination of available resources. This includes an estimation of both physical and human resources. The determination of these factors requires the answers to questions like how many workers are presently employed, how many will be required in the future, what will be expected of them in the way of performance, and what is their projected availability in the job market? It should be noted that the results of the resource analysis should be used to identify those problems specifically related to training needs, as well as problems that may not be remedied by the training program. Clearly, training cannot always solve all of an organization's problems, and the resource analysis will help to isolate those problems that it can solve. It also provides information about where problems exist and therefore about what other organizational actions may be necessary.

Also, the organization analysis must consider the entire setting in which the worker will be expected to perform. This means that there must be some under-standing of the organizational climate. The climate of the organization may determine whether the goals and objectives of the training program are ultimately transferred to the on-the-job setting. The assessment of the climate should exam-ine not only the formal organization—its policies and rules—but also the infor-mal organization that includes the leadership, coworkers, working conditions, etc.

A later section of this chapter offers the hypothesis that many instructional programs fail because of organizational problems that existed and should have been resolved before the training program commenced. This view emphasizes that organizational analysis is a critical component in the successful design and implementation of instructional program. Unfortunately, although this view has been previously expressed in McGehee and Thayer's (1961) classic book on training and reemphasized by recent texts (Goldstein, 1974), there is virtually no information available on the procedures necessary to accomplish this task. Re-cent work in organization development (Alderfer, 1977) and the measurement of organizational climate (Schneider, 1973) certainly indicate a concern with these types of variables. However, the search for and measurement of these variables as related to instructional processes remain problems.

Task Analysis

Just as an organizational analysis is necessary to determine the organizational objectives, a task analysis is necessary to determine the objectives in terms of performance standards for the skills, knowledge, and attitudes required to perform the task successfully. The task analysis consists of several components, each of which further delineates the performance required to succeed at the task. Thus, the analysis begins with a behavioral description and is completed with a detailed specification of the behaviors to perform each task.

Task Description. The description is a statement about the activities performed on the job, and the conditions under which the job is performed. It is not a description of the worker but rather a description of the task or job. The statement should completely describe all the essential activities of the job including the: "workers actions and the results accomplished; the machines, tools, and equipment; and/or work aids used; materials, products subject matter, or services involved and the requirements made of the worker" (U.S. Department of Labor, 1972, p. 30)." The statement includes a description of the conditions under which the job is performed, the characteristics of the environment (e.g., noise, extreme temperature variations), and any special features (e.g. stress) that further delineates the job. Some of the environmental conditions and physical demands that should be examined are presented in Table 5.2. As Thorndike (1949) said: "A job description should provide an accurate picture of significant factors in the

TABLE 5.2
Environmental Conditions and Physical Demands

Environmental Conditions			*Physical Demands*
1. Environment			1. Strength (lifting, carrying
Inside _____%	Teamwork _____%		pushing, and/or pulling)
Outside _____%	Proximity _____%		Sedentary work
	Isolation _____%		Light work
2. Extreme cold with or without temperature changes			Medium work
3. Extreme heat with or without temperature changes			Heavy work
4. Wet and/or humid			Very heavy work
5. Noise			2. Climbing and/or balancing
Estimated maximum number of decibels			3. Stooping, kneeling,
6. Vibration			crouching, and/or crawling
7. Hazards			4. Reaching, handling, fingering,
Mechanical	Explosives		and/or feeling
Electrical	Radiant Energy		5. Talking and/or hearing
Burns	Other		6. Seeing
8. Atmospheric conditions			
Fumes	Gases		
Odors	Poor ventilation		
Dusts	Other		
Mists			

Note: Reprinted from Manpower Administration. U.S. Department of Labor, *Handbook for Analyzing Jobs.* Washington, D.C.: U.S. Government Printing Office, 1972.

TABLE 5.3
Frequency, Importance, and Difficulty Ratings for Police Office Tasks

	Frequency	Importance	Difficulty
Using firearms	1.21	3.48	2.15
Writing traffic violations	2.69	2.12	1.00
Checking supplies	.91	1.05	1.19

Note: The actual rating task involved carefully specified definitions of frequency, importance, and difficulty at each of the specified levels. For summary purposes, it can be indicated that the scores for each of the dimensions ranged from 0 (never performed, of no importance, very easy) to 4 (frequently performed, of critical importance, very difficulty). In this study, the ratings were obtained from all officers who actually performed the job. From Bartlett, C. J., and Goldstein, I. L. A validity analysis of a selection program in a police organization. Training and Educational Research Programs, Inc., College Park, Md, 1978.

physical, social and psychological environment in which the work must be carved out [p. 15]." The description should contain material about each of the kinds of activities either in order of their importance or in the chronological order in which they are performed.

Task Specification.   The next step in the task analysis is to specify the tasks performed, determine their importance, and detail the actual steps necessary to perform each important task. The determination of the significance of these tasks represents the next major step in the analysis. Three criteria with which to judge the significance are:

1. Frequency of performance in terms of how often the activity is performed.
2. Importance of the activity in terms of the potential consequences in negative or positive terms, if the worker is not as capable of performing that aspect of the job.
3. The learning difficulty in terms of how difficult it will be for the potential trainee to perform that component of the job.

An illustration of this approach is presented in Table 5.3. In this study, Bartlett and Goldstein (1978) collected frequency, importance, and difficulty ratings for tasks performed by police officers. There are many procedures that can be used to obtain similar information including the critical incident technique, actual observation of the job, etc. The important point is that these types of indices are critical to the actual design of the training program. For example, a task that is performed frequently, but that is not very important and extremely easy to learn, would not require the attention that should be given to an infrequently performed, but critical, task that is very difficult to learn.

The final step in terms of the task specification is to break down the components for each of the tasks into the steps involved in performing that task. Thus, for example, a gas-station attendant to clean and replace spark plugs would take the steps listed in Table. 5.4.

From this specification of tasks (such as the example in Table 5.4) and the determination of their importance, determination can be made of the behavioral objectives that specify the terminal behaviors required to perform the job, as well as the criteria that will be used to measure the performance. It should also be possible to start considering the types of behaviors necessary to perform the job and the instructional media and learning variables that best support these types of behaviors.

While this type of analysis is clearly easier to complete on a service-station attendant than on corporate-executive personnel, the proper design of a training program requires similar analyses for each case. Interestingly, any review of need assessment techniques must conclude that task analysis is the most highly developed procedure. Unfortunately, most of the development has not been guided toward training needs but rather toward the development of selection devices. For example, several job-analysis techniques are directed at defining task characteristics that are generalizable across jobs (McCormick, Jeanneret, & Mecham, 1969). These procedures involve the validation of test batteries developed to measure various task components of jobs. Subjects currently performing the job being examined are administered the tests. Then a factor analysis yields the relevant tests that represent the task components of that particular job. This approach is currently more widely used for determining synthetic validity, but research remains to be done on its usefulness for determining training needs.

Currently, the best strategy calls for training development to analyze each job individually by considering each task required for performance and the frequency, importance, and difficulty of the tasks. The exact interrelationship

TABLE 5.4
Task Listing for Cleaning and Replacing Spark Plugs

(1) Note plug location relative to the cylinder; remove plug cover, leads.
(2) Remove all spark plugs.
(3) Identify the type of plugs.
(4) Decide whether to clean, adjust, and/or replace plugs.
(5) Adjust and clean plugs, if appropriate.
(6) Reinsert plugs in engine.
(7) Connect ignition wire to appropriate plugs.
(8) Check engine firing for maximum performance.
(9) Clean and replace equipment and tools.

Note: Adapted from Mager, R. F. and Beach, K. M., Jr. *Developing Vocational Instruction.* Belmont, Calif.: Fearon, 1967.

among these components as well as the procedures for establishing the components remain empirical questions that require further research.

Person Analysis

The organizational and task analyses provide specifications of the required behaviors regardless of the individual performing the task. There remains a very critical part of the total process, the reason why a training program is being designed in the first place—the human being. There are two populations that the analysis must consider. The first population consists of those persons who are already performing the job, whereas the second group comprises those persons who are to be trained. In some instances, these are the same individuals, but, in other cases, new trainees will be entering the training program. To the extent that these new individuals differ from those already performing the task, it is necessary to examine both populations. Thus, the procedure requires a performance analysis of those individuals already performing the job and an analysis of the actual target population for training.

The purpose of the performance analysis is to determine whether performance is acceptable and, certainly, to identify substandard performance. In a sense, this type of analysis determines if there is a significant difference between what the incumbent is able to do, and what he is expected to do. Few, if any, organizations can afford instructional programs on every aspect of the task. Performance analysis is used to determine where the resources should be spent. The knowledge tests, performance reports, supervisory evaluation, and observation techniques employed to obtain performance measures also help specify which objectives are important to achieve, and what criteria or measures of success are useful in determining whether the objectives have been achieved.

If the program is intended for those persons already on the job, data from the performance analysis and the specification of desirable performance traits provide the required information for the analysis of the target population. However, if the target population is a new group of students or employees, the analyses are necessarily incomplete. The instructional program must be based on the characteristics of the group that will be placed in the training environment. Many observers have commented on the differences in values between those students entering school and work situations today from those of preceding generations. These types of factors must be considered in the design of any training program. For example, particular errors may appear on the job due to difficulties related to mathematical ability. However, entering trainees may have the prerequisite skills in mathematics, so that their training need not emphasize those particular skills. Thus, the organization may be faced with different training programs for the population presently employed and those coming to the job.

At the present time, the state of the art for person analysis is at a point where the need for it is recognized, and the most obvious types of person analyses could be accomplished. Thus, for example, were person analysis included as part of the need assessment technique, there would not be training manuals written for high school graduates at a level for college graduates. However, procedures for carefully matching the capabilities of individuals to the requirements of the job are sorely lacking, and research along these lines should produce beneficial results.

Derivation of Objectives

The organizational analyses, task analyses, and person analyses provide the information necessary for the assessment of instructional need. This assessment makes it possible to specify the objectives of the training program. The objectives provide the direct input for the design of the training program and help specify the criterion measures that will be used to evaluate the performance of the trainees at the end of the training program and in the transfer setting (on the job, in the next program, etc.). The assessment of instructional needs tells the trainer where to begin, and the specification of the objectives specifies the completion point of the program. The characteristics of behavioral objectives are presented in Table 5.5.

Sound objectives communicate to the learner what he is expected to be able to do when he finishes the program. Some professionals believe that one of the most difficult student problems is determining what they are supposed to do at the end of the program to demonstrate their proficiency. Some trainers have suggested (not without a note of sarcasm) that if the instructor communicated the terminal objectives, it would not be necessary to do very much else to achieve the success of the program. The importance of specifying objectives can be documented by the example—"to appreciate safety." Unfortunately, that goal does not state

TABLE 5.5
Characteristics of Behavioral Objectives

(a) An objective is a statement about a student, not the text or teacher.

(b) The objective refers to the behavior of the student. It does not just specify what a student is to know but instead further describes what you mean by *knowing* by indicating what the student will be doing to reflect the fact that he knows.

(c) An objective is stated in terms of terminal performance. Thus, it is a description of the end product, not the method for reaching the end product.

(d) An objective describes the conditions under which the student will perform. Thus, if the student is expected to perform with the use of a training aid (e.g., calculator), the objectives specify its use.

(e) An instructional objective further indicates the level of performance necessary to achieve that objective. Thus, statements related to the number of errors permitted and speed of performances are included as part of the objective.

Note: Adapted from Mager, R. F., and Beach, K. M., Jr. *Developing Vocational Instruction.* Belmont, Calif.: Fearon, 1967.

what the learner should be doing when he "appreciates safety," nor does it state the desired terminal behavior or the conditions under which the behavior should occur. Thus, any of the following behaviors could be considered as meeting the goals of the program, although it is doubtful that any represent what safety directors would have in mind.

1. The employee passed a safety knowledge test with a minimum score of 75%.
2. The employee bought a Red Cross handbook on safety.
3. The employee wears safety goggles when the foreman is present.
4. The employee indicates that safety is important on questionnaires handed out by top management.

Clearly, the goal to appreciate safety is not a concrete safety objective and is open to varying degrees of interpretation. Also, it becomes quite difficult to develop particular training programs to meet that objective. Instead of "to appreciate safety," consider the following safety objective designed to minimize the danger of an exploding grinding wheel.

When the trainee turns on the grinding wheel, the trainee should always stand to the left of the wheel and out of the path of any exploding particles for the 30 seconds necessary for the wheel to reach maximum velocity.

This safety objective clearly states in behavioral terms the terminal performance expected of the trainee. It also states the level of performance required by indicating that the trainee should always perform the task, and it indicates the conditions of performance by noting that this behavior should be performed in the first 30 seconds while the wheel is warming up. The safety objective also provides guidance about the type of training program necessary to teach that behavior. Thus, a simulator where the trainee can practice that behavior as well as all other safety behaviors for the task and be informed about mistakes is one method of training for the objective.

Similar objectives can be written for all the important aspects of the training program. In many cases, the trainer will discover that the objectives of the training program can be related to, but may not be exactly the same as, those for successful job performance. When the job is complex, the trainee cannot be expected to exhibit the same behaviors as persons who have been performing the task for many years. Thus, one group of objectives and criteria are designed for the initial training analyses, and other objectives and criteria are designed to be used at a later time on the job. However, it should be clear that the specification of these different objectives will, in itself, clear up many misunderstandings about trainee requirements upon completion of the program.

Thus far, the objectives discussed are related to specific aspects of trainee behavior. These represent only one level of analysis. There are also objectives that are concerned with more than the behavior of trainees (e.g., the performance of an entire educational system). Some observers (Cogan, 1971) have suggested that two organizational objectives of educational systems should be to individualize instruction and to prevent ''drop outs.'' These objectives must also be specified through behavioral outcomes, conditions, and criteria of successful performance. Although this is a difficult exercise, the determination of the achievement of policy and organizational objectives is dependent on such specifications.

The importance of this latter procedure has been recognized by industry for a number of years and is typically called *management by objectives* (MBO). Strauss (1972) states that:

> MBO (at least when it works as it should) requires management to define exactly what it wants to accomplish and to specify all important objectives, expecially those commonly ignored. It reduces the emphasis on short-run profits, increases the number of managerial goals and forces the explicit consideration of exactly what steps must be taken if these goals are to be fulfilled. In this way, it helps subordinates learn what is required of them, thus reducing their need for guesswork. As a result, it makes decision-making more rational, both for boss and subordinate. In sum, MBO can become a coordinated process of planning that involves every management level in determining both the goals that it will meet, and the means by which they are to be met [p. 11].

The difficulties associated with this process are accented by the controversies provoked by the MBO system. One group of conflicts is related to the procedures used in implementing the system. There are complaints about the amount of paper work as well as the great flourish with which objectives and goals are announced, only to be forgotten 6 months later. These complaints appear related to the failure to carry out the program properly. Another more serious criticism is related to who determines the objectives. Critics have stated that the determination of objectives often leads to conflict between personal and corporate goals, and the information gathered is simply used to exercise a greater degree of control over the organization. The latter issues pertain to the controversy over participative action, where all individuals have an opportunity to help in the determination of goals and objectives. Whether the system is participative or not, goals and objectives are still designed by someone at the policy level. If there are policies, it is as important to determine their success as it is to determine the success of an individual worker performing his task. Certainly, the specification of the goals provides information that can lead to changes in the objectives as well as their achievement.

Relationship of Need Assessment to Other Model Components

The need assessment phase of ISD specifies the requirement for a planning stage. The purposes of the planning analyses are twofold.

First, as noted in Fig. 5.2, the need assessment provides the information around which the training environment is to be built. Thus, the determination of the most productive training environment results from a careful examination of the training objectives to determine the type of learning necessary to acquire the essential behaviors. There is still considerable controversy about the number and kinds of learning necessary to describe performance. In one system, Gagné (1965, 1967, 1970) formulates eight types of learning including concept learning, rule learning, and problem solving. Another method (Harmon, 1968) divides the objectives into three groups including verbal, physical, and attitudinal performance. In each of these systems, the researcher analyzes his objectives and determines the required behaviors. Then, the behavior is matched to the most appropriate learning environment and instructional media. By learning environment, the reference is to the dynamics of the instructional setting with particular emphasis on learning variables (e.g., knowledge of results, massed and spaced practice). Instructional media refer to particular devices and techniques like simulators, programmed instruction, films, and lectures. In some cases, the instructional media themselves help predetermine the learning variables. It is relatively easy to provide individual feedback with a teaching machine, but it is difficult to do so with lecture material. However, this is not always the case. Teaching machines can be used without individual feedback, and simulators may present the entire task (whole learning) or components of the task (part learning). In either case, it is important for the learning environment and instructional media to be determined by the objectives and the form of performance required.

Secondly, it is not difficult to successfully convince training sponsors that the instructional media fit the behavior. They understand that simulators are not the best techniques available for foreign-language drills but may be excellent for learning driving skills. As later sections of this chapter indicate, this has not necessarily prevented training designers from utilizing inappropriate techniques simply because the techniques were readily available. Unfortunately, the design of the learning environment and the selection of the appropriate instructional variables have not been treated with the same degree of awareness. It is not unusual for a training designer to insist that knowledge of results or feedback must be part of the instructional system without first determining the kinds of behavior necessary, and whether feedback is appropriate for learning those particular behaviors. Such analysis often leads to inaccurate assessments, in which the adequacies of a device are evaluated solely by whether or not the device provides for various learning variables. On the other hand, the approach emphasized here stresses the determination of objectives through need assessment and the analyses of those objectives to determine the behaviors required. After that has been accomplished, the proper learning environment with appropriate learning variables, as well as particular media and techniques, can be selected.

TRAINING EVALUATION

The other side of the ISD equation to the development of training programs is the evaluation phase. Examination of the ISD model indicates that the need assessment directly enters into the evaluation process by providing the information necessary for the development of criteria. The section presents the basic components of training evaluation models from the perspective of the current state of the art. Comments about the way the state of the art capabilities are being employed in training research are reserved, wherever possible, for a later section.

In an earlier section, information was presented relevant to the potentials of training. A reconsideration of that material plus an examination of the various instructional programs that have produced a variety of benefits (from lowering accident rates to increasing production) should lead to the conclusion that the effort necessary to design training programs is worthwhile. Additionally, the previous sections indicated that training programs must begin with a careful need assessment of organizational, task, and person attributes. Then the training environment should be carefully matched to meet the objectives determined by the need assessment process. If this carefully designed process is properly completed, trainees should be able to perform well on the job, and evaluation should be unnecessary. Unfortunately, such is not often the case. The need assessment process is at present more of an art than a technology, and it is quite possible that important job components or organization goals are omitted. Also, there are always questions about the relation of the training media to the particular objectives of the program. Instructional programs are typically multifaceted with objectives including organizational goals (e.g., low cost), as well as a variety of learner performance goals. The success of these training programs is not apparent from casual observation.

These types of programs must be designed and evaluated according to a feedback model that permits the reevaluation of programs. Thus, the information obtained from the program evaluation should provide information on where and how to revise the training instruction to achieve even better results.

Finally, assumptions about the quality of instructional programs without evaluation displays a naive understanding of the relationship between instructional programs and organizational environments. There is growing evidence that indicates that trainee achievement in the classroom may bear no relation to the performance of the trainee on the job. Basically, there is little to be gained from the enormous efforts placed in instructional programs unless there is data to advice the analyst on where to revise and where to proceed. This view is particularly well stated by Stake (1967) as follows:

> Folklore is not a sufficient repository. In our data banks we should document the causes and effects, the congruence of intent and accomplishment, and the panorama

of judgments of those concerned. Such records should be kept to promote educational action, not obstruct it. The countenance of evaluation should be one of data gathering that leads to decision making, not troublemaking [p. 539].

Evaluation methodology centers around two interacting concerns. One, *the establishment of measures of success (criteria)*, and the other, *the particular research designs* that will be utilized to gain information about the training process. The connection between these two aspects of evaluation makes it necessary to consider them as interacting components. Thus, if it is not possible to obtain prelearning and postlearning criteria, then it also becomes rather difficult to utilize a pre-post experimental design. The present section first considers the evaluation of criterion measures and then treats some of the basic issues in evaluation methodology. It should also be noted that these two topics have a substantive literature, and this presentation is only designed to review briefly the major issues.

Criteria

The previous section on behavioral objectives indicated that objectives stem from a properly designed need assessment, and that the objectives clearly state the criterion by which the student is judged. These steps provide much of the basic information necessary to begin to develop actual criteria of success. However, the choice of criteria must consider the constraints imposed on the use of such measures in real world environments. Thus, a behavioral objective may be stated, but then it is necessary to develop criteria that not only measure the objective but also are free from bias and reliable. The relationship of measures of performance in the learning environment to measures of performance in the on-the-job setting must also be determined. In addition, there is the issue of the complex criteria necessary to measure organizational objectives as well as trainee performance. The problems encountered in this difficult process are described with pointed humor by Guion (1961). The following is a concise version:

1. The psychologist has a hunch (or insight) that a problem exists, and that he can help solve it.
2. He reads a vague, ambiguous description of the job.
3. From these faint stimuli, he formulates a fuzzy concept of an ultimate criterion.
4. He formulates a combination of measures that will give him a satisfactory composite for the criterion he desires.
5. He judges the relevance of this measure (i.e., the extent to which it is neither deficient nor contaminated).
6. He then finds that the data required for his carefully built composite are not

available in the company files, nor is there any immediate prospect of having such records reliably kept.

7. Therefore, he will then select the *best available criterion*.

Guion's version of the criterion selection process points to the major concerns in the steps necessary to establish relevant measures of training performance. They include the following.

The Establishment of Relevant Criteria.   The chosen criteria are judged relevant to the degree that the components (knowledge, skills, attitudes) required to succeed are the same as those required for the ultimate task (Thorndike, 1949). Unfortunately, the determination of relevance must often be made on the basis of judgment rather than empirical evidence, because the ultimate criteria are unavailable. However, the relevance of training criteria could be judged against the criteria established for measuring on-the-job performance by content validity measures. Unfortunately, the procedure for performing this task remain to be established. Thus, the judgment of relevance of a criterion has typically been based upon the reduction of two other components: *criterion deficiency* and *criterion contamination*.

Criterion deficiency is the degree to which there are components in the ultimate criteria that are not present in the actual criteria being employed. Again, this establishes the relationship between the need assessment process and the evaluation. The better the need assessment, the less likely that important components will be left unrecognized.

The construct of criterion contamination pertains to extraneous elements present in the actual criteria that are not part of the ultimate criteria. The existence of such elements that contaminate the criteria can lead to incorrect conclusions regarding the validity of the training program. For example, supervisors may give better work stations to those individuals who participated in the new training program, because they are judged equipped to handle the assignment better than those persons who have simply been placed on the job. In this case, the training program may demonstrate its validity, because the participants had better assignments. Blum and Naylor (1968) and Goldstein (1974) outline various types of contamination and note that many of these problems as well as the difficulties of criterion deficiency can be avoided so that more relevant criteria are established.

The Breadth of Criteria.   The typical judgment regarding deficient criteria is related to the adequacy of criteria in measuring a particular process. Thus, it questions the extent to which the chosen criteria are adequate to the degree that the components required to succeed are represented. In the evaluation of training programs, there are also the issues related to obtaining criteria that represent all the objectives, including organizational goals or trainer acceptance as well as learning. A study by O'Leary (1972) further illustrates the importance of considering the many different criterion dimensions. She utilized a program consisting of role playing and group problem-solving sessions with hard-core unemployed women. At the conclusion of the study, the trainees had developed greater positive changes in attitude toward self, but these were not accompanied by positive attitudes toward their tedious, structured job. Rather, these trainees apparently raised their levels of aspirations and subsequently left the work environment to seek employment in a work setting consistent with their newly found expectations. In this instance, it may have been obvious that the trainees were leaving the job as well as experiencing positive changes in attitude. However, there are many other cases where the collection of a variety of criteria related to the objectives are the only way that such data will be available to evaluate the training program.

One interesting scheme that suggests the degree of breadth possible is described by Kirkpatrick (1959). He indicates that training analysts should consider measuring reactions, learning, behavior, and results. Kirkpatrick defines "reaction" as what the trainees thought of the particular program; it does not include a measure of the learning that takes place. The reaction of the participants is often a critical factor in the continuance of training programs. These types of instruments help ensure against decisions based upon the comments of a few very satisfied or disgruntled participants. Most trainers believe that favorable reactions provide a good atmosphere for the learning of the material in the instructional program. However, favorable reaction will not necessarily result in high levels of learning. Thus, a second criterion suggested is based on "learning." Here, the training analyst is concerned with measures of learning of the principles, facts, techniques, and attitudes that were specified as the objectives of the training program. These measures must be objective and quantifiable indicants of the learning that has taken place during training. They are not measures of performance on the job. There are many different measures of learning performance including paper and pencil tests, learning curves, and job-sample tests. The objectives determine the choice of the most appropriate measure.

Kirkpatrick uses the term *behavior* to refer to the measurement of job performance. Just as favorable reaction does not necessarily mean that learning will occur in the training program, superior training performance does not always result in similar behavior in the transfer setting. Thus, it is important to examine the learning that takes place in a special reading lab and then examine the behavior in the classroom where the learning is expected to produce a variety of changes. Kirkpatrick uses his last category, "results," to relate the results of the training program to the organizational objectives. Some of the results that could be examined include costs, turnover, absenteeism, grievances, and morale. The difficulties in determining organizational objectives have been previously described. These difficulties are further compounded by the determination of criteria that measure the achievement of these objectives. Moreover, as previously noted, achievement of these organizational objectives are often critical components of the decisions that determine the fate of the training program.

Reliability. Reliability is a necessary condition to obtain stable criterion measures, but it is important to recognize that reliability will not replace the need for a relevant criterion. Reliability can be measured statistically, and this has led some evaluators to emphasize reliability rather than relevance. Wherry (1957) warns us that choosing what is available is often dictated by measurement considerations that are no more valid than choosing those criteria that happen to be lying around. Whereas arguing strenuously for measuring carefully, Wherry (1957) notes that the selection of a criterion just because it is measurable says: "We don't know what we are doing, but we are doing it very carefully, and hope you are pleased with our unintelligent diligence [p. 1-2]." We gain very little understanding by carefully measuring the wrong thing.

Process and Outcome Measures. Outcome measures refer to critera like "learning" and "performance" that represent various levels of achievement. Although such measures are critical in determining the viability of instructional programs, strict reliance on outcome measures often make it difficult to determine why these results were achieved. The view is especially well expressed by Cronbach (1963):

> Insofar as possible, evaluation should be used to understand how the course produces its effects and what parameters influence its effectiveness. It is important to learn, for example, that the outcome of a programmed instruction depends very much upon the attitude of the teacher; indeed, this may be more important than to learn that on the average such instruction produces slightly better or worse results than conventional programs [p. 675].

Evaluation Methodology

There are various procedures to be considered in selecting an evaluation methodology. For example, it is possible to consider training as a predictor and job performance as a criterion. In this instance as discussed earlier, the methodology employed would be similar to the selection evaluation procedures utilized in evaluating a test. Another potential procedure is the methodology of content validation, where the components of the training program are expected to represent the content domain of the job. However, these methodological procedures and their utility for evaluating training programs remain uncertain. There are virtually no empirical tests and also very little thought about the development of such techniques. Thus, most of the development in evaluation methodology have been related to experimental and quasi-experimental designs as originally organized by Campbell and Stanley (1963). These designs are concerned with the establishment of both internal and external validity. Internal validity questions the extent to which the treatment makes a difference in the specific situation. External validity questions the extent to which inferences can be made; it deals with the issues of generalizeability.

As presented by Campbell and Stanley (1963) and Cook and Campbell (1976), there are numerous threats to both internal and external validity and a large number of different experimental designs that are useful for many different organizational settings. It is only recently that evaluation methodologists have begun to appreciate the fact that training represents an organizational intervention that can produce a variety of problems. For example, Cook and Campbell (1976) discuss the threat to validity resulting from trainees who receive less desirable treatments being demoralized. They express some of the complexities of design issues as follows:

> Improvements on design need to be made, can be made, and should be made in order to facilitate better casual inferences. But we would delude ourselves if we believed that a single experiment, or even a research program of several years' duration, would definitely answer the major questions associated with confidently inferring a causal relationship, naming its parts, and specifying its generalizeability [p. 227].

Whereas all these concerns should be eventual goals, the use of basic research designs adjusted for the difference between research in a controlled laboratory and research in organizational environments still offers the best hope for the near future. Thus, at the very least, it is possible to begin answering the question, "Does exposure to the instructional material result in a change in performance?" A design to answer this question would use a pretest administered before the instructional program begins, and then a posttest following exposure to the instructional program. The timing of the posttest for the evaluation of an instructional program is not easily specified. One posttest at the conclusion of the training program provides one measure of the changes that have occurred during instruction, but it does not give any indication of later transfer performance. Thus, other measures must be employed at a later time when the participant has been in the transfer situation for a reasonable time period. Comparisons can then be made between the pretest and the first posttest, pretest and second posttest, and between the posttest themselves.

Pretest and Posttest Measurement.   The variables measured in the pretests and posttests must be associated with the objectives of the training program. The expected changes associated with the instructional program should be specified so that statistically reliable differences established between the tests can confirm the degree to which the objectives have been achieved. It should be emphasized that the measurement of changes between the instructional group and a control group is not a simple matter. Often the measures used in the pretest are inappropriate for the posttest. There are also problems associated with the relations among the initial levels of performance (pretest) and the degree of success on the posttest. Some researchers (Mayo & DuBois, 1963) have suggested that it is necessary to partial out the effects of initial pretest differences on the posttest. Such statistical considerations are not treated in this chapter, except to warn the reader that such statistical expertise is necessary in order to properly evaluate programs.

Control Groups.   The specification of changes indicated by pre and posttest measurements are only one consideration. The determination that these changes occurred as a result of the instructional treatment is another matter. Basic methodology, as practiced in laboratory research where experimental control is easier to achieve, suggests the use of a control group. The classical use of the control group requires that it be treated just like the experimental group on all variables that might contribute to pre-post differences except for the independent variable being investigated. Thus, medical researchers have employed control groups to separate the effects of the actual drug from the reactions induced by the patients' expectations and suggestibility. In training research, similar cautions are necessary to separate the background effects of instructional treatments. Thus, the presence of observers and the excitement of a new training methodology may mislead the evaluator in determining the source of the treatment effects. To the extent that participants in the control condition can be included as part of the study, some of these contaminants are controlled.

A more serious evaluation concern for training researchers is whether the classical use of control groups is meaningful. In many instances, the appropriate comparison for a training group does not appear to be a do nothing control but rather a comparison group that was trained utilizing the previous or other alternative instructional methods. Few persons would be interested in flying across the Atlantic ocean with a pilot who was randomly placed in the uninstructed control group. In some situations, the comparison group may appear to be individuals who have not received any formalized training. However, even in these instances, the individuals probably received some previous on-the-job type instruction that could make them appropriate for a comparison group.

Obviously, the better the control procedures employed, the more the threats to the internal validity (e.g., passage of time, maturation factors, or events in the outside world) are controlled as alternate sources of the effect. For example, the random assignment of subjects to the instructional treatment and the control or comparison groups help to eliminate sources of error related to initial trainee differences. It is also important to note that evaluation methodologists (Cook & Campbell, 1976) have begun to work with many types of quasi-experimental designs that can control particular types of threats to validity. In other instances, training researchers have been equally ingenious in using designs to fit particular environmental constraints. Thus, Komaki, Waddell and Pearce (1977) have introduced an operant-conditioning model employing baseline measurements on small samples of subjects. In their studies, positive reinforcers are introduced for target behaviors. Differences were obtained between initial base rates and later target behavior while other behaviors did not change. These types of efforts are important to the development of research procedures that permit the specification of treatment effects.

It is clear from these considerations of the evaluation issues that there remain many serious problems that require research consideration. The same point can be made for most of the components in the ISD model. Fortunately, considerable information has been published regarding training and its evaluation, and given the state of the art assessment presented, it is now appropriate to consider the question ''what have we learned about the use of training programs?''

VALIDITY ISSUES IN TRAINING PROGRAMS

The issue of validity can be addressed from two perspectives, both of which are discussed here; namely: (1) "How much of the presently available information about instructional design and evaluation is used"; and (2) "Where is more information required?" The focus must concentrate on several types of analyses. As indicated, it must consider not only how well the present knowledge is being used but also how much the area is affected by lack of knowledge about certain issues. One particular difficulty in accomplishing this type of analysis is that there are exceptions to nearly all generalizations that can be made. Thus, a review of the evaluation techniques employed must conclude with a sense of despondency about the willingness of training directors to evaluate their own products. However, there are some very creative examples of evaluation of training techniques. This presentation acknowledges these accomplishments while also focusing on the general state of the field.

The Use of Need Assessment Techniques

Training analysts are somewhat unique in their treatment of need assessment techniques. For some reason, they have tended to emphasize instructional techniques rather than the needs and the matching of instructional techniques with the training needs. Thus, instead of careful need assessment, the training field appears dominated by a fads approach. Children go from yo-yos to hoola hoops to skate boards, while training directors move from sensitivity training to organizational development to computer-assisted instruction (CAI). Each of these techniques probably has a place (for the children, also), but analysts never seem to find out very much about their approach before they are off examining another type of program. This type of fads approach places a heavy emphasis on the development of techniques without consideration of needs assessment or the matching of the technique to the needs. It is interesting to note that machinists examine the job they must perform before choosing their tools, and a gardener usually chooses a sprinkling system rather than a bucket to water a half acre lawn. Yet analysts still have to be warned about selecting tools and finding something they fit by quotes like the following by Gilbert (1961):

> If you don't have a gadget called a teaching machine, don't get one. Don't buy one; don't borrow, one; don't steal one. If you have such a gadget, get rid of it. Don't give it away, for someone else might use it. This is a most practical rule, based on empirical facts from considerable observation. If you begin with a device of any kind, you will try to develop the teaching program to fit that device [p. 478].

Gilbert is not saying that teaching machines or sensitivity training or CAI or any other technique doesn't work. He is saying that the design of change programs cannot begin with instructional media. Instead, we must, through need assessment, determine the objectives of our programs so that our criteria for evaluation and the choice of instructional program are based upon sound decisions.

This problem has become so serious that Campbell (1971) was actually able to discern the following pattern in the fads approach:

1. A new technique appears with a group of followers who announce the success of the technique.
2. A new group of followers develops modifications of the technique.
3. A few empirical studies appear supporting the technique.
4. There is a backlash. Critics publish articles questioning the usefulness of the new techniques but rarely produce any data.
5. The techniques survive until a new technique appears. Then, the whole procedure is repeated.

The consequences of failing to carry out need assessment approaches was amply demonstrated in an investigation of 418 hard-core unemployed trainees in a program to train highway construction machinery operators (Miller & Zeller, 1967). The authors were able to obtain information from 270 graduates. Of this group, 61% of the graduates were employed and 39% unemployed at the time of the interview. In addition, more than half of the employed group said they were without jobs more than 60% of the time. Some of the reasons for the unemployment situation were inadequacies in training, such as not enough task practice and insufficient training time. The details showed that the program was not based upon a consideration of the job components. According to Miller and Zeller (1967), one trainee noted that: "the contractors laughed when I showed them my training diploma and said, 'come back after you get some schooling buddy' [p.

32-33]." In a now familiar lament, the authors of the report wonder how a training program could be designed without a thorough analysis of the skills required.

The reason for this state of affairs is probably rather complex. Training analysts appear to have adopted the fads approach based upon a forelorn belief that the next toy they purchase will provide the answers to their training problem. This approach appears to have resulted in an approach dominated by ancedotal testimonials rather than a research approach. Campbell, Dunnette, Lawler, and Weick (1970) expressed this problem especially well as follows:

> First, we must state quite bluntly that there is simply a great need for more research and for a wider variety of research. This may sound trite, but we are frankly surprised by the extremely limited nature of managerial training studies done thus far [p. 480-481].

As far as need assessment is concerned, it is especially important to begin establishing techniques that help to determine what behaviors are necessary for job performance. Then, there is the additional question of determining which of these behaviors should be taught in the training program, and which techniques are most likely to impact those skills. Again, this point is well expressed by Campbell et al. (1970) for managerial training:

> Taken together, questions related to what techniques are best for what kinds of content and how such combinations are related to managerial behavior show that the need for more and broader research has reached alarming proportions [p. 481].

Annett and Duncan (1967) reach a similar conclusion for training in general. They note that a method for analyzing tasks that suggests training procedures is a critical issue. That the task analysis method should also specify which behaviors should be treated in training is also a further conclusion that can be reached on the basis of the analysis and review presented in this chapter. Additionally, person analysis procedures that attend to the capabilities of entering trainees require considerable attention. For example, data related to the appropriate training methodologies for aged individuals is basically nonexistent. The matching of training techniques for particular behaviors for particular individuals requires considerable work on need assessment methodology.

Also, the design of training programs has not considered time perspectives. Thus, some programs train to unrealistically high levels for jobs that, at best, will not be performed by trainees for many years (Alluisi, 1976), and other programs train an individual for the first job without considering other early job transfer requirements. Need assessment approaches that examine these concerns are sorely lacking.

Organizational analysis that constituted another aspect of need assessment has not been discussed here but will be separately addressed in a later section.

The Use of Evaluation Techniques

Evaluation, as described by Goldstein (1974), is considered to be an information-gathering process that should not be expected to lead to decisions that declare a program as all good or all poor. Instructional programs are never complete; instead, they are designed to be revised on the basis of information obtained from evaluations based on relevant multiple criteria that are both free from contamination and reliable. The better experimental procedures control more of the potentially disruptive variables, thereby permitting a greater degree of confidence in specifying program effects. Although the constraints of the training environment may make laboratory type evaluations impossible to achieve, an awareness of the important factors in experimental design makes it possible to conduct useful evaluations even under adverse conditions.

If this particular philosophy is considered reasonable, then the state of training evaluation must be assessed as absolutely deplorable. A review by French in 1953 indicated that only one company in 40 made any scientific evaluation of supervisory training programs, whereas an examination of 476 studies by Castle in 1952 failed to find any research that examined both pretraining and on-the-job performance. In 1961, Shafer found that most companies still spent less than 5% of their training budget on evaluation (with assuredly corresponding low amounts of time). In 1970, Cohen, commenting on the evaluation reports of the federally financed innovative school program known as "Title I," stated that the national evaluations of these programs were little more than annual reports. There was nothing wrong with the annual reports except that they were not evaluations. Meanwhile, the U.S. Civil Service Catalogue of Basic Education Systems (1971) listed 55 basic reading programs for educationally disadvantaged employees. For these programs, four publishers listed some type of validation program, two publishers offered case studies, and the other 49 indicated that validation data were not available. Similar commentary on the lack of sound empirical data for managerial training programs has also been published (Campbell, Dunnette, Lawler, Weick, 1970), and a recent analysis of the Department of Defense training effort (Orlansky, 1977) suggests that efforts to examine the cost effectiveness of major flight-simulation efforts are minimal.

Additionally, examinations of the types of criteria employed to provide evaluation data are consistent with the previous commentary. For example, Catalanello and Kirkpatrick (1968) found that of 154 companies surveyed, the largest number (77%) stressed studies related to reactions. Even in those instances where reaction data are collected, some investigators (Mindak & Anderson, 1971) have suggested that most of these measures were "eyeball" attempts to measure reactions. Few studies have bothered to measure learning, behavior, or results. It is probably not unreasonable to suspect that these investigations did not consider criterion relevance and reliability.

Two recent developments indicate an increasing concern over these criterion problems. First, there has been increased attention to criterion-referenced measures that are dependent on an absolute standard of quality (Swezey, 1978) rather than norm-referenced measures that are dependent on a relative standard. Criterion-referenced measures provide a standard of achievement for the individual based upon specific behavioral objectives and thereby provide an indicant of the degree of competence attained by the trainee. The characteristics of criterion-referenced measures, including methods of content validity to determine relevance as well as the design of methods to determine reliability indices, need attention.

Secondly, there has been some pioneer efforts that have begun to attend to diverse criterion measures of training success. The best illustration of these efforts is provided by Orlansky and String's (1977) examination of the cost effectiveness of flight simulators in military training. These authors examined both performance and cost data and conclude that flight simulators are cost effective. However, they also concluded that simulator extras such as motion cues were not cost effective. Similar innovative types of analyses of training effectiveness should be strongly encouraged.

Authors who have commented on evaluation methodology with regard to specific techniques have also expressed concern about the lack of information. For example, in 1961, McGehee and Thayer reached the following conclusion concerning the use of business games: "For all we know, at this time, there may be a negative or zero relationship between the kinds of behavior developed by business game training and the kinds of behavior required to operate a business successfully [p. 223]." Unfortunately, the conclusion is still valid today.

The complexity of the research questions requiring evaluation efforts are made obvious by studies of machine simulation efforts. The development of simulation efforts are closely tied to the basic learning literature on transfer of training. In many cases, studies of simulation efforts have contributed to that body of knowledge. Yet, despite the accomplishments in the academic and applied laboratories, the degree of understanding that might be expected has not been achieved. In part, the limitations are a result of inadequate evaluation efforts. For example, Blaiwes and Regan (1970) suggest that evaluation efforts must consider three criteria: (1) original learning efficiency; (2) transfer of learning to the new task; and (3) retention of original learning. Yet, in the area of flight simulation where the greatest effort has been expended, the emphasis has been on the most immediate criteria—original learning, and even those studies have been plagued by serious problems.

Williges, Roscoe, and Williges (1972) note that there is little agreement on what constitutes ideal pilot performance, and the reliability of most pilot-performance grading systems has been disappointing. Thus, even studies of original learning are difficult to complete, because there is little agreement on what constitutes terminal performance. Studies investigating the transfer of skills from simulation to on-the-job efforts are less frequent and suffer from serious design flaws usually led by the lack of a control group. As far as retention measures are concerned, they are virtually nonexistent. There is little information on whether the skills obtained through simulation efforts are maintained over a period of time, or whether many of the learning variables (massed versus spaced, amount of original learning) make any difference in long-term retention.

Similar commentary can be offered about almost all training techniques currently being used: CAI, sensitivity training, role playing, lecture methods, on-the-job training, etc. However, a fair appraisal should indicate that there are some properly designed studies attempting to examine every one of these techniques. Unfortunately, such studies are few and far between, and as a result, there are few generalizations concerning particular techniques for particular behaviors. Potentially, an interesting exception to this viewpoint might be offered by recent research on the newest popular training technique known as role modeling (Moses, 1978). This procedure is based upon careful job analysis and techniques designed to specify particular objectives. Also, the proponents of the technique are especially concerned about transfer of training and thus have instituted systematic evaluation procedures. The results of these efforts may prove to be a real contribution that hopefully will be adopted by the proponents of other procedures.

Another major concern that has not yet been addressed deals with the development of evaluation procedures that permit greater understanding of the meaning of training results. The evaluation designs and criteria (when they are employed) have been based upon a product or outcome view of training validity. Thus, researchers collected pre and posttraining measures, compared them with control groups, and discovered that the results they had obtained were not understood. This problem was especially apparent when the collectors of these data were outside consultants, who appeared only to collect the pre- and posttraining data but had little or no conception of the processes that had occurred in the training between the two measurements.

A recent event experienced by this author illustrates this issue. In a study of CAI in a school setting (Goldstein & Rosenberg, 1978), two teachers each agreed to instruct a geometry class by traditional methodology and by CAI methods. Thus, each teacher taught one traditional and one CAI class. Further, the teachers agreed to work together to design an examination that would cover the material presented in each of the classes. At the end of the early testing period, the traditional classes taught by each teacher significantly outperformed the CAI group taught by these same teachers. However, at the third testing, one of the CAI groups improved to the point of being equivalent to the two traditional groups; the other CAI group performed significantly worse than the other three instructional groups.

One reasonable conclusion for this series of events is that one of the teachers finally learned how to instruct the CAI group so that it was now equivalent to the two traditional groups, but that the other teacher had not been able to perform that task with his CAI group. Indeed, if the investigators had only collected the outcome measures, the previous or other similar *erroneous* conclusions would probably have been offered as explanations for the data. In this case, the investigators also observed the instructional process to acquire information about the program. They learned that the instructor of the CAI group that eventually improved had become disturbed over the performance of his students and had offered remedial tutoring. He had essentially turned his CAI class into a traditional group.

Thus, from an organizational behavior perspective, process measures might provide important insights for the analysis of instructional programs. As indicated above, process measures can help determine the source of the effect. If it is found that the trainers' attitudes or the trainees' expectations account for a substantial portion of the variance in the outcomes, those variables must be considered in the design of the instructional programs. The utilization of process measures may provide all sorts of unanticipated dividends. The author will never forget the look of astonishment on the faces of a number of high-level executives, who had just discovered the reason entry-level grocery clerks couldn't operate the cash register—the instructional sequences for that task was no longer included in their carefully designed instructional program.

The view of process variables presented here suggests that there are many instances of interactions between training systems and the rest of the organization. In this sense, training is an intervention, and it is necessary to begin understanding the effects of this intervention, a point that is further emphasized in the next section.

First, it is also appropriate to note here that in addition to a need for more evaluation research, there is also a need for more research on evaluation. As indicated earlier, Cook and Campbell (1976) have outlined some of the threats to validity that result from the training type of intervention. There is also some reason to believe that the decision to examine data in an organization actually changes the form and quality of the data. Thus, Cochran (1977) suggests that all activity, including the production of objective indices, have unintended as well as intended effects. For example, data omissions and changes in the way data are categorized in order to meet various sets of objectives are not unusual. Thus, when police departments have an objective "to lower crime," there may be tendencies to classify more larcenies as involving less than $50, a classification that is not counted in the Uniform Crime Report (Cochran, 1977).

These types of variables require further study. Also, it is necessary to consider other methods of evaluation including content and predictive validity studies. There is now a clear indication that training programs are being scrutinized to determine if they meet fair employment-practices guidelines (Bartlett, 1978). Unless there are considerable advances both in the implementation of the methodology presently available and in the development of additional methodological strategies, the law courts will dictate the rules to the profession in a fashion similar to the way this happened to researchers who study selection techniques.

The Use of the Training Subsystem in an Organization

The discussion of process variables suggests the necessity of understanding that training programs are simply one part of an organization. It is necessary to realize that analyses of training programs force consideration of the fact that something learned in one environment (training) will be performed in another environment (on the job). Thus, the trainee will enter a new environment subject to the effects of all of the interacting components that represent organizations today. Certainly, there are some aspects of the environment that help determine the success or failure of the training programs—aspects that go beyond the attributes the trainee gains as a result of the instructional program completed. Also, judgments about the success of a training program involve variables other than the performance of the trainee. Goldstein (1978) has categorized two major types of problems that affect training programs: unspecified goals and organizational conflicts.

Unspecified Goals. When organizational goals are not considered in the implementation of training programs, the objectives and criteria that ensue from the need assessment process are not evaluated. Later, the organizations are not able to specify their achievements, because they have not collected the necessary criterion information. For example, Lynton and Pareek (1967) have described a program that "successfully" results in training foreign-born engineers in American universities. However, failure to specify the organizational objectives and their consequences permitted the program to "succeed" without meeting the needs of the original country. In this case, an organizational objective was to have the trained engineers return home. Any examination of that objective would have shown the program to be unrealistic, because the training qualified the individuals for jobs that simply did not exist in their native environments.

Similarly, organizations might expect training programs to provide trainees with expectations about the job or particular views toward performance requirements. It is not unusual, for example, to discover that police training programs are devoted to skill requirements (e.g., operating a police vehicle or using firearms) or information requirements (e.g., knowing the difference between a felony and misdemeanor). Yet, organizational analyses often show that there are organizational expectations concerning interpersonal relations with the public and a concern for all citizens regardless of race, color, or creed. Obviously, if these organizational philosophies and emphases are not clearly defined and specified during the need assessment phase, they will not be considered in the design of the training program and at best will receive only passing attention in the instructional sequence.

The problems are further complicated in such cases by the fact that it is a lot easier to teach weapons procedure than to train interpersonal relations. Thus, certain topics may be deemphasized. Sometimes, the organizations become aware that they have problem areas only when they are faced with a series of complaints. At that point in time, everyone wonders why the organizational objectives were not translated into training and job requirements. In short, many training programs are based upon meeting skill requirements only rather than including other important but unspecified and unidentified organizational objectives. Yet paradoxically, organizations and their managers often judge the value of training programs on the basis of their own particular objectives, many of which were never specified, never considered in the design of the program, and never utilized in designing the evaluation model. For example, the high financial cost of some instructional programs leads to their early demise, because the instructional system analysis failed to identify the cost variable as related to any of the organizational objectives listed for the program.

The Problems of Organizational Conflicts.   In some instances, there are organizational dynamics that affect training programs but that cannot be simply described as unspecified goals. The most insidious of these types of problems are organizational conflicts that the training program is somehow (with a magic wand) supposed to resolve. More likely, the training program succumbs to the conflict. A good illustration of these problems is offered in a training program designed by Fleishman, Harris, and Burtt (1955) to produce more considerate foremen. At the end of the program, the foremen had become more considerate than a comparable control group. At a later time, these investigators collected further data that indicated the positive changes were not maintained on the job. An investigation determined that the supervisors of the trainees were not supportive of these new behavior patterns. In this nonsupportive climate, the foremen reverted back to their old behavior. Some analysts use these data to support the adage that training should start at the top.

Another perspective is that conflict between the goals of the organization and the training program must be discovered and corrected before training begins. In instances marked by conflict, complete success in training (high training validity) could still result in a program that failed (low-performance validity). It is also likely that most programs are not as carefully analyzed as the Fleishman, Harris, and Burtt study, so that few persons would realize the training program had failed.

The history of training programs for the hard-core unemployed (HCU) reflects similar problems. First, many programs failed to specify organizational objectives that went beyond the components of work ordinarily stemming from job analysis. Miller and Zeller (1967) state the problem this way: "It might have been helpful to have included within the training experience itself practice in job hunting, assistance in contacting employers before the end of training, and following-up counseling and job-placement help [P. 31]."

The themes of job placement, counseling, and attention to the needs of the trainee are included in most programs that have evidence of success. In some cases, the attention is manifested by health care for individuals who previously were not able to attend training because of their ills. In other cases, the consideration is shown in detailed and careful transportation directions to help the trainees find their way to the training or job site. It appears that training programs cannot just attend to job skills but must also consider the trainee as an individual within a social system. In many instances, the trainee not only lacks job skills but also is not knowledgeable about many aspects of being a worker (e.g., health care, transportation, baby sitters, promptness on the job, etc.). Such factors make careful organizational analysis and need assessment procedures mandatory.

In addition to issues such as these, another peripheral problem that appears to have developed as a result of the failure to have developed appropriate need assessment procedures is the belief that training programs can solve any problem. Thus, many programs are designed to solve problems that are related to more internal organizational conflict, human-factors problems, or other difficulties unrelated to the design of an instructional program. A good illustration of this difficulty is Sheridan's (1975) description of the American Telephone and Telegraph Company attempt to comply with a government order to place 19% females in outside craft jobs. Despite rigorous recruiting and comprehensive training efforts, the women they did manage to recruit into the job dropped from training at an average rate of 50%. The individuals who completed training usually didn't last a full year on the job. The analysis of the situation indicated that the physical differences between men and women made the job extremely difficult for women to perform. Some of the most serious problems centered upon the use of the ladder that was both long and heavy. Applying basic human-factors principles, the job was redesigned so that it could be performed by women.

At this point in time, there is virtually no basic information available on the appropriate techniques for performing organizational analyses or analyses of the ways in which such variables affect training programs and trainee performance. However, the developing concern for these issues is a hopeful sign. Perhaps, training research is finally beginning to recognize that the data produced in the training program are only the beginning steps toward an understanding of the role of such programs in the total organization.

CONCLUSION

An analysis of both financial and personnel resources directed to the development and implementation of training programs is a direct testimonial to the positive benefits ascribed to training programs by the providers of instructional materials. Thus, training programs are expected to benefit productivity directly as measured by a large number of criteria (e.g., increased work quantity and quality, and reduced turnover, absenteeism, and accidents). Whereas training programs are a potentially powerful technique that can achieve positive results, few programs are designed appropriately so that positive benefits are likely to accrue, and even fewer are evaluated to determine whether they achieved specified goals and objectives. Instead, the choice of procedures and design of programs are based upon which new technique happens to be the latest fad.

Recent concern over these issues has been partially responsible for the specification of *Instructional Systems Development* (ISD) models as a procedure for conceptualizing the interacting components in the design and evaluation of training programs. Although the individual components included in these models are not new, this approach provides a framework that specifies issues that require further research attention as well as indicating where knowledge exists that is not fully utilized by the training community. From this perspective, the following concerns have been identified:

1. As noted by many researchers (Campbell, Dunnette, Lawler, & Weick, 1970; Goldstein, 1974), there is simply a great need for a wide variety of research. The training community has been misled by a fads approach that has emphasized the nonempirical development of new techniques. This has resulted in a dearth of knowledge about which techniques are most appropriate for different content, behaviors, or situations. Thus, there is little taxonomic information available to help the thoughtful training analyst choose the appropriate training methodology.

2. Research on the design of need assessment procedures to provide information for program design and evaluation is required. Task analysis procedures specific to the identification of training needs must be considered as well as procedures that identify the appropriate entering abilities of trainees. With this information, it will be possible to match the most relevant instructional components to the capabilities of trainees.

3. It is important to support research that treats training programs as an intervention in an organizational environment. Thus, the failure to specify organizational goals and conflicts within the organizations often predetermines the failure of training programs. The methodology necessary for the design of organization analysis as a part of need assessment procedure requires research effort.

4. Similarly, the treatment of training programs as interventions demands a concern for the development of evaluation methodology appropriate for research in organizational environments. Thus, it is necessary to recognize threats to validity and to design research methods that help control the threat as well as help specify the effects of intervention programs. Additionally, the type of internal and external validity threats that results from the introduction of training studies

in organizations should be studied as a source of information about the effects of interventions in real-world environments. Various research strategies that permit relevant data-collection efforts within the constraints of organizational environments must also be considered. Thus, it is necessary to begin exploring precise procedures for determining the content validity of training programs, as well as the examination of other evaluation strategies like operant baseline investigations.

5. Research is needed on the specification of relevant criteria for evaluation judgments. The development and examination of criterion procedures like criterion-referenced measurement and cost-effectiveness measurements need support. Presently, relevance is considered achieved by the elimination of criterion deficiency and criterion contamination. It is important to begin developing content-validity procedures that can be used to examine the relevance of actual criteria employed. Additionally, it is necessary to examine the usefulness of process criteria, both as a procedure to check on the content of training programs and as a procedure to collect information that helps in the interpretation of outcome measures.

6. Training should be examined as a rich source of information concerning individuals who enter organizations. In this regard, research is needed on the expectancies of trainees and the effect of these expectancies on performance. In addition, the use of training programs as a source of realistic and unrealistic expectations should be explored. Also, research that examines training performance as a predictor of future performance, as well as training as a criterion to examine previously collected entry-level data, should be encouraged.

ACKNOWLEDGMENT

Some of the concepts presented in this chapter (especially the material found in the section on the instructional model) are adapted from Goldstein, I.L. *Training: Program Development and Evaluation.* Monterey, California: Brooks/Cole, 1974. Copyright by Brooks/Cole Publishing Co., 1974. All rights reserved. The chapter was originally edited for volume 3 of this series, *Human Performance and Productivity: Stress and Performance Effectiveness,* Alluisi, E. A. & Fleishman, E. A. (Eds.), but was felt more appropriate for inclusion in the present volume.

REFERENCES

Alderfer, C. P. Organization development. *Annual Review of Psychology.* Palo Alto, Calif.: Annual Reviews, 1977.

Alluisi, E. A. Summary report of the task force on training technology. *Defense Science Board Task Force on Training Technology.* Washington, D.C., 1976.

Annett, J., & Duncan K. D. Task analysis and training design. *Occupational Psychology,* 1967, *41,* 211-221.

Bartlett, C. J. Equal employment opportunity issues in training. In I. L. Goldstein (Ed.), Training: Methodological Considerations and Empirical Approaches. Special Issue *Human Factors Journal, 1978, 20.*

Bartlett, C. J., & Goldstein, I. L. A validity analysis of employment tests for bus drivers. *Training and Educational Research Program, Inc., College Park, Md., 1974.*

Bartlett, C. J., & Goldstein, I. L. *Analysis of a selection program in a police organization.* Unpublished manuscript, College Park, Md.: University of Maryland, 1978.

Blaiwes, A. S., & Regan, J. J. *An integrated approach to the study of learning, retention, and transfer—A key issue in training-device research and development* (NAVTRADEVCEN1H-178). Naval Training Device Center, Orlando, Fla., 1970.

Blum, M. L., & Naylor, J. C. *Industrial psychology.* New York: Harper & Row, 1968.

Bray, D. W., & Campbell, R. J. Selection of salesman by means of an assessment center. *Journal of Applied Psychology,* 1968, *52,* 36-41.

Bray, D. W., & Grant, D. L. The assessment center in the measurement of potential for business management. Psychological Monographs, 1966, *80,* (17, Whole No. 625).

Campbell, D. T., & Stanley, J. C. *Experimental and quasi-experimental designs for research.* Chicago: Rand McNally, 1963.

Campbell, J. P. Personnel training and development. In *Annual Review of Psychology.* Palo Alto, Calif.: Annual Reviews, 1971.

Campbell, J. P., Dunnette, M. P., Lawler, E. E. III, & Weick, K. E., Jr. *Managerial behavior, performance, and effectiveness.* New York: McGraw-Hill, 1970.

Castle, P. F. C. Evaluation of human-relations training for supervisors. *Occupational Psychology,* 1952, *26,* 191-205.

Catalanello, R. F., & Kirkpatrick, D. L. Evaluating training programs—the state of the art. *Training and Development Journal,* 1968, *22,* 2-9.

Cochran, N. *Reactivity of data and alternatives for data use.* Paper presented at the American Psychological Association, 1977.

Cogan, E. A. *Systems analysis and the introduction of educational technology in school* (HumRRo Professional paper 14-71). Human Resources Research Organization, Alexandria, Va. 1971.

Cohen, D. K. Politics and research: Evaluation of social action programs in education. *Review of Educational Research,* 1970, *40,* 213-238.

Cook, T. D., & Campbell, D. T. The design and conduct of quasi-experiments and true experiments in field settings. In M. P. Dunnette, *Handbook of industrial and organizational psychology.* Chicago: Rand McNally, 1976.

Cronbach, L. J. Course improvement through evaluation. *Teachers College Record,* 1963, *64,* 672-683.

Fleishman, E. A. On the relationship between abilities, learning, and human performance. *American Psychologist,* 1972, *27,* 1017-1032.

Fleishman, E. A., Harris, E. F., & Burtt, H. E. *Leadership and supervision in industry.* Columbus, Ohio: Bureau of Educational Research, Ohio State University, 1955.

French, S. H. Measuring progress toward industrial-relations objectives. *Personnel,* 1953, *30,* 338-347.

Gagné, R. M. Instruction and the conditions of learning. In L. Siegel (Ed.), *Instruction: Some contemporary viewpoints.* San Francisco: Chandler, 1967.

Gagné, R. M. The conditions for learning. New York: Holt, Rinehart, & Winston, 1965, 1970.

Ghisell, E. E. *The validity of occupational aptitude tests.* New York: Wiley, 1966.

Gilbert, T. F. On the relevance of laboratory investigation of learning to self-instructional programming. In A. A. Lumsdaine & R. Glaser (Eds.), *Teaching machines and programmed instruction.* Washington, D.C.: National Education Association, 1960.

Goldstein, I. L. *Training: Program development and evaluation.* Monterey, Calif.: Brooks/Cole, 1974.

Goldstein, I. L. The pursuit of validity in the evaluation of training programs. In I. L. Goldstein

(Ed.), Training: Methodological Considerations and Empirical Approaches. Special Issue *Human Factors Journal,* 1978, *20.*

Goldstein, I. L., & Rosenberg, B. *An evaluation of a computer-assisted instruction program.* Unpublished manuscript. College Park, Md.: University of Maryland, 1978.

Gordon, M. E., & Cohen, S. L. Training behavior as a predictor of trainability. *Personnel Psychology,* 1973, *26,* 261-272.

Grayson, L. P. Costs, benefits, effectiveness: Challenge to educational technology. *Science,* 1972, *175,* 1216-1222.

Guion, R. M. Criterion measurement and personnel judgements. *Personnel Psychology,* 1961, *14,* 141-149.

Harmon, P. A classification of performance objective behaviors in job training programs. *Educational Technology,* 1968, *8,* 11-16.

Hinrichs, J. R. Comparisons of "real life" assessments of management potential with situational exercises, paper and pencil ability tests, and personality inventories. *Journal of Applied Psychology,* 1969, *53,* 425-432.

Hoiberg, A., & Berry, N. H. Expectations and perceptions of Navy life. *Organizational Behavior and Human Performance,* 1978, *21,* 130-145.

Holt, H. O. An exploratory study of the use of a self-selection instruction program in basic electricity. In J. L. Hughes (Ed.), *Programmed learning: A critical evaluation.* Chicago: Educational Methods, 1963.

Kirkpatrick, D. L. Techniques for evaluating training programs. *Journal of the American Society of Training Directors,* 1959, *13,* 3-9, 21-26; 1960, *14,* 13-18, 28-32.

Komaki, J., Waddell, W. M., & Pearce, M. G. The applied behavior analysis approach and individual employees: Improving performance in two small businesses. *Organizational Behavior & Human Performance,* 1977, *19,* 337-352.

Kraut, A. I. Prediction of managerial success by peer and training-staff ratings. *Journal of Applied Psychology,* 1975, *60,* 14-19.

Lindahl, L. G. Movement analysis as an industrial training method. *Journal of Applied Psychology,* 1945, *29,* 420-436.

Lynton, R. P., & Pareek, U. *Training for development.* Homewood, Il.: Irwin, 1967.

Mager, R. F., & Beach, K. M. Jr. *Developing vocational instruction.* Belmont, Calif.: Fearon, 1967.

Mayo, G. D., & Dubois, P. H. Measurement of gain in leadership training. *Educational and Psychological Measurement.* 1963, *23,* 23-31.

McCormick E. J., Jeanneret, P. R., & Mecham, R. *A study of job dimensions as based on the Position Analysis Questionnaire.* Lafayette, Indiana: Purdue University, Report No. 6, 1969.

McGehee, W., & Thayer, P. W. *Training in business and industry.* New York: Wiley, 1961.

Miller, R. W., & Zeller, F. H. *Social psychological factors associated with responses to retraining.* Final Report, Office of Research and Development, Appalachian Center, West Virginia University, U.S. Department of Labor, 1967.

Mindak, W. A., & Anderson, R. E. Can we quantify an act of faith? *Training and Development Journal,* 1971, *25,* 2-10.

Moses, J. Behavior modeling for managers. In I. L. Goldstein (Ed.), Training: Methodological Considerations and Empirical Approaches. Special Issue *Human Factors Journal,* 1978, *20.*

O'Leary, V. E. The hawthorne effect in reverse: Effects of training and practice on individual and group performance. *Journal of Applied Psychology,* 1972, *56,* 491-494.

Orlansky, J. *The RDT and E program of the DoD on training.* IDA (Log No. HQ 77-19304). Institute for Defense Analysis Science and Technology Division, Arlington, Va., 1977.

Orlansky, J., & String, J. *Cost effectiveness of flight simulators for military training.* IDA (Log No. HQ 77-19470). Institute for Defense Analysis Science and Technology Division, Arlington, Va., 1977.

Shafer, C. I. *A study of evaluation in management education and development programs in selected U.S. companies:* Doctoral dissertation, Michigan State University, 1961.

Schneider, B. *The perceived environment: Organizational climate.* Paper presented at the Midwestern Psychological Association, May, 1973.

Sheridan, J. A. *Designing the work environment.* Paper presented at the American Psychological Association, 1975.

Siegel, A. I. Miniature Job Training and Evaluation as a Selection/Classification Device. In I. L. Goldstein (Ed.), Training: Methodological Considerations and Empirical Approaches. Special Issue *Human Factors Journal*, 1978, *20*.

Siegel, A. I., & Bergman, B. A. A job learning approach to prediction. *Personnel Psychology*, 1975, *28*, 325-339.

Stake, R. E. The countenance of educational evaluation. *Teachers College Record*, 1967, *68*, 523-540.

Strauss, G. Management by objectives: A critical view. *Training and Development Journal*, 1972, *26*, 10-15.

Swezey, R. Criterion-referenced measurement in performance. In I. L. Goldstein (Ed.), Training: Methodological Considerations and Empirical Approaches. Special Issue *Human Factors Journal*, 1978, *20*.

Thorndike, R. L. *Personnel selection.* New York: Wiley, 1949.

U.S. Civil Service Commission. *Catalog of basic education systems.* U.S. Government Printing Office, 1971.

U.S. Department of Labor, Manpower Administration. *Handbook for analyzing jobs.* Washington, D.C.: U.S. Government Printing Office, 1972.

Wanous, J. P. Organizational entry: Newcomers moving from outside to inside. *Psychological Bulletin*, 1977, *84*, 601-618.

Wernimont, P. F., & Campbell, J. P. Signs, samples, and criteria. *Journal of Applied Psychology*, 1968, *52*, 372-376.

Wherry, R. J. The past and future of criterion evaluation. *Personnel Psychology*, 1957, *10*, 1-5.

Williges, B. H., Roscoe, S. N., & Williges, R. C. Synthetic flight training revisited (Tech. Rep. ARL-72-21/AFOSR-72-10). Aviation Research Laboratory, Savoy, Ill., 1972.

6 Individual Capability, Team Performance, and Team Productivity*

Bernard Bass
School of Management
State University of New York at Binghamton

BACKGROUND AND PURPOSE

Work in teams is commonplace at all levels in all types of organizations. Why? A first reason is that modern technology usually makes it difficult for one person to assemble, organize, and digest the facts necessary to make an appropriate decision or complete an operation. Individuals must, therefore, often depend on others in order to complete their mutual tasks successfully. An operator of a new electrocardiogram unit in a hospital may be puzzled about the unusual behavior of an instrument metering the input of voltage. Consultation may be needed with the hospital electrician, a cardiologist from the medical staff, other instrument operators, the supervisor, and possibly also a representative of the firm that sells and services the machine. A meeting may be called to discuss the problem. No one person may have the knowledge or capability to deal with the problem alone (Bass & Ryterband, 1979).

Nearly 90% of companies larger than 250 employees reported regular use of committees. Fifty% of lower-middle management, 76% of upper-middle management, and 81% of top management among several thousand readers of the Harvard Business Review reported that they served on standing committees in their organization. Only 8% would abolish them (Tillman, 1960). A majority saw committees as the best way to ensure informed decisions, to promote creativity through the exchange of ideas, and to coordinate departments. Yet, a majority also believed committees waste too much time. There was seen to be considerable room for improving their interaction processes.

---

*Some of the material presented in this chapter has appeared in Bass (1980).

Complexity of technology puts a premium on team effort. For example, the design, implementation, and effective utilization of a computer system requires the services of system analysts, programmers, and operators, who must interact with each other in varying degrees, as well as with users and supervisors.

How do we achieve the optimal utilization of the individual talents available for the total effort? Napoleon is said to have stated that he would rather have an army of rabbits led by a lion than an army of lions led by a rabbit. Although the validity of the proposition is questionable, it does point up the importance to team performance of matching role assignments with individual differences in talent.

There are a number of self-evident truths about how the talent of the individual members of a team affect outcomes of the team effort. For example, all other things being equal:

1. The team product will be better, the more capable the average member.

However, it should be noted that although a team comprised of low-ability members has little likelihood of producing good products, the converse is not necessarily true; that is, a team of high-ability members may produce products low in quality and/or quantity.

2. For a set of nonredundant individuals (or individuals diversified in skills) performing independently, the group product will reflect some simple sum of their pooled performance. The greater the interdependence of the nonredundant individuals, the greater the opportunity for the group product to be more (or less) than the simple sum of their pooled performance.

3. If members of a team are performing tasks in series, the team ouput will be only as fast or as good as the "weakest link in the chain."

4. If the team's performance depends on discovering the right answer, then team performance will be as good as its best member.

There are also some empirically established truths about individuals performing in problem solving teams. For example:

1. Where the team task requires shared decision making among members, the team solution will be better than that of the *average* individual member but not necessarily better than that of the *best* individual member.

2. Like-minded individual members can work together more easily but are likely to be less creative. Members with diverse attitudes will generate more conflict but also more often hammer out more creative solutions.

3. The optimum size of a group depends on its task. Each additional member above one adds the need to involve an additional interaction (in a geometric increase) and an additional resource for solving the problem or completing the task. The optimum size for most problem-solving discussions seems to be reached with five or six members, but for many production tasks, the optimum size may be two (e.g., a carpenter and his helper) or even one (e.g., brainstorm-

ing ideas). (In the case of brainstorming, even adding a second participant interferes with, rather than enhances, the productivity of each participant working alone.)

The purpose of this chapter is to provide a framework for examining in detail what we know and what we don't know about how the distribution of available individual capabilities on a team, the distribution of work assignments, and the organization of the parallel distributions of roles and individual capabilities contributing to team productivity.

The plan of this chapter is to present a list of classes of variables that may affect team productivity; then, to review the empirical evidence available on the actual relations of these variables to team productivity. Since understanding and control can only be achieved by going beyond the listing of variables related to team effectiveness, we also present a complex model linking the classes of variables on the list. Such a model should generate hypotheses about the nature of expected linkages, which can then be tested against available empirical evidence. Finally, implications of the model for immediate actions relevant to productivity enhancement are suggested, and areas are discussed where further basic research is required.

Limits Set

Team productivity is assumed to be a product of its members' capabilities and effort. Such effort is a consequence of a variety of motivational phenomena ranging from conformity to intergroup competition. To keep the chapter manageable, we concentrate on team performance as a function of the level, interaction and utilization of the capabilities of its members, singly or collectively. Motivation, as such, is given somewhat less attention. We also focus less on various social-influence processes that make a difference in problem solving and decision making in groups. Attention is given to that part of productive effort that is a function of internal team resources available to the teams and the conditions imposed on the teams.

IMPORTANT VARIABLES

From the scheme for the study of small groups developed by McGrath and Altman (1966), we have chosen the following sets of variables and their intercorrelations:

State Variables

100 Properties of group members
110 Biographical Characteristics
130 Abilities of members

131 General abilities of members
132 Task-relevant proficiencies of members

150 Positions of members
151 Social position
152 Task or physical position

200 Properties of the group
220 Group capabilities
221 Group abilities
222 Group training and experience
230 Interpersonal relations in the group
240 General structural properties of the group
300 Conditions imposed on the group
320 Task and operating conditions
321 Stimulus properties of the task
322 Feedback and reinforcement conditions
323 Induced task conditions

Action Variables

400 Interaction process
410 Content
420 Patterns of interaction
430 Outcomes of interaction

600 Measures of performance
620 Task performance of members: global and specific
630 Task performance of groups: global and specific

IMPORTANT STATE VARIABLES

Following are brief descriptions of the classes of state variables in the list.

Biographical Characteristics of Members

Biographical characteristics of members include such variables as sex, age, education, marital status, race, religious affiliation, geographical region of birth and/or upbringing, weight, and height.

Obtained by self-report, these measures usually can be assumed to be accurate portrayals of a person's background. Puffing up of responses occurs mainly when respondents are applying for a job, *and* if they believe that their responses cannot or will not be independently verified.

Abilities of Members

Two classes of abilities are of consequence here—the general level of abilities and abilities relevant to the task.

General Abilities of Members.   As is used in psychological research, general abilities of members include such objective measures of ability as intelligence test scores and records of adademic and/or military-training course grades or class rankings. Also included are peer ratings of athletic ability, intelligence, expertness in music, and leadership potential (McGrath & Altman, 1966, p. 110). Various personality traits, such as sociability, task orientation, ascendancy, authoritarianism, and emotional stability can be subsumed here as general abilities likely to be of consequence to performance involving interpersonal competence.

Task-Relevant Abilities of Members.   The second set of abilities are relevant to the task itself. We conceive an aptitude to be illustrative of a general ability. An *aptitude* is an ability to deal with a wide range of related real-life problems. Thus, spatial visualization is the ability to put parts of objects together, to manipulate objects in space, to judge size, spaces, and shapes, and to visualize in three dimensions, two-dimensional displays. On the other hand, a task-relevant *proficiency* is an ability to deal with a more limited range of problems, such as blueprint reading (Bass & Barrett, 1981).

Ability can be tested or demonstrated. It can also be estimated. Self-estimates of general aptitude seem to be fraught with a high degree of error. Correlations as low as .05 were found when college students tried to assess their own tested aptitudes (De Nisi & Shaw, 1977). On the other hand, self-estimates of specific proficiencies may be much more accurate. For example, typing test scores correlated .62 or better with self-assessments of typing proficiency among 569 applicants for clerical jobs (Levine, Flory, & Ash, 1977).

The members' ability to contribute to the team effort as estimated by their colleagues is also important. This perception of the worth of the members to the team is of particular importance for understanding their influences on others on the team The members' self-estimates, or self-esteem, are equally important in understanding their attempts to be influential as team members (Bass, 1960a).

Positions in the Team

Social position refers to the status of members on the team—the value or importance of their positions regardless of who they are (Bass, 1960a). In hierarchical teams, it is their rank or level in the hierarchy. How such status is distributed is obviously an important group property. Thus, we can organize a flat organization with all team members reporting to one supervisor. Or we can arrange for an autonomous group (Herbst, 1954) with all members at the same level. Or a taller pyramidal organization of the team may be put in place, where team members are at several different levels in status.

Task or physical position in the group describes whether the member is *central* or *peripheral* to the operations of the team. One's position may be *independent* or *dependent* on the team as a whole or specifically on other members or equipment. If *dependent*, positions of members can differ in responsibilities. They may differ where they are in sequence in the total operation, and whether they are reciprocal in chains that are in series.

These interdependencies of members are properties of the group and are of particular significance to us.

Properties of the Group

These include group capabilities and interpersonal relations.

Group Capabilities. Group capabilities include the mean or summed abilities of the individual members and their variance in ability. In addition, transcending these summaries of members' biodata, ability, and position are group properties, such as group training and experience, reports of time of the team in combat or on the job, stage of the team in training, and amount of team training or practice. Also included are ratings by member, observer, and supervisor of group capabilities of performance potentiality, flexibility, team comparability, team work, and value to firm.

Group biodata summarized for several different teams can be used to compute the variance *between* teams in age, seniority, and the like. Variances of members *within* teams in ability and in position also are of consequence. Particularly significant are the *congruence* of the distributions within the team of biodata, ability, and position.

Interpersonal Relations. Interpersonal relations in the group include sociometric choices and ratings of absolute or differential liking of other group members, preference for them as social companions, roommates, confidants, and so on. It also contains ratings of liking for the group as a whole, willingness to work with this group again, morale, satisfaction with group, pride in group, pleasantness of group, and similar attitudes (McGrath & Altman, 1966, p. 133).

Structure. General structural properties of the group include variables, such as group size, communication nets, unity, and permanency of the group.

Conditions Imposed on the Group

Stimulus properties of the task include experimental variations in nature and difficulty of task or stimulus materials. These materials include differences of subject matter, familiarity of objects, clarity of stimulus, nature of stimulus, and relevancy of task information.

Feedback and reinforcement conditions include whether or not critiques are held.

Induced task conditions include the team's requirements to reach a decision as a team, the time limitations imposed, the opportunities for team mobility, and whether the team has to follow standard operating procedures. The team may be part of a larger organization that imposes order, structure or constraints, as well as goals, and a climate of trust or suspicion on the team.

IMPORTANT ACTION VARIABLES

So far we have looked only at *state variables*, descriptive of conditions, attributes for a particular period of time. Now we turn to action varibles, variables describing events, dynamics, and processes.

Interaction Processes

Interaction processes relevant to team effort include the *contents* of the interaction. These are the substantive elements in the interactions between the members, such as goal setting, information sharing, and consulting with others.

Patterns of interaction include number of communications (overall, by a particular member, or between a particular pair of members), length of time spent talking, time for making a decision, number of simultaneous conversations, and numbers of participating members.

Outcomes of interaction include measures of task versus interpersonal focus of activity, employee turnover, copying of other members' behavior, adaptability or flexibility of group, formation of cliques or coalitions, and communication effectiveness.

Measures of Performance

Measures of performance can be global or specific. They may be objective or subjective. They may be the product of a single member, the pooled product of all team members, or a group product that represents a joint effort of two or more members. Typically, the basic psychologist looks at speed of response and accuracy and the human costs in energy of response as the criteria of interest. Management looks at the quality and quantity of productivity, and the economic costs.

Efficiency of performance can be seen in terms of speed of response and accuracy of response as a function of economic and human costs (in energy, accidents, scrap rates, turnover, etc.). Or, it can be seen in terms of quality and quantity of production as a function of costs. Many other relevant criteria of performance are available, such as amount of services rendered, goods sold, time required for training, loads handled, and bonuses earned.

RELATIONS BETWEEN THE LISTED CLASSES OF VARIABLES AND TEAM PRODUCTIVITY

We now review to what extent correlations exist between each of the classes of variables and team productivity. This is the next step up in the elucidation of the relation of individual capabilities to team performance.

Member Biodata and Team Performance

It is obvious that a team's performance can be raised or lowered by selecting members for it according to their biographical characteristics. Adolescents and young adults will make better athletic teams. Male teams will be physically stronger than female teams. Office employees residing within the city will form more stable clerical teams with less turnover than office employees from outlying suburbs (Fleishman & Berringer, 1960). After studying 12 work groups in a research organization, Friedlander (1966) noted that group effectiveness was negatively correlated with the occupational and educational level of the group.

The success of biodata in forecasting individual performance as a supervisor, salesperson, and professional would suggest that Life History items (Owens & Henry, 1966), pooled for teams, would also be likely to relate to team performance. For example, a crew in which all members had held part-time jobs as adolescents might be expected to work harder as a team than a crew in which none of the members had held part-time jobs.

But the association of biodata with team performance depends on culture. In the U.S., it might not matter if the more important position on the team were assigned to a younger member, but in Japan, it might lead to considerable conflict and reduced efficiency. Traditionally, it was the usual thing in U.S. industry for men to supervise women. Increasingly, women are supervising men. Evidence is sparce concerning the effects on efficiency of such role-status reversals. (See Bass, B. M., 1981, Chapter 30).

Abilities of Members and Team Performance

Reviews by Gibb (1954), Hesling (1964), and Mann (1959) have shown that the abilities of its members generally are positively related to a team's productivity. Correlations between measures of task-relevant abilities and group productivity are typically small, however. Illustrating this relationship, in a longitudinal field experiment Terborg, Castore, and De Ninno (1976) organized 43 three- and four-person teams of undergraduates to complete six projects, covering the basic techniques in land surveying. Students rotated through each of three team positions. Following discussions with course instructors, scores on the quantitative section of the Scholastic Aptitude Test (SATQ) and cumulative Grade Point Average (GPA) were selected on a logical basis as indices of task-relevant abilities.

The level of these abilities on each team were associated to a small extent (3%) with team performance rated by the instructor.

Task Proficiency of Individual Members and Team Performance

Graham and Dillon (1974) showed that "supergroups" composed of individually productive brainstormers did far better than brainstorming groups composed of individuals who were low in the generation of ideas. Similarly, Weist, Porter, and Ghiselli (1961) found that 128 undergraduates who worked at four jigsaw puzzles alone, and then in pairs yielded multiple correlations as high as .85 when their speed of performance as individuals was pooled to forecast the performance of their teams. The faster member contributed somewhat more to team performance than the slower member. Comrey (1953) demonstrated comparable results for individuals and team dexterity on the Purdue Pegboard. Yet as Comrey noted:

> Less than half of the group performance variance could be predicted from a knowledge of the individual performances, even with the effect of errors removed. It is suggested that manifest differences between the "individual" and "group" tasks, interactions among individuals, and a constellation of abilities in the general area of cooperation may account for the variance not predicted by perfectly reliable individual performance scores [p. 210].

Position of Members and Team Performance

As already noted, the ability level of the individual members is of consequence to team performance. But the status of the members also make a difference.

Consistently observed differences in the character of 300 groups in 30 industrial plants made it possible to distinguish different types. Much of the difference was associated with the importance of the members' positions in the total operation. The importance of members' roles affected the observed performance of the groups in their cooperation and competition with other constituent parts of the organization. If all members of a team held unimportant jobs, they were likely to be apathetic as a team. They took little concerted action against management. Neither were they a bother to the union. If all members of a team held important assignments with the firm, the team exerted strong and continuous pressure on management (Ronan, 1963).

Properties of the Team, Per Se, and Team Performance

Apart from overall level of abilities and position, a variety of other attributes of groups have been found to associate with the performance of the groups. Such attributes include the size of the group, heterogeneity or homogeneity in composition of the membership in attitudes, ability or influence, the congruence of status, esteem, and ability of the membership.

Group Size.   The relative output of 239 work groups in two British automobile factories was generally greater in the smaller groups. The groups varied in size from 10 to 50 men each (Marriot, 1949).

Sears, Roebuck surveys concluded likewise that small units had higher morale and were more productive (Worthy, 1950). In all, McGrath and Altman's (1966) review of 250 studies concluded that smaller groups generally perform better in operational settings and on laboratory tasks than larger ones assigned to the same tasks, although members feel they are going to be less competent as a group compared to larger groups.

What size groups organizations establish cannot tell us much about what is optimum, but they can provide clues as to what at least is satisfactory as far as their managements are concerned. The average size of work groups seems to vary with the industry, but they are on the order of 15 to 25 at blue-collar levels, much larger than optimum for fostering effective interaction processes.

A survey of 910 American work groups suggested that the group can be even larger if the foreman has an assistant. But it is likely to be smaller than average when workers operate as a gang, or if they are highly skilled (Guion, 1953).

As one proceeds up the management hierarchy, the size of the team of a manager and his immediate subordinates decreases, until the typical higher level executive is expected to deal with only 3 to 7 immediate subordinates.

Group Composition.   Whether homogeneity or heterogeneity of membership is more conducive to team performance will depend on the variables on which the members are the same or different and the nature of the task. If the task with which a team must cope is a simple one, say, folding and packing equipment into containers, where a variety of resources are not needed to complete the task but merely several pairs of hands instead of one pair, then a homogeneous team is likely to be productive. For example, 64 pairs of subjects completed nine jigsaw puzzles, alone and in pairs. The speed of the pair was greater, the greater the speed of each partner working alone, and the less the difference in speed between the partners when they worked alone (Wiest, Porter, & Ghiselli, 1961).

Where a group must work in a chain, the total chain depends on the adequacy of each link. This is labeled as a *conjunctive* task by Steiner (1972). Again homogeneity is favored, for the group is no better than its poorest member. The chain fails if one link fails. The group can proceed no faster than its slowest member. One member can veto the decisions of the entire group. One member can block a group that cannot convert him (other), compromise with him, or expel the member from the group. In such chains, such as when subjects had to coordinate completely an interlocking system of levers to turn on lights of a group maze, the typical group did worse than its average member working alone (McCurdy & Lambert, 1952). Presumably the more varied the abilities of members in such circumstances, the more likely the group is to contain an extremely poor member who would drag the performance of the group down to his or her level (Bass & Ryterband, 1979). If the task is complex and the main reason for grouping is because no single individual has the varied resources to deal with such complexity, then heterogeneity may prove more productive.

Whereas people who are alike may do a better job facing assignments requiring routine, coordinated, or linked efforts, people who are different are likely to be more creative as a group (Hoffman, 1961; Maier & Hoffman, 1960). Trios of participants in a management training laboratory were composed of those with the same or different values and opinions. The most creative trios, ones that could generate additional alternatives, were those whose members differed initially in values but subsequently could reach a team decision. At least two-thirds of these trios came up with one or more additional solutions, whereas only half of those with members alike in values and opinions did so. Least creative were those trios whose members disagreed initially and could never reach a team decision. Only about a third of these could think up other alternatives when pressed to do so.

The importance of heterogeneity in resources to creativity is illustrated by comparing open groups where members change from time to time, with closed groups where members remain the same. Teams were asked to compose captions for a cartoon. The captions were evaluated for fluency and originality. Where a team added, removed, or replaced members during its efforts, fluency and originality were higher than when it remained the same in membership (Ziller, Behrringer, & Goodchilds, 1962).

A key feature of much human-relations training and organizational development is power equalization—the power of the positions of all team members should be equalized. This is based on the presumed utility of self-management and of participation in decisions affecting oneself. Nevertheless, with 224 management-level units, Bass, Farrow, and Valenzi (1979) have found positive correlations of .24 between the size of the power difference between leader and subordinates, according to the subordinates' and the leader's ratings of the effectiveness of the work group. A parallel correlation of .20 was found between the leader's estimates of the power differences in the group and the subordinates' evaluations of the group's effectiveness. Information differences among team members are also important, but in the opposite direction. Large differences in amount of information available to the team leader and the rest of the team seem to result in less effective operations. For the 224 work groups, negative correlations of −.14 and −.22 were obtained.

Congruence of Status, Esteem, and/or Ability. Haythorn (1968) noted that air crew effectiveness was lower if the formal organization (status hierarchy) and the informal organization (esteem hierarchy) were incongruent. Similarly, Slusher, Van Dyke and Rose (1972) showed that among 9 leaders of 30 engineers, group productivity suffered when the most technically competent tended to reject the role of manager. Conversely, Rock and Hay (1953) found that when the committee leader is esteemed according to sociometric assessment, the committee is more effective. Palmer and Myers (1955) reported a correlation of .38 between the effectiveness with which 40 antiaircraft radar crews maintained their equipment and their level of esteem for their key noncommissioned officer. Bass, Flint, and Pryer (1957) found a correlation of .25 between the degree to which status was correlated with esteem in a group and the subsequent effectiveness of the group in reaching the correct ranking of the familiarity of words. Finally, Shaw and Harkey (1976) demonstrated that group effectiveness was enhanced if leader roles in problem solving groups were assigned to be congruent with the extent individual members were socially bold and likely to take the initiative, according to their scores on a scale of Individual Prominence.

Conditions Imposed on the Team and Team Performance

Organizational formalization, task demands, and required team structure have been found to relate to team productivity.

Organizational Formalization. Teams can be handed plans of action, standard operating procedures, and decision rules, which if obeyed to the letter will produce the requisite coordination between teams. Programming can be effective to the extent that unit activities are simple and routine. This formalization of relationships can be seen in the extent to which jobs are codified and tolerances established for what deviation will be permitted. According to Pugh, Hickson, Minings and Turner (1968), formalization involves: "statements of procedures, rules, roles, and operation of procedures which deal with decision seeking (applications for capital, employment, and so on), conveying of decisions and instructions (plans, minutes, requisitions, and so on), and conveying of information including feedback." Formalization includes: (1) concretely defined positions; (2) written job descriptions; (3) a clearly defined hierarchy of authority; (4) a written description of the hierarchy; (5) emphasis on written communications; (6) emphasis on following established channels of clearly stated penalties for violating rules; (7) a written code of penalties for violations; (8) formalized orientation programs for new members; and (9) formalized in-service training programs for new members (Hall, Haas, & Johnson, 1967).

Bass, Farrow, and Valenzi (1979) correlated the ratings of effectiveness of 224 management teams by their leaders' and subordinates' ratings of imposed conditions. They also correlated subordinates' ratings of effectiveness with their

TABLE 6.1
Correlations Between Rated Effectiveness and Conditions Imposed
on 224 Work Groups
(Data from Bass, Farrow & Valenzi, 1979)

| | *Correlations of*
Ratings of Group Effectiveness | |
	By Superior *With Subordinates* *Ratings of Conditions* *Imposed on Group*	*By Subordinates* *With Superior's* *Ratings of Conditions* *Imposed on Group*
Condition		
Organizational		
Constraints	−.17	.00
Clarity of goals	.23	.41
Warmth and trust	.25	.39
Order	.27	.28
Task		
Clear objectives	.29	.37
Routine	.07	.11
Discretionary opportunities	−.14	.00
Complexity	.00	−.01
Managerial activity	−.01	−.07
Transforms		
Structure	−.24	−.25
Interdependence	.12	.16

Note: Correlations in italics are significant at $p < .01$ or $p < .001$.

superior's ratings of imposed conditions. The correlations, as such, are free from the halo that would be due to correlating the ratings of the same raters for both effectiveness and conditions. (The tasks of these teams were unlikely to be routine.)

Table 6.1 shows the results obtained. It can be seen that the clarity of the goals of the larger organization of which the team is a part, its climate of warmth and trust, and its orderliness all correlate positively with judged effectiveness. On the other hand, how much organizational structuring is imposed by the organization is not associated with the effectiveness of these management teams dealing with nonroutine work.

Task Demands.   Steiner (1972) conceived of three types of task demands. For additive tasks, the success of the group depends on the summation of individual products. Team performance will depend on the average competence of the individuals composing the group. A *conjunctive* task is one that requires each member to perform the task so that the team mission can be accomplished. Performance here cannot be any better than that of the least competent member. A *disjunctive* task is one that requires a team choice among alternatives. Performance is expected to depend on the most competent person. Some experimental support has been obtained for Steiner's propositions.

McGrath & Altman's (1966) review reported mixed results. For instance, unambiguous tasks generally were more effectively handled by teams. Familiar tasks were handled better than unfamiliar ones. The presence or absence of feedback critiques didn't make a consistent difference to effective team performance. Personal feedback and praise helped, but frequency of explanations and illustrations did not.

Shiflett (1976) failed to find that difficult tasks enhanced the team effect on what the most competent member could contribute to the team, although several other experiments had shown this assembly effect. *Dividing the labor* was found to be more efficient (production for time spent) in the performance on puzzles and analogies of 72 U.S. Army enlisted men, but shared labor produced the greatest total performance.

A More Complex Model Needed

So we see both theories and research relating a host of variables to team productivity in varying degrees. Nevertheless, logically, ignoring motivation, the only possible causal effects on team productivity are the resources and capabilities of the individual members as modified with how they interact with each other. What we are saying is that we need to show how such interaction processes actually enhance or inhibit how the individual member resources are effectively brought to bear to yield team productivity above and beyond what each could do alone.

Actually, many of the available empirical studies provide some insight into how interaction processes modify team productivity, but one needs to carefully read the "discussion and implications" sections where the investigators speculate on why they obtained the results they did.

For example, Terborg, Castore, and DeNinno (1975), in looking at how the tested abilities of their surveying teams of three students each affected the team performance, commented:

> successful performance on the (team) task was largely determined by the ability of the person working the transit. Since all group members rotated through this position, it is clear that homogeneously high ability groups would perform better than homogeneously low ability groups. However, if students were allowed to permanently place the most capable group member behind the transit, then it would no longer be necessary for groups to be composed of all high ability members. In this

case, the ability of one group member could compensate for the lack of abilities of other group members. Therefore, it would appear that the demands and characteristics of the task be considered so as to better specify the technical skill mix required for optimal group performance [pp. 11-12].

Again after showing that whether or not member ability contributed to group productivity depended on the task organization required, O'Brien and Owens (1969) declared:

> In tasks where there is high degree of collaboration (or integrated effort), it appears that members are unable to contribute significantly because the organization involves a great deal of interaction and prevents the group from organizing the best contributions in a systematic fashion... collaborative organizations generated more comments and more disagreements than organizations requiring only coordination... A high level of interaction was associated with significantly lower productivity (O'Brien & Ilgen, 1968). Organizations involving some degree of coordination had... less interaction (but higher productivity) than collaborative organizations.
>
> In a task where there is low collaboration but high coordination, each member must make some contribution to the formation of the group product. Under these conditions, it is not possible for a single person to make the only major contribution, but it is possible for the group to organize systematically the contributions of the group members. For a task of this kind, the principle—a chain is only as strong as its weakest link—seems appropriate. Poor work by a relatively dull person may severely limit the performance of brighter members. Only when all members have high ability for their particular task is it possible for group performance to reach a maximal level (pp. 529-530].

A MORE COMPLEX MODEL

A team will be more effective if its individual members are capable, skillful, and knowledgeable about what needs to be done. In addition, the success of the group effort also will depend on how much and how well they interact with each other. A disaster will ensue if the crane follower or hoistman helper fails to signal the hoist operator or, in turn, if he misreads one of their signals. The team's speed and accuracy will be high when signals are on time, are clear and complete, and are accepted or trusted as reliable.

Consider what it means to be an effective team. A total of 250 respondents were each asked to use a checklist to describe an efficient and inefficient work group to which they had belonged. They described clerical, sales, manufacturing, business, maintenance, and military work groups. Among the five clusters of statements that best discriminated the effective from the ineffective work groups, one dealt with available resources, three dealt with interaction processes:

Available Resources

The members have the equipment, tools, and skills necessary to attain the group's goals. The group members are taught various parts of their jobs by experts. The group is not shorthanded. . . .

Interaction Processes

The members function as a unit. The group works as a team. The members do not disturb each other. . . .

The members are oriented toward a single goal. They work for common purposes. . . .

Members ask and receive suggestions, opinions, and information from each other. If a member is uncertain about something, he stops working and finds out. The members talk to each other frequently . . . (Bass, 1954a).

The fifth cluster dealt with motivation.

The members participate fully in group effort. They work hard when there is something to do. Members do not loaf if they get the opportunity . . . (Bass, 1954a).

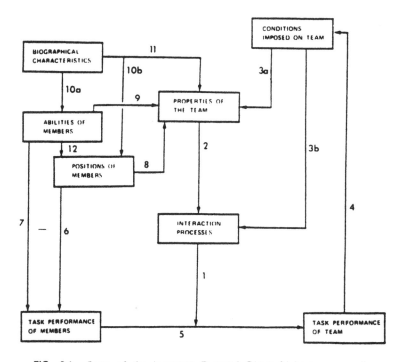

FIG. 6.1. Some of the important Expected Direct Linkages among the McGrath-Altman Classes of Variables Selected for Study.

Thus the effective work group is one in which the individual members are highly interdependent, coordinated, and cooperative in their efforts. They are capable and highly motivated as individuals, and information flows freely between them.

In Fig. 6.1, we sum up our purposes by noting that team performance logically should depend on the performance of its individual members. Yet, this dependence is modified by the interaction processes between the members, which in turn are affected by the conditions imposed on the team and various properties of the team, as a team. In turn these properties and conditions can be linked to attributes of individual team members.

We now note and briefly discuss each of the expected linkages shown in Fig. 6.1. To keep the model manageable, we ignore possible links not shown that are of secondary importance for our purposes here. For instance, not shown is the link of ability to biographical characteristics; yet generally, it is the more able member who advances further in the occupational hierarchy and in education. The causal links of Fig. 6.1 are as follows:

Link 1. Interaction processes are expected to modify how the task performance of individual members contribute to the task performance of the team. For example, a team of highly capable individual members can fail to accomplish its task, because one member monopolizes the discussion necessary to pool the available knowledge of all the members.

Link 2. Interaction processes depend on properties of the group. If members are homogeneous in status and power, they may combine to silence the monopolizer to give other members a chance to participate.

Link 3a. Conditions imposed on the group determine its properties. A policy of higher authority may specify everyone's role in the group, so that all are equal in importance and in the sources of information required to accomplish the team task. The property of homogeneity is a consequence of a condition imposed on the group.

Link 3b. Conditions imposed can also directly affect interaction processes. For instance, imposition of a more difficult task may generate more consultation among members than imposition of an easy task.

Link 4. Task performance of the team feeds back to affect conditions imposed on the group. Team failure, as a consequence of an inability of all members to contribute their unique information about how to accomplish the team's mission, can lead to a structural imposition on the team that members must take turns in presenting their respective viewpoints. The team now has among its properties, a rule requiring equal time for each member.

Link 5. As we have already noted, as much as half the variance in team performance can be attributed to the task performance of members, as individuals.

Link 6. Task performance of individuals may be due to the position to which they are assigned. A member assigned the central position in a communication network acquires more information relevant to the team task than do members assigned to peripheral positions.

Link 7. Individual differences in task performance of team members are dependent on their individual differences in general and specific abilities. (Aptitude and proficiency tests are valid.)

Link 8. The positions assigned members collectively become a property of the team. For example, the positions can differ in importance to the team effort. Therefore, the team property will feature a status hierarchy.

Link 9. The abilities of members of a team when summarized by measures of central tendency or dispersion are team properties.

Link 10a. Biographical characteristics of members are associated with their abilities. For example, younger workers may learn faster. Rapid learning may be important in dealing with the task.

Link 10b. Biographical characteristics include data about the previous history of the individual members and as such will affect what a member can do and the position in which he is placed.

Link 11. Biographical characteristics of members pooled for the team are a team property.

Link 12. More capable members may be assigned to more important positions, less capable members to less important positions.

Any appreciation of what team effort does to individual performance has to consider more than merely mechanical interaction effects. Team membership transforms the individual members. The cues and reinforcements of their behavior are likely to stem from each other as well as the task.

The character, composition, and history of a team strongly affects the performance of its members. Although individuals may be somewhat ambivalent and indirect by themselves, the actions of the team to which they belong are typically more direct, less ambivalent, less hesitant, and less confused (Weick, 1969). Individuals behaving as a part of a team demonstrate different kinds of behavior than they would if they were alone, even if they were assigned the same task as individuals. The nature of these differences between individuals working alone and on a team can be traced to conditions imposed on the team, properties of the team, and the resulting interaction processes within the team (Bass & Ryterband, 1979).

We begin by looking at Link 1, interaction processes as the modifier of the contribution of the individual member to the team performance.

INTERACTION PROCESSES AS MODIFIERS

One can readily describe ways in which faulty interaction processes reduces team effectiveness below what could have been predicted from the ability level of the average team member. For instance, trouble arises in teams when members are unclear about what others expect of them. Members become defensive if they are unable to forecast what other members are likely to do. Thus, when accomplices of an experimenter remained silent, the groups in which they are supposedly members remained more dissatisfied, defensive, and less productive. When these silent accomplices clarified the reasons for their silence, and the rules under which they operate became predictable and understandable, their groups improved in effectiveness and satisfaction (Gibb, 1954).

Conversely, the modest talent available to a group can be marshalled effectively to complete challenging team assignments through the development and maintenance of efficient interaction processes.

Nevertheless, in a sample of 250 small group studies, McGrath and Altman reported no relation in four operational investigations between *patterns* of interraction and team task performance. However, in 14 of 25 studies, team performance was moderately related to the *outcomes* of interaction processes. For example, team performance in training and in operations tended to improve with team discussions about effective coordination and utilization of its resources.

The McGrath–Altman sampling was for studies completed before 1960. Since then, additional ones can be cited of consequence and consistant with the obtained moderate relations. Results with 224 management teams by Bass, Farrow, and Valenzi (1979) strongly suggest that harmony in interaction is conductive to team effectiveness.

In a series of studies in the 1950s, Bass and colleagues (Bass, Gaier, Flint, & Farese, 1957) engaged student teams in what would now be called *disjunctive* tasks (Steiner, 1972). Students first alone ranked the order of the size of cities. Or, they first alone ranked sets of words like ROAD-TARPULIN-CAMISOLE-FERRULE-KETTLE in order of familiarity to them. Then they reached a group decision about the ranking. The rank difference correlation between the true task order and individual rankings indexes each individual's proficiency. The correlation of the true and group rankings indexed the group's task performance. *Almost invariably,* (for example, on 199 problems out of 200), the group decision was more accurate than would have been forecast from the average member rankings. But beyond this, Pennington, Haravey & Bass (1957) showed that the group decision was even more accurate if a group discussion preceded it. The group decision's accuracy was enhanced further over that of the average individual, if all member's individual rankings were made public. Just knowing what other members had done was helpful. In addition, further improvement was obtained, if discussion was permitted prior to the group decisions.

This "assembly bonus effect" (Collins & Guetzkow, 1964) is an important element in group dynamics training. A central theme involves "building on each other's ideas."

Yet, such interaction can be detrimental to team performance. Steiner (1972), in fact, concentrated on the subtractive outcome when individuals must interact. He looked for "faulty group processes." Thus, the degree of crew work in 44 departments of an automobile plant employing 7000 employees correlated .33 with frequency of accidents. More required interaction with others, coordination and carrying responsibility in departments resulted in considerably higher accident rates (Keenan, Kerr, & Sherman, 1951).

Other workers evidently were a distraction contributing to inattention and accidents. On additive tasks such as brainstorming, pooling the production of ideas of individuals working alone yields more in total quality and quantity than if those same individuals brainstormed in groups. The interaction is a negative modifier for such *additive* tasks.

Based on experiments with 80 students, Shaw and Ashton (1976) suggest that on disjunctive tasks, to obtain the assembly bonus effect one must be dealing with difficult tasks. They state:

> easy tasks will be completed relatively quickly by the most competent group member, who will have relatively less difficulty getting the solution accepted by other group members. Consequently, there is less need or opportunity for the information and ideas of some group members to stimulate other group members. On the other hand, when the task is difficult, the group will spend more time attempting to complete the task and interpersonal stimulation should be greater [p. 471].

Initial ability also involves difference on disjunctive tasks on whether an assembly effect will occur (Laughlin & Bitz, 1975). Further elucidation about interaction processes as modifiers of the individual-to-team proficiency comes, as we explore how the next links influence interaction processes. We show how imposed conditions and group properties affect interaction processes to the enhancement or detriment of team performance.

Suggestions for Research: Interaction Process as Modifiers

As noted earlier, there is little solid information on what interaction processes are helpful or detrimental to increasing or decreasing individual members' contributions to team productivity. Most of what is available is ex post facto speculation about why some experimental treatment did or did not work. We need to consider, among choices available for study of interaction processes, which conceptual frameworks (Bales, 1950) and which methods of observation and measurement provide the greatest understanding of this link between interaction processes and productivity.

One kind of specific investigation that is needed concerns what particular content, patterns, and outcome of interaction processes statistically interact with, or modify, individual member task performance (and position and individual abilities that lie behind the performance). For example, we might first obtain individual performance of subjects. Then, the subjects could freely, as teams, coordinate efforts to develop the team scores. The content, patterns, and outcomes of their interactions before and during the team effort would be examined partialing out the effects of their initial individual scores.

Here are some hypotheses about what we might find:

1. As for content of interaction processes, the greater the total amount of consultation, two-way communications and questioning during discussion prior to team performance, the greater the effect on team performance above and beyond expected from individual member scores.

2. As for patterns of interaction, the observed verbal conflict before the team effort, the less the team is effective.

3. As for outcomes of interaction, the more modeling of one member's behavior by another, if the model was above average in individual task performance, the greater than expected would be the team's task performance.

Answers to many practical questions remain unresolved. For a given task, if A's performance is X, and B's performance is Y, when they work alone without interaction, how much can we raise X and Y, if:

1. A works side-by-side with B; each provides only visual stimulation (or interferences) not particularly related to the task.

2. A works side-by-side with B; there is social, nonverbal or verbal interstimulation, not particularly relevant to the task.

3. A works with B. There is stimulation (or interference) or positive or negative transfer of knowledge between A and B.

Will results be task specific, or can they be generalized? What properties of A and B as a team are relevant? What conditions imposed on the Team AB are relevant?

How much can we train A and B to be good team members above and beyond training them in their task proficiencies?

Team-building success (Bass & Barrett, 1981) suggests A and B be trained as teams rather than first trained as individuals, then as team members. Yet this may not be as efficient as first training A and B in their respective tasks, then training them as a team.

2. PROPERTIES OF THE TEAM ⟶ INTERACTION PROCESSES

Interaction processes are obviously strongly affected by properties of the group. A cocktail party that begins with pairs of spouses often quickly breaks into two subgroups: one male; the other female. Who talks to whom, how long and how often is strongly associated with the existence or absence of status differentials in a group. The author has been in an off-site training group where "spontaneously" all first-line foremen chose to sit on one side of a long table, whereas all higher level supervisors sat across from them on the other side of the table. Black students have resegregated themselves on college campuses.

Illustrating how team properties influence the team's interaction processes, Bowers (1969) showed that the assigned leader as the source of influence will loom larger for teams composed of some persons rather than others. His analysis of 1700 work groups from 22 organizations of all types and sizes indicated that groups made up of longer service, older, and less educated members attached greater importance to the supervisor and his direct influence on their behavior. This condition was especially true in administrative, staff, production, and marketing groups. In better educated, shorter service, younger groups, especially those largely female in composition (for example, clerical and service groups), somewhat less importance was given to the role of the supervisor per se and greater importance to the behavior of peer members in the group. Again, Goldman (1971) showed that groups homogeneous in ability but differing from each other in mean ability level (little variance within groups, much variance between groups) underwent their own unique patterns of improving themselves.

Among the many properties of the groups singled out for investigation of their effects on interaction processes have been group size, group composition, and congruence in the group of status, esteem, and ability.

Group Size

After so much mixed empirical results (Goldman, 1971) there should be a moratorium on further atheoretical studies of team size and team productivity, for the evidence suggests the effects of size on productivity will depend on other factors. Nevertheless, as a property of a group, size has logical implications (Steiner, 1966). Additional members above one may add resources or be completely redundant. At the same time, they complicate the amount of possible simple interactions in the team. Only one interaction is possible in a 2-person team; 3 in a 3-person team, 6 in a 4-person team and 10 in a 5-person team. Moreover, cliques with more complex interactions can form in the 3-, 4-, 5-person or larger team.

Cliques occur in larger teams because of communication barriers more likely in such groups. In addition, control, affection, and trust are easier to maintain in a smaller subgroup than in the larger total group. Moreover, on any issue where differences of opinion are involved, like-minded members holding a minority opinion will coalesce into a clique, and the clique can become isolated, competitive, even conflicting as time passes (Bass & Ryterband, 1979).

As the team is enlarged to increase its total resources, the frequency of interaction between any two members decreases, for, in the larger group, more competition is possible in who will send and who will receive. If only one person can "send" signals in a 10-person team at any one time, then the chance to send at that moment is denied to nine-tenths of the team. In a 2-person team, only half the team must wait. In the same way, if all 10 can signal at once, then there is 100 times the interference among signals in the 10-person team as among the 2-person team.

We need to know more about how the group property of size affects the group's interaction processes before trying to assess the more remote connection between size and effectiveness. Yet, there is some survey and experimental evidence available about how size affects interaction processes. In the previously cited survey by Marriot (1949), foremen and workers favored the smaller of the work groups, because better relations could be obtained among members of the smaller groups. They could see each other and what each was contributing to the group effort.

Again, Scott *et al* (1956) showed that it was in the smaller among 228 work groups varing in size from 5 to 50 that men were likely to be more attached to the group and committed to its goals. Members feel less sense of belonging to larger discussion groups (Miller, 1950). In addition, role expectations are less clear in larger groups. This results in frustrations for the members of larger groups and a tendency to form cliques (McDavid & Harari, 1966). Members of larger groups are less expressive and helpful and are more likely to agree with others publicly, even if they do not privately accept the judgments they publicly accept (Gerard, Wilhelmy, & Conolley, 1968).

The severe disrupting effects of size on the interaction processes of members was shown by Gibb (1954), when 48 groups varying in size up to 96 were presented with a public relations problem. The first 30 minutes was spent listing suggested solutions and the next 30 minutes evaluating them. As can be seen in Fig. 6.2, in the larger groups there was a larger percentage of team members who reported that they had ideas they did not express, and a larger percentage of members who never talked directly. Members who failed to interact felt more threatened in the larger groups. According to Gibb (1954), they stated that more often they did not express themselves for fear that: "I might be misinterpreted by the group"; "someone else said it before I had thought of it clearly enough to express it in words before the group"; "it is easier to let someone else express his ideas"; or, "I thought my idea might sound silly."

A number of other indications suggest that members have fewer difficulties interacting with each other in smaller groups. More ideas per member are expressed, and more mutual influence occurs in smaller groups. Also smaller groups see less need for guidance from higher authority. Less efforts to maintain coordination of member efforts are required. There is less need to clarify rules and standards (McGrath, 1962).

Yet, smallness is no panacea for team effort. Rather, if the team is too small, it lacks the resources to do the job adequately. If the team is too large, interaction difficulties interfere with performance.

But although some tasks may call for larger groups, possibilities for redesign-

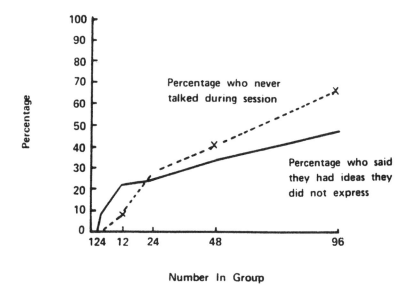

FIG. 6.2. Percentages of Members Who Are Unable to Express Their Ideas Because of the Size of the Group. (Data from Gibb. 1964)

ing them to adapt to smaller groups seems worth the effort, because smaller groups on balance yield interaction processes likely to positively rather than negatively modify team performance. (Bass & Ryterband, 1979).

If smaller units yield interaction processes more conducive to team productivity, what reinforces policies to maintain large shop-floor work units and to establish and maintain groups considerably larger than optimum? First, it is probable that management pays more attention to what appears to be the engineering and technical aspects of designing an organization. It considers what resources must be brought to bear and the minimum amount of administrative superstructure required. Smaller worker units require more units. More units require more supervisors and more interunit coordination. Less attention is paid to what is likely to happen to interaction processes.

We can speculate that the total organizational operations are likely to be more efficient and satisfying, if work groups generally are made smaller than now is current practice. The technological imperatives, which led to the seemingly efficient assembly line of say 30 workers responsible for a particular section along one of the lines, caused management to ignore the psychological imperatives; that is, the same worker will be far more effective as a member of a 5-person than a 30-person work group. Smaller groups are likely to learn tasks faster (Cattell, 1953) and to perform them faster (Lichtenberg & Deutsch, 1954).

Although with such smaller teams, more attention must be paid to intergroup cooperation and coordination.

Group Composition

Haythorn (1968) has enumerated why the composition of the membership is important above and beyond the pool of talent it represents.

1. The inability to "get along" frequently results in failure of the team or ineffectiveness in achieving the team's goals. Members of staff conferences often cite conference failure to "personality clashes." Task-oriented members tend to fight in group settings, interaction-oriented members tend to play, and self-oriented members tend to introspect on why they were placed on the team (Bass, 1967). Authoritarian-submissive members create authoritarian-submissive team climates (Haythorn, 1968). In a variety of ways associated with the personality, attitudes, values, and training, individual members will serve as "good" group members or "poor" group members.

2. Composition determines the team's adequacy of communications. Differences of members in socioeconomic level, educational level, verbal fluency, general intelligence, not to mention native language (all group properties) will affect communications among the members. Individuals with different professional backgrounds use words differently, with different meanings and objectives.

3. Diverse rather than shared values, goals, and norms will make for systematic differences in interaction processes. Deviant members in conflict with the group majority are likely to appear when members differ in social interests, hobbies, and politics. They will be rejected if they cannot be converted.

4. Interaction processes will reflect the extent that the individual members can complement each others' skills, because labor is divided and the members can play the requisite roles.

5. In staffing a team, heterogeneity or homogeneity of skills and abilities may be sought. A social action team may represent similar or diverse interest groups from business, church, and political establishments. Accumulated evidence suggests heterogeneous teams will experience more conflict at first in their interaction processes, but in the long run, such heterogeneity may be necessary to reach creative problem solutions. Yet, a group may also be too diverse in terms of the expertise various members have. If such task-related expertise is seen to vary, it can inhibit those who feel more knowledgeable and those who feel less so (Collaros & Anderson, 1969).

Effects of Homogeneity.   Interaction processes are better in teams of persons who are alike in interests and abilities. Members can communicate more easily with each other. There will be less conflict, fewer differences in opinions, standards, and ways of doing things (Bass, 1965, Hoffman, 1959).

Members who are like-minded can influence each other more easily. They are mutually attracted. (I like me. I like you, if you are similar to me.) (Lott & Lott, 1965).

We tend to like those who hold similar opinions to us and to reject those whom we think are unlike us. Therefore, members who have like opinions or who think they are alike will be more satisfied with the group as well as with each other, than members who see differences between themselves and others in the group. Such concordance of attitudes will result in less conflict and smoother interaction processes (Byrne, 1971).

For instance, 11 teams of managers in a training laboratory were composed of participants who beforehand agreed that a particular one of five alternatives should be employed to handle ethical problems in education and politics. Another 13 teams were composed so that each participant on a team favored a different alternative. Interaction difficulties and dissatisfaction were obviously much greater in those teams that began with decided differences of opinion (Bass, 1965).

It follows that if task accomplishment depends on smooth, cooperative, conflict-free, coordinated efforts among the members, all of whom have been highly trained to interact routinely and automatically, then homogeneous membership, a membership where members are alike, should prove more productive. Thus, teams were clustered to work on assembly problems on the basis of whether or not they were compatible; that is, subjects were grouped according to whether they agreed on how much power, status, and affection should be used to maintain satisfactory interpersonal relations. The compatible teams were more productive than incompatible teams on the assembly tasks that required a high degree of cooperation under pressure (Schutz, 1955).

Compatibility acts like homogeneity in its effects on interaction processes. If one partner of a dyad wants to control and the other partner needs to be controlled, cooperation is more easy between them. Compared to incompatible teams of managers, Reddy and Byrnes (1972) found groups of compatible managers on the FIRO-B dimensions of control and affection able to complete more rapidly a LEGO block task requiring cooperative efforts. But compatibility was less important if the tasks did not require as much cooperation among the members of a team (Lodahl & Porter, 1961, Schutz, 1958).

Effects of Heterogeneity.   Where speedy, smooth interactions are less important than a creative solution of a complex problem, a heterogeneous group is more desirable than a homogeneous one (Hoffman, 1961). The very speed with which a homogeneous group can reach decisions can be a handicap to creativity. If members already have reached the same opinion even before they have discussed an issue, they are less likely to reach a good decision as a group, than if they are in disagreement when they begin deliberations (Marston, 1924). Like odd groups compared to even, groups homogeneous in opinion may close debate too quickly with a decisive vote (Bass & Ryterband, 1979). Heterogeneous groups seem less likely to unquestioningly accept wrong responses (Goldman, Dietz, & McGlynn, 1968; Hoffman & Maier, 1961).

Effects of Familiarity.   A property of the group, how familiar members are with each other, fosters the ease with which people can work together. Such familiarity is due to two independent factors: length of acquaintanceship and amount of daily or weekly contact (Bass, Klauss, & DeMarco, 1977).

Familiar members are more likely to be able to communicate fluently, accurately, and rapidly with each other (Newcomb, 1961). Such familiarity in turn, leads to more frequent interactions (Bass, 1960a; Bass, Klauss, & DeMarco, 1977); for if we are intimate, familiar, or experienced with other persons, we feel more comfortable about initiating and maintaining interaction with them. This comfort is most likely to occur in those circumstances where mutually held important attitudes or values become known to those interacting. Homogeneity promotes interaction; interaction promotes familiarity. Members' similarities bind them together. Thus, students living together in dorms were more likely to form attachements to others who were similar to them in attitudes that they considered important (Newcomb, 1961). And because they interact more readily, friends can work together faster than strangers. Thus, pairs of close friends were able to solve codes, puzzles, and arithmetic problems more quickly than pairs of strangers (Husband, 1940).

Effects of Mutual Esteem.   This group property, based on how much team members value each other, is seen in cohesive teams. Such teams are more likely to perform well, if the members subscribe to the goal of accomplishing their team task, but they can just as readily sabotage such efforts, if they collectively reject the task objective (Seashore, 1954).

Members who esteem each other are more attracted to each other. If given the opportunity, they will choose each other as work partners. Such mutually chosen work partners will interact more effectively. This was determined in a field experiment by Van Zelst (1952) where costs of labor and materials to construct rows of housing units were reduced significantly when carpenters and bricklayers were allowed to choose their work partners.

The workers were union men on fixed wages with at least 7 years' experience, who had been working on a current housing development for an average of 5 months. During this period, they had considerable opportunity to learn much about each other on different job assignments and at lunch. Workers were asked to nominate the first, second, and third persons with whom they would most like to work. All but eight were paired or grouped with their first, second, or third choices who, in turn, had chosen them as well. Mutual esteem of the pairs were thus close to maximum. Compared to earlier performance measures, sociometrically assembled crews took less time to complete a unit, reducing labor costs. They wasted less material, reducing material costs. Efficiency continued to improve for quite a while before leveling off on a higher continuing level. At no time did the mutually chosen crews ever slip back to operating at the previous costs. There was about a 5% overall savings in total production costs, and the turnover index dropped from 3.11 per production period to .27 per period.

The impact of mutual esteem on interaction processes is seen in the following worker comment about the sociometrical arrangements: "Seems as though everything flows a lot smoother. It makes you feel more comfortable working—and I don't waste any time bickering about who's going to do what and how. We just seem to go ahead and do it. The work is a lot more interesting when you've got your buddy working with you. You certainly like it a lot better anyway [p. 184]."

Congruence or Incongruence of Status, Esteem, and Abilities

Although status and esteem tend to correlate positively in the usual group, discrepancies do arise and produce conflict in the team's interaction processes. This is readily explainable.

The tendency to lead is greater among those of higher status as well as those of higher esteem. Suppose that the person of higher esteem in a group is not the same as the member with highest status. The occurrence of two or more individuals with equal leadership potential is likely to promote conflict in interaction. For instance, the higher status of the foreman of a department permits him to serve as a leader. But if the most-esteemed member is someone other than the foreman, this other member of the department also has potential to influence the team. As long as the foreman and the most esteemed department member agree on the solutions to the group's problems, no conflict occurs. But if disagreement arises between those two members, both with power to influence the department, conflict is likely. Thus, if the correlation between the esteem and status of members in a group is high, little conflict is likely in the interaction processes. But if the correlation is low, that is, if different members in the group have potential to be the most influential, conflict results if they do not share the same approaches to the group's problems. We can express the same conclusions in terms of formal and informal organization. Formal organizations provide occupants of its positions with varying status. Yet much of the interaction between persons may occur regardless of position, because of esteem. Thus, the divergence of the informal from formal organization is another way of conceiving status-esteem congruence (Bass, 1960a). Moreno (1953) noted that formal groupings are a chronic source of conflict if they are superimposed by some authority upon informal, spontaneous groupings.

Naval and Air Force surveys by Stogdill and Koehler (1952) revealed the effect. Stouffer, Suchman, DeVinney, Starr and Williams (1949) observed that discussions went smoother when the most esteemed were given higher status by being placed in the position of discussion leader. A naval air squadron of high morale was contrasted by Jenkins (1948) with one of low morale. (Elements of high morale included effective and satisfying interaction processes; elements of low morale included conflict, diversion, and dissatisfaction with interaction.) In the high-morale group, the squadron commander and executive officer, men of high status, were also esteemed; that is, they were often nominated as individuals with whom others would want to fly. But, in the low-morale squadron, esteem as measured by these nominations were unrelated to status, based on positions as commander or executive officer.

The impact on interaction of an elected, hence, more esteemed supervisor was contrasted with the impact of a leader with lower esteem who usurped the status of leader. Under the usurper's occupancy of the leadership position, there was greater private rejection of his acts compared with those of the legitimately elected supervisor and more discrepancy between public and private compliance of the membership (Institute for Social Research, 1954).

Finally, Shaw and Harkey (1976) set up congruent and incongruent groups. In the congruent groups, and status of leader was assigned to the member high in self-reported initiative and social boldness. In the incongruent group, such a person was assigned the status of a follower. As expected, congruent groups were more effective in accomplishing the group task. The one effect on interaction processes observed was the tendency of the leaders of incongruent groups to interrupt discussions more frequently than leaders of congruent groups. According to Shaw and Harkey (1976):

> This finding probably reflects interpersonal tension resulting from the difficulty of coordinating member actions in the noncongruent groups. When the occupants of the various positions in the group behave in accord with expectations, as in the congruent groups, group members may be expected to be more relaxed (at least, relatively so), and the followers may not feel as restrained from interrupting the leader to make a point, to facilitate task completion, etc. At the same time, the leader may not feel a need to impose his/her will upon the group. On the other hand, when the occupant of the leadership position does not typically enact leadership behaviors, as in the noncongruent condition, some tension is likely to be aroused; the leader may feel a need to exert some influence upon the group (hence tending to interrupt others), whereas the followers may not feel free to interrupt the leader [p. 417].

Suggestions for Research:
Team Properties ⟶ Interaction Processes

A variety of applied and basic research needs are apparent, dealing with how group properties affect interaction processes. A handbook detailing optimum size teams for given tasks suitably conceptualized and measured seems technically feasible. Some tasks are best done by eliminating any required interaction with others. Single workers, working alone, would be optimal. Pairs may be optimal for tasks requiring continuous feedback from another person. Empirically, five or six persons have often been shown to produce the most effectively interacting discussion groups, in comparison with smaller or larger groups. For difficult tasks requiring a group decision, even-sized groups do better than odd-sized groups, presumably because the even-sized groups cannot achieve superficial resolution of problems when there is a 50–50 split on what to do. Some changing of minds is required. An odd-sized group can always settle matters quickly with a vote (Frye & Stritch, 1960).

Most of what Haythorn (1968) said about the potential payoff but the lack of research on group composition is still true over a decade later. For some tasks, we expect that compatibility, homogeneity, and familiarity will yield the most effective interaction processes. For other tasks, complementarity and heterogeneity will be more useful. Again, as with size effects, whether or not task taxonomies (e.g., Shaw's 1963 or Steiner's, 1972 can serve the purpose remains to be seen. We have more to say about this in the next section.

Finally, implementation of procedures for ensuring group congruence between status, esteem, and ability and policies fostering mutual choice seem likely to have immediate payoff for more effective interaction processes and consequential team productivity.

3a. CONDITIONS IMPOSED ON THE TEAM ⎯⎯⎯➤ PROPERTIES OF THE TEAM

Logically, we can readily link the conditions imposed on a team to its size and composition.

Goal Specifications

Directives from higher authority or selection policies in force can restrict the range of members in biographical characteristics and abilities. Age, sex, and educational limits may have been more operative in the past than currently, with affirmative action in force.

Directives clarifying team goals give rise to team properties. With clear goals, the group is likely to be composed of members more purposively selected. Their training is likely to have been more relevant.

Thanks to Locke (1968), there is a growing literature on how clear goals relate to a team's effectiveness. For example, Bass, Farrow, and Valenzi (1979), for 224 management teams, have found (as seen in Table 6.1) correlations of .23 and .41 between clarity of organizational objectives and independent ratings of unit effectiveness. Corresponding correlations of .29 and .37 have been found between clarity of task objectives and unit effectiveness assessed independently. But, there is little data on how such group clarity affects group properties. We would expect, for instance, that a team faced with unclear goals would be more likely to organize itself with less relevance to the team task requirements. Incongruence of ability and status would be more likely, because the requisite abilities would be uncertain.

Some evidence suggests that if demands on a team are ambiguous, it will fall back to its old structure that has worked in the past. It will use previously successful rituals to handle problems. Ambiguity in the environment gives rise to teams devoted to ritual. Thus, in an experimental comparison, groups tended to maintain obsolete, irrelevant procedures rather than form new methods, when new conditions they had to learn were unclear. On the other hand, when the new signals were distinct in meaning, there was more innovation and less ritualism in the group. (Behling & Hopple, 1967).

Existing group properties affect the extent to which environmental demands will produce subsequent effects on the group. Thus, whenever an unexpected problem or need for change arises, new goals are to be selected and old goals are to be abandoned, the norms of the team concerning change may be more influential than members' skills in handling the changing demands (Fleishman, 1965). If they are afraid of change, they may withdraw from opportunities to influence it (Bass & Ryterband, 1979).

Task Specifications

It is most obvious that the task and technology of the team determines what a team can and does become as a group, and how members interact as a consequence.

A team formed to polish and grind auto bumpers will be of extremely different composition, as well as different in arrangement of how the work is to be accomplished, than a team formed to launch a sales campaign. Steel production demands that work be carried out by integrated teams working closely together. According to Walker (1950), steel workers are seen to say: "working with men I know and working like a team . . . we carry on a lot of conversation and joke and time passes very quick. . . . Every man works as a member of a team and tries to turn out as much steel as possible [p. 61]." On the other hand, such integrated team work is impossible on the automobile assembly line. Only loose ties between men on the line can occur during work. Although assembly workers can talk with the men nearest them on the line, no set of workers will maintain the same contacts to form a stable, informal group (Walker & Guest, 1952).

An aspect of the task of particular consequence to the team's organization is the coordination required of its members.

Coordination Requirements. Three levels of interdependence, each requiring more coordination, can be specified: *pooled, sequential,* and *reciprocal* (Thompson, 1967). In pooled interdependence, each team member contributes to the whole, and the whole supports each member. Coordination requires standard routines and expectations that all members will generally follow the routines. It is relatively easy to accomplish. Consider the cooperating efforts of several snow-removal plows. Each plows different sections of a main thoroughfare. When each has done its own section, the entire route is clear.

In sequential interdependence, one member's activities must follow another's. In addition to following standard routines, the team must plan and schedule for line balancing. More communications are required between members. Aircraft ground controllers are sequentially interdependent. As an airplane leaves one traffic space, ground control of the plane is transferred to another station in charge of the space the aircraft is now entering.

Reciprocal interdependence requires even more coordination. Mutual adjustments must be maintained in addition to standard routines, planning, scheduling, and communicating. A five-man basketball team plays in reciprocal interdependence (Thompson, 1967).

In aircrew operations, some positions may be in reciprocal interdependence because one crew member can compensate for another. In the B-29, because the navigator could perform some of the same functions and simplify the work of other bomb team members, his proficiency was likely to be more important in determining bomb scores, if one or more of the other team members were below average in proficiency. In a study of the relationship between individual crew member proficiencies and radar bombing accuracy, Voiers (1956) noted that the individual proficiencies of B-29 bomb team members tended to combine in ways in some operations, so that the aircraft commander, radar observer, and bombardier were in sequential interdependence; that is, the proficiency of any one of these three was reflected in the team's bomb score (computed distance of the bomb from the target) only to the extent that other bomb team members were proficient. The proficiency of the aircraft commander depended on whether the radar observer was of above-average proficiency. On the other hand, how well the plane was flown had little importance, if the man on the bomb site was of relatively low competence.

There has been little explanation of how these levels of interdependence influence various properties of the team. However, one would immediately think of the following likely associations:

| | Required Level of Interdependence | | |
Impact On:	Pooled	Sequential	Reciprocal
Coordination Required will be . . .	Low	Medium	High
Need for Open Communications will be . . .	Low	Medium	High
Alertness to Other Team Members will be . . .	Low	Medium	High
Flexibility will be . . .	Low	Medium	High
Minimum Standards For All Members Critical For Team Success?	No	Yes	Yes
Correlation of Mean Ability With Team Performance will be . . .	High	Low	Low

O'Brien and Owens (1969) allocated different tasks to different positions, and the tasks were then ordered to be completed sequentially. Under these conditions of sequential interdependence, all members not only had an opportunity to influence the group product but were actually required to contribute. The investigators found that the group product was proportional to the average members' abilities. Furthermore, because of the definite task sequencing, the quality of the group product was particularly sensitive to poor performance by any one person. They noted the similarity of their findings to observations about assembly lines, where shoddy performance by one worker often results in an inferior product, even though the remaining members are quite competent.

On the other hand, when members were asked to cooperate and pool their efforts in a freer form of collaboration, the better members could compensate for the less capable ones, so that team output was unrelated to the average or the dullest members. This was made even clearer by Weinstein and Holzbach (1973), who placed 72 undergraduates in one of two conditions: handling problems in pooled interdependence or in sequential interdependence. Rewards were equal or differential. Task ability was assessed with the Minnesota Clerical Test.

Results in Table 6.2 show how tested ability correlated with team productivity under the four conditions. It can be seen that individual ability was strongly associated with team productivity, only when members' performance could be added under the pooled conditions and where rewards to members were equalized. The more able members of teams in sequential interdependence evidently were constrained by their needing to wait for the member in front of them in production to complete work.

TABLE 6.2
Correlations of the Minnesota
Clerical Test with Productivity
Measures under Different
Reward and Levels of
Interdependence
Adapted from Weinstein and
Holzbach, 1973, p. 299.

	Level of Interdependence	
	Pooled	*Sequential*
Reward		
Differential	.24	.16
Equal	*.67*	− .23

Note: Correlation in italics significant at $p < .01$.

Suggestions for Research

Immediate payoff is likely from efforts to specify goals and to increase goal clarity of teams. Further research simulating different team arrangements found in industry would also seem profitable. Needed are comparisons of the effects on team properties of required pooled, sequential, and reciprocal coordination.

3b. CONDITIONS IMPOSED ON THE TEAM ———▶
INTERACTION PROCESSES

Even without change in the team's properties, we expect and obtain differences in the team's interaction processes as a consequence of conditions imposed on the team. Mann (1961) obtained such differences on six of seven categories of interaction, when he compared groups working on tasks compared to groups discussing their own socioemotional processes. Morris and Fiedler (1964) compared groups composing a fable with groups solving a difficult problem. More than half the interaction categories yielded significantly different frequencies for the two kinds of groups.

Shaw's (1963) factor analysis of 104 group tasks yielded task factors particularly useful for understanding interaction processes:

1. Difficulty—the amount of effort required to complete the task.
2. Solution multiplicity—the degree to which there is more than one correct solution.
3. Cooperation requirements—degree to which integrated efforts are required.

Morris (1966) contrasted the performance of 108 groups working on three types of problems: production, discussion, and problem solving:

> On production tasks the ideas and materials which the group produces and works with are images. Examples of tasks in this category are the TAT or tasks which essentially ask: "Write a story . . ."; "Draw a picture of . . .", etc. These are the so called creativity tasks whose goal is the production of images. On discussion tasks the ideas and materials with which groups work are issues. Examples are: "What makes for success in our culture?"; "Takes a stand on capital punishment"; "Birth control is . . ."; "Foreign aid is . . ." Here the group materials are aspects of the issue which are evaluated, interpreted, reformulated, etc. The group is not required to put their beliefs into practice. Problem-solving tasks concern implementations as the ideas with which the group works. Examples are: "How can you do . . ."; "Develop a procedure for . . ."; "Devise a way to . . ." [p. 547].

Each type of task was also systematically varied in difficulty.

Table 6.3 shows the impact of type of task on interaction processes. Table 6.4 shows the impact of task difficulty. It can be seen that problem structuring was highest for the discussion tasks, whereas structuring answers was highest for production tasks. Clarification was highest for discussion tasks; repetition for production tasks. Irrelevancies occured most frequently on problem-solving tasks. The type of task accounted for 60% of the interaction process. Morris felt the results could be best understood, if he looked at groups whose tasks led them primarily to focus on production or primarily to focus on process.

Difficult tasks yielded more structuring of answers; easy tasks produced more irrelevancies. Morris (1966) concluded that we need more extensive mapping of how task attributes affect interaction processes, as well as team output. Hackman (1968) found strong associations between task difficulty, task type, and outputs. For example, easy tasks were conducive to avoidance of points of view in the group product that was prepared. A proposed course of action appeared more often in dealing with problem-solving tasks than in discussions or production tasks. But, there continues to be a sparcity of information on how interaction processes are influenced by type of task.

TABLE 6.3
Effects of Task Type on Categorized Interaction Processes

	Production	Discussion	Problem Solving	F Ratio
Structure problem	11.6	19.0	14.9	11.43**
Structure answer	8.6	5.2	5.4	11.09**
Propose solution	19.4	9.8	13.4	28.71**
Clarify	11.6	17.2	14.8	15.81**
Defend	2.0	3.5	3.5	6.5**
Repeat	4.6	2.1	2.3	29.71**
Agree	13.8	14.6	15.9	2.06
Disagree	4.7	3.2	4.2	5.47*
Seek structuring	3.2	2.9	2.4	2.58
Seek solution proposals	1.7	1.2	1.3	2.00
Seek clarify-defend-repeat	2.9	2.7	2.6	0.47
Seek evaluation	1.6	1.4	1.6	0.99
Procedure	2.0	1.4	1.4	5.89*
Seek procedure	0.5	0.4	0.4	1.48
Irrelevant	5.9	8.6	10.8	4.29*
Fragmentary	5.8	6.5	5.0	2.00
Total base activity	205.8	198.6	214.8	0.66

*$p < .05$, df = 2,27.
**$p < .01$, df = 2,27.
(After Morris, 1966, p. 550)

TABLE 6.4
Effects of Difficulty on Categorized Interaction Processes

	Difficulty[a]			
	Low	Medium	High	F Ratio
Structure problem	13.3	17.3	14.9	3.46*
Structure answer	3.5	5.7	8.1	6.20**
Propose solution	14.6	13.5	14.5	0.46
Clarify	13.1	15.1	15.2	2.82
Defend	2.7	3.4	2.9	0.89
Repeat	3.4	2.4	3.1	3.84*
Agree	14.0	14.6	15.7	1.46
Disagree	4.1	3.8	4.2	0.30
Seek structuring	2.6	2.9	3.0	0.84
Seek solution pro- posals	1.4	1.3	1.5	0.27
Seek clarify-defend- repeat	2.7	2.6	2.8	0.26
Seek evaluation	1.5	1.3	1.8	3.36*
Procedure	1.6	1.7	1.6	0.07
Seek procedure	0.5	0.4	0.4	0.18
Irrelevant	12.9	8.3	4.1	14.55**
Fragmentary	6.3	5.6	5.4	0.80
Total base activity	201.9	197.1	220.3	1.50

[a]Preexperimental judgments of task difficulty.
*$p < .05$, $df = 2.27$.
**$p < .01$, $df = 2.27$.
(After Morris, 1966, p. 550)

Team Training.   Much of organizational development efforts centers around team-building activities. Training is a condition imposed on teams that may have direct impact on its interaction processes. Or, we can argue that training is an acquired group property that can result in interaction processes more conducive to team productivity.

Although team training has been practiced with particular diligence since the advent of the OD movement, it remains more of an art than a science.

To facilitate team interaction, team training should depend on a diagnosis of the team's interaction problems. There may be lack of clarity about the conditions imposed on the team. The team may lack response capability. Feedback may be missing. Individual team members may represent sources of conflict as a consequence of deviance from team norms in history, ability, or position. Team norms may foster rigidity in the face of changing external conditions that are occurring. The team's boundaries with the larger organization of which it is a part may be too impenetrable, unclear, or weak.

Trainers usually encourage members to design their own remedial efforts, although a variety of specific interventions by the trainers may be attempted, ranging from brief exercises to a full-fledged sensitivity training program. Aims include educating individual members about group dynamics, as well as better understanding of themselves in interaction situations (Bass & Barrett, 1981).

Such training to facilitate interaction may fail to produce the expected improvements in team performance. If the team is a part of a centralized organizational hierachy, much of its training may conflict with the organization's requirements. Or, as Deep, Bass, and Vaughan (1967) suggested, trained teams may depend too much on the adequacy of their informal interaction processes and fail to make sufficient use of formal management controls required by the complex tasks they face.

Imposed Conditions Permitting Team Improvement.   Above and beyond formal team training, conditions may permit team learning. The team can modify its own processes as a consequence of its available internal resources to learn how to cope best with the demands of it. Thus, when groups of 40 operators each were assigned to operate a simulated air defense system, they were permitted to develop ''organically'' rather than ''mechanically.'' They could do more than just continue to follow the routines originally given them. By being given the opportunity to learn and develop themselves, a team eventually could handle several times the load that had originally been planned for the system of operators and machines (Chapman, Kennedy, Newall, & Biel, 1962). Operators first fell back on their own previous experiences in relating to others. Following some trial and error, team members invented new ways of interacting with each other, not foreseen by the system designers (Weinber, 1960).

Team Design.   In addition to giving members opportunities to participate in the design of their working relationships (Bass, 1977) and in their redesign in the light of learning and changing conditions, a variety of other principles have been propounded for imposing conditions on a team to improve its interaction processes:

Time-and-motion study pushes for job specifications for individual team members, written job specifications, clarity about organizational structure, and individual authority, so members can coordinate easily and avoid duplication of effort and idle time.

Human factors engineering introduces designs for team interaction to make better use of known operator capacities based on knowledge about how individuals process information.

Sociotechnical systems weigh both the social and technical aspects of team design. The design must be compatible with the team's objectives. If an objective is team development, then the design must include member participation in decisions. Only what is absolutely essential needs to be specified. Individual discretionary opportunities should be maximized. Responsibility for control of technical variances in quality should be vested in the operators themselves rather than in quality control inspectors. Team members should be cross-trained. Team boundaries should be drawn, so they do not interfere with the inflow of information. There should be congruence between what is demanded and what is rewarded. The design should be compatible with human needs and provide for an effective quality of working life. For instance, each job on the team should be big enough to provide its job holders with meaningful work and identification of their contribution to the team effort. The design should have "built-in" the potential for its own improvement (Bass & Barrett, 1981).

Suggestions for Research:
Conditions Imposed ⎯⎯→ Interaction Processes

How much to specify in advance, how much to build into the task and job requirements, on the one hand, and how much to allow for team learning is largely unknown. It is the philosophical watershed between the older approaches of time-and-motion economy and the newer concepts of sociotechnical systems.

Analogous to the part versus whole learning of individuals is the question of how much each individual should be trained alone before joining the team, and how much should members who must work together be trained together. It seems obvious that if the coordination required is reciprocal interdependence, it is probably best to emphasize team training. But pooled interdependence may not require much more than individual learning.

4. TASK PERFORMANCE OF THE TEAM ⎯⎯→
CONDITIONS IMPOSED ON THE TEAM

The presence or absence of this feedback loop is of central importance to whether the team can respond flexibly to changing task demands. In an effective team, negative feedback should have immediate effects on the team's perceptions.

Ordinarily, effective teams will suffer if they must operate without knowledge of whether or not they are performing adequately. Thus, Johnston and Briggs (1968) found that if members are not allowed to correct or counteract one another after errors are committed, mistakes would continue to occur more frequently. They also noted that groups are less likely to solve problems effectively, and members are likely to be more dissatisfied with their work, if they receive no feedback indicating the success with which the group is carrying out its assignments. They actually don't do much better if all they receive is feedback continuously pointing to unfavorable aspects of the group performance. Yet, learning about the group's success only contributes slightly to team performance. On the other hand, the performance of individual members working as a group improves the most when they receive constructive information about their individual efforts along with the group's success as a whole, particularly if faced with difficult problems. Equally useful is personal feedback of one member to another in improving problem-solving efficiency of all (Bass & Ryterband, 1979).

The task performance of the team can alter subsequent conditions imposed on the group by higher authority or other sources external to the team. For example, the team may have to work overtime because it failed to meet its quota.

Many other such feedback loops can be identified but are not essential to our future discussion. For example, current biodata could alter conditions imposed on the group. Thus, it might be discovered that women are underrepresented on the team. A condition might be imposed that all new hires for the team will be women, until they achieve 50% representation.

Suggestions for Research:
Team Task Performance ──→ Conditions Imposed

What we need to know is how members perceive different kinds of feedback. For example, are they more responsive to computer-based feedback, quantitative data, or qualitative reports? What about the timing and display of feedback information? How can "active" rather than "passive" reception of the feedback be promoted? How much feedback should be public to the whole team or private to specific team members? Does this depend on their level of interdependence?

TASK PERFORMANCE OF MEMBERS ──→
TASK PERFORMANCE OF TEAM

We have already discussed this link as part of the simple model relating the list of group variables to team performance.

Suggestions for Research:
Member Task Performance ──→ Team Task Performance

We need to catalog for different individual and team tasks how much of the variance in team performance is due to individual task competence and individual task performance. Thus, for some tasks, to guarantee adequate team output may only require that we select proficient team members. For other team tasks, individual team member proficiency may be irrelevant. Again, a required taxonomy of tasks seems of central importance to the effort. A significant start in this direction has been made by Nieva, Fleishman, & Rieck (1978).

6. POSITIONS OF MEMBERS ——→
TASK PERFORMANCE OF MEMBERS

The importance of one's position to the team effort is likely to be strongly linked to one's individual performance as a team member. In a line of investigations in the early 1950s, Bass and co-workers repeatedly demonstrated correlations as high as .88 between status of members in an initially leaderless group and their subsequent leadership behavior (Bass & Wurster, 1953).

In the laboratory studies of communication networks, Shaw (1954) noted that subjects placed in central positions with more access to the communication channels were more likely to influence those who were placed in peripheral positions, rather than vice versa. Generally, the centrally located subjects could make more relevant and larger contributions to the team task, because they had a better understanding of what was happening.

Suggestions for Research:
Member Positions ——→ Member Task Performance

Terborg, Castore, and DiNinno (1975) noted that in three-person survey teams there is acutally one critical job, that of working the transit. The team did well if that job was performed well. This concept of the critical job for various types of team effort should be explored further.

The profitability of optimizing the assignments of team members to the respective individual tasks to be performed seems to be a course worth pursuing.

7. ABILITIES OF MEMBERS ——→
TASK PERFORMANCE OF MEMBERS

This linkage of member ability to member performance is a reaffirmation that behavior is predictable. The sampling (and signs) we use in valid tests of aptitude and proficiency correlate substantially with the individual performance of the same extended behaviors we observe in training and on the job. The general level of competence of individual members may have considerable effect. It is obvious that members reading at the level of college graduates will deal differently with most intellectual tasks than members who are illiterate. Their differential reading comprehension may not be directly related to the task of the team; nevertheless, their ability to receive instructions will be strongly affected by their literacy, or lack of it.

One may ask whether the validity of a test for predicting successful performance on a job is altered if the job is worked on alone or as a member of a team. If there are team effects, are they related to team properties and conditions imposed on the team?

8. POSITIONS OF MEMBERS ———►PROPERTIES OF THE TEAM

Positions of members can be arranged in status hierarchies. Or, all positions can be equal in importance to the team effort. Team properties, such as star, wheel, yoke, and other networks, are particular arrangements of positions into communication networks of consequence to subsequent interaction processes (i.e., the star takes less interaction time than the wheel to complete the team task) (Shaw, 1954).

Suggestions for Research:
Member Position ———►Team Properties

The redesign of individual jobs creates comparable changes in team properties. Positions can be assigned to overlap, so that one member serves as backup to another to promote team reliability. This obviously becomes especially important in sequential or reciprocal interdependence. Positions can be rearranged so as to provide more variety to job holders. For example, job rotation (a team property) can be practiced. If this results in cross-training, team flexibility is enhanced. Task identity can be provided job holders by assigning them a complete, whole task to do. This may lessen the need for coordination (a team property) between the job occupants. More autonomy can be provided job occupants, reducing their dependency on peers and supervisors. (Porter, Lawler, & Hackman, 1975).

9. ABILITIES OF MEMBERS ———►PROPERTIES OF THE TEAM

The general and specific abilities of members obviously are the source of the means and variances in the same abilities of their teams. But, member abilities also have some impact on other more remote properties of the team and subsequent interaction processes. For example, Russ and Gold (1975) found that when they planted a task expert and a task bungler on a team, the result was a centralization of team communications and an overall lowering of communications.

If the abilities of consequence are personality traits, then it becomes necessary to detail more fully the linkages between individual attributes and team properties. As Haythorn (1968) notes, individuals' traits may be similar, matching each other; they may be complementary or they may be competing. Two sociable individuals produce a sociable team. One individual expressing the need for control and the other expressing the need to control will produce a compatible team. Two socially bold individuals may produce a team in conflict.

Haythorn and Altman (1966) showed that greatest subjective stress was produced when pairs of men, studied for 10 days in social isolation or in nonisolated conditions, were competitive (both high in dominance), differed in need for achievement, and were competitive in task orientation.

Research Needed

Haythorn's conclusions in 1968 are still pertinent about what we don't know about this linkage and its effects on interaction processes:

> relatively little is known about the interplay of personalities in groups.... Although better than chance predictions of interpersonal compatibility in the interaction process can apparently now be made, such predictions fall short of the precision needed to claim a valid theory of personality interactions, or to provide the basis for a satisfactory rational group assembly process.
>
> (We need to identify) the more important personality characteristics in the interpersonal interaction process; developing better measures of them than are now available; developing better techniques for describing relationships between personality profiles... achieving a better understanding of the interaction process over time; and obtaining more reliable information regarding the relationships between the expressed behavior of one individual and the perceived behavior of another as both of these relate to the personality characteristics of the individuals involved [p. 121].

10   BIOGRAPHICAL CHARACTERISTICS ⟶ ABILITIES OF MEMBERS

We would expect varieties of direct linkages between biodata and abilities of members. College graduates are literate; adults who never went beyond the fourth grade are less likely to be. Literacy is a general ability having sweeping effects on trainability as a team member for coping with complex tasks. On average, female finger dexterity is better than male. For tasks specifically requiring fine finger dexterity, whereas some men will do better than some women, women will usually do better than men.

Obviously, we can complete or locate many empirical studies showing no relation between biodata and ability. It is a question of sampling the possibilities. Logically, it is easy to conceive such a relation. It may or may not be of practical importance in a given situation. In their survey of 250 studies, McGrath and Altman (1966) found slightly positive associations between biodata and abilities in 13 of 51 investigations, and no significant associations in seven operational studies. It is probable that biodata has more effect on ability than appears in validity studies of actual recruiting, selection, and placement. Restriction in range occurs. It has been difficult to show that height is important to success in police work, because most police officers already have been preselected on the basis of height.

Suggestions for Research: Biodata ———➤ Member Abilities

To the degree that biodata offers an indirect approach for measuring abilities, it has utility for assessment purposes. Particularly useful would be the search for biodata that can serve as indicators of interpersonal competence and other types of general ability of importance for serving as a "good" team member. But care must be taken that the biodata does not become an unfair discrimination tool.

11.   BIOGRAPHICAL CHARACTERISTICS ———➤ PROPERTIES OF THE TEAM

The second logical linkage for biodata is with its collective aspect as a group property. For instance, the age of team members takes on particular significance, when they all are nearing retirement or when they, as a team, vary from young adult to senior citizen.

Suggestions for Research: Biodata ———➤ Team Properties

Much of what we have just stated about personality can be restated here. Teams can be composed of individuals similar, compatible, or competitive in their biographical characteristics. Alexander's Macedonian army was strengthened by teaming up an older experienced soldier with a compatible young recruit. We are changing from all male to mixed sex teams in many aspects of work.

Many countries are faced with trying to minimize the competitiveness arising within teams composed of persons from different cultures within their country: Blacks–Whites; French–English; Walloons–Flemings; Catalans–Castillians, and so forth. Multinational corporations face comparable problems trying to team host-country nationals, third-country nationals, and parent-country nationals.

NEEDED: INNOVATIVE RESEARCH STRATEGIES

A thorough search of the research literature for the period 1968 to 1978 has failed to reveal much about how interaction processes between members of teams actually change as a function of such important elements in our model as task characteristics (i.e., conditions imposed on the teams), abilities of members, or many of the other key factors shown there. And, to make matters worse, the area is barren with respect to any basic knowledge concerning explicit "rules" or principles about how the elements of the model may combine in a complex way to affect the nature of either team performance or of the performance of team members as individuals. Even when results of this last decade are combined with those of earlier literature searches (Bass 1960a, McGrath & Altman 1966), the terrain of knowledge is sparsely settled.

This state of affairs is *not* due to lack of research attention. In fact, literally thousands of small group experiments have been carried out in social science laboratories all over the world. Unfortunately, it appears that the emphasis on rigorous experimentation, and the presumed need for tight control over variables has resulted, in most instances, in severe oversimplification of the concepts, measures, and complexities of linkages suggested by the complex model we have presented and discussed in this chapter. What is needed are *not* more rigorous or larger experimental investigations in the standard laboratory mold. Instead, we need innovative and different research strategies that can encompass more fully the many variables and the complexities of interaction shown in our model. Standard field experiments of broader scope than that contained within Zajonc's (1965) standard group task need to be designed. Presumably, an important feature of such field experiments would be that persons would actually be hired to do jobs and be observed under various conditions, instead of being brought together in ad hoc settings to serve merely as laboratory guinea pigs.

Obviously, what has just been proposed is much easier said than done. However, two research strategies are proposed here to serve as beginning alternatives to the classic laboratory experiment. These two strategies—*complex simulation* and *compilation of field study results*—may serve, at least, to stimulate the beginning of thinking about approaches that have greater likelihood of producing the type of "reality based" knowledge demanded by the complex model shown in Fig. 6.1. Readers may, therefore, regard what is offered in the following as likely candidates for new beginnings in this difficult area. It is hoped that readers will develop their own new research strategies within the context of the model.

Outlined in the following, then, are the rudiments of two approaches that may add needed knowledge to the area of Individual Capability, Team Performance, and Team Productivity.

Complex Simulations

A complex simulation, such a business game, could be developed and used with MBA students who are about to gradutae. Such participants are, of course, prospective employees in business or government agencies. All have been educated in various specialties, such as marketing, finance, and production. It becomes possible with simulation to introduce a variety of experimental variables and laboratory-like conditions; nevertheless, the behaviors observed contain considerable fidelity for the real world of business. For example, for an under-graduate honors thesis of SUNY-Binghamton, while this chapter was being completed, Susan Kreutzberger spent 15 weeks using Bale's (1950) analyses of the interaction processes of nine second year MBA "companies" engaged in competition in a complex business game. Team market share gained and profitability were found strongly associated with widespread team participation in decision-making rather than monopolistic decision-making by dominating "company" presidents.

Each of the classes of variables of the model can be varied simultaneously. Path analyses can be used to explore ways to best trim the model, or, a number of the classes can be controlled. It should be possible to impose various conditions on teams of participants. Measures of inputs and performance outcomes are fine tuned. Teams report to Boards of Directors composed of retired business executives and are counseled by them. Fidelity is enhanced further, when teams interested in acquiring another firm must apply for a loan from a real former loan officer from a bank. Teams can be balanced with specialists from production, finance, accounting, and marketing. Teams of equal mean capability can be formed to be heterogeneous or homogeneous in verbal, numerical, and intellectual aptitude, and patterns of background characteristics.

Currently available computerized response capabilties and videotape laboratories make possible manipulation of the quality and quantity of the measurement and feedback of team productivity and team interaction processes. Almost any of the hypotheses presented in this article can be tested in the simulation environment now available. Even more important, the interplay of variables can be studied in a highly involving setting where real time is compressed but fidelity remains high.

Compilation of Uncontrolled Field Studies

Another research opportunity lies in the reports of the uncontrolled field experiments in teamwork (usually quasi-experiments) being conducted in ever-increasing numbers in this country and abroad. Actually, a good start has already been made by Katzell, Brenstock & Faerstein (1977) with their *Guide to Worker Productivity Experiments in the United States, 1971-1975.* They present abstracts and an index of 103 published studies. Of these, 18 involved changing jobs from individual to team designs or improving team performance. Nevertheless, a great deal more such data could be accumulated from unpublished internal reports both in the United States and abroad. In one Volvo plant in Gothenberg that I visited in 1974, 41 such experiments, or quasi-experiments, were in progress (for a description of the Volvo experiment at Kalmar, see Gyllenhammer, 1977). Many more of these studies will never be reported in the literature. We are probably ready for the equivalent of a Human Area Research Files that was accumulated for anthropological studies of primitive societies. These uncon-

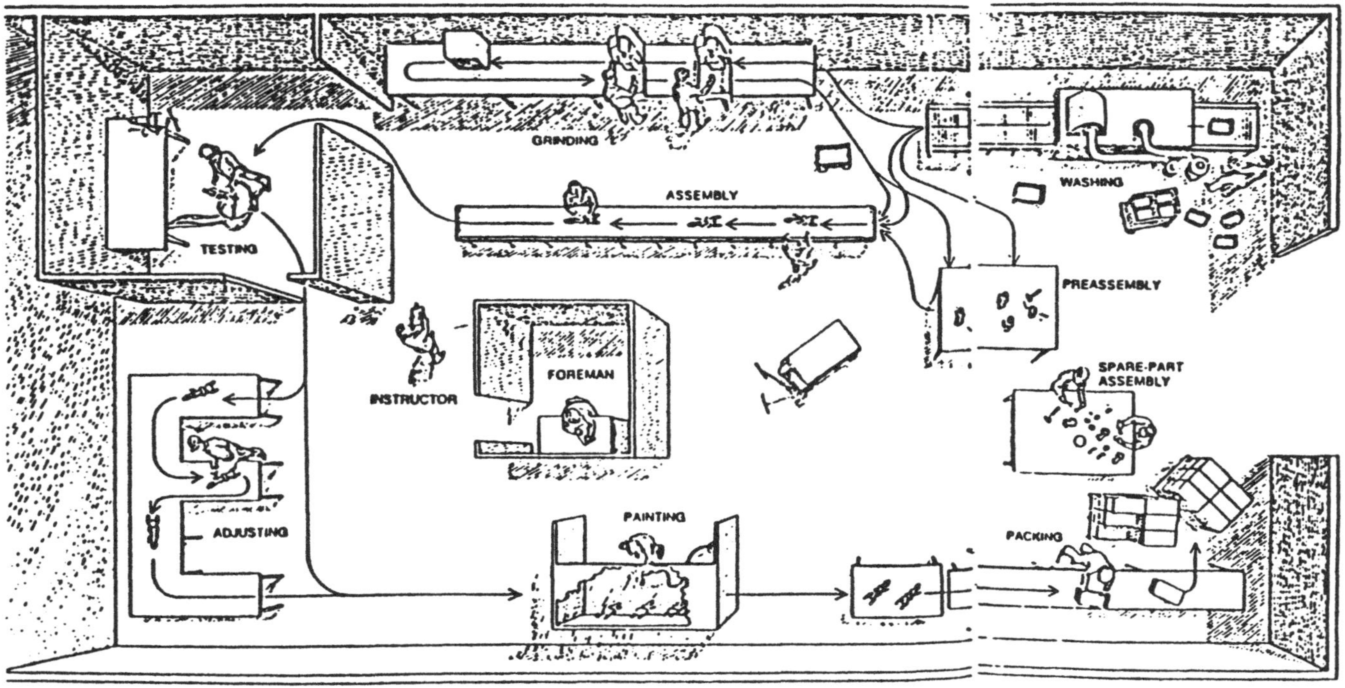

Department 698 is pictured as it was before the experiment in work satisfaction began. The twelve men and their foreman, engaged in the final assembly of rock-drilling machines, were typically disposed as shown here, with each man working at a fixed station. Parts were delivered (top right), put through a degreasing machine, and then transported to the next stage; some parts required grinding or preassembly before moving to the conveyor-belt assembly line. Once assembled, each drill was tested, painted, and packed. The "instructor" handled difficulties in production and, along with the adjuster, was responsible for quality and the correction of errors. Apart from these two men, the workers were each assigned a single task. Their pay was based on some form of piecework, and so each man was primarily interested in keeping his own output at a high level.

FIG. 6.3. Department 698 (From Björk, 1975, p. 18).

trolled single cases, by themselves, can prove nothing. But collectively, they can be used in the same way as the Human Area Research Files to extract generalizations of consequence. The Case of Department 698 for assembling rock-drilling machines in a Swedish firm is illustrative of the uncontrolled field study. A single group is used, and comparison is made between conditions before and after the changeover from individual to team effort. Originally, as seen in Fig. 6.3, Department 698 was run like Adam Smith's pin factory. Each of the 12 employees worked at a fixed station. Figure 6.4 shows the original linear flow *from person to person*. Here, each worker was passively bound to a specific task, location, and the parts that passed by him. Each employee's self-interest was the prime motivator. His pay depended solely on his individual output. Figure 6.4 then shows that the individuals were rearranged into teams of two to four. Since the changeover, each team is responsible for assembling a single lot of drills. Each worker has learned to do most jobs in the department. The team takes the lot through the entire process. Wage agreements have been changed. Each worker continues to receive his guaranteed hourly rate, but instead of increments for individual productivity, increments are now to be made for team productivity exceeding established levels.

The old approach produced dull, tiring, monotonous jobs, destructive to self-esteem. Worker apathy was the rule. Work was sloppy. Absenteeism was high. Quit rates were high. Morale was low. Conflict between the individually oriented, self-interested workers was high.

The new approach makes more use of employees' capacity to plan as team members, as well as to execute plans developed as part of a team. They have to learn about how to apply new technological developments throughout the production process for which the team is responsible. The new approach increases the variety of individual activities. Cooperation rather than competition with fellow workers is encouraged. The new approach gives employees a sense of completion, or wholeness, or identity with the fully assembled rock-drilling machine that appears at the end of the production run. The new approach given employees a greater sense of autonomy to choose to work on within the constraints of what the team has to accomplish. The supervisor now is a source of technical information rather than solely a director or controller of activities.

In the 1920s, the solution to the apathy and sloppy work would have been to create even simpler, individualized jobs and tighter controls that could lead to further monotony and resentment. In the 1970s, the team approach in Department 698 resulted in a 5% increase in productivity, higher employee satisfaction and morale, less conflict among employees, and a greater sense of influence and participation in what was taking place in the work situation (Bjork, 1975).

Most Likely Areas for Immediate Payoff

The previous research approaches are but two of many that can and should be developed. The important point, of course, is that real breakthroughs in increased

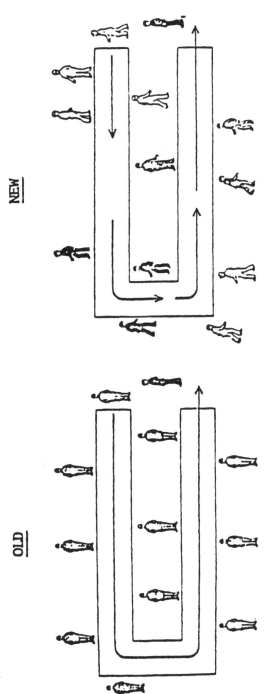

OLD

NEW

Flow of Production changed in the course of the experiment as shown in these highly schematic diagrams. Before the experiment (left) the flow was linear; the men were passively bound in specific tasks and locations and the drill moved past them. During the experiment the workers were divided into four groups of two to four men (right). Each group (shown by different shading) is responsible for a single lot of drills and, with each worker able to do most jobs, takes the lot through the entire process.

FIG. 6.4.   Flow of production in department 698 under the old and new arrangements (From Bjork, 1975. p. 20.).

226

team productivity are most likely to come about by recognizing and taking advantage of the full complexity of the model in Fig. 6.1. Because of its complexity, however, the planning of research activities should focus on those areas likely to yield the most useful immediate results. To this end, we suggest some of the areas that seem to us to hold greatest potential for most immediate payoff, in the form of increased productivity and/or reduced costs in actual work settings:

1. For teams with disjunctive tasks, studies of the effects of reorganizing teams in such a way that each team contains at least one member with above-average capability for doing the task should be undertaken.

2. For teams with conjunctive tasks, the expectation that teams should be comprised of members in such a way that no area of expertise known to be required for task accomplishment is missing needs to be confirmed.

3. Studies should be carried out to discover the types of constraints on individual member performance that may come about in teams where members are essentially carrying out their functions independently.

4. Investigations are needed of approaches that may be used (e.g., promotion, training, etc.), and the effects likely to be produced by increasing the intraindividual congruence within team members of such factors as status, esteem, influence, and ability.

5. When cohesion among team members is important for productivity, the possibility should be studied of using sociometric choice as a basis for assigning members to teams. Studies should be be carried out of the ways in which sociometric choice may be most effectively undertaken and implemented.

6. Obviously much research still is required to learn both the effects and the means by which team performance and productivity goals may be effectively clarified and communicated to team members.

7. Related to the previous, research also needs to be carried out to learn both the most effective means and the effects of clarifying the nature of rewards to be derived from particular types and/or levels of both individual member and team performance.

Overall, of course, the most obvious long-term research need is to learn much more about exactly what interaction processes result from properties of the team and the conditions imposed on it, and what types of interaction processes are likely to be conducive to, or detrimental to, team productivity for members with certain capabilities.

REFERENCES

Bales, F. *Interaction process analysis: A method for the study of small groups.* Cambridge: Addison-Wesley Press, 1950.

Bass, B. M. Feelings of pleasantness and work group efficiency. *Personnel Psychology,* 1954, 7, 81-91. (a)

Bass, B. M. The leaderless group discussion. *Psychological Bulletin*, 1954, *51*, 465–492. (b)

Bass, B. M. *Leadership, psychology, and organizational behavior.* New York: Harper & Row, 1960. (a)

Bass, B. M. Measures of average influence and change in agreement of rankings by a group of judges. *Sociometry*, 1960, *23*, 195–202. (b)

Bass, B. M. *Organizational psychology.* Boston: Allyn & Bacon, 1965.

Bass, B. M. Social behavior and the orientation inventory: A review. *Psychological Bulletin*, 1967, *68*, 260–292.

Bass, B. M. Utility of managerial self-planning in a simulated production task in twelve countries. *Journal of Applied Psychology*, 1977, *62*, 506–609.

Bass, B. M. Team productivity and individual member competence. *Small Group Behavior*, 1980, *11*, 431–504.

Bass, B. M. *Stogdill's handbook of leadership.* (*Revised Edition*). New York: Free Press, 1981.

Bass, B. M., & Barrett, G. V. People, work, and organizations. Boston: Allyn & Bacon, 1981.

Bass, B. M., Farrow, D., & Valenzi, E. *Analyses of PROFILE data.* Florida International University, Miami, 1979.

Bass, B. M., Flint, A. W., & Pryer, M. W. Effects of status-esteem conflict on subsequent behavior in groups (ONR Technical Report 10, Contract N70NR 35609). Louisiana State University, Baton Rouge, 1957.

Bass, B. M., Gaier, E. L., Flint, A. W., & Farese, F. J. An objective method for studying group behavior. *Psychol. Report. Monograph*, 1957, *3*, 265–280.

Bass, B. M., Klauss, R., & De Marco, J. J. Impact model of managers' interpersonal communication styles on an industrial and a navy civilian organization (ONR Technical Report 3, Contract No. N0001476-C-0912), Syracuse University, Syracuse, N.Y., 1977.

Bass, B. M., & Ryterband, E. *Organizational psychology.* Boston: Allyn & Bacon, 1979 (Second Edition).

Bass, B. M., & Wurster, C. R. Effects of company rank on LGD performance of oil refinery supervisors. *Journal of Applied Psychology*, 1953, *37*, 100–104.

Behling, C., & Hopple, F. G. Small group adaptation to unprogrammed change. *Organizational Behavior & Human Performance*, 1967, *2*, 73–83.

Bjork, L. E. An experiment in work satisfaction. *Scientific American*, 1975, 232(3), 17–23.

Bowers, D. G. *Work organizations as dynamic systems* (Technical Report) Office of Naval Research, September 30, 1969.

Byrne, D. *The attraction paradigm.* New York: Academic Press, 1971.

Cattell, R. B. On the theory of group learning. *Journal of Social Psychology*, 1953, *37*, 27–52.

Chapman, R. L., Kennedy, J. L., Newall, A., & Biel, W. C. The System Research Laboratory's air-defense experiments. In H. Guetzkow (Ed.), *Simulation in social science: readings.* Englewood Cliffs, N.J.: Prentice-Hall, 1962.

Collaros, P. A., & Anderson, L. R. Effect of perceived expertness upon creativity of members of brainstorming groups. *Journal of Applied Psychology*, 1969, *53*, 159–163.

Collins, B. E., & Guetzkow, H. *A social psychology of group processes for decision-making.* New York: Wiley, 1964.

Comrey, A. L. Group performance in a manual dexterity task. *Journal of Applied Psychology*, 1953, *37*, 207–210.

DeNisi, A. S., & Shaw, J. B. Investigation of the uses of self-reports of abilities. *Journal of Applied Psychology*, 1977, *62*, 641–644.

Deep, S. D. Bass, B. M., & Vaughan, J. A. Some effects on business gaming of previous quasi-t group affiliations. *Journal of Applied Psychology*, 1967, 51, *5*, 426–431.

Fleishman, E. A. Attitude versus skill factors in work group productivity. *Personnel Psychology*, 1965, *18*, 253–266.

Fleishman, E. A., & Berringer, J. One way to reduce office turnover. *Personnel*, 1960, *37*, 63–69.

Friedlander, F. Performance interactional dimensions of organizational work groups. *Journal of Applied Psychology*, 1966, *50*, 257-65.

Frye, R. L., & Stritch, T. M. *Effect of group size on public and private coalescence* Technical Report 24. Contract N70NR 35609, Mississippi Southern College, Hattiesburg, 1960.

Gerard, H. B., Wilhelmy, K. A., & Connolley, E. S. Conformity and group size. *Journal of Personality & Social Psychology*, 1968, *8*, 79-82.

Gibb, J. R. *Factors producing defensive behavior within groups* (Ann. Tech. Rep.), Hum. Relat. Lab., University of Colorado, Boulder, 1954.

Gibb, J. R. *The effects of group size and threat reduction upon creativity in a problem-solving situation.* Technical Report 7, Contract NONR-3088(00). Western Behavioral Science Institute. La Jolla, CA, 1964.

Goldman, M. Group performance related to size and initial ability of group members. *Psychological Reports*, 1971, *28*, 551-557.

Goldman, M., Dietz, D. M., & McGlynn, A. Comparison of individual and group performance related to heterogeneous-wrong responses, size, and patterns of interaction *Psychological Reports*, 1968, *23*, 459-465.

Graham, W. K., & Dillon, P. C. Creative supergroups: Group performance as a function of individual performance on brainstorming tasks. *Journal of Social Psychology*, 1974, *93*, 101-105.

Guion, R. M. The employee load of first line supervisors. *Personnel Psychology*, 1953, *6*, 223-244.

Gyllenhammar, P. G. *People at work.* Reading, Mass.: Addison-Wesley, 1977.

Hackman, J. R. Effects of task characteristics on group products. *Journal of Experimental Social Psychology*, 1968, *4*, 162-187.

Hall, R. H., Haas, E. J., & Johnson, W. J. Organizational size, complexity, and formalization. *American Sociological Review*, 1967, *32*, 903-912.

Haythorn, W. W. The composition of groups: A review of the literature. *Acta Psychologica*, 1968, *28*, 97-128.

Haythorn, W. W., & Altman, I. Personality factors in isolated environments. In: M. Appley & R. Trumbull (eds.), *Psychological Stress*, New York: Appleton-Century-Crofts, 1966.

Herbst, P. G. The analysis of social flow systems. *Human Relations*, 1954, *7*, 327-336.

Hesling, R. Predicting group task effectiveness from member characteristics. *Psychological Bulletin*, 1964, *62*, 248-256.

Hoffman, L. R. Conditions for creative problem-solving. *Journal of Psychology*, 1961, *52*, 429-444.

Hoffman, L. R. Homogeneity of member personality and its effect on group problem solving. *Journal of Abnormal and Social Psychology*, 1959, *58*, 27-32.

Hoffman, L. R., & Maier, N. R. F. Quality and acceptance of problem solutions by members of homogeneous and heterogeneous groups. *Journal of Abnormal and Social Psychology*, 1961, *62*, 401-407.

Husband, R. W. Cooperative versus solitary problem solution. *Journal of Social Psychology*, 1940, *11*, 405-409.

Institute for Social Research. *Ann. Rept.* (ONR Contract 232, Task Order 2), University of Michigan, Ann Arbor, 1954.

Jenkins, J. G. The nominating technique, its uses and limitations. Unpublished manuscript reported in D. Krech & R. S. Cruchfield (eds.), *Theory and problems of social psychology.* New York: McGraw-Hill, 1948, 405-407.

Johnston, A. W. & Briggs, E. Team performance as a function of team arrangement and work load. *Journal of Applied Psychology*, 1968, *52*, 89-94.

Katzell, R. A., Brenstock, P. & Faerstein, P. H. *A guide to worker productivity experiments in the United States.* 1971-75, New York: New York Press, 1977.

Keenan, V., Kerr, W., & Sherman, W. Psychological climate and accidents in an automobile plant. *Journal of Applied Psychology*, 1951, *35*, 108-111.

Laughlin, P. R., & Bitz, D. S. Individual versus dyadic performance on a disjunctive task as a function of initial ability level. *Journal of Personality & Social Psychology*, 1975, *31*, 487-496.

Levine, E. L., Flory, A., & Ash, R. A. Self-assessment in personnel selection. *Journal of Applied Psychology*, 1977, *62*, 428-435.

Lichtenberg, P., & Deutsch, M. *A descriptive review of research on the staff process of decision-making* (AFPTRC-TR-54-129), San Antonio, Texas, 1954.

Locke, E. A. Toward a theory of task motivation and incentives. *Organizational Behavior and Human Performance*, 1968, *3*, 157-190.

Lodahl, T. M., & Porter, L. W. Psychometric score patterns, score characteristics, and productivity of small industrial work groups. *Journal of Psychology*, 1961, *45*, 73-79.

Lott, A. J., & Lott, B. E. Group cohesiveness and interpersonal attraction: A review of relationships with antecedent and consequent variables. *Psychological Bulletin*, 1965, *14*, 259-309.

Mann, R. D. A review of the relationships between personality and performance in small groups. *Psychological Bulletin*, 1959, *56*, 241-270.

Mann, R. D. Dimensions of individual performance in small groups under task and social-emotional conditions. *Journal of Abnormal and Social Psychology*, 1961, *62*, 674-682.

Maier, N. R. F., & Hoffman, L. R. Quality of first and second to group problem solving. *Journal of Applied Psychology*, 1960, *44*, 278-283.

Marriott, R. Size of working group and output. *Occupational Psychology*, 1949, *23*, 47-57.

Marston, W. M. Studies in testimony. *Journal of Criminal Law & Political Science*, 1924, *15*, 5-31.

McCurdy, H., & Lambert, W. E. The efficiency of small human groups in the solution of problems requiring genuine cooperation. *Journal of Personnel*, 1952, *20*, 478-494.

McDavid, J. W., & Harari, H. Stereotyping of names and popularity in grade-school children. *Child Development*, 1966, *37*, 453-459.

McGrath, J. E. *A summary of small group research studies*. Arlington, Va.: Human Sciences Research, Inc., 1962.

McGrath, J. E., & Altman, I. *Small group research: a synthesis and critique*. New York: Holt, Rinehart & Winston, 1966.

Miller, N. E. Effects of group size on group process and member satisfaction. *Process of Admin. Conf.* Ann Arbor: University of Michigan, 1950. (Abstract)

Moreno, J. L. *Who shall survive?* Beacon, N.Y.: Beacon House, 1953.

Morris, C. G. Task effects on group interaction. *Journal of Personality and Social Psychology*, 1966, *4*, 545-554.

Morris, C. G., & Fiedler, F. E. Application of a new system of interaction analysis to the relationships between leader attitudes and behavior in problem solving groups (*Technical Report No. 14*), University of Illinois, Group Effectiveness Research Laboratory (Contract No. NR 177-472, NONR-1834 [36]), Office of Naval Research, 1964.

Newcomb, T. M. *The acquaintance process*. New York: Holt, Rinehart, & Winston, 1961.

Nieva, V. F., Fleishman, E. A., & Rieck, A. Team Dimensions: Their identity, their measurement, and their relationships. Washington, D.C.: Advanced Research Resources Organization, 1978.

O'Brien, G. E., & Ilgen, D. Effects of organizational structure, leadership style, and member compatibility upon small group creativity. *Proceedings of the American Psychological Association*, 1968, *3*, 555-556.

O'Brien, G. E., & Owens, A. G. Effects of organizational structure on correlations between member abilities and group productivity. *Journal of Applied Psychology*, 1969, *53*, 525-530.

Owens, W. A., & Henry, E. R. *Biographical data in industrial psychology*. Creativity Research Institute, Richardson Foundation, 1966.

Palmer, F. H., & Myers, T. I. Sociometric choices and group productivity among radar crews. *American Psychologist*, 1955, *10*, 441-442. (Abstract)

Pennington, D. F., Jr., Haravey, F., & Bass, B. M. Some effects of decision and discussion on coalescence, change, and effectiveness. *Journal of Applied Psychology*, 1958, *42*, 404–408.

Porter, L. W., Lawler, E. E., & Hackman, J. R. *Behavior in Organizations*. New York: McGraw-Hill, 1975.

Pugh, D. S., Hickson, D. J., Minings, C. R., & Turner, C. Dimensions of organization structure. *Administrative Science Quarterly*, 1968, *13*, 66–105.

Reddy, W. B., & Byrnes, A. Effects of interpersonal group composition on the problem-solving behavior of middle managers. *Journal of Applied Psychology*, 1972, *56*, 516–517.

Rock, M. L., & Hay, E. N. Investigation of the use of tests as a predictor of leadership and group effectiveness in a job evaluation situation. *Journal of Social Psychology*, 1953, *38*, 109–119.

Ronan, W. W. Work group attributes and grievance activity. *Journal of Applied Psychology*, 1963, *47*, 38–41.

Russ, R. C., & Gold, J. A. Task expertise and group communication. *Journal of Psychology*, 1975, *91*, 187–196.

Seashore, S. *Group cohesiveness in the industrial work group*. Ann Arbor: SRC, University of Michigan, 1954.

Schutz, W. C. What makes groups productive? *Human Relations*, 1955, *8*, 429–465.

Schutz, W. C. *FIRO: a three dimensional theory of interpersonal behavior*. New York: Rinehart, 1958.

Scott, W. H., et al. *Technical change and industrial relations: a study of the relations between technical change and social structure in a large steelworks*. Liverpool: Liverpool University, 1956.

Shaw, M. E. Some effects of problem complexity upon problem solving efficiency in different communication nets. *Journal of Experimental Psychology*, 1954, *48*, 211–217.

Shaw, M. E. *Scaling group tasks: a method for dimensional analysis* (Technical Report No. 1). University of Florida (Contract No. NR 170-266, NONR-580 [11]), Office of Naval Research, 1963.

Shaw, M. E., & Ashton, N. Do assembly bonus effects occur on disjunctive tasks? A test of Steiner's theory. *Bulletin of the Psychonomic Society*, 1976, *8*, 469–471.

Shaw, M. E., & Harkey, B. *Some effects of congruency of member characteristics and group structure upon group behavior*, 1976.

Shiflett, S. Dyadic performance on two tasks as a function of task difficulty, work strategy, and member ability. *Journal of Applied Psychology*, 1976, *61*, 455–462.

Slusher, A., Van Dyke, J., & Rose, G. Technical competence of group leaders, managerial role, and productivity in engineering design groups. *Academy of Management Journal*, 1972, *15*, 197–204.

Steiner, I. D. Models for inferring relationships between group size and potential group productivity. *Behavioral Science*, 1966, *11*, 273–283.

Steiner, I. D. *Group processes and productivity*. New York: Academic Press, 1972.

Stogdill, R. M., & Koehler, K. *Measures of leadership structure and organization change*. Personnel Research Board, Ohio State University, Columbus, 1952.

Stouffer, S. A., Suchman, E. A., Devinney, L. C., Starr, S. A., & Williams, R. M. The American soldier (Vol. 1). Adjustment during army life. Princeton, N.J.: Princeton University Press, 1949.

Terborg, J. R., Castore, C. H., & DeNinno, J. A. A longitudinal field investigation of the impact of group composition on group performance and cohesion (Technical Report No. 80). Lafayette, Indiana: Purdue, 1975.

Terborg, J. R., Castore, C., & DeNinno, J. A. A longitudinal field investigation of the impact of group composition on group performance and cohesion. *Journal of Personality & Social Psychology*, 1976, *34*, 782–790.

Thompson, J. D. *Organizations in action*. New York: McGraw-Hill, 1967.

Tillman, R., Jr. Problems in review: committees on trial. *Harvard Business Review*, 1960, *38*, 7–12, 162–172.

Van Zelst, R. H. Sociometrically selected work teams increase production. *Personnel Psychology,* 1952, *5,* 175-185.

Voiers, W. D. *Bombing accuracy as a function of the ground-school proficiency structure of the B-29 bomb team.* Lackland Air Force Base, Texas: Air Force Personnel and Training Research Center (Research Report AFPTRC-TN-56-4). 1956.

Walker, C. R., & Guest, R. H. *The man on the assembly line.* Cambridge, Mass.: Harvard University, 1952.

Walker, C. R. *Steeltown.* New York: Harper, 1950.

Weick, K. E. *The social psychology of organizing.* Reading, Mass.: Addison-Wesley, 1969.

Weinber, M. G. Observations on the growth of information-processing centers. In A. H. Rubenstein & C. J. Haverstroh (Eds.), *Some theories of organization.* Homewood, Ill.: Irwin, 1960.

Weinstein, A. G., & Holzbach, R. L. Impact of individual differences, reward distribution, and task structure on productivity in a simulated work environment. *Journal of Applied Psychology,* 1973, *58,* 296-301.

Wiest, W. M., Porter, L. W., & Ghiselli, E. E. Relationships between individual proficiency and team performance and efficiency. *Journal of Applied Psychology,* 1961, *45,* 435-440.

Worthy, J. C. Organizational structure and employee morale. *American Sociological Review,* 1950, *15,* 169-179.

Yuker, H. E. Group atmosphere and memory. *Journal of Abnormal and Social Psychology,* 1955, *51,* 17-23.

Zajonc, R. B. The requirements and design of a standard group task. *Journal of Experimental Social Psychology,* 1965, *1,* 71-88.

Ziller, R. C., Behringer, R. D., & Goodchilds, J. E. Group creativity under conditions of success or failure and variations in group stability. *Journal of Applied Psychology,* 1962, *46,* 43-49.

7

Fitting People to Jobs: The Impact of Personnel Selection on National Productivity

John E. Hunter
Department of Psychology
and
Department of Mathematics
Michigan State University

Frank L. Schmidt
Personnel Research and Development Center
U.S. Civil Service Commission
and
Department of Psychology
George Washington University

INTRODUCTION

It has long been recognized that one of the variables determining aggregate productivity and organizational efficiency is the degree of fit between the capacities of individuals and the demands of the jobs they hold. This idea is at least as old as Plato's *Republic*. Most previous research on this question has focused on the selection process.

In selection, the problem is to select for the job that subset of applicants that will yield the highest subsequent average level of job performance. Well-elaborated models and equations have been worked out for determining the impact of selection procedures on productivity (i.e., the practical utility of selection procedures). Another important decision problem is that of classification. In classification, there are a number of jobs rather than a single job, and each applicant must be assigned to one of these jobs or rejected. The objective is to make the assignments in such a way as to maximize productivity in the group of jobs, while at the same time ensuring that each job receives the predetermined required number of workers. Some quantitative work has been done on the

233

classification problem, although not as much as in the case of selection. In this chapter, we first review previous work on the selection and classification problems and explore some problems and difficulties that have prevented widespread utilization of these models. We then introduce a modified classification model suitable for the economy as a whole and use this model to estimate the implications of job assignment strategies for national productivity. To our knowledge, no such estimates have previously been made. Finally, we suggest additional research that is needed to further clarify the impact of individual differences and job assignment strategies on aggregate national productivity and to provide policy guidance in this area.

History of the Development of Selection Utility Models

The evaluation of benefit obtained from selection devices has been a problem of continuing interest in industrial psychology. Most attempts to evaluate benefit have focused on the validity coefficient, and at least five approaches to the interpretation of the validity coefficient have been advanced over the years. The oldest of these is the Index of Forecasting Efficiency, symbolized E. $E = 1 - \sqrt{1 - r_{xy}^2}$, where r_{xy} is the validity coefficient. This index compares the standard error of job performance scores predicted by means of the test (the standard error of estimate) to the standard error that results when there is no valid information about applicants, and one predicts the mean level of performance for everyone (the standard deviation of job performance). This index describes a test correlating .50 with job performance as predicting only 13% better than chance, a very unrealistic and pessimistic interpretation of the test's value. The index of forecasting efficiency was heavily emphasized in early texts (Kelley, 1923; Hull, 1928) as the appropriate means for evaluating selection procedures. Actually, it has no direct relationship to the economic value of a selection test.

The index of forecasting efficiency was succeeded by the coefficient of determination, which became popular during the 1930s and 1940s. The coefficient of determination is simply the square of the validity coefficient or r_{xy}^2. This coefficient is called "the proportion of variance in the job performance measure accounted for" by the test. The coefficient of determination describes a test of validity of .50 as "accounting for" 25% of the variance of job performance. Although r_{xy}^2 is still occasionally referred to by selection psychologists—and has surfaced in litigation on personnel tests—the "amount of variance accounted for" has no direct relationship to the actual economic value of a selection device.

Both E and r_{xy}^2 lead to the conclusion that only tests with relatively high correlations with job performance—that is, validities high enough to be quite rare—will have any significant practical value. Neither of these interpretations recognizes that the value of a test varies as a function of the parameters of the situation in which it is used. They are general interpretations of the correlation coefficient and have been shown to be inappropriate for interpreting the validity coefficient in selection (Brogden, 1946a; Cronbach & Gleser, 1965, p. 31; Curtis & Alf, 1969).

The well-known interpretation developed by Taylor and Russell (1939) goes beyond the validity coefficient itself and takes into account two properties of the selection problem—the selection ratio (the proportion of applicants hired) and the base rate (the percentage of applicants who would be "successful" without use of the test). This model yields a much more realistic interpretation of the value of selection devices. The Taylor-Russell model indicates that even a test with a modest validity can substantially increase the percentage who are successful among those selected when the selection ratio is low. For example, when the base rate is .50 percent and the selection ratio is .10, a test with validity of only .25 will increase the percentage among the selectees who are successful from 50 to 67%, a gain of 17 additional successful employees per 100 hired.

Although an improvement, the Taylor–Russell approach to determining selection utility does have disadvantages. Foremost among them is the need for a dichotomous criterion. Current employees and new hires must be sorted into an unrealistic two-point distribution of job performance: "successful" and "unsuccessful" (or "satisfactory" and "unsatisfactory"). As a result, information on levels of performance within each group is lost (Cronbach & Gleser, 1965, 123–124, 138). All those within the successful group, for example, are implicitly assumed equal in value, whether they perform in an outstanding manner or barely exceed the cutoff. This fact makes it difficult to express utility in units that are comparable across situations.

A second disadvantage of the Taylor-Russell model results from the fact that the decision as to where to draw the line to create the dichotomy in job performance is arbitrary. Objective information on which to base this decision is rarely available, and thus different individuals may draw the line at very different points. This state of affairs creates a problem because the apparent usefulness of the selection procedure depends on where the line is drawn. For example, suppose both the selection ratio and the validity are .50. If the dichotomy is drawn so that 90% of non-test-selected employees are assigned to the successful category, the test raises this figure to 97%—a gain of only seven successful employees per 100 hired, or an 8% increase in the success rate. However, if the dichotomy is drawn so that 50% are considered successful, this same test raises the percentage successful to 67, a gain of 17 successful employees per 100 hired, or a 34% increase in the success rate. Finally, if the line is drawn so that only 10% of employees are considered successful, use of the test raises this figure to 17%. Here the gain is 7 additional successful employees per 100 hired, as it was when 90% were considered successful. But here the percentage increase in the success rate is 70% rather than 8%. Thus the Taylor-Russell approach appears to give different answers to the question of how useful a test is, depending on where the arbitrary dichotomy is drawn.

The next major advance was left to Brogden (1949), who used the principles of linear regression to demonstrate how the selection ratio (SR) and the standard deviation of job performance in dollars (SD_y) affect the economic utility of a selection device. Despite the fact that Brogden's derivations are a landmark in the development of selection utility models, they are very straightforward and simple to understand.

Let r_{xy} = the correlation between the test (x) and job performance measured in dollar value. The basic linear model is:

$$Y = \beta Z_x + \mu_y + e$$

Where:

Y = job performance measured in dollar value;

β = the linear regression weight on test scores for predicting job performance;

Z_x = test performance in standard score form *in the applicant group;*

μ_y = mean job performance (in dollars) of randomly selected employees; and

e = error of prediction.

This equation applies to the job performance of an individual. The equation that gives the *average* job performance *for the selected (s) groups* (or for any other subgroup) is:

$$E(Y_s) = E(\beta Z_{xs}) + E(\mu_y) + E(e)$$

Since $E(e) = 0$, and β and μ are constants, this becomes:

$$\hat{Y}_s = \beta \bar{Z}_{xs} + \mu_y$$

This equation can be further simplified by noting that $\beta = r_{xy}(SD_y/SD_x)$ where SD_y is the standard deviation of job performance measured in dollar value among randomly selected employees. Since $SD_x = 1.00$, $\beta = r_{xy}SD_y$. We thus obtain:

$$\hat{Y}_s = r_{xy}SD_y\bar{Z}_{xs} + \mu_y$$

This equation gives the *absolute* dollar value of average job performance in the selected group. What is needed is an equation which gives the *increase* in dollar value of average performance that results from using the test. Note that if the test were not used, $\hat{Y}_s$ would be μ_y. That is, mean performance in the selected group is the same as mean performance in a group selected randomly from the applicant pool. Thus the increase due to use of a valid test is $r_{xy}SD_y\bar{Z}_{xs}$. The equation we want is produced by transposing μ_y to give:

$$\hat{Y}_s - \mu_y = r_{xy}SD_y\bar{Z}_{xs}$$

The value on the right in the above equation is the difference between mean productivity in the group selected using the test and mean productivity in a group selected without using the test, that is, a group selected randomly. The above equation thus gives mean gain in productivity per selectee resulting from use of the test, i.e.,

$$\Delta \bar{U} / \text{selectee} = r_{xy} SD_y \dot{Z}_{xs} \tag{1}$$

Where U is utility and ΔU is marginal utility.

Equation (1) states that the average productivity gain in dollars per person hired is the product of the validity coefficient, the average standard score on the test of those hired, and the SD of job performance in dollars. The value $r_{xy} \dot{Z}_{xs}$ is the mean standard score on the dollar criterion of those selected, $\dot{Z}_y$. Thus, utility per selectee is the mean Z score on the criterion of those selected times the standard deviation of the criterion in dollars. The only assumption that Equation (1) makes is that the relation between the test and job performance is linear. If we further assume that the test scores are normally distributed, the mean test score of those selected is ϕ/p, where:

$p = $ the selection ratio, and
$\phi = $ the ordinate in N (0, 1) at the point of cut corresponding to p.

Thus equation (1) can be written

$$\Delta U / \text{selectee} = r_{xy} \phi / p SD_y \tag{2}$$

The previous equations illustrate the critical role of SD_y and suggest the possibility of situations in which tests of low validity have higher utility than tests of high validity. For example:

	r_{xy}	$\bar{Z}_x$	SD_y	$\Delta U/\text{selectee}$
Mid-level job (e.g., systems analyst)	.20	1.00	25,000	$5,000
Lower-level job (e.g., janitor)	.60	1.00	2,000	1,200

The total utility of the test depends on the number of persons hired. The total utility (total productivity) gain resulting from use of the test is simply the mean gain per selectee times the number of people selected, N_s. That is, the total productivity gain is:

$$\Delta U = N_s r_{xy} SD_y \bar{Z}_{x_s}.$$

In this example, the average, marginal utilities are $5,000 and $1,200. If 10 people were hired, the actual utilities would be $50,000 and $12,000 respectively. If 1,000 people were to be hired, then the utilities would be $500,000 and $120,000, respectively. Obviously the *total* dollar value of tests is greater for large employers than for the local shoeshine stand. However, this is misleading, because on a *percentage* basis it is average gain in utility that counts; and that's what counts to each individual company.

Equations (1) and (2) clearly illustrate the basis for Brogden's (1946), conclusion that the validity coefficient itself is a direct index of selective efficiency. Brogden (1946a) showed that given only the assumption of linearity, the validity coefficient is the proportion of maximum utility attained, where maximum utility is the productivity gain that would result from a perfectly valid test. A test with a validity of .50, for example, can be expected to produce 50% of the gain that would result from a perfect (validity = 1.00) selection device used at that same selection ratio. A glance at Equation (1) or (2) verifies this verbal statement. Because the validity coefficient enters the equation as a multiplicative factor, increasing or decreasing the validity by any factor will increase or decrease the utility by the same factor. For example, if we increase validity by a factor of two by raising it from .20 to .40, Equation (2) shows that utility doubles. If we decrease validity by a factor of one-half by lowering it from 1.00 to .50, utility is cut in half. Equations (1) and (2) also illustrate the fact that there are limitations on the utility of even a perfectly valid selection device. If the selection ratio is very high, the term ϕ/p approaches zero, and no test has much value. If the selection ratio is 1.00, even a perfect test has no value. Likewise, as SD_y decreases, the utility of even a perfect test decreases. If SD_y should somehow happen to be zero (a very unlikely event), then even a perfect test would have no value.

Brogden (1946) further showed that the validity coefficient could be expressed as the following ratio:

$$r_{xy} = \frac{\bar{Z}_{y(x)} - \bar{Z}_{y(r)}}{\bar{Z}_{y(y)} - \bar{Z}_{y(r)}},$$

where $\bar{Z}_{y(x)}$ = the mean job performance (y) standard score for those selected using the test (x).

$\bar{Z}_{y(y)}$ = the mean job performance standard score resulting if selection were on the criterion itself, at the same selection ratio.

$\bar{Z}_{y(r)}$ = the mean job performance standard score resulting if selection decisions were made randomly (from among the otherwise screened pool of applicants).

r_{xy} = the validity coefficient.

This formulation has implications for the development of new methods of estimating selection procedure validity. If reasonably accurate estimates of both $Z_{y(x)}$ and $Z_{y(y)}$ can be obtained, validity can be estimated without conducting a traditional validity study. Further, estimates produced by a procedure of this kind would be unaffected by criterion unreliability.

In Equations (1) and (2), the values for r_{xy} and SD_y should be those that would hold if applicants were hired randomly with respect to test scores; that is, they should be values applicable to the applicant population, the group in which the selection procedure is actually used. Values of r_{xy} and SD_y computed on incumbents will typically be underestimates, because of reduced variance among incumbents on both test and job performance measures. Values of r_{xy} computed on incumbents can be corrected for range restriction, producing estimates of the value in the applicant pool (Thorndike, 1949, 169–176). The applicant pool is made up of all who have survived screening on any prior selection hurdles that might be employed (e.g., minimum educational requirements or physical examinations).

The correlation between the test and a well-developed measure of job performance (y') provides a good estimate of r_{xy}, the correlation of the test with job performance measured in dollars (productivity). It is a safe assumption that job performance and the value of that performance are at least monotonically related. It is inconceivable that lower performance could have greater dollar value than higher performance. Ordinarily, the relation between y' and y will be not only monotonic but also linear. If there are departures from linearity, the departures will typically be produced by leniency in job performance ratings that lead to ceiling effects in the measuring instrument. The net effect of such ceiling effects is to make the test's correlation with the measure of job performance smaller than its correlation with actual performance, its true value, making $r_{xy'}$ an underestimate of r_{xy}. An alternative statement of this effect is that ceiling effects due to leniency produce an artificial nonlinear relation between job performance ratings and the actual dollar value of performance. A nonlinear relation of this form would lead to an underestimation of selection utility, because the performance measure underestimates the relative value of very high performers.

Values of $r_{xy'}$ should also be corrected for attenuation due to errors of measurement in the criterion. Random error in the observed measure of job performance causes the test's correlation with that measure to be lower than its correlation with *actual* job performance. Because it is the correlation with actual performance that determines test utility, it is the attenuation-corrected estimate that is needed in the utility formulas. This estimate is simply $r_{xy'}/\sqrt{r_{y'y'}}$ where $r_{y'y'}$, is the reliability of the performance measure. (See Schmidt, Hunter, & Urry, 1976, for further discussion of these points.)

The next major advance in this area came in the form of the monumental work by Cronbach and Gleser (1957/1965), *Psychological Tests and Personnel Decisions*. First published in 1957, this work was republished in 1965 in augmented form. The book consists of detailed and sophisticated application of decision theory principles, not only to the single-stage fixed-job selection decisions that we have thus far discussed, but also to placement and classification decisions and sequential selection strategies. In these latter areas, many of their derivations were indeed new to the field of personnel testing. Their formulas for utility in the traditional selection setting, however, are, as they note (Cronbach & Gleser, 1965, chap. 4), identical to those of Brogden (1949), except that they formally incorporate cost of testing (information gathering) into the equations. This fact is not obvious.

Brogden, it will be recalled, approached the problem from the point of view of mean gain in utility per selectee. Cronbach and Gleser (1965, chap. 4) derived their initial equation in terms of mean gain per applicant. Their initial formula was (ignoring cost of testing for the moment):

$$\Delta \bar{U}/\text{applicant} = r_{xy}SD_y\phi.$$

All terms are as defined earlier. Multiplying by the number of applicants, N, yields total or overall gain in utility. The Brogden formula for overall utility is:

$$\Delta \bar{U} = N_s\Delta \bar{U}/\text{selectee} = N_s r_{xy}SD_y\phi/p \qquad (3)$$

N_s, it will be recalled, is the number selected. If we note that $p = N_s/N$, that is, the ratio of selectees to applicants, we find that Brogden's equation immediately reduces to the Cronbach-Gleser (1965) equation for total utility:

$$\Delta U = Nr_{xy}SD_y\phi$$

Role of the Cost of Testing

The previous section ignored the cost of testing, which is small in most testing situations. For example, in a typical job situation, the applicant pool consists of people who walk through the door and ask for a job (i.e., there are no recruiting costs). Hiring is then done on the basis of an application blank and tests, administered by a trained clerical worker at a cost of $10 or so. If the selection ratio is 10%, then the cost of testing per person hired is $10 for each person hired and $90 for the nine persons rejected in finding the person hired, or $100 altogether. This is negligible in relation to the usual magnitude of utility gains. Furthermore, this $100 is a one-time cost, whereas utility gains continue to accumulate over as many years as the person hired stays with the organization. When cost of testing is included, Equation (2) becomes:

$$\Delta \bar{U}/\text{selectee} = r_{xy}SD_y\phi/p - C/p, \qquad (4)$$

where C is the cost of testing one applicant.

Although cost of testing typically has only a trivial impact on selection utility, it is possible to conjure up hypothetical situations in which cost plays a critical role. For example, suppose an employer were recruiting one individual for a sales position that would last only 1 year. Suppose further that the employer decided to base the selection on the results of an assessment center that costs $1,000 per assessee and has a true validity of .40. If the yearly value of SD_y for this job is $10,000, and 10 candidates are assessed, the expected gain in productivity is .4 × $10,000 × 1.758 or $7,032. However, the cost of the assessment center is 10 × 1,000 = $10,000, which is $2,968 greater than the expected productivity gain; that is, under these conditions it would cost more to test 10 persons than would be gained in improved performance. If the employer tested only 5 candidates, then the expected gain in performance would be $5,607 whereas the cost of testing would be $5,000 for an expected gain of $607. In this situation, the optimal number to test is 3 persons. The best person of 3 would have an expected gain in performance of 4,469 with a cost of testing of $3,000, for an expected utility of $1,469.

Relation Between SR and Utility

In most situations, the number to be hired is fixed by organizational needs. If the applicant pool is also fixed, the question of which selection ratio (SR) would yield maximum utility becomes academic. The SR is determined by circumstances and is not under the control of the employer. However, employers can often exert some control over the size of the applicant pool by increasing or decreasing recruiting efforts. If this is the case, the question is then how many applicants the employers should test to obtain the needed number of new employees in order to maximize productivity gains from selection. This question can be answered using a formula given by Cronbach and Gleser (1965, p. 309):

$$\phi - pZ_x = C/(r_{xy}SD_y) \tag{5}$$

where Z_x is the cutting score on the test in Z score form. This equation must be solved by iteration. Only one value of the SR (i.e., p) will satisfy this equation and p will always be less than or equal to .50. The value computed for the optimal SR indicates the number that should be tested in relation to the number to be selected. For example, if the number to be selected is 100 and Equation (3) indicates that the optimal SR is .05, the employer will maximize selection utility by recruiting and testing 2000 candidates (100/.05 = 2000). The cost of recruiting additional applicants beyond those available without recruitment efforts must be incorporated into the cost of testing term C. C then becomes the average cost of recruiting and testing one applicant. The lower the cost of testing and recruiting, the larger the number of applicants it is profitable to test in selecting a given number of new employees. Because the cost of testing is typically quite low relative to productivity gains from selection, the number tested should typically be large relative to the number selected.

In situations in which the applicant pool is constant, statements about optimal SRs typically do not have practical value, because the SR is not under the control of the employer. Given a fixed applicant pool, $\Delta\bar{U}$/selectee increases as SR decreases, if cost of testing is not considered. Brogden (1949b) showed that, when cost of testing is taken into account and when this cost is unusually high, $\Delta\bar{U}$/selectee will be lower at very low SRs than at somewhat higher SRs. If cost of testing per applicant is very high, cost of testing *per selectee* can become greater at extremely low SRs than $\Delta\bar{U}$/selectee, producing a loss rather than a gain in utility. In practice, however, the combination of extremely high testing costs and extremely low SRs that could lead to negative utilities occurs rarely, if ever. When the applicant pool is fixed, the SR that is optimal for $\Delta\bar{U}$/selectee is not necessarily the optimal SR for total gain in utility. Cronbach and Gleser showed that total utility is always greatest when the SR falls at .50. As SR decreases from .50, $\Delta\bar{U}$/selectee increases until it reaches its maximum, the location of which depends on the cost of testing. But as $\Delta\bar{U}$/selectee increases, the number of selectees, N_s, is decreasing, and the product N_s $\Delta\bar{U}$/selectee (total utility) is also decreasing. In a fixed applicant pool, total gain is always greatest when 50% are selected and 50% are rejected (Cronbach & Gleser, 1965, pp. 38–40).

REASONS FOR FAILURE TO EMPLOY SELECTION UTILITY MODELS

Despite the availability since 1949 of the utility equations discussed previously, applied differential psychologists have been notably slow in carrying out decision-theoretic utility analyses of selection procedures. This fact may be attributable in part to a lack of interest in economic questions. In our judgment, the sparcity of work in this area is primarily traceable to three facts.

First, many psychologists believe that the utility equations presented earlier are of no value unless the data *exactly* fit the linear homoscedastic model, and all marginal distributions are normal. They reject the model in the belief that their data do not perfectly meet the assumptions.

Second, psychologists once believed that validity is situationally specific, that there are subtle differences in the performance requirements of jobs from situation to situation that produce (nontrivial) differences in test validities. If this were true, then the results of a utility analysis conducted in a given setting could not be generalized to apparently identical test-job combinations in new settings. Combined with the belief that utility analyses must include costly cost accounting applications, it is easy to see why belief in the situational specificity of test validities would lead to reluctance to carry out utility analyses.

Third, it has been extremely difficult in most cases to obtain all the information called for by the equations. The selection ratio and cost of testing can be determined reasonably accurately and at relatively little expense. The item of information that has been most difficult to obtain is the needed estimate of the standard deviation of job performance (SD_y) (Cronbach & Gleser, 1965, p. 121). It has generally been assumed that SD_y can be estimated only by the use of costly and complicated cost accounting methods. These procedures involve first costing out the dollar value of the job behaviors of each employee (Brogden & Taylor, 1950) and then computing the standard deviation of these values. We were able to locate only two studies in which cost accounting procedures were used to estimate SD_y. We present in the following an alternative to cost accounting estimates of SD_y.

Are the Statistical Assumptions Met?

The linear homoscedastic model includes three assumptions:

1. Linearity.
2. Equality of variances of conditional distributions.
3. Normality of conditional distributions.

As we have shown previously, the basic selection utility equation [Equation (1)] depends only on linearity. Equation (2) does assume normality of the test-score distribution. However, Brogden (1949b) and Cronbach and Gleser (1965) introduced this assumption essentially for derivational convenience: It provides an exact relation between the selection ratio (SR) and the mean standard score test performance ($\dot{Z}_r$). One need not use the normality-based relation $\phi/p = \dot{Z}_r$ to compute $\dot{Z}_r$. The value of $\dot{Z}_r$ can be computed directly. Thus, in the final analysis, linearity is the only required assumption.

To what extent do data in differential psychology fit the linear homoscedastic model? To answer this question, we must of necessity examine sample rather than population data. However, it is only conditions in populations that are of interest; sample data are of interest only as a means of inferring the state of nature in populations. Obviously, the larger the sample used, the more clearly the situation in the sample will reflect that in the population, given that the sample is random. A number of researchers have addressed themselves to the question of the fit of the linear homoscedastic model to data in differential psychology.

Sevier (1957), using Ns from 105 to 250, tested the assumptions of linearity, normality of conditional criterion distributions, and equality of conditional variances. The data were from an education study, with cumulative grade-point average being the criterion and high school class rank and various test scores being the predictors. Out of 24 tests of the linearity assumption, only 1 showed a departure significant at the .05 level. Out of the eight samples tested for equality of conditional variances, only one showed a departure significant at the .05 level. However, 25 of the 60 tests for normality of the conditional criterion distributions were significant at the .05 level. Violation of this assumption throws interpretations of conditional standard deviations based on normal curve tables into some doubt. However, this statistic typically is not used in practical prediction situations, such as selection or placement. Sevier's study indicates that the assumptions of linearity and equality of conditional variances may be generally tenable.

Ghiselli and Kahneman (1962) examined 60 aptitude variables on one sample of 200 cases and reported that fully 40% of the variables departed significantly from the linear homoscedastic model. Ninety % of these departures were reported to have held up on cross validation. Tupes (1964) reanalyzed the Ghiselli and Kahneman data and found that only 20% of the relationships departed from the linear homoscedastic model at the .05 level. He also found that three of the "significant" departures from linearity were probably due to typographical or clerical errors in the data. Later Ghiselli (1964) accepted and agreed with Tupes' reanalysis of his data. Tupes' findings must be interpreted in light of the fact that the frequency of departure from the linear homoscedastic model expected at the .05 level is, in fact, much greater than 5%. Tupes carried out two statistical tests on each test-criterion relation: one for linearity and one for equality of conditional variances. Thus, the expected proportion of data samples in which at least one test is significant is not .05 but rather a little over .09. If three statistical tests are run at the .05 level—one for linearity, one for normality of conditional distributions, and one for homogeneity of conditional distributions, the expected proportion of data samples in which at least one of these tests is significant is approximately .14 when relations in the parent populations are perfectly linear and homoscedastic.

Tiffin and Vincent (1960) found no significant departures from the bivariate normal model in 15 independent samples of test-criterion data, ranging in size from 14 to 157. In each set of data, a chi-square test was used to compare the percent of employees in the "successful" job performance category in each fifth of the test-score distribution to the percentages predicted from the normal bivariate surface (which incorporates the linear homoscedastic model) corresponding to the computed validity coefficient. Surgent (1947) performed a similar analysis on similar data and reported the same findings.

Hawk (1970) reported a major study searching for departures from linearity. The data were drawn from 367 studies conducted between 1950 and 1966, on the General Aptitude Test Battery (GATB), used by the U.S. Department of Labor. A total of 3,303 relations, based on 23,428 individuals, between the nine subtests of the GATB and measures of job performance (typically supervisory ratings) were examined. The frequency of departures from linearity significant at the .05 level was .054. Using the .01 level, the frequency was .012. Frequencies closer to the chance level can hardly be imagined. If any substantial proportion of the relations in the Hawk study had in fact been nonlinear, statistical power to detect this fact would have been high—even if statistical power were low for each of the individual 3,303 relations. For example, suppose statistical power to detect nonlinearity had been as low as .30 in each of the individual tests. Then if 40% of the relations were in fact nonlinear, the expected proportion of significant tests for nonlinearity would have been .30 × .40 + .05, or 17%. If only 20% of the relations were truly nonlinear, the expected proportion significant would have been .30 × .20 + .05, or 11%. If only 10% of the relations were truly nonlinear, the expected proportion significant would have been 9%. The obtained proportion was 5.4%. Thus the Hawk study provides extremely strong evidence against the nonlinearity hypothesis.

During his years as technical director of what is now the Army Research Institute for the Behavior and Social Sciences, Brogden and his research associate Lubin spent a considerable amount of time and effort attempting to identify nonlinear test-criterion relationships in large samples of military selection data. Although quadratic and other higher-order nonlinear equations sometimes provided impressive fits to the data in the initial sample, not one of the equations cross-validated successfully in a new sample from the same population. In cross-validation samples, the nonlinear functions were never superior to simple linear functions (Brogden, 1967).

These findings, taken in toto, indicate that the linear homoscedastic model generally fits the data in this area well. The linearity assumption, the only truly critical assumption, is particularly well supported.

We turn now to the question of normality of marginal distributions. In certain forms [see Equation (2)], the Brogden-Cronbach-Gleser utility formulas assume, in addition to linearity, a normal distribution for predictor (test) scores. The Taylor-Russell tables, based on the assumption of a normal bivariate surface, assume normality of total test-score distribution also. One obviously relevant question is whether violations of this assumption seriously distort utility estimates. Van Naerssen (1963; cf. also Cronbach & Gleser, 1965) found that they do not. He derived a set of utility equations parallel to the Brogden-Cronbach-Gleser equations, except that they were based on the assumption of a rectangular distribution of test scores. He found that when applied to the same set of empirical data, the two kinds of equation produced very similar utility estimates (p. 288). Cronbach and Gleser (1965) point out that this finding "makes it possible to generalize over the considerable variety of distributions intermediate between normal and rectangular" (p. 160). Results from the Schmidt and Hoffman (1973) study suggest the same conclusion. In their data, neither the predictor nor the criterion scores appeared to be normally distributed. Yet, the utility estimates produced by the Taylor-Russell tables were only off marginally: 4.09% at $SR = .30$ and 11.29% at $SR = .50$.

Thus, it appears that an obsessive concern with statistical assumptions is not justified. This is especially true in light of the fact that for most purposes, there is no need for utility estimates to be accurate down to the last dollar. Approximations are usually adequate for the kinds of decisions that these estimates are used to make (Van Naerssen, 1963, p. 282; Cronbach & Gleser, 1965, p. 139). Alternatives to use of the utility equations will typically be procedures that produce larger errors, or even worse, no utility analyses at all. Faced with these alternatives, errors in the 5%–10% range appear negligible. Further, if overestimation of utility is considered to be more serious than underestimation, one can always employ conservative estimates of equation parameters (e.g., r_{xy}, SD_y) to virtually guarantee against overestimation of utilities.

Are Test Validities Situationally Specific?

The third reason that we postulated for the failure of personnel psychologists to exploit the Brogden–Cronbach utility models was belief in the doctrine of the situational specificity of validity coefficients. This belief precludes generalization of validities from one setting to another, making criterion-related validity studies—and utility analyses—necessary in each situation. The empirical basis for the principle of situational specificity has been the fact that considerable variability in observed validity coefficients is typically apparent from study to study, even when jobs and tests appear to be similar or essentially identical (Ghiselli, 1966). However, there are a priori grounds for postulating that this variance is due to statistical, measurement, and other artifacts unrelated to the underlying relation between test and job performance. There are at least seven such sources of artifactual variance:

1. Differences between studies in criterion reliability.
2. Differences between studies in test reliability.
3. Differences between studies in range restriction.
4. Sampling error (i.e., variance due to $N < \infty$).
5. Differences between studies in amount and kind of criterion contamination and deficiency (Brogden & Taylor, 1950).
6. Computational and typographical errors (Wolins, 1962).
7. Slight differences in factor structure between tests of a given type (e.g., arithmetic reasoning tests).

In a purely analytical substudy, Schmidt, Hunter, Pearlman, and Shane (1979) showed that the first four sources alone are capable, under specified and realistic circumstances, of producing as much variation in validities as is typically observed from study to study. They then turned to analyses of empirical data. Using 14 distributions of validity coefficients from the published and unpublished literature for various tests in the occupations of clerical worker and first-line supervisor, they found that artifactual variance sources (1) through (4) accounted for an average of 62% of the variance in validity coefficients, with a range from 43% to 87%. Thus there was little remaining variance in which situational moderators could operate. Similar results were obtained in Pearlman, Schmidt, and Hunter (1980) and in Schmidt, Gast-Rosenberg, and Hunter (1980). If one could correct for all seven sources of error variance, one would, in all likelihood, consistently find that the remaining variance was zero or near zero. That is, it is likely that the small amounts of remaining variance in the studies cited here are due to the sources of artifactual variance not corrected for. Thus, there is now strong evidence that the observed variation in validities from study to study for similar test-job combinations is artifactual in nature. These findings cast considerable doubt on the situational specificity hypothesis.

Rejection of the situational specificity doctrine obviously opens the way to validity generalization. However, validity generalization is possible in many cases even if the situational specificity hypothesis cannot be definitively rejected. After correcting the *mean* and variance of the validity distribution for sampling error, for attenuation due to criterion unreliability, and for range restriction (based on average values of both), one may find that a large percentage, say 90%, of all values in the distribution lie above the minimum useful level of validity. In such a case, one can conclude with 90% confidence that true validity is at or above this minimum level in a new situation, involving the same test type and job without carrying out a validation study of any kind. Only a job analysis is necessary, in order to ensure that the job at hand is a member of the class of jobs on which the validity distribution was derived. In Schmidt and Hunter (1977), two of the four validity distributions fell into this category, even though only three sources of artifactual variance could be corrected for. In Schmidt et al. (1979), it was possible to correct for four sources of error variance, and 12 of the 14 corrected distributions had 90% or more of validities above levels that would typically be indicative of significant practical utility. Similar findings are reported in Pearlman et al. (1980) and Schmidt et al. (1980).

When validity generalization is possible, the best estimate of test validity is the mean of the corrected validity distribution, not the value at the foot of the 95% confidence interval. In addition to validities for individual tests and test types, validities for test combinations or batteries can also be estimated. This can be done in one of two ways. In some cases, distributions of validity coefficients will be available for test combinations or sums. These coefficients can be used with the validity generalization model in the usual manner. For exmaple, Schmidt et al. (1979) report 53 validity coefficients for tests for which total scores were a composite of verbal, quantitative, and perceptual speed subscores. The mean of this corrected distribution was .60 and the value at the 10th percentile was .20. Validities for composite scores will rarely be available from the literature in sufficient numbers, however, and therefore researchers will typically have to rely on the second approach. This procedure requires that one be able to obtain estimates of predictor intercorrelations in the applicant pool. Data on predictor intercorrelations is typically more readily available than validity data. In addition, N's are usually larger. In most cases, published correlations (e.g., from test manuals) computed on similar groups will be sufficiently accurate. Criterion validities are, of course, estimated for each predictor from the validity generalization model. One then has all the information necessary to estimate multivariate validities, based on either rational (including equal) or least squares regression weights. If regression is used, little or no shrinkage would be expected, assuming the predictor intercorrelations were based on a large sample; validities will have been based on samples in the thousands. On the other hand, equal weighting of predictors is apt to produce validities as high as those produced by regression weights (Schmidt, 1971, 1972).

These methods and findings indicate that in the future validity generalization will be possible for a wide variety of test-job combinations. Such a development will do much to encourage the application of decision-theoretic utility estimation tools.

Difficulties in Estimating SD_y

The generally recommended procedure for estimating SD_y is that used by Roche (1961; summarized in Cronbach & Gleser, 1965, pp. 254-266). Cost accounting procedures are supposed to be used to estimate the dollar value of performance of a number of individuals (Brogden & Taylor, 1950), and the SD of these values is then computed. Roche's dissertation illustrates well the tremendous time and effort such an endeavor entails. Even given great effort and expense, the final product nevertheless is far from perfect. Roche (1961) used a cost accounting procedure called "standard costing" to determine the contribution of radial drill-press operators to the profits of the company. The procedure was extremely detailed and complex, involving cost estimates for each piece of material machined, direct and indirect labor costs, overhead, perishable tool usage, etc. There was also a "burden adjustment" for below-standard performance. But despite the complexity and apparent objectivity, Roche, in Cronbach and Gleser (1965), is compelled to admit that: "many estimates and arbitrary allocations entered into the cost accounting [p. 263]." After discussing the study with Roche, Cronbach states that some of the cost accounting procedures used are unclear or questionable (Cronbach & Gleser, 1965, pp. 266-267), and that the accountants perhaps did not fully understand the utility estimation problem. The fact that Roche's study is one of only two studies we could locate that even attempted to apply cost accounting to the estimation of SD_y further points up the difficulty of this approach.

Recently, we have developed a procedure for obtaining rational estimates of SD_y. This method was used by 62 experienced supervisors of budget analysts to estimate SD_y for that occupation. Supervisors were used as judges, because they have the best opportunities to observe actual performance and output differences between employees on a day-to-day basis. The method is based on the following reasoning: If job performance in dollar terms is normally distributed, then the difference between the value to the organization of the products and services produced by the average employee and those produced by an employee at the 85th percentile in performance is equal to SD_y. Budget analyst supervisors were asked to estimate both these values; the final estimate was the average difference across the 62 supervisors. The estimation task presented to the supervisors may appear difficult at first glance. but only one out of 62 supervisors objected and stated that he did not think he could make meaningful estimates. Use of a carefully developed questionnaire to obtain the estimates apparently aided significantly. Instructions to the supervisors were as follows:

> Now, based on your experience with agency budget analysts, we would like for you to estimate the yearly value to your agency of the products and services produced by the average budget analyst. Consider the quality and quantity of output typical of the average budget analyst and the value of this output. In placing an overall dollar value on this output, it may help to consider what the cost would be of having an outside consulting firm produce these products and services.

> Based on my experience, I estimate the value to my agency of the average budget analyst at _____ dollars per year.

> We would now like you to consider the "superior" budget analyst. Let us define a superior performer as a budget analyst who is at the 85th percentile; that is, his performance is better than that of 85% of his fellow budget analysts, and only 15% of budget analysts turn in better performances. Consider the quality and quantity of the output typical of the superior budget analyst. Then estimate the value of these products and services. In placing an overall dollar value on this output, it may again help to consider what the cost would be of having an outside consulting firm provide these products and services.

> Based on my experience, I estimate the value of a superior budget analyst to be _____ dollars per year.

The final estimate of SD_y for the budget analyst occupation was 11,327 per year (standard error of the mean = $1,120). This figure is approximately 60% of the average yearly salary for budget analysts at this level. This estimate is based on incumbents rather than applicants and must therefore be considered to be an underestimate.

This procedure assumes that dollar outcomes are normally distributed; this assumption has now been evaluated in another study. One hundred and five supervisors of computer programers estimated values for the 15th as well as the 85th and 50th percentiles, providing two estimates of SD_y. Each estimate allows prediction of the value for the other. If the distribution is approximately normal, these two estimates will be similar in value. The average estimated difference between the 15th and 50th percentiles was $9,955 (standard error of the mean = $1,035); for the difference between the 50th and the 85th percentiles, this figure was $10,871 (standard error of the mean = $1,673). The difference of $826 is roughly 8% of each of the estimates and is not statistically significant. These findings provide strong support for the normality assumption. These values of

SD_y are approximately 55% of the average yearly salary for government computer programers at the level specified in the questionnaire. Once again, this estimate applies to incumbents rather than applicants, and is therefore an underestimate.

Let us briefly examine the productivity implications of a SD_y of $11,327 per year, as found in the budget analyst study. If we assume that budget analysts selected remain on the job for an average of 4 years (Cronbach & Gleser, 1965, p. 126), then the 4-year SD_y is 4($11,327) or $45,308. Application of the utility equation to a hypothetical example illustrates the very real practical implications of a SD_y of $45,308. Suppose that the selection ratio is .50, 2,000 budget analysts are selected, cost of testing is $10.00 per applicant, and the validity is .45. Total gain in utility from use of the selection procedure is then:

$$\Delta U = 2,000(.45)(\$45,308)(.3989/.50) - 2,000 (10.)/.50$$
$$\Delta U = \$32,492,050$$

The value of the productivity gains to be expected from the use of the test in hiring these budget analysts is over 32 million dollars.

Suppose this were the validity for one selection procedure. Suppose, further, that the estimated true validity for an alternate selection procedure were .20. Applying the same formula, the gain in utility from using the alternate procedure would be $14,418,688. The difference between these two figures is $18,073,362, which is an estimate of the dollar utility of substituting the more valid for the less valid procedure.

As noted earlier, it is generally not critical that estimates of utility be accurate down to the last dollar. Although our purpose in this chapter is broader, utility estimates are typically used to make decisions about selection procedures, and for this purpose only errors large enough to lead to incorrect decisions are of any consequence. Such errors may be very infrequent. Further, they may be as frequent—or more frequent—when cost accounting procedures are used. Roche (1961) found that, even in the case of the simple and structured job he studied, the cost accountants were frequently forced to rely on subjective estimates and arbitrary allocations. This is generally true in cost accounting and may become a more severe problem as one moves up the occupational hierarchy. What objective cost accounting techniques, for example, can be used to assess the dollar value of an executive's impact on subordinate morale? It is the jobs with the largest SD_y values (i.e., the jobs for which ΔU/selectee is potentially greatest) that are handled least well by cost accounting methods. Rational estimates—to one degree or another—are virtually unavoidable at the higher job levels.

Our procedure has at least two advantages in this respect. First, the mental standard to be used by the supervisor-judges is the estimated costs to the company of having an outside consulting firm provide the same products and/or services. In many occupations, this is a relatively concrete standard. Second, the idiosyncratic tendencies, biases, and random errors of individual experts can be controlled for by averaging across a large number of judges. In our initial study, the final estimate of SD_y was the average across 62 supervisors. Unless this is an upward or downward bias in the group as a whole, such an average should be quite accurate. In our example, the standard error of the mean was $1,120. This means that the interval $9,480 to $13,175 should contain 90% of such estimates. (One truly bent on being conservative could employ the lower bound of this interval in his or her calculations.)

Methods similar to the one described here have been used successfully by the Decision Analysis Group of the Stanford Research Institute (Howard, 1966) to scale otherwise unmeasurable but critical variables, and the resulting measures have been used in the application of decision-theoretic principles to high-level policy decision making, in such areas as nuclear power plant construction, corporate risk policies, investment and expansion programs, and hurricane seeding (Howard, 1966; Howard & Matheson, 1972; Matheson, 1969; Raiffa, 1968). All indications are that the response to the work of this group has been quite positive; these methods have been judged by high-level decision makers to contribute valuably to the improvement of socially and economically important decisions.

In most cases, the alternatives to use of a procedure like ours to estimate SD_y are unpalatable. The first alternative is to abandon the idea of a utility analysis. This course of action will typically lead to gross (implicit) underestimates of the economic value of valid selection procedures. This follows from the fact that the empirical studies that are available indicate much higher dollar values than psychologists have expected. The second alternative in most situations is use of a less systematized, and probably less accurate, procedure for estimating SD_y. Both these alternatives can be expected to lead to more erroneous decisions about selection procedures.

REVIEW OF EMPIRICAL RESEARCH ON SELECTION UTILITY

In reviewing the sparse empirical literature on selection utility, it rapidly became apparent that all available studies suffered from deficiencies that produce systematic underestimates of utility. These deficiencies are:

1. Failure to correct validities for range restriction.
2. Failure to correct validities for criterion unreliability.
3. Falsely dichotomizing the job performance continuum into "successful" and "unsuccessful" groups.
4. Use of partial measures of job performance rather than measures of overall performance.

The need for corrections for range restriction and criterion unreliability were explained earlier. Every study reviewed failed to make these corrections. The third and fourth deficiencies were not universal but were very common. Artificial dichotomization of the criterion measure, the third deficiency, leads to considerable information loss (Cronbach & Gleser, 1965, pp. 123-124, p. 138). All individuals in the "successful" group are assigned the same "high" value and all in the "unsuccessful" group are assigned the same "low" value. This result has been interpreted as indicating that dollar values need be attached to only two levels of performance. Each decision to select or reject an applicant can be classified as either "correct" or "incorrect." The number of correct and incorrect decisions that would result from use of different cutting scores on the predictor can then easily be calculated, and a dollar value attached to each "decision strategy." The difference between this dollar value and that resulting when the predictor is not used is the estimate of gain in utility due to use of the test.

Examples of the fourth deficiency, the use of partial measures of job performance, include criteria of training success and turnover. The costs (or savings) that accrue to the organization as a result of an employee's tenure are obviously not the sum total of the employee's value to the organization. In the case of the training criterion, if selection reduces average training costs from $5000 to $2000, for example, the saving is $3000. This figure is likely to be only a fraction of the utility that would result if selection were against a criterion of total job performance. This is especially obvious when we consider that productivity gains due to increased job performance continue to accumulate for as long as the employee remains in the job. Further, the savings figure of $3000 underestimates even the gains produced by that particular selection usage. Empirical evidence indicates that success in training usually correlates positively with later performance on the job (Severin, 1952). Thus, in selecting those who perform best in training, the employers are also to some extent selecting those who will perform better on the job. The value of higher job performance is not reflected in our figure of $3000.

Lee and Booth (1974) used a weighted application blank to predict tenure among clerical workers. Employees were trichotomized into "long-term," "intermediate-term," and "short-term" employees. The negative value of a turnover was estimated from costs of recruiting, hiring, and training a replacement for a resigning clerk. Scores on the predictor correlated .56 with the turnover measure. Calculations by us using their data produce an estimate of $\Delta \bar{U}/$ selectee of $1,020 at a SR of .17. The authors forecast the hiring of 245 clerical workers over the upcoming 25-month period, for a total utility of 245 × ($1,020), or about $250,000. Cost of scoring the weighted application blank—which would be minimal—was not considered.

Although Lee and Booth do report overall ΔU, they do not compute $\Delta \bar{U}/$ selectee. Instead, they calculate dollar savings *per long-term selectee*. This is a common practice in utility studies characterized by dichotomized criteria and partial measures of job performance. In three studies reported by Doppelt and Bennett (1953), savings in training costs due to testing were reported in dollars saved *per satisfactory selectee*. However, the data presented is again sufficient to allow computation of $\Delta\bar{U}$/selectee. For example, for check-out clerks in a grocery chain, $\Delta\bar{U}$/selectee is $197 at $SR = .10$ (with cost of testing considered). For adding machine operators, this figure was $180 at $SR = .13$, and for produce workers, $116 at the SR of .07. Corrected for inflation since 1953, all figures would be approximately tripled. Of course, as shown previously, both $\Delta\bar{U}$/selectee and total ΔU vary with SR. Another study of this same nature is that of Rusmore and Toorenaar (1956), who report only total gain in utility. Use of a battery of tests in selecting telephone operators led to a reduction of $28,000 per year in training costs. Adjusted for inflation, this figure would be approximately $80,000. Schmidt and Hoffmann (1973) report total gain in utility at two SR's and the number hired, making computation of $\Delta\bar{U}$/selectee quite straightforward. This study examined savings resulting from use of a weighted application blank to predict turnover among nurses aides in a large hospital. At $SR = .30$, $\Delta\bar{U}$/selectee was $424 and total utility overall a 2-year period, assuming hiring of 380 new aides, was $161,243. At $SR = .50$, $\Delta\bar{U}$/selectee was $372, and total utility was estimated at $233,920. These latter two figures are hypothetical, because they assume the hiring of 629 new aides, whereas the hospital anticipated only 380 openings over the upcoming 2-year period.

Because of the idiosyncratic and ad hoc methods of utility calculation, studies like these are difficult to relate in any precise manner to the Brogden–Cronbach utility models. But because the unit of measurement for utility in these studies is the dollar, it is often possible to derive rough approximations of SD_y from the data presented. We examine some of these estimates of SD_y in a later section.

Finally, we mention the study by Curtis (1966) on the determination of optimal strategies for selection of seamen into Navy technical schools. In this study, unlike those mentioned earlier, the utility scale used was not the dollar but rather a scaling of subjective utilities based on application of psychophysical scaling methods to the judgments of Naval personnel officers. It is thus difficult to relate these values to our present concern with the impact of selection methods on economic productivity.

Methods have been proposed for conducting utility analyses of the kind reviewed previously. These procedures generally contain an algorithm for maximizing some utility index. The most complex of these procedures is that of Sands (1973), the Cost of Attaining Personnel Requirements model (CAPER). This model assumes an organization that requires a specific number, say 200, of "successful" new employees over an upcoming time period. The overall base rate of successful employees in the applicant pool must be specified, as well as the proportion successful at each test score level. In addition, costs must be known: costs of recruiting, testing, and training. Finally, the costs of an erroneous rejection and an erroneous acceptance must be estimated. Using this information, the model determines the test cutoff score that will minimize the total cost of obtaining the 200 "successful" employees.

This model well illustrates the problems that plague all approaches that artificially dichotomize the job performance dimension (Cronbach & Gleser, 1965, pp. 123-124, p. 138). As the cutoff score decreases from high values, total cost of "attaining personnel requirements" (i.e., obtaining the needed number of successful employees) decreases until it hits its minimum value (after which it again increases). Because it is known what proportion of the applicant pool exceeds the minimum cost (or any other) test cutoff, and what proportion of this group is successful, it is an easy matter to compute the number that must be selected.

The problem with the model is that, as SR increases (i.e., minimum test score is decreased), the model assumes a constant mean value to the organization for the successful employees (200 in our example). But because job performance is really continuous in nature, and linearly related to test scores, the 200 successful employees obtained at a high-minimum test score (with the aid of increased recruiting and a larger applicant pool) will average higher in job performance than the 200 successful employees obtained (with less recruiting and fewer applicants tested) using the lower minimum cutoff score. The latter group of 200 will contain more employees who are near the successful-unsuccessful dividing line (i.e., are just barely "successful"). The model, however, does not take this fact into account. It assumes that any 200 "successful" employees are equal in value to any other 200 successful employees. It thus fails to correctly indicate the minimum test-scores cutoff that will maximize utility or savings. The computed optimal cutting score is lower than the true optimum, perhaps by a substantial amount. The Sands model also falsely assumes that the cost of erroneous rejections (false negatives), the cost of erroneous acceptances (false positives), and the value of correct rejections (true negatives) remain constant as the SR changes. Actually, all four values in the 2 by 2 utility matrix vary with the SR. Sands (1975) has acknowledged these problems but states that he has not been able to modify the model to alleviate them. Other decision-theoretic models involving dichotomized criteria are presented by Schmidt (1974), Alf and Dorfman (1967), Darlington and Stauffer (1966), and Curtis (1966). These models are only tangentially related to the concerns of this chapter and are, therefore, not pursued further here.

We could locate only two studies of selection utility that set out specifically to apply the Brogden-Cronbach equations and that used cost accounting methods to estimate SD_y. The first of these is the doctoral dissertation of Roche (1961). Earlier in this chapter, we described the many practical difficulties that Roche encountered in attempting to apply cost accounting procedures. In addition to these problems, his approach is deficient on a logical basis. The index of utility he computed for each employee was the individual's contribution to company *profits*. An employee's contribution to company profits is only a percentage of his productivity. This fact means that the *SD* of contribution to profits underestimates SD_y. For example, if contribution to profits averages 10% of workers' productivity (with the other 90% going to pay costs of various kinds), then the *SD* of contribution to productivity would be only 10% as large as SD_y. Finally, Roche failed to correct the observed validity coefficient for range restriction and criterion unreliability. Roche's final conclusion is that $\Delta \hat{U}$/selectee from the use of a mechanical comprehension test is 20 cents per hour per selectee. This is about $400 per year per selectee. If the average selectee remains on the job 4 years, $\Delta \hat{U}$/selectee is $1600. Then if, for example, 100 radial drill-press operators are selected, total ΔU comes to $160,000. Obviously, these utility estimates are quite substantial, despite the fact that they are almost certainly gross underestimates.

Van Naersson (1963) estimated the utility of procedures used to select drivers in the Dutch Royal Army. All utilities are given in Dutch guilder but have been converted to dollars for our discussion. The conversion is based on the 1963 official exchange rate of 1 : 3.4. Although the guilder was then officially worth only about 30 cents, its actual purchasing power was considerably higher. All dollar figures should be more than doubled to allow for inflation. Van Naersson costed out the monetary value of improvements on three criterion measures: reductions in accidents, failure rates, and training time. For the first of two criterion measures, however, his methods were those of Taylor and Russell (1939), with the reduction in frequency of accidents and failures being converted to monetary units. Only in the case of the criterion of training time did he apply the Brogden–Cronbach utility formulas.

The reduction in accident frequency from 25 to 22% of the selectees was found to be worth less than it cost to administer the test battery. Testing led to approximately five fewer accidents per 170 drivers successfully completing the training program, but cost of testing, at $3 per applicant, was $675 per bimonthly draft of 225 applicants. This meant that the test battery would have positive utility, only if the loss from the average accident was greater than $675/5 or $135. Most accidents were minor, and losses averaged less than $135 per accident. However, the conclusion that the battery lacks positive utility is to a great extent a function of the fact that the tenure for drivers, because of military regulations, was only 22 months. Longer tenure as drivers would mean reduction in accidents by a larger number and thus positive utility.

Use of a test battery correlating .67 with the success–failure training criterion and a *SR* of .75 led to a reduction in the proportion of failures from .07 to .025. This meant approximately eight fewer failures per class of 183. The cost of a failure was estimated at $240, producing a bimonthly savings of $1,920. Cost of testing per draft was $73.00, for a total utility of $1,847. Assuming 24 drafts per year, total annual utility would be about $44,330. In 1980 dollars, this would be considerably over $88,000 per year. It is not clear, however, why Van Naersson used .75 as the figure for the *SR*. The mean number of applicants from which classes of 183 were selected was 225, for a *SR* of .81.

The *SD* of training time across selectees was determined to be 12.9 hours. Cost of training was found to be $6 per hour, for a SD_y of approximately $77.00. The test used in this case correlated .66 with training time; the cost of testing was 30 cents per examinee, and the *SR* was .81. The average gain per selectee was therefore:

$$
\begin{aligned}
\Delta \dot{U}/\text{selectee} &= r_{xy} SD_y \ \phi/p \ - \ C/p \\
&= .66(77) \ .271/.81 \ - \ .30/.81 \\
&= \$17
\end{aligned}
$$

Because there were 183 selectees per draft, total ΔU per draft was 183 (17) or $3,111. Assuming 24 drafts per year, this figure rises to $74,664. In 1980 dollars, this is approximately $190,000 per year.

This analysis by Van Naersson is remarkable only for the ease with which the dollar *SD* of his partial measure of job performance was calculated. The amount of training time required for each trainee was available from routine records, allowing ready calculation of the *SD* in hours. Van Naersson then used relatively straightforward methods to estimate the cost per hour of training. His SD_y was then simply the product of these two figures. Corrected for inflation since 1963, SD_y of training time would be approximately $200. The SD_y for job performance as a whole is certainly much higher.

ESTIMATES OF SD_y DERIVED FROM EMPIRICAL STUDIES

Let us see what information can be derived from published studies about values of SD_y. The reader recalls that, when cost of testing is not considered, the formula for mean gain per selectee is:

$$
\Delta \dot{U}/\text{selectee} = r_{xy} \ \phi/p \ SD_y
$$

Solving for SD_y, we get:

$$
SD_y = p(\Delta \dot{U}/\text{selectee})/(r_{xy}\phi) \tag{6}
$$

In four of the studies we have reviewed, estimates of all the terms in the right-hand side of the previous equation are available. To be sure, these estimates are somewhat crude. Values for r_{xy} are underestimates because of failure to correct for criterion unreliability. Range restriction corrections are never applied, even though they were appropriate. Estimates of $\Delta \dot{U}/\text{selectee}$ are only approximate because of the methods used in calculating utility. Computed values of SD_y

apply to incumbents rather than applicants and are thus likely to be underestimates. In all but one of the studies providing the information necessary for the calculations, the job performance criteria are only partial—either tenure or training success measures. Finally, all the jobs concerned are relatively low level. Thus, the resulting estimates of SD_y can serve as *lower-bound estimates* of what should be expected even *in lower-level jobs*. Nevertheless, these estimates may be instructive.

Estimates of SD_y, calculated from six studies, are shown in Table 7.1. The second column shows the estimates in 1980 dollars. For the clerks in the Lee and Booth (1974) study, SD_y at $1812 is at least 20%—perhaps 25%—of average annual salary ($1812 is 20% of $9060). For the nurse's aides in Schmidt and Hoffman (1973) and the grocery clerks in Doppelt and Bennett (1953), SD_y appears to be in the neighborhood of 15% of average annual salary, assuming average salaries of about $6,100 and $7,500 for nurse's aides and grocery clerks, respectively. For adding machine operators and produce workers, SD_y appears closer to 10% of estimated annual salaries. Because Roche based his SD on employee differences in contribution to profit rather than productivity, his SD_y figure also applies to only a partial measure of job performance. Nevertheless, it appears to be about 25% of annual salary, assuming an annual salary of about $12,200 for the semiskilled job of radial drill-press operator.

The average value of SD_y as a percentage of salary for the studies reviewed here is 16%. The fact that these SD_y refer to only partial measures of value to the organization is very relevant here. Values of SD_y based on all facets of job performance would certainly be higher as a percentage of salary. In our study of budget analysts, we found the yearly SD_y to be approximately 60% of annual

TABLE 7.1
Estimates of SD_y Calculated from Six Studies

Study	Occupation	Performance Dimension	SD_y	SD_y-adj.[a]
Lee and Booth (1974)	Clerks	Tenure	$1238	$1812
Schmidt and Hoffman (1973)	Nurse's aide	Tenure	624.	914.
Doppelt and Bennett (1953)				
	Grocery check-out clerks	Training Costs	308.	1,127
	Adding machine operators	Training Costs	214.	·783.
	Produce workers	Training Costs	179.	655.
Roche (1961)	Radial drill-press operators	Overall Performance	1152	3049

[a]In 1980 dollars.

salary. For computer programmers, this figure was 55%. Based on these two studies and the information from the Table 7.1 studies, we estimate that the true average for SD_y falls somewhere in the range of 40 to 70%. But even if one assumes that in the economy as a whole, SD_y is only 16% of salary, the utility implications of improved selection procedures are quite significant, as we show later. The impact of job assignment strategies on national productivity is enormous, even under the most conservative of assumptions.

THE IMPACT OF JOB ASSIGNMENT STRATEGIES ON NATIONAL PRODUCTIVITY

The empirical studies of selection utility reviewed previously make it clear that the savings and/or productivity increases resulting from use of a valid selection procedure can be substantial in individual jobs, even in lower-level jobs. This finding quite naturally raises the question of what the productivity implications are of job assignment strategies on an economy-wide or national basis. How much would national productivity increase if jobs were allocated to individuals using more valid procedures than those currently in use? What would the implications of random assignment of people to jobs be for productivity levels? If the impact in the case of individual jobs is substantial, it seems likely that the impact on the economy as a whole must be quite significant. It is to this question that we now turn.

It is probably a rare job in which performance is so constrained by situational determinants (be it from labor or management) that no individual differences in performance are permitted to emerge, and we ignore such jobs in our analysis. It is probably also true that jobs for which no known psychological ability is relevant are rare (though considerable uncertainty on this issue was resolved only recently by the validity generalization studies discussed earlier) and we ignore such cases in the following.

The Classification Model

When considering the impact of job assignment strategies on the economy as a whole, the relevant model is no longer the selection model but the classification model. In selection, the focus is on a single employer, who seeks to select the best possible workers from the existent applicant pool. The selection model assumes that available applicants will be evaluated for only a single job, whereas the classification model assumes each applicant will be assigned to one of several jobs. The task of the classification model is to assign individuals to jobs in such a way as to maximize overall productivity, while ensuring that each job receives the required number of workers. Classification always involves two or more real jobs. In addition, there may be a "reject" category; that is, the organization can reject at least some of the applicants rather than assigning them to one of the jobs.

Selection can be carried out with only one test or predictor (Schmidt & Kaplan, 1971). But classification may use a separate equation for predicting success for each job (Brogden, 1955, 1964). The weight for a given test may differ from job to job, and may be zero for some jobs. The case in which one predictor is used for multiple jobs is called "placement." In placement, if there is no reject category, the value $r_{xv_i}SD_{v_i}$ must differ from job to job in order for the gain in utility to be greater than zero (Cronbach & Gleser, 1965, Chapter 5). The greater these differences, the greater is the gain in utility. Even if r_{xv_i} is the same for all jobs, the utility of placement can still be substantial, if jobs differ significantly on SD_{v_i}. If there is a reject category, utility gains may stem primarily from rejection of poor prospects. In this case, the major determinant of utility gains is r_{xv_i}, independent of differences between jobs in $r_{xv_i}SD_{v_i}$.

The mathematical and measurement problems in the classification problem are considerably more complex than in selection. However, Brogden (1946b, 1954) has developed an iterative procedure that provides an optimal solution. In addition to estimates of SD_y for each job, the classification model also requires estimates of the average dollar value of the performance of randomly selected applicants for each job. In selection, we need deal only with increments over this value and thus need not estimate absolute mean productivity values for jobs. In the terms of the economist, we need deal only with marginal utility in selection; in classification, we must deal with both marginal and absolute utility.

In a classic study, Brogden (1959) sought to determine average productivity as a function of the validity of the estimates of job performance, the degree of intercorrelation of these estimates, the number of jobs involved, and the proportion of the total group rejected. He made a number of simplifying assumptions in order to make the problem mathematically tractable. The most important of these assumptions are:

1. All jobs are assumed to be of equal importance; that is, the value of mean productivity of applicants selected at random is assumed to be the same for all jobs.

2. SD_y is assumed equal for all jobs.

3. The validity of test composites or regression equations is assumed to be the same for all jobs. Brogden had in mind the case in which job performance is predicted using regression equations derived on a common battery of tests. However, the model also holds when a different test is used to predict performance on each job.

4. The correlation between each pair of test composites is assumed to be the same for all pairs of jobs. This is equivalent to the assumption that a single common factor is responsible for all the correlations among the $\hat{y}$s. ($\hat{y}$ = predict job performance.)

5. *SR* is the same for all jobs; that is, the same number of applicants are to be assigned to each job.

6. All prediction composites and job performance measures are assumed to be normally distributed with mean of zero and standard deviation of 1.00. Further, all correlations surfaces are assumed to be normal and all relations linear.

Brogden (1959) first solved for utility under the assumptions that: (1) the prediction composites for different jobs are uncorrelated; and (2) the validity of each predictor composite is 1.00. Let this utility be denoted U_n. He then showed that the general solution is:

$$U = v\sqrt{1 - r\,U_n}$$

where v is the actual predictor validity and r is the actual level of correlation between the predictors. Values of U_n are presented in Table 7.2 for varying numbers of jobs and for varying proportions assigned to the reject category.

Brogden (1959) proved that it was not necessary to know correlations among measures of job performance to solve the classification problem; correlations among predictions of job performance are sufficient. Because job performance measures are rarely available on the same individual for different jobs, this is an important finding. Brogden's major conclusions about classification can be summarized as follows:

TABLE 7.2
Mean Job Performance Standard Scores as a Function of Number of
Jobs and Percent of Applicant Pool Rejected

Number of jobs	When $v = 1.00$ and $r = 0$[a] Percent Rejected									
	0	10	20	30	40	50	60	70	80	90
1	.00	.20	.35	.50	.64	.80	.97	1.16	1.40	1.75
2	.56	.73	.85	.97	1.09	1.22	1.37	1.54	1.75	2.07
3	.85	.99	1.10	1.21	1.32	1.44	1.57	1.73	1.93	2.23
4	1.03	1.17	1.27	1.37	1.48	1.59	1.71	1.86	2.05	2.35
5	1.16	1.29	1.39	1.49	1.59	1.70	1.82	1.95	2.14	2.43
6	1.27	1.38	1.48	1.58	1.68	1.78	1.90	2.04	2.22	2.51
7	1.35	1.46	1.56	1.65	1.75	1.86	1.97	2.10	2.28	2.55
8	1.42	1.53	1.63	1.72	1.81	1.91	2.03	2.16	2.33	2.60
9	1.49	1.59	1.68	1.77	1.86	1.96	2.07	2.20	2.38	2.64
10	1.54	1.65	1.73	1.82	1.91	2.01	2.11	2.24	2.41	2.68

[a]To calculate average gains for other specified values of v (validity) and r (performance prediction correlation), multiply table entries by $v\sqrt{1-r}$. Adapted from Brogden (1959), p. 189.

1. Other factors constant, utility gains from classification vary directly with the validity of estimates of job performance.

2. Other factors constant, the utility gain from classification varies with the correlation between predictor composites by the function $\sqrt{1-r}$. The implications of this finding are very important: Significant gains in utility from classification do not begin to disappear until correlations between job performance predictions become quite high. For example, with a correlations of .80, classification gains can still be 45% as great as with a correlation of zero. This finding verifies Brogden's earlier (1951) suggestion that correlations between predictor composites might not reduce utility to the extent usually imagined.

3. Other factors constant, the gain from classification increases in a negatively accelerated function with the number of jobs. Utility gains are highly dependent on the number of jobs. Holding other factors constant, gains will double in moving from two to five jobs; they will triple in going from two to thirteen jobs.

4. The larger the percentage of the applicant pool that is rejected, the greater are the utility gains. However, this effect decreases as the number of jobs increases. Conversely, as the percent rejected increases, the utility gain from increasing the number of jobs decreases.

As an example of the productivity implications of Brogden's (1959) findings, let us consider an economy in which: (1) there are only 10 different jobs (i.e., 10 unique regression equations for predicting job performance); (2) yearly SD_y is $7,000 for all jobs; (3) validity is .45 for all jobs, (4) the average correlation among prediction composites (mean $r_{y_i y_j}$) is .85; and (5) the labor force is 90 million strong. If we further assume that every member of the labor force will be assigned a job (i.e., there is no reject category), we see from Table 7.3 that the mean standard job performance score when validity = 1.00 and $r_{y_i y_j}$ = 0 is 1.54. The difference in yearly productivity between random assignment of the 90 million workers to jobs and assignment based on the classification model is then:

$$\Delta U = .45\sqrt{1-.85}\ (1.54)\ (\$7,000)\ (90,000,000)$$
$$\Delta U = 169 \text{ billion dollars}$$

Obviously, the productivity implications of appropriate ability—job requirement matching can be substantial. This figure is, of course, constrained by Brogden's somewhat unrealistic simplifying assumptions (e.g., SD_y, mean productivity, and number of incumbents are assumed the same for all jobs). But, as we show later, models that provide a better fit to empirical reality also indicate that the ability-job fit has substantial implications for national productivity.

Classification has received practical application primarily in the military. We could locate only one classification study carried out in an industrial setting: Selover and Vogel (1948). By contrast, a considerable number of military studies are available. Examples include Abellera, Mullins, and Earles (1975), DuBois (1947), Helm, Gibson, and Brogden (1957), and Maier and Fuchs (1972).

The Hierarchical Model of Talent Allocation

In order to obtain a tractable model of the nation as a whole, we must make some categorization of jobs. For our calculations in this chapter, we have chosen a four-class categorization scheme: management–professional, skilled trades (including crafts, such as bricklaying, as well as industrially defined trades, such as tool and die making), clerical (here we actually mean all white-collar work at a nonmanagerial level), and semiskilled and unskilled labor (the residual blue-collar and farm-labor workers); that is, we are assuming that, in terms of ability correlates, there are only four distinct "kinds" of jobs in the economy. Because estimated productivity gains are an increasing function of the number of jobs, as we have just seen, our assumptions are very conservative. Based on U.S. Bureau of the Census (1977) figures, the proportion of the labor force in each of these is 24, 12, 24, and 40%, respectively. For our preliminary calculations, we have taken mean output to be equal to median income in these groups. The Census Bureau places median 1976 incomes at $12,818, $11,476, $6668, and $4883 for these four groups, respectively. All Census figures include both full- and part-time workers, and our results apply to this composite labor force. Inclusion of part-time workers accounts for the relatively low average salaries reported by the Census. These lower salaries lead to smaller SD_y estimates and, thus, lower estimates of productivity gains per worker. However, this effect is offset by the fact that the number of workers in the composite labor force (104 million) is greater than the number in the full-time labor force (90 million).

For any given job we can write:

$$y = \mu + r_{xy}SD_y Z_x + e$$

where

Z_x is ability expressed in standard score units (mean 0, standard deviation 1),
y is individual performance on the job expressed in dollars,
μ is the mean performance in dollars of individuals selected to the job *without* use of the test,
SD_y is the performance standard deviation in dollars of persons selected to the job *without* use of the test,
r_{xy} is the population correlation between ability and performance (for the entire working population), and
e is the residual error of prediction.

If a group of persons is selected to a job on the basis of ability, and if the mean ability of that group is given by $\bar{Z}_x$, then the mean performance, y, is given by $\bar{y} = \mu + r_{xy}SD_y\bar{Z}_x$. This equation differs from our earlier equations for $\Delta \bar{U}/$

selectee in that it includes the term μ. This equation gives the mean absolute level of productivity rather than the increment in productivity (i.e., marginal utility) resulting from use of the selection device. The term $r_{xy}SD_y\dot{Z}_x$ is, of course, that increment (ignoring testing costs). This equation omits the term for testing costs, and we will not, in general, consider testing costs in our analysis of selection impact on the gross national product. This omission is justified by the fact that costs for the kinds of test we postulate—ordinary paper-and-pencil group tests of aptitude and ability—are negligible relative to utility gains. This is especially true in light of the need to pro-rate over the average tenure of the selectee. (Our utility estimates will be on a *per year* basis.) Mean performance on the job will be increased by use of the test to the extent that the numbers r_{xy}, SD_y, and $\dot{Z}_x$ are high (i.e., to the extent that job performance is highly related to ability, to the extent that there are great individual differences in performance, and to the extent that those selected have high mean ability).

For random selection, mean ability of those selected is the same as the mean for the population as a whole, which is zero if ability is expressed in standard scores. Thus, for random selection, mean productivity for a given group is simply given by the constant μ for that group, which is the mean output assumed earlier (i.e., $12,818 for the managerial-professional group, $11,476 for the skilled-trades group, etc.). The mean output for the country as a whole is the weighted average of these means, where each group is weighted by the number of persons in that group. For our figures, this comes to $8,007 per year.

The problem of determining the impact of the U.S. job assignment strategies on national productivity is in theory a classification problem, although there is no national agency or organization responsible for job assignments. Instead, a mechanism of another sort operates. The wide differences in pay and status set up a multiple-ordered selection process; that is, institutions hiring people for managerial-professional positions have first choice of workers, because workers prefer these highest paid jobs. For those who do not land a job in the top paying category, there is a similar selection for the skilled trades. Finally, although there is not such a large differential in pay between clerical and unskilled labor, there is a considerable differential in job security and in working conditions and some differential in status. The model we employ is designed to capture the essence of this process. In our model, we assume that each successive job category selects its workers from those remaining after the previous category has attracted those it requires. We also assume there is no reject category, that is, everyone must be assigned to a job. This model is similar to the job assignment strategy described by Ghiselli (1956) as being a realistic model of industrial selection. Within these constraints, the job allocation model can be either univariate or multivariate.

Univariate Selection. If job assignments are all made on the same ability, gains due to selection for one job are partially offset by losses due to application of the same selection process to other jobs. Thus, if high-ability workers are assigned to one job, increasing productivity on that job, the remaining lower-ability workers must be assigned to other jobs, resulting in decreased productivity on those jobs. However, this cancellation effect will not be complete unless $r_{xv_i} SD_{v_i}$ is equal for all jobs. The univariate model requires that the labor force be broken into four categories on that test score: the top 24% who go to managerial and professional jobs, the next 12% go to skilled trades, etc. For purposes of comparison, we will call this model the "univariate selection" model. The specific mathematical computations for this model are given in the appendix. For this model, there is a maximum of counterbalancing between the gains produced by selecting the brightest for managerial–professional jobs, and the losses produced by selecting the dullest for unskilled labor. However, because our review of utility studies suggests that individual differences in output in dollars in high-paying jobs (i.e., absolute values of SD_y) are greater than such differences in lower-paying jobs, the gains at the top will be larger than the losses at the bottom. Thus, because our model assumes that the standard deviation in dollar output is proportional to mean dollar output, our model predicts that univariate selection will yield higher utility than does random selection.

Multivariate Selection.   The univariate selection model assumes that all selection is to be done on one ability, but, in fact, it is well-known that optimal prediction of job performance requires different ability combinations for different jobs. It is true that general ability is predictive of success on all jobs, but most jobs also require more specialized abilities as well. Our multivariate model crudely but faithfully preserves these distinctions. We assume that skilled-trades jobs depend on spatial as well as general ability, and we assume that clerical ability depends on perceptual speed as well as general ability. Because we have not yet successfully measured special skills for managerial–professional jobs (presumably emotional control, social skills, etc.), we will assume that selection at this level is done solely on general ability. However, this is reasonably consistent with present practices, because initial selection for such jobs in our economy rests primarily on school achievement, which is highly correlated with general ability. Unskilled and semiskilled labor presents a very heterogeneous set of jobs requiring a wide range of special abilities (many noncognitive) that vary sharply from job to job. We will code this heterogeneity into our model by assuming that performance in unskilled and semiskilled labor (on the average) depends only on general ability. A complete correlation matrix of the type implied by these assumptions is portrayed in path analytic form in Fig. 7.1. All correlations are assumed to be based on the entire U.S. work force and validities are assumed to be corrected for criterion unreliability.

Figure 7.1 assumes that general ability correlates .40 with performance in all jobs. However, for skilled labor, spatial ability is correlated with performance to the same extent as general ability; and for clerical work, perceptual speed is as highly correlated with performance as is general ability; that is, spatial ability

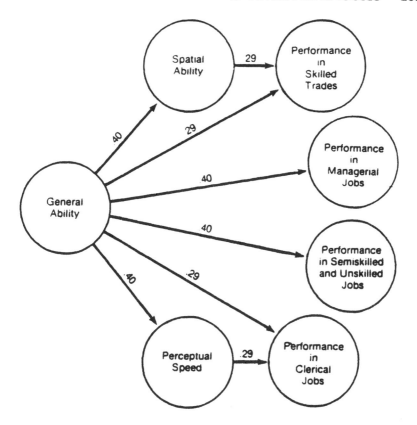

Figure 1. The correlational assumptions in the multivariate selection model in path analytic form.

was assumed to correlate .40 with performance in skilled trades, whereas perceptual speed was assumed to correlate .40 with performance on clerical level white-collar jobs. Spatial ability and perceptual speed were each assumed to be correlated .40 with general ability, but no more correlated with each other than would be predicted from their relationship to general ability [i.e., .16 (= .40 times .40)]. Our assumed correlation of .16 is consistent with the empirical literature, which generally indicates only a low relation between perceptual speed and more "cognitive" abilities.

If different abilities are required in different jobs, then to the extent that those abilities are less than perfectly correlated, multivariate selection (i.e., selection on combined ability test scores) will be less prone to losses due to selection; that is, gains from selecting high-ability people for one job will be less offset by selection of low-ability people to other jobs than in the case of univariate selection (Brogden, 1959). Thus our model predicts greater gains in overall utility for multivariate selection than for univariate selection. The specific mathematical calculations for this model are given in the appendix.

RESULTS PRODUCED BY THE HIERARCHICAL MODEL
OF TALENT ALLOCATION

For purposes of our analysis, people can be assigned to jobs in three different ways: random selection, univariate selection, and multivariate selection. Table 7.3 presents the mean output under all three conditions under the most conservative assumption about individual differences in job performance: that SD_y is only 16% of the mean output. The reader recalls that the 16% figure is the average across the studies summarized in Table 7.1.

As can be seen in Table 7.3, the mean output in goods and services, if people were randomly assigned to jobs, would be $8,007 per person per year. However, if persons were assigned on the basis of general ability, then average production would be $8,137 per year per person. This figure is a compromise between the increase in production for those in high-output jobs and the decrease in average production for those in low-output jobs (i.e., because better than average workers are assigned to the high-output jobs, the resulting average output improves). But then this means that lower than average workers are left to do the lower-output jobs and, hence, average output on those jobs decreases. This is an increase of $130 per person per year. Calculated across 104 million workers, this means a difference of $13.5 billion in the productivity of the nation as a whole. If multivariate selection is used, then the mean output rises to $8,265 per person per

TABLE 7.3
Mean Annual Output of Workers in 1976 Dollars in Four Occupational
Categories With Three Different Personnel Assignment Strategies
and $SD_y = .16u$

Occupation Class	No. of Persons[a]	Percent	Random Selection	Univariate Selection	Multivariate Selection
Professional/ managerial	25,085	24	12,818	13,815	13,815
Skilled	12,593	12	11,476	11,766	12,137
Clerical	25,040	24	6,668	6,627	6,847
Semiskilled and unskilled	41,605	40	4,883	4,549	4,625
Total–	104,323	100	8,007	8,137	8,265

[a] In thousands.

year, or an increase of $26.8 billion per year, even under our most extremely conservative assumptions.

These figures are extremely conservative for a number of reasons. First, and most obvious, is the fact that our figure of SD_y as 16% of mean salary is low. The true value is probably in the 40 to 70% range. Another important reason is that both the number of "jobs" and the number of abilities assumed are unrealistically low. Because we have assumed that the ability correlates of job performance are the same for the professional–managerial group and the semiskilled and unskilled group, our analysis assumes that the economy contains only three different kinds or groupings of jobs with different patterns of ability-performance correlations (i.e., with different regression equations for predicting y). This is obviously an unrealistically small number. As we saw earlier, utility increases (though not linearly) with increases in the number of jobs, other factors constant. Although this principle was ennunciated for the traditional classification model, it applies to our hierarchical model also. Use of a larger number of abilities increases the probability of holding the $r_{v_i v_j}$ to lower levels as the number of jobs is increased. The lower the $r_{v_i v_j}$ values are for any given number of jobs, the higher is the overall productivity gain. This follows from the fact that lower $r_{v_i v_j}$ values reduce the productivity gain tradeoff between jobs; that is, to the extent these values are low, high performance in some jobs is less offset by low performance in other jobs. Alternatively, lower $r_{v_i v_j}$ values mean lower effective selection ratios for each of the jobs and, thus, higher mean job performance. In addition, use of a larger number of abilities could be expected to lead to higher validities ($r_{v_i v_j}$'s), and, as we have seen, utility in classification— as in selection—is a direct linear function of validity, other factors constant. As we saw earlier, increases in validity are more important in increasing utility than are reductions in mean $r_{v_i v_j}$.

Of the occupational categories shown in Table 7.3, perhaps the best candidate for further breakdown is the semiskilled and unskilled group. On one hand, this group contains 40% of the work force. On the other, it is highly likely that success in different semiskilled and unskilled jobs depends on different, somewhat narrow abilities, making possible relatively low $r_{v_i v_j}$ values.

Finally, U.S. Census figures for mean income are underestimates (U.S. Census, 1977), as the reader might have surmised from the figures in Table 7.3. The bias results from a tendency to underreport income—for example, leaving out consideration of benefits, the value of overtime, etc. In addition, there have been salary increases since 1976—which essentially just offset inflation—and there should be adjustments for this fact.

To provide a more accurate, though still conservative, estimate of the impact of selection, let us set SD_y at 40% of mean salary and adjust all incomes upward by 10% to allow for underreporting and by 20% to allow for inflation since 1976. (This adjustment for inflation is obviously a gross underestimate.) The figures resulting from these adjustments are shown in Table 7.4. Under these assumptions, the average productivity difference between random selection and univariate selection is approximately $423 per worker per year ($10,832-10,409), or 44.1 billion dollars per year for the labor force as a whole. Similarly, the difference between random and multivariate selection is $839 per worker per year ($11,248-10,409), or $87.5 billion per year economy wide. If SD_y is taken as 70% of mean salary, these figures are $76.9 billion and $152.6 billion per year, respectively. These results are summarized in Table 7.5 Because the impact of individual differences increases as the potential productivity of the job increases, these figures will rise exponentially over the years at a rate equal to the rate of increase in the gross national product. Indeed, because loss in productivity also represents a loss in investment (i.e., an opportunity loss in increased product), the cumulative loss over time is far more than our calculations indicate, because it is compounded exponentially.

Wages and Output.   Our model has assumed that mean output is equal to mean income, yet any accountant would assure you that a business in which dollar value of output is equal to wages would be unable to pay costs and overhead, must less profit. Consider a plumbing contractor. He may pay his plumber $20 per hour, but he must charge the customer $40. The other $20 an hour pays for materials, equipment, office work, rent, interest, and profit for the contractor.

In 1970, the gross national product of the United States was $974 billion, although wages and compensation came to only $541 billion. Thus, in 1970, on the average, wages were only 57% of output. Using this estimate for 1980, we would obtain output figures in Tables 7.3 and 7.4 by multiplying all figures by 1.75.

TABLE 7.4
Mean Annual Output of Workers in 1980 Dollars in Four Occupational
Categories With Three Different Personnel Assignment Strategies
and $SD_y = .40u$

Occupational Class	No. of Persons[a]	Percent	Random Selection	Univariate Selection	Multivariate Selection
Professional/ Managerial	25,085	24	16,663	19,902	19,902
Skilled	12,593	12	14,919	15,859	17,065
Clerical	25,040	24	8,668	8,534	9,251
Semiskilled and Unskilled	41,605	40	6,348	5,262	5,508
Total	104,323	100	10,409	10,832	11,248

[a] In thousands

TABLE 7.5
Estimated Productivity Differences Between
Selection Strategies
(In Billions of Dollars)

	SD_y as Percent of Salary		
	16%	40%[a]	70%[a]
Univariate vs. Random	13.5	44.1	76.9
Multivariate vs. Random	26.8	87.5	152.6
Multivariate vs. Univariate	13.3	43.3	54.2

[a] 1976 salaries adjusted upward by 10% to allow for underreporting
and by 20% to allow for inflation between 1976 and 1980.

This disparity between salaries and output also explains an anomaly in our utility estimates. We found that supervisors of budget analysts and computer programmers gave estimates of the standard deviation of output in dollar terms that were large relative to salaries—as high as 60% of salaries. This would be very strange if output were equal to wages, because it would imply that people two standard deviations below average actually cause a negative output for the company. This anomaly vanishes if we use output as sold rather than wages as our base. If average output is, for example, 1.75 times salary, a SD_y that is 60% of mean salary is only 34% of output.

A CRITIQUE OF THE HIERARCHICAL MODEL

Our model contrasts a society in which all jobs are allocated on the basis of a few relevant abilities to a society in which all jobs are assigned randomly to members of the labor force. Given two such admittedly hypothetical societies, the estimates of productivity differences produced by our model can be accepted as reasonably accurate, within the limitations discussed earlier. Of these two hypothetical societies, the first is by far the most realistic. Although not all jobs in our society are allocated on the basis of ability, it is certainly possible that they could be; that is, there is no reason in principle why selection procedures of the kind we assume could not be used by virtually all employers.

It appears that our contrast between random selection and selection on the basis of ability directly addresses a current controversy. In recent years, random selection has frequently been advocated as a means of reducing adverse impact of selection on minority groups. However, random selection in this context generally refers to random selection from the applicant pool rather than the entire labor force. For most jobs—especially higher- and lower-level jobs—ability distributions in applicant pools differ systematically from ability distributions in the labor force. In terms of general ability, the mean level in the applicant pool is probably correlated with job level; that is, people of high general ability tend to seek higher-level jobs at an above chance frequency, and vice versa for people of low general ability. In terms of specific aptitudes (to the extent that they are independent of general ability), mean applicant pool level is probably, to some extent, correlated with the relevance (validity) of the ability to the job; that is, general ability constant, people often attempt to capitalize on their special abilities when seeking employment. Under these conditions, random selection from applicant pools will result in higher levels of productivity than random selection from the work force, making random selection from the work force an inappropriate basis for evaluating proposed random selection strategies. However, two considerations are relevant here. First, this difference will not be particularly large. Random selection from applicant pools will result in levels of productivity far below those produced by our univariate selection model. Second, the difference described here would almost certainly be reduced and perhaps eliminated if it became widely known that selection was on a random basis. Applicant pools for different jobs could be expected to become pretty nearly a random sample of the work force. The difference between the univariate and the multivariate models is therefore an *extremely conservative* estimate of the price in productivity that would have to be paid for choosing random selection from applicant pools over multivariate ability-based assignment. The difference between our random and multivariate job allocation models is a more accurate estimate of this price. Under any of these assumptions, it is evident that proposals for random selection from among applicants entail substantial productivity losses when projected for the economy as a whole. Productivity losses of this magnitude could have significant implications for the ability of U.S. products to compete with those of other nations in foreign (export) and domestic markets. Such losses would also lead to a substantial lowering of the U.S. standard of living.

What are the real-world implications for productivity improvements of the multivariate selection model when compared to selection practices current in the American economy? Except for the facts that too few abilities and occupational categories were used and lower than possible validities were assumed, the multivariate selection model is a reasonable approximation to an optimal procedure for job assignment in the U.S. economy. And, as indicated previously, it is a potentially attainable state of nature. Employers do not select randomly from among applicant pools. Instead, they base decisions on a whole gamut of selection aids, ranging from graphology, through the interview, to batteries of valid tests of the kind assumed in our model of multivariate selection. Many of these procedures have only low levels of validity, but average productivity levels associated with current methods are certainly above those that would result from random selection from applicant pools, though less effective than our univariate selection strategy. The yearly productivity difference between the univariate and multivariate selection models is thus a conservative estimate of the productivity improvement that could be realized by moving from current procedures to the multivariate selection model. This figure is between 43 and 54 billion dollars per year. Thus, it appears that improvements in current selection procedures could have substantial effects on the gross national product.

CONCLUSIONS

The analysis of the impact of job allocation procedures on national productivity presented in this chapter is, to our knowledge, the first of its kind. Therefore, it should not be surprising that our analysis is neither definitive nor complete. Despite its limitations, it nevertheless demonstrates some important facts. Most important is the fact that the way in which talent is allocated to jobs in the economy does have a significant impact on national productivity. Individual differences in abilities make a difference in economic productivity. This finding contrasts with the dominant emphasis in economics on technological improvements as essentially the sole route to increased productivity. The wise use of human resources does lead to significant productivity payoffs. This conclusion holds even without consideration of the indirect effects of selection systems on productivity. For example, a random system of selection—or even a system with large random components—is apt to be perceived as arbitrary, irrational, unfair, and perhaps even dangerous (e.g., consider airline pilots). The same is true of nonrandom systems that are perceived to be invalid or arbitrary. Objective measures of ability, such as those employed in our univariate and multivariate selection models, are apparently perceived by most people as fairer and more valid than most other procedures (Gallup, 1977). The effects of these perceptions on work motivation, job involvement, and overall job performance are not considered in our model, although these effects are probably substantial.

FUTURE RESEARCH NEEDS

Available information on individual differences in productivity in dollar terms is very limited. There is little information at present on the size of SD_y for different kinds of jobs. More detailed and specific information on the impact of talent allocation on national productivity will have to come from future research. We recommend that future research be interdisciplinary, that economists as well as psychologists be included on the research teams. Model refinements should include increased numbers and specificity of job classes, increased numbers of abilities, and projections over longer time frames.

Research on methods of validity generalization and techniques for improved estimation of true validities of predictors will provide useful payoffs for the national utility estimation problem. Promising beginnings have been made in this area (Curtis, 1967; Schmidt & Hunter, 1977; Schmidt et al., 1979; Pearlman et al., 1980; Schmidt et al., 1980), but much remains to be done. Accurate estimates of test validities for different occupations are critical to accuracy of model output. In this connection, we also recommend support for research efforts to develop valid nontest predictors of job proficiency. Productivity on many jobs may be determined not only by cognitive skills of the kind measured by most psychometric tests but also by motivational, personality, and behavioral propensity dimensions that are not very well assessed by presently available instruments. Procedures based on the measurement of past achievements and behaviors similar to those needed for superior performance on the job may provide an answer to this deficiency (Wernimont & Campbell, 1968).

Finally, we recommend research on the major information gap affecting solutions to this problem: the standard deviation of job performance. Studies comparing rationally derived estimates of SD_y—using our procedure or similar procedures—with estimates derived using cost accounting methods should prove informative. Such comparisons should begin with jobs that allow a relatively unambiguous application of cost accounting methods.

APPENDIX

Throughout this appendix certain notations will be held constant. The predictors are

x = general intelligence
y = spatial ability
z = perceptual speed

The criterion is denoted U and is defined to be dollar output. For this model it is assumed that in each of the occupational categories, the proportion of workers is P_i. The abilities are assumed to have a multivariate normal distribution. Each is correlated r with utility, y and z are correlated r with x, and y and z are correlated r^2 with each other.

In this appendix, the standard normal density function will be denoted by ϕ and the standard normal distribution function will be denoted by Φ. All the computations in this appendix are included in the computer program NATUTIL available from the senior author.

Random Selection

If workers were randomly assigned to jobs in all categories, then there would be some mean and some standard deviation in utility in each category. These means will be denoted μ_i and the standard deviations will be denoted σ_i. Overall average output will be the frequency weighted average of these means.

$$E(U) = \sum_{i=1}^{4} \mu_i P_i$$

Univariate Selection

The mathematics of univariate selection has been presented many times (see Brogden, 1946a, for example). The top paying jobs get the top ability applicants, the next level gets the next set of applicants, etc. Thus the distribution of x is divided by three cut points c_1, c_2, c_3, so that the correct proportion of persons is in each category. That is,

$$P_1 = \int_{c_1}^{\infty} \phi(x)dx = 1 - \Phi(c_1)$$

$$P_2 = \int_{c_2}^{c_1} \phi(x)dx = \Phi(c_1) - \Phi(c_2)$$

$$P_3 = \int_{c_3}^{c_2} \phi(x)dx = \Phi(c_3) - \Phi(c_2)$$

$$P_4 = \int_{-\infty}^{c_3} \phi(x)dx = \Phi(c_3)$$

For ease of notation below, we will use $c_0 = +\infty$ and $c_4 = -\infty$. The cut points c_i can be calculated using the inverse normal ogive function Φ^{-1} or by using the following Newton-Raphson iterative procedure. Let P be the number of persons who lie above the cut point and define the function f by

$$f(c) = \int_{c}^{\infty} \phi(x)dx - P = 1 - P - \Phi(c)$$

Then

$$f'(c) = -\phi(c)$$

and the recursive formula for the nth estimate of c is

$$c_{m+1} = c_m - \frac{f(c_m)}{f'(c_m)} = c_m + \frac{1 - P - \Phi(c_m)}{\phi(c_m)}$$

The mean output in each occupational category can be calculated from the formula

$$E(U)_i = \mu_i + r\sigma_i E(x)_i$$

$$= \mu_i + r\sigma_i \left[\int_{c_i}^{c_{i-1}} x\, \phi(x)\, dx \, / \, \int_{c_i}^{c_{i-1}} \phi(x)\, dx \right]$$

$$= \mu_i + \frac{r\sigma_i}{P_i} \int_{c_i}^{c_{i-1}} x\phi(x)dx$$

$$= \mu_i + \frac{r\sigma_i}{P_i} \{\Phi(c_i) - \Phi(c_{i-1})\}$$

The overall mean utility is

$$E(U) = \sum_{i=1}^{4} P_i\, E(U)_i$$

$$= \sum_{i=1}^{4} P_i \left[\mu_i + r\, \frac{\sigma_i}{P_i} \{\Phi(c_i) - \Phi(c_{i-1})\} \right]$$

$$= \sum_{i=1}^{4} \mu_i P_i + r \sum_{i=1}^{4} \sigma_i \{\Phi(c_i) - \Phi(c_i)\}$$

The gain in mean utility using univariate rather than random selection is the marginal utility

$$E(\text{gain}) = r \sum_{i=1}^{4} \sigma_i \{\Phi(c_i) - \Phi(c_{i-1})\}$$

Multivariate selection: introduction

The computations for multivariate selection become progressively more difficult as we move down the occupational scale. The top group is selected on general intelligence alone and hence is identical to the group that would be selected by univariate selection. The mean performance for this group is

$$E(U)_1 = \mu_1 + r\, \sigma_1\, \phi(c_1) \, / \, P_1$$

However the computations for the technical-skilled worker classification is complicated in two ways. First, two predictors x and y are used. Second, this next group must be chosen from the distribution left after the top group is taken out. This computation is a bivariate normal distribution calculation which has no closed analytic solution and must be integrated numerically. The computations for the clerical category are also complicated in two ways: First, two predictors x and z are used; and second, the clerical group must be chosen from the distribution left after the top two groups are taken out. This computation is a trivariate normal distribution calculation which has no closed analytic solution and must also be numerically integrated. Finally the unskilled workers are those left after the top 3 groups are taken out and their mean output is given by a trivariate normal distribution integral which must be computed numerically.

Multivariate selection: technical-skilled workers

For the technical or skilled workers, the regression equation for utility is

$$\hat{U} = \mu_z + \frac{r}{1 + r} \, \sigma_2 \, x + \frac{r}{1 + r} \, \sigma_2 \, y$$

$$= \mu_2 + \frac{r}{1 + r} \, \sigma_2 \, (x + y)$$

Therefore the workers selected for this group must satisfy two inequalities: They must have general ability scores less than c_1 or they would have been selected for the top group and they must be among the top P_2 of those left on the sum score $x + y$. Thus there will be a cut off score c_2 such that those selected will have scores such that $x \leq c_1$ and $x + y \geq c_2$. The first problem is to determine that second cutoff score c_2. Since there is no analytic solution for this, it will be found using a Newton-Raphson iteration. The equation for the Newton-Raphson iteration is obtained by computing the probability that both $x \leq c_1$ and $x + y \geq c_2$.

$$P \, \{x + y \geq c_2 \text{ and } x \leq c_1\}$$

$$= P \, \{y \geq c_2 - x \text{ and } x \leq c_1\}$$

$$= \int_{-\infty}^{c_1} \int_{c_2-x}^{\infty} f(x,y) \, dy \, dx$$

where x and y have a bivariate normal distribution with correlation r.

$$P \, \{x + y \geq c_2 \text{ and } x \leq c_1\}$$

$$= \int_{-\infty}^{c_1} \phi(x) \int_{c_2-x}^{\infty} f(y|x) \, dy \, dx$$

$$\int_{c_2-x}^{\infty} f(y|x) \, dy = P \, \{y \geq c_2 - x | x\}$$

where the conditional distribution of y is normal with mean rx and standard deviation $\sqrt{1 - r^2}$. Thus

$$P\{y \geq c_2 - x | x\} = P \left\{ \frac{y - rx}{\sqrt{1 - r^2}} \geq \frac{c_2 - x - rx}{\sqrt{1 - r^2}} \, \bigg| x \right\}$$

$$= P \left\{ \text{st. normal} \geq \frac{c_2 - [1 + r]x}{\sqrt{1 - r^2}} \right\}$$

$$= P \left\{ \text{st. normal} \leq -\frac{c_2 - [1 + r]x}{\sqrt{1 - r^2}} \right\}$$

$$= \Phi \left(\frac{[1 + r]x - c_2}{\sqrt{1 - r^2}} \right)$$

The original probability is then given by

$$P\{x + y \geq c_2 \text{ and } x \leq c_1\} = \int_{-\infty}^{c_1} \phi(x) \, \Phi(u) dx$$

where u is defined by

$$u = \frac{[1 + r]x - c_2}{\sqrt{1 - r^2}}$$

This integral has no closed analytic form and must be calculated numerically. Thus there is a numerical integration within each Newton-Raphson iteration. The Newton-Raphson function and its derivative are defined by

$$f(c) = \int_{-\infty}^{c_1} \phi(x) \, \Phi(u) dx - P_2$$

$$f'(c) = \int_{-\infty}^{c_1} \phi(x) \, \phi(u) \, \frac{du}{dc} \, dx$$

$$\frac{du}{dc} = -\frac{1}{\sqrt{1 - r^2}}$$

where $f'(c)$ can also be numerically integrated. The Newton-Raphson iteration is given by

$$c_{m+1} = c_m + \sqrt{1 - r^2} \left[\frac{\int_{-\infty}^{c_1} \phi(x) \, \Phi(u) dx - P_2}{\int_{-\infty}^{c_1} \phi(x) \, \phi(u) dx} \right]$$

Once the cutoff c_2 is known, then the next step is to calculate the average sum score for the selected group.

$$E(x + y)_2 = \frac{\int_{-\infty}^{c_1} \int_{c_2-x}^{\infty} (x + y) f(x,y) \, dy \, dx}{\int_{-\infty}^{c_1} \int_{c_2-x}^{\infty} f(x,y) \, dy \, dx}$$

The denominator is P_2; the numerator can be calculated in two parts.

$$\int_{-\infty}^{c_1} \int_{c_2-x}^{\infty} xf(x,y)\ dy\ dx$$

$$= \int_{-\infty}^{c_1} x\phi(x) \int_{c_2-x}^{\infty} f(y|x)\ dy\ dx \quad = \int_{-\infty}^{c_1} x\phi(x)\ \Phi(u)\ dx$$

which must be integrated numerically.

$$\int_{-\infty}^{c_1} \int_{c_2-x}^{\infty} yf(x,y)\ dy\ dx = \int_{-\infty}^{c_1} \phi(x) \int_{c_2-x}^{\infty} yf(y|x)\ dy\ dx$$

$$= \int_{-\infty}^{c_1} \phi(x) \int_{c_2-x}^{\infty} y\ \frac{1}{\sqrt{1-r^2}}\ \phi\left(\frac{y-rx}{\sqrt{1-r^2}}\right)\ dy\ dx$$

The inner integral can be calculated using the substitution

$$w = \frac{y-rx}{\sqrt{1-r^2}} \text{ or } y = rx + \sqrt{1-r^2}\ w$$

$$\int_{c_2-x}^{\infty} y\ \frac{1}{\sqrt{1-r^2}}\ \phi\left[\frac{y-rx}{\sqrt{1-r^2}}\right]\ dy$$

$$= \int_{-u}^{\infty} (rx + \sqrt{1-r^2}\ w)\ \phi(w)dw$$

$$= rx \int_{-u}^{\infty} \phi(w)dw + \sqrt{1-r^2} \int_{-u}^{\infty} w\phi(w)dw$$

$$= rx\ \Phi(u) + \sqrt{1-r^2}\ \phi(-u)$$

$$= rx\ \Phi(u) + \sqrt{1-r^2}\ \phi(u)$$

Thus the original integral is

$$\int_{-\infty}^{c_1} \int_{c_2-x}^{\infty} yf(x,y)\ dy\ dx$$

$$= \int_{-\infty}^{c_1} [rx\phi(x)\Phi(u) + \sqrt{1-r^2}\ \phi(x)\phi(u)]dx$$

and the numerator of $E(x+y)_2$ is

$$\int_{-\infty}^{c_1} \int_{c_2-x}^{\infty} (x+y)\ f(x,y)\ dy\ dx$$

$$= \int_{-\infty}^{c_1} [(1+r)x\phi(x)\Phi(u) + \sqrt{1-r^2}\ \phi(x)\phi(u)]\ dx$$

which must be integrated numerically.

$$E(U)_2 = \mu_2 + \frac{r\sigma_2}{P_2} \int_{-\infty}^{c_1} \int_{c_2-x}^{\infty} (x + y) f(x,y) \, dy \, dx$$

Multivariate selection: clerical-white collar workers

For clerical workers, the multiple regression equation for utility is

$$\hat{U} = \mu_3 + \frac{r^{\cdot}}{1 + r} \sigma_3 x + \frac{r}{1 + r} \sigma_3 z = \mu_3 + \frac{r}{1 + r} \sigma_3 (x + z)$$

Thus the sum score $x + z$ must be as high as possible for persons selected to this group. This means that there must be a third cutoff score c_3 such that $x + z \geq c_3$. However, a person selected to this group cannot belong to the top two groups; hence their scores must also satisfy $x \leq c_1$ and $x + y \leq c_2$. The first step required then is to find the cutoff score c_3 so that

$$P(x \leq c_1 \text{ and } x + y \leq c_2 \text{ and } x + z \geq c_3) = P_3$$

This is the triple integral

$$\int_{-\infty}^{c_1} \int_{-\infty}^{c_2-x} \int_{c_3-x}^{\infty} f(x,y,z) \, dz \, dy \, dx$$

$$= \int_{-\infty}^{c_1} \int_{-\infty}^{c_2-x} f(x,y) \int_{c_3-x}^{\infty} f(z|x,y) \, dz \, dy \, dx$$

$$\int_{c_3-x}^{\infty} f(z|x,y) dz = P\{z > c_3 - x|x,y\}$$

$$= P\{z > c_3 - x|x\}$$

The conditional distribution of z given x is normal with mean rx and standard deviation $\sqrt{1 - r^2}$. Hence

$$P\{z > c_3 - x|x\} = P \left\{ \frac{z - rx}{\sqrt{1 - r^2}} > \frac{c_3 - x - rx}{\sqrt{1 - r^2}} \middle| x \right\}$$

$$= P \left\{ \text{st. normal} > \frac{c_3 - [1 + r]x}{\sqrt{1 - r^2}} \right\}$$

$$\underline{} = P \left\{ \text{st. normal} < \frac{[1 + r]x - c_3}{\sqrt{1 - r^2}} \right\}$$

$$= \Phi(v)$$

where v is defined by

$$v = \frac{[1 + r]x - c_3}{\sqrt{1 - r^2}}$$

The triple integral is thus reduced to

$$P_3 = \int_{-\infty}^{c_1} \int_{-\infty}^{c_2-x} f(x,y)\, \Phi(v)\, dy\, dx$$

$$= \int_{-\infty}^{c_1} \Phi(v)\, \phi(x) \int_{-\infty}^{c_2-x} f(y|x)\, dy\, dx$$

$$= \int_{-\infty}^{c_1} \Phi(v)\, \phi(x)\, \Phi(-u)\, dx$$

$$= \int_{-\infty}^{c_1} \phi(x)\, \Phi(v)\, [1 - \Phi(u)]\, dx$$

which must be integrated numerically. The Newton-Raphson iterative procedure to obtain the cutoff c_3 is determined from the functions

$$f(c) = \int_{-\infty}^{c_1} \phi(x)\, \Phi(v)\, [1 - \Phi(u)]dx - P_3$$

$$f'(c) = \int_{-\infty}^{c_1} \phi(x)\, \phi(v) \left[-\frac{1}{\sqrt{1 - r^2}} \right] [1 - \Phi(u)]\, dx$$

and is given by the recursion

$$c_{m+1} = c_m + \sqrt{1 - r^2}\; \frac{\displaystyle\int_{-\infty}^{c_1} \phi(x)\, \Phi(v)\, [1 - \Phi(u)]dx - P_3}{\displaystyle\int_{-\infty}^{c_1} \phi(x)\, \phi(v)\, [1 - \Phi(u)]dx}$$

Once the cutoff is known, the average sum score $x + z$ is given by

$$E(x + z)_3 = \frac{1}{P_3} \int_{-\infty}^{c_1} \int_{-\infty}^{c_2-x} \int_{c_3-x}^{\infty} (x + z)\, f(x,y,z)\, dz\, dy\, dx$$

$$\int_{-\infty}^{c_1} \int_{-\infty}^{c_2-x} \int_{c_3-x}^{\infty} xf(x,y,z)\, dz\, dy\, dx$$

$$= \int_{-\infty}^{c_1} \int_{-\infty}^{c_3-x} x\, f(x,y) \int_{c_3-x}^{\infty} f(z|x,y)\, dz\, dy\, dx$$

$$= \int_{-\infty}^{c_1} \int_{-\infty}^{c_2-x} x\, f(x,y)\, \Phi(v)\, dy\, dx$$

$$= \int_{-\infty}^{c_1} x \; \Phi(v) \; \phi(x) \int_{-\infty}^{c_2-x} f(y|x) \; dy \; dx$$

$$= \int_{-\infty}^{c_1} x \; \Phi(v) \; \phi(x) \; [1 - \Phi(u)] \; dx$$

which must be integrated numerically.

$$\int_{-\infty}^{c_1} \int_{-\infty}^{c_2-x} \int_{c_3-x}^{\infty} z \, f(x,y,z) \; dz \; dy \; dx$$

$$= \int_{-\infty}^{c_1} \int_{-\infty}^{c_2-x} f(x,y) \int_{c_3-x}^{\infty} z \, f(z|x,y) \; dz \; dy \; dx$$

$$\int_{c_3-x}^{\infty} z \, f(z|x,y) \; dz = \int_{c_3-x}^{\infty} z \, f(z|x) \; dz$$

$$= \int_{c_3-x}^{\infty} z \; \frac{1}{\sqrt{1-r^2}} \; \phi\left[\frac{z - rx}{\sqrt{1-r^2}}\right] dz$$

Using the substitution

$$w = \frac{z - rx}{\sqrt{1-r^2}} \text{ or } z = rx + \sqrt{1-r^2} \; w$$

we have

$$\int_{c_3-x}^{\infty} z \, f(z|x) \; dz = \int_{-v}^{\infty} (rx + \sqrt{1-r^2} \; w) \; \phi(w) \; dw$$

$$= rx \; \Phi(v) + \sqrt{1-r^2} \; \phi(v)$$

The triple integral is

$$\int_{-\infty}^{c_1} \int_{-\infty}^{c_2-x} \int_{c_3-x}^{\infty} z \, f(x,y,z) \; dz \; dy \; dx$$

$$= \int_{-\infty}^{c_1} \int_{-\infty}^{c_2-x} f(x,y) \; [rx \; \Phi(v) + \sqrt{1-r^2} \; \phi(v)] \; dy \; dx$$

$$= \int_{-\infty}^{c_1} [rx \; \Phi(v) + \sqrt{1-r^2} \; \phi(v)] \; \phi(x) \int_{-\infty}^{c_2-x} f(y|x) \; dy \; dx$$

$$= \int_{-\infty}^{c_1} [rx \; \Phi(v) + \sqrt{1-r^2} \; \phi(v)] \; \phi(x) \; [1 - \Phi(u)] \; dx$$

which must be numerically integrated. The expected value of $x + z$ is

$$E(x + z)_3 = \frac{1}{P_3} \int_{-\infty}^{c_1} \phi(x) \left[1 - \Phi(u) \right] \left[(1 + r) x \Phi(v) + \sqrt{1 - r^2} \phi(v) \right] dx$$

The mean output is then given by

$$E(U)_3 = \mu_3 + \frac{r}{1 + r} \sigma_3 E(x + z)_3$$

Multivariate selection: unskilled workers

The regression of output for unskilled workers is given by

$$\hat{U} = \mu_4 + r \sigma_4 x$$

and hence mean output is given by

$$E(U)_4 = \mu_4 + r \sigma_4 E(x)_4$$

However the mean of x must be calculated for those who were not selected for the top 3 groups and hence this mean must be calculated as a triple integral over the set determined by $x \leqslant c_1$ and $x + y \leqslant c_2$ and $x + z \leqslant c_3$.

$$P_4 E(x)_4 = \int_{-\infty}^{c_1} \int_{-\infty}^{c_2-x} \int_{-\infty}^{c_3-x} x f(x,y,z) \, dz \, dy \, dx$$

$$= \int_{-\infty}^{c_1} \int_{-\infty}^{c_2-x} x f(x,y) \int_{-\infty}^{c_3-x} f(z|x,y) \, dz \, dy \, dx$$

$$= \int_{-\infty}^{c_1} \int_{\infty}^{c_2-x} x \Phi(-v) f(x,y) \, dy \, dx$$

$$= \int_{-\infty}^{c_1} x \Phi(-v) \phi(x) \int_{-\infty}^{c_2-x} f(y|x) \, dy \, dx$$

$$= \int_{-\infty}^{c_1} x \Phi(-v) \phi(x) \Phi(-u) \, dx$$

$$= \int_{-\infty}^{c_1} x \phi(x) \left[1 - \Phi(u) \right] \left[1 - \Phi(v) \right] dx$$

which must be integrated numerically.

Multivariate selection: overall mean output

The overall mean output is given by the frequency weighted average of the mean output in each occupational category.

$$E(U) = \sum_{i=1}^{4} P_i E(U)_i$$

REFERENCES

Abellera, J. W., Mullins, C. J., & Earles, J. A. *Value of personnel classification information.* Air Force Human Resources Laboratory (Technical Report 75-2). Lackland Air Force Base, Texas, 1975.

Alf, E. F., & Dorfman, D. D. The classification of individuals into two criterion groups on the basis of a discontinuous payoff function. *Psychometrika,* 1967, *32,* 115-123.

Brogden, H. E. On the interpretation of the correlation coefficient as a measure of predictive efficiency. *Journal of Educational Psychology,* 1946, *37,* 65-76. (a)

Brogden, H. E. An approach to the problem of differential prediction. *Psychometrika,* 1946, *11,* 139-154. (b)

Brogden, H. E. A new coefficient: Application to biserial correlation and to estimation of selective efficiency. *Psychometrika,* 1949, *14,* 169-182. (a)

Brogden, H. E. When testing pays off. *Personnel Psychology,* 1949, *2,* 171-183.

Brogden, H. E., & Taylor, E. K. The dollar criterion: Applying the cost accounting concept to criterion construction. *Personnel Psychology,* 1950, *3,* 133-154.

Brogden, H. E. Increased efficiency of selection resulting from replacement of a single predictor with several differential predictors. *Educational and Psychological Measurement,* 1951, *11,* 173-196.

Brogden, H. E. A simple proof of a personnel classification theorem. *Psychometrika,* 1954, *19,* 205-208.

Brogden, H. E. Least squares estimates and optimal classification. *Psychometrika,* 1955, *20,* 249-252.

Brogden, H. E. Efficiency of classification as a function of number of jobs, percent rejected, and the validity and intercorrelation of job performance estimates. *Educational and Psychological Measurement,* 1959, *19,* 181-190.

Brogden, H. E. Simplified regression patterns for classification. *Psychometrika,* 1964, *29,* 393-396.

Brogden, M. E. *Personal communication,* 1967.

Cronbach, L. J., & Gleser, G. C. *Psychological tests and personnel decisions.* Second Edition. Urbana, Illinois: University of Illinois Press, 1965. Originally published, 1957.

Curtis, E. W. *The application of decision theory and scaling methods to selection test evaluation.* San Diego, California: U.S. Naval Personnel Research Activity (Technical Bulletin, STB 67-18). February 1967. (See also *Dissertation Abstracts,* 1966, 26, 4794.)

Curtis, E. W., & Alf, E. F. Validity, predictive efficiency, and practical significance of selection tests. *Journal of Applied Psychology,* 1969, *53,* 327-337.

Darlington, R. B., & Stauffer, G. F. Use and evaluation of discrete test information in decision making. *Journal of Applied Psychology,* 1966, *50,* 125-129.

Doppelt, J. E., & Bennett, G. K. Reducing the cost of training satisfactory workers by using tests. *Personnel Psychology,* 1953, *6,* 1-8.

DuBois, P. H. (Ed.). *The classification program.* AAF Aviation Psychology Program (Research Reports Rep. No. 2.). Washington, D.C.: Government Printing Office, 1947.

Gallup, G. 80% majority favors ability as criteria for admissions. *Washington Post,* November 20, 1977.

Ghiselli, E. E. The placement of workers: concepts and problems. *Personnel Psychology,* 1956, *9,* 1-16.

Ghiselli, E. E., & Kahneman, Daniel. Validity and nonlinear heteroscedastic models. *Personnel Psychology,* 1962, *15,* 1-11.

Ghiselli, E. E. Dr. Ghiselli's comments on Dr. Tupes' note. *Personnel Psychology,* 1964, *17,* 61-63.

Ghiselli, E. E. *The validity of occupational aptitude tests.* New York: Wiley, 1966.

Guion, R. M. *Personnel Testing.* New York: McGraw-Hill, 1965.

Hawk, J. Linearity of criterion-GATB aptitude relationships. *Measurement and evaluation in guidance*, 1970, *2*, 249–251.

Helm, W. E., Gibson, W. A., & Brogden, H. E. *An empirical test of shrinkage problems in personnel classification research*. U.S. Army, Adjunct General's Office. Personnel Research Board (Technical Research Note 84), October 1957.

Howard, R. A. *Decision analysis: applied decision theory presented at the Fourth International Conference on Operational Research*. Boston, 1966.

Howard, R. A. Proceedings of the fourth international conference on operational research. New York: Wiley, 1966.

Howard, R. A., Matheson, J. E., & North, D. W. The decision to seed hurricanes. *Science*, 1972, *176*, 1191–1202.

Hull, C. L. *Aptitude testing*. Yonkers, N.Y.: World Book, 1928.

Jarrett, R. F. Percent increase in output of selected personnel as an index of test efficiency. *Journal of Applied Psychology*, 1948, *32*, 135–145.

Kelly, T. L. *Statistical method*. New York: Macmillan, 1923.

Lee, R., & Booth, J. M. A utility analysis of a weighted application blank designed to predict turnover for clerical employees. *Journal of Applied Psychology*, 1974, *59*, 516–518.

Maier, M. H., & Fuchs, E. F. *Development and evaluation of a new Army Classification Battery and aptitude area system*. U.S. Army Research Institute for the Behavioral and Social Sciences (Technical Research Note 239), September 1972.

Matheson, J. E. Decision analysis practice: Examples and insights. In *OR 69: Proceedings of the Fifth International Conference on Operational Research*. Venice: Tavistock Publications, 1969.

Pearlman, K., Schmidt, F. L., and Hunter, J. E. Validity generalization results for tests used to predict proficiency and training criteria in clerical occupations. *Journal of Applied Psychology*, 1980, *65*, 373–406.

Raiffa, H. *Decision analysis: Introductory lectures on choices under uncertainty*. Reading, Mass.: Addison-Wesley, 1968.

Rusmore, T. T., & Toorenaar, G. J. Reducing training costs by employment testing. *Personnel Psychology*, 1956, *9*, 39–44.

Roche, U. F. The Cronbach-Gleser utility function in fixed treatment employee selection. Unpublished doctoral dissertation. Southern Illinois University, 1961. (Portions reproduced in L. J. Cronbach & G. C. Gleser (Eds.), *Psychological Tests and Personnel Decisions*, Urbana, Ill., University of Illinois Press, 1965, pp. 254–266.)

Sands, W. A. A method for evaluating alternative recruiting-selection strategies: The CAPER model. *Journal of Applied Psychology*, 1973, *57*, 222–227.

Sands, W. A. *Personal communication*. May 7, 1975.

Schmidt, F. L. The relative efficiency of regression and simple unit predictor weights in applied differential psychology. *Educational and Psychological Measurement*, 1971, *31*, 699–714.

Schmidt, F. L. The reliability of differences between linear regression weights in applied differential psychology. *Educational and Psychological Measurement*, 1972, *32*, 879–886.

Schmidt, F. L. Probability and utility assumptions underlying use of the Strong Vocational Interest Blank. *Journal of Applied Psychology*, 1974, *59*, 456–464.

Schmidt, F. L., Gast-Rosenberg, I., & Hunter, J. E. Validity generalization results for computer programmers. *Journal of Applied Psychology*, 1980, *65*, 643–661.

Schmidt, F. L., & Hoffman, B. Empirical comparison of three methods of assessing the utility of a selection device. *Journal of Industrial and Organizational Psychology*, 1973, *1*, 13–22.

Schmidt, F. L., & Hunter, J. E. Development of a general solution to the problem of validity generalization. *Journal of Applied Psychology*, 1977, *62*, 529–540.

Schmidt, F. L., Hunter, J. E., Pearlman, K., & Shane, G. S. Further tests of the Schmidt-Hunter validity generalization model. *Personnel Psychology*, 1979, *32*, 257–281.

Schmidt, F. L., Hunter, J. E., & Urry, V. W. Statistical power in criterion-related studies. *Journal of Applied Psychology*, 1976, *61*, 473–485.

Schmidt, F. L., & Kaplan, L. B. Composite vs. multiple criteria: A review and resolution of the controversy. *Personnel Psychology*, 1971, *24*, 419-434.

Selover, R. B., & Vogel, J. The value of a testing program in a tight labor market. *Personnel Psychology*, 1948, *1*, 447-456.

Severen, D. The predictability of various kinds of criteria. *Personnel Psychology*, 1952, *5*, 93-104.

Sevier, Francis A. C. Testing the assumptions underlying multiple regression. *Journal of Experimental Education*, 1957, *25*, 323-330.

Surgent, L. V. The use of aptitude tests in the selection of radio tube mounters. *Psychological Monographs*, 1947, *61*, 1-40.

Taylor, H. C., & Russell, J. T. The relationship of validity coefficients to the practical effectiveness of tests in selection. *Journal of Applied Psychology*, 1939, *23*, 565-578.

Thorndike, R. L. *Personnel selection*. New York: Wiley, 1949, 169-176.

Tiffin, J., & Vincent, N. L. Comparison of empirical and theoretical expectancies. *Personnel Psychology*, 1960, *13*, 59-64.

Tupes, E. C. A note on "validity and nonlinear heteroscedastic models." *Personnel Psychology*, 1964, *17*, 59-61.

U.S. Bureau of Census. *Current population reports: Consumer income*. Department of Commerce (Series P-60, No. 107), September 1977 (Table 7).

Van Naersson, R. F. Selectie van chauffeurs. Gronigen: Wolters, 1963. Portions translated in L. J. Cronbach & G. C. Gleser (eds.), *Psychological tests and personnel decisions*. Urbana, Illinois. University of Illinois Press, 1965, pp. 273-290.

Wernimont, P. F., & Campbell, J. Signs, samples, and criteria. *Journal of Applied Psychology*, 1968, *52*, 372-376.

Wolins, L. Responsibility for raw data. *American Psychologist*, 1962, *17*, 657-658.

Author Index

Subject Index